To T.
In ...
Canc...
Upper Missouri River with
your brother, Jason.
Glenn Monahan

Montana's Wild and Scenic Upper Missouri River

written and edited by

Glenn Monahan
and
Chanler Biggs

Northern Rocky Mountain Books

First Edition ©1997
Second Edition ©2001

Northern Rocky Mountains Books
315 West Fourth Street
Anaconda, Montana 59711
(406) 563-2770
www.uppermissouri.com

Front Cover photography ©David Matherly Photography
Rear Cover Photography © Glenn Monahan
Cover Design by Glenn Monahan
Printed in the United States of America

Library of Congress Control Number: 2001117705

ISBN 0-9711214-0-0

For Nancy

Table of Contents

UPPER MISSOURI NATIONAL WILD & SCENIC RIVER

LEWIS & CLARK NATIONAL HISTORIC TRAIL

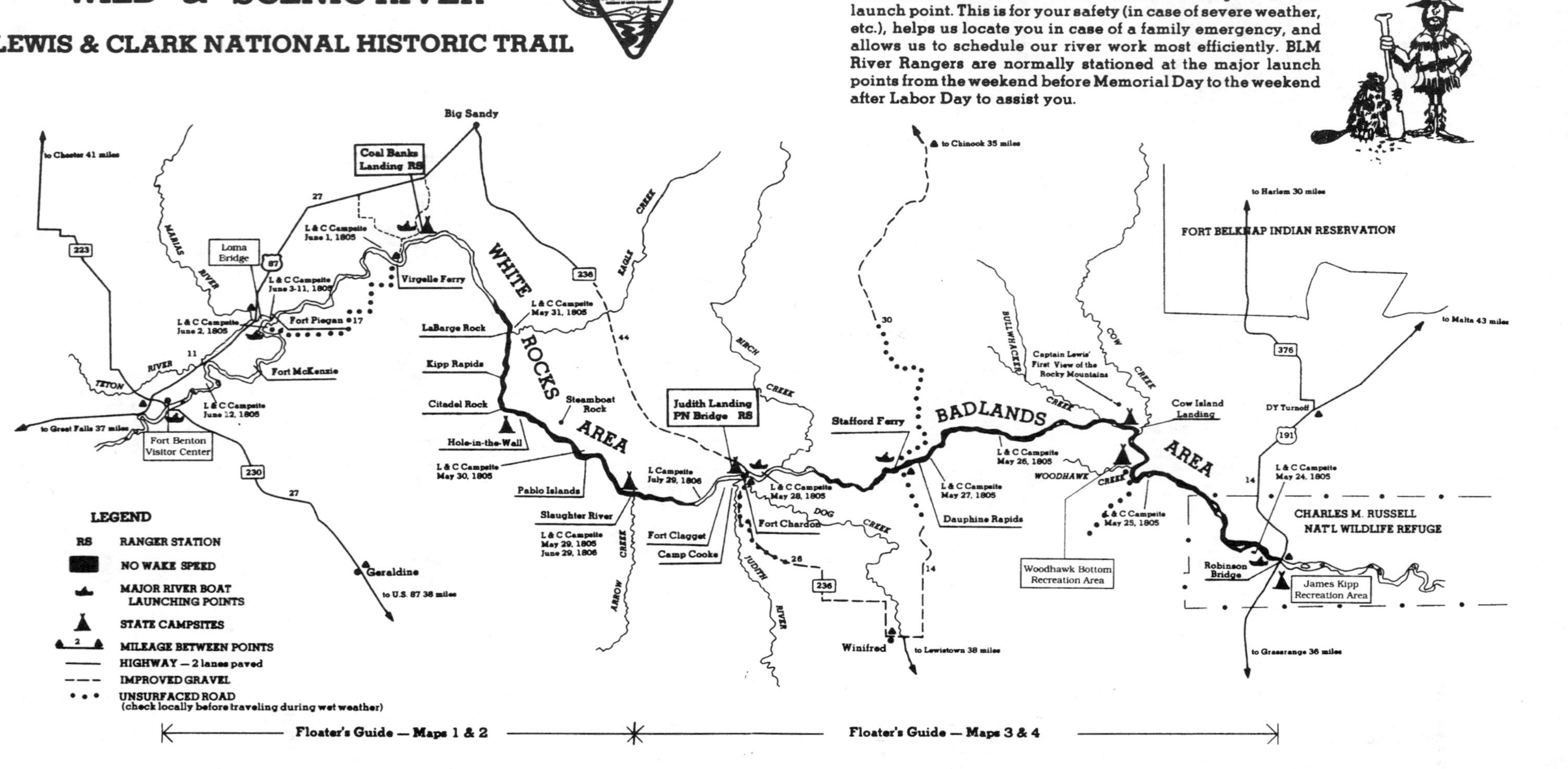

TRIP REGISTRATION — Boaters are asked to register at their launch point. This is for your safety (in case of severe weather, etc.), helps us locate you in case of a family emergency, and allows us to schedule our river work most efficiently. BLM River Rangers are normally stationed at the major launch points from the weekend before Memorial Day to the weekend after Labor Day to assist you.

Introduction

"It is hereby declared to be the policy of the United States that certain selected rivers of the nation, which with their immediate environments, possess outstandingly remarkable scenic, recreational, geological, fish and wildlife, historic, cultural, or other similar values, shall be preserved in free-flowing condition, and that they and their immediate environments shall be protected for the benefit and enjoyment of present and future generations." . . . . *from the National Wild and Scenic Rivers Act.*

With the above words, the Congress of the United States made it possible to set aside exceptional stretches of rivers for the enjoyment and appreciation of the people. As a result, in 1976, with the urging of Montana Senator Lee Metcalf, the Upper Missouri National Wild and Scenic River was created, effectively preserving for posterity a one-hundred forty-nine mile stretch of the river. It was not easily accomplished. At the time, opposing forces were promoting a much different use for the Upper Missouri - a dam located at Cow Creek.

In January of 2001, President Bill Clinton, working with Interior Secretary Bruce Babbitt, created the Upper Missouri River Breaks National Monument, recognizing the uniqueness of the tens of thousands of acres of wilderness quality public land that border the river. As in 1976, the opposition to monument designation was intense - this time from stockgrowing interests, highlighting the fact that preserving special places will always be a battle - but one worth fighting.

Those who enjoy the river today owe a debt of gratitude to those who have worked for the protection that it so eminently deserves. The Upper Missouri easily fulfills all of the conditions of the Wild and Scenic Rivers Act: it is remarkably scenic; it provides recreation and serenity for thousands every year; its geology is fascinating, and its wildlife abundant; and it has played a leading role in the history of Montana, and of the West.

This book is intended as a resource for individuals wishing to learn about the Upper Missouri River in Montana, with the focus being on the 149 mile stretch that falls within the Wild and Scenic corridor. It includes information about the river's historic, geologic, and biologic resources, and it includes a section about floating the river.

Acknowledgments

I would like to recognize and thank a number of individuals and institutions for their assistance in the second edition of this book, and for their efforts over the years to protect and preserve the Upper Missouri River.

Chanler Biggs carried out the historical research for Chapters 2, 3, and 4, and the material produced from his research forms the core of the book. I am indebted to Chan for allowing me to publish this material. Mr. Biggs was assisted in his research by Edrie Vinson.

Lory Morrow and Becca Kohl at the Montana State Historical Society were very helpful in my research and procurement of historical photos.

Sandra Padilla from the Bureau of Land Management's Lewistown Field Office has been most helpful in providing me with information about the river, and giving me access to BLM research materials.

David Matherly, photographer and friend, provided help in preparing photographs for publication, and also is the photographer for the front cover photograph.

Larry Cook of Fort Benton, Montana has been crusading to protect and preserve the Upper Missouri for many years, and is herein nominated for the Upper Missouri's "best friend" award.

Artists Glenn West, Robert Neaves, and Joe Thornbrugh for allowing me to use their works in the Wildlife Chapter.

John Rimel of Mountain Press for permission to use diagrams that appear in the Geology Chapter.

Karen Porter, geologist with the Montana Bureau of Mines and Geology, provided valuable insight into some of the finer points of Central Montana's geology.

My wife Nancy has supported me immeasurably throughout both editions of this book and I thank her for her help, suggestions, energy, and inspiration.

Using This Book

The majority of individuals who use this book will likely be those planning a canoe trip on the Upper Missouri, which is the only way to experience most of the river. This book is not a paddler's guide that describes every inch of the river, and tells for example, where to camp, hike, fish, eat lunch, swim, watch wildlife, et cetera. - the river is a wilderness and part of enjoying it is in the unknown. Chapter Seven, "Floating the Missouri", does provide pertinent information of a somewhat general nature that will give individuals a feel for the Upper Missouri and should help greatly in planning a trip.

Chapter One is an overview of the significant episodes in the history of Montana's Upper Missouri River, and will help readers understand the important role that the river played in the settling of Montana.

The core of this book is the History Digest, which makes up Chapters Two, Three, and Four. The History Digest is a mile-by-mile log of important and interesting events which have occurred along the Upper Missouri since the Lewis and Clark Expedition came up the river in 1805. When used in combination with the Bureau of Land Management maps of the Wild and Scenic Upper Missouri individuals who are floating the river will be able to identify the locations of scores of historic sites, and learn about the particular event(s) that occurred there.

Chapter Five, Geology, if read prior to floating the river, should help paddlers understand how geologic processes contribute to the beautiful and varied landscape of the Upper Missouri.

Chapter Six, Wildlife, is a short survey of the fauna of the Upper Missouri, and includes a bird checklist.

Several Lewis and Clark Journal entries are included, and to a great extent the Captains' original spelling is retained; some minor editing has been done to make the journal entries more readable, and in a number of cases information has been inserted in parentheses that helps the reader identify a geographic location whose present-day name is different than the one assigned it by Lewis and Clark.

Throughout the book references are made to specific sites on the Upper Missouri River. These references are usually accompanied with the location of the site on the Bureau of Land Management maps that are commonly used by floaters; these maps delineate every mile of river from Fort Benton - which is river mile 0, to James Kipp Recreation Area - which is river mile 149. When referring to the location of a site this book will either state the location of the site with the words "river mile", or it will use the abbreviation "rm"; each of these will be followed by a number designating the river mile, and in many cases the number will be followed by the letters "L" or "R", which designate the left or right side of the river as seen when looking downriver. An example would be, "rm 99.3 R".

The book is not footnoted, but the bibliography lists numerous sources of additional information about the Upper Missouri.

Captains Meriwether Lewis, left, and William Clark, right, with Sacagawea and her infant son, as depicted by Montana sculptor Bob Scriver. This larger-than-life rendition is located in Fort Benton, overlooking the Upper Missouri River. Courtesy Bob Scriver.

Chapter 1

The Upper Missouri: Historical Overview

Introduction

In 1976, a one-hundred forty-nine mile segment of Montana's Upper Missouri River was designated as the Upper Missouri National Wild and Scenic River, exending from Fort Benton to James Kipp Recreation Area; in 2001, the river and adjacent public lands were designated as the Upper Missouri River Breaks National Monument. Both of these designations were based, to a large extent, in recognition of the important role that the river played in our country's history, and the fact that the river is changed but little since Lewis and Clark first saw it in 1805. Important historic sites exist around every bend of the Upper Missouri, and include native American habitation sites, Lewis and Clark campsites, steamboat landings, and old homesteads. These historic sites, when combined with the Upper Missouri's outstanding natural beauty and the large tracts of surrounding public land, make the monument a national treasure, that is enjoyed by thousands each year.

In prehistoric times, Native Americans situated their villages along the Upper Missouri, taking advantage of the supplies of wood, shelter, and food sources. For whites, the river became the highway of exploration and commerce into Northern Plains, as well as into the Northern Rocky Mountains. Lewis and Clark, in 1805, were the first whites to experience the grandeur of the Upper Missouri. In 1831, the American Fur Company built Fort Piegan, located on the Missouri at its confluence with the Marias River, to trade with the Blackfeet Indians; it was followed in 1832 by Fort McKenzie, six miles upriver. Both of these posts were serviced by man-powered keelboats which were largely crewed with St. Louis-based "voyageurs" of French decent. In 1833, German scientist Maximilian of Wied accompanied by artist Karl Bodmer made their exceedingly valuable ethnologic observations of the Upper Missouri. A new era began in 1860, when the first steamboats succeeded in navigating the river to Fort Benton, which became the head of navigation, and an important fur trade post. In 1862, gold was discovered in Montana and steamboats began bringing large numbers of white settlers to Fort Benton, which boomed as it became the take-off point, and the supply center for the Montana gold fields. In the 1880's the completion of the Great Northern Railroad brought thousands of settlers into Montana to take advantage of the Homestead Act, a trend which continued through the early 1900's along the Upper Missouri.

This chapter is intended as an overview of the Upper Missouri's history, from its earliest native inhabitants, to its exploration by Lewis and Clark, and to the various stages of white settlement in Montana. Following this history overview, Chapters Two through Four provide locations and descriptions of specific historic sites along the entire river.

The Lewis and Clark Expedition

Introduction

The Upper Missouri River Breaks National Monument includes a149-mile section of the eight thousand mile Lewis and Clark Trail, which traces the expedition's entire route from St. Louis to the Pacific, and back. There are thirteen Lewis and Clark campsites within the monument. The Expedition entered the monument, traveling upriver, on May 25, 1805, and passed through Fort Benton on June 12, one day before discovering the Great Falls of the Missouri. The captain's journals for this period record many challenges and milestones, including hazardous encounters with Plains Grizzly Bears, the first view of the imposing Rocky Mountains, extreme physical challenges posed by the river, a significant navigation decision at the Marias River, and - on the return voyage, a hurried escape from a violent encounter with a band of Blackfeet Indians.

The purpose and goals of the Lewis and Clark Expedition were complex and varied, and involved more than simply exploring unknown territory. There were several exceedingly important political objectives that the expedition had as goals, and Meriwether Lewis, having lived in the White House as President Jefferson's personal secretary, was keenly aware of the potential contribution that the expedition could make to the future of the United States. Following is an overview of the geo-politics of the early 19th century which helps to explain why Lewis and Clark came up the Missouri.

Overview

The driving force behind initiating the Lewis and Clark Expedition was President Thomas Jefferson. Even before the United States negotiated the purchase of the Louisiana territory from France in 1804, President Jefferson had visions of the borders of the United States stretching from coast to coast; but other countries with colonialistic goals, such as Spain, France, and England, posed a threat to such plans. Lewis and Clark knew the potential of their expedition to significantly strengthen America's claim to vast areas of the North American continent.

The Lewis and Clark Expedition spent approximately one-fourth of its time in Montana, and traveled on the Missouri River both on its outbound journey and on its return trip. The expedition's primary objective was the discovery of a theorized mostly-water route to the Pacific, which involved traveling up the Missouri, and then gaining easy access to the headwaters of the Columbia via a (hopefully) short land portage. Although is seems absurd today, in the latter part of the eighteenth century, some geographers even considered it possible that the Missouri and the Columbia might join in a lake in the Rocky Mountains.

Although the water route to the Pacific was found to be non-existent, Lewis and Clark accomplished several major geo-political objectives which were important to President Jefferson, and which ultimately led to the United States claiming all of the lands through which the captains passed.

Summary of the Lewis and Clark Expedition

The following summary of the Lewis and Clark Expedition is taken from the National Park Service publication "Lewis and Clark", by Roy E. Appleman. It provides a concise and comprehensive discussion of the expedition.

The Lewis and Clark Expedition was one of the most dramatic and significant episodes in the history of the United States. In 1804-06 it carried the destiny as well as the flag of our young Nation westward from the Mississippi across thousands of miles of mostly unknown land - up the Missouri, over the Rocky Mountains, and on to the Pacific. This epic feat not only sparked national pride, but it also fired the imagination of the American people and made them feel for the first time the full sweep of the continent on which they lived. Equally as important, the political and economic ramifications of the trek vitally affected the subsequent course and growth of the Nation.

In its scope and achievements, the expedition towers among the major explorations of the North American Continent and the world. Its members included the first U.S. citizens to cross the continent; the first individuals to traverse it within the area of the present United States; and the first white men to explore the Upper Missouri area and a large part of the Columbia Basin as well as to pass over the Continental Divide within the drainage area of the two rivers.

Before Lewis and Clark, the trans-Mississippi West was largely a virgin land. British, Spanish, and French explorers and traders had barely penetrated it. Apart from a tiny fringe of French-American settlement in the St. Louis area and elsewhere along the Mississippi and small Spanish colonies in the Rio Grande Valley of New Mexico and in California, the region was virtually uninhabited by whites. For the most part enveloped in rumor, fantasy, and mystery, it was almost as strange as outer space would be to the later generation that was first to orbit the earth and put a man on the moon.

The men of the expedition made their way through this vast land, living mainly off its resources and superbly adapting themselves to the new conditions it imposed. They encountered alien tribes and menacing animals. On foot, on horseback, and by boat, they pushed over jagged mountain ranges, across seemingly endless plains, through tangled forests, against powerful currents and raging waters. Under two determined captains and three hardy sergeants, the explorers met danger as a matter of course and suffered hunger, fatigue, privation, and sickness.

Despite all these obstacles, the project was brilliantly managed and executed. Few, if any, comparable explorations have been so free of blunders, miscalculations, and tragedy. Its leaders were masters of every situation. Only one individual lost his life, but of a disease that could not have been cured in the best hospitals of the day. Clashes with the Indians were limited to two unavoidable instances - with the Teton Sioux and a small party of Blackfeet - but in both cases Lewis and Clark triumphed and their firmness won the respect of the natives.

Considering the frequent stress and their close association over a long period of time, relations between the two captains were remarkably harmonious. This was also true of their party, which when fully assembled consisted of a mixture of white, black, and Indian from various sections of the country and Canada.

Not many explorers in the history of the world have provided such exhaustive and accurate information on the regions they probed. Assigning high priority to the quest for knowledge, Lewis and Clark laboriously recorded in their journals and notebooks observations about the characteristics, inhabitants, and resources of the country through which they passed. All told, they amassed far more reliable data on the West than had ever been acquired before.

In a broad sense, too, Jefferson was continuing the centuries-long search for a Northwest Passage to the riches of the Orient - an all-water or nearly all-water route from the Atlantic to the Pacific through or around northern North America that would obviate the need for U.S. and European ships to make the long voyages around South America and Africa. In 1778 the English explorer Capt. James Cook had made an inconclusive search for the passage along the Pacific coast of the continent, but in 1792-94 the Vancouver Expedition had demonstrated that for all practical purposes an all-water route through the continent did not exist. Jefferson hoped that the Lewis and Clark Expedition might still find a nearly all-water passage, but it made no such discovery. As a matter of fact, the pathway it charted was not even economically feasible because of the long portages required and serious navigational problems.

If Lewis and Clark did not discover the Northwest Passage or a practicable transcontinental channel of commerce, their other accomplishments were formidable. The significance of their exploration extends over a broad and interrelated gamut - in geopolitics, westward expansion, and scientific knowledge. From the standpoint of international politics, the expedition basically altered the imperial struggle for control of the North American Continent, particularly the present northwestern United States, to which the U.S. claim was substantially strengthened.

The westward expansion that ensued in the wake of Lewis and Clark would provide substance to that claim. The wealth of detailed information they acquired about the climate, terrain, native peoples, plants, animals, and other resources of the princely domain they had trodden represented an invitation to occupy and settle it. In their footsteps, came other explorers, as well as trappers, traders, hunters, adventurers, prospectors, homesteaders, ranchers, soldiers, missionaries, Indian agents, and businessmen.

Many of these people followed for part of the way the Missouri River route that Lewis and Clark had pioneered - a waterway that became one of the major westward routes, though the complications of traveling it by steamboat restricted the flow of traffic to its lower reaches and rendered it less useful than the major overland trails.

The initial spur to westward expansion was the news the explorers brought back about the rich potentialities of the western fur trade, which were concentrated in the Upper Missouri-Yellowstone River-Rocky Mountain area. This trade was the first means of exploiting the resources of the newly discovered land. Trappers and traders were the first to penetrate it in detail, and these mountain men laid the groundwork for the miners and settlers who followed.

... hostilities, mainly limited to spasmodic outbreaks of the Teton, Sioux, Arikaras, and Blackfeet, were undoubtedly far less severe than they might have been were it not for the reservoir of goodwill the expedition had left with nearly all the western tribes. This reservoir, which Clark deepened during his long and distinguished post-expedition career as Superintendent of Indian Affairs in St. Louis, contributed to the success of the early westward movement.

Blending fairness, honesty, and strength with patience, respect, and understanding, Lewis and Clark recognized the personal dignity of the Indians, honored their religion and culture, sincerely proffered aid from the U.S. Government, and tried to establish intertribal peace. Masters of primitive psychology, they instinctively and unerringly always seemed to make the right decision and rarely offended the natives.

Tragically, this heritage of friendliness was not to prevail for more than a few decades ...

The Lewis and Clark Expedition also made major contributions to the fields of geography-cartography, ethnography, and natural history. Scientists were kept busy for a long time digesting the mass of raw information, studying plant and animal specimens, analyzing descriptions and translating them into the appropriate technical language, and classifying and correlating data.

Except in cartography, Lewis was primarily responsible for most of the scientific contributions. He was better educated than Clark and during two years of residence with President Jefferson prior to the expedition had enjoyed access to his fine library and been able to draw on his extensive knowledge of zoology and botany. Lewis had also enjoyed the benefit of a cram course in science at Philadelphia and Lancaster that Jefferson arranged for him.

The geographical findings were in themselves of outstanding significance. Lewis and Clark determined the true course of the Upper Missouri and its major tributaries. They discovered that a long, instead of short, portage separated it from the Columbia, which proved to be a majestic stream rivaling the Missouri itself rather than a short coastal river. Neither the Missouri nor the Columbia was found to be navigable to its source, as many had believed. The explorers also learned that, instead of a narrow and easily traveled mountain range, two broad north-south systems, the Rockies and the Cascades, represented major barriers.

Passing for the most part through country that no Americans and few white men had ever seen, the two captains dotted the map with names of streams and natural features. Some of the designations that have survived to this day include the Jefferson, Madison, Gallatin, Milk, Marias, and Judith Rivers, Beaverhead Rock, Rattlesnake Cliffs, White Bear Islands, York Canyon, and Baptiste Creek. Unfortunately, many other names that were bestowed have faded out of existence.

Clark made his scientific mark primarily in the field of cartography, for which his training consisted mainly of some experience in practical surveying and a limited amount of Army mapping. Yet his relatively crude maps, prepared under field conditions, enriched geographical knowledge and stimulated cartographical advances.

Of particular importance were the three progressively improved maps Clark drew between 1804 and 1810 of the Western United States and lower Canada. These were mainly based on the observations of the two captains, data provided by the Indians, earlier maps of the West, and the journals of preceding explorers. According to historical cartographer Carl I. Wheat, the last of the three (ca. 1809) was of 'towering significance' and was 'one of the most influential ever drawn' of the United States. Although deficient in its non-expedition data, provided to Clark by others, for three decades it represented some of the best knowledge available about the West and practically all other maps were based on or influenced by it. Also valuable to geographers and cartographers were the detailed local and regional maps that Clark sketched in his journals or on separate sheets of paper. They provided valuable information on hydrography and relief.

The second scientific field on which the Lewis and Clark Expedition exerted a major impact was ethnography. Although the two captains' comprehensive descriptions of the natives and their way of life contained some errors and misconceptions, as a whole they were so astonishingly accurate and complete that they provided a basic document for western ethnologists.

Previously, almost nothing had been known of the Indians westward from the Mandan villages, in present North Dakota, to the Upper Columbia. Native groups residing in that area, whom the explorers were undoubtedly the first white men to encounter and describe included the Northern Shoshoni, Flatheads, Nez Perces, Cayuses, Yakimas, and Walla Wallas. Although the expedition did not meet any Crows, their presence was noted.

Even for those tribes that traders had contacted and casually reported on - those on the Lower Missouri from St. Louis to the Mandan villages and those at the mouth of the Columbia - Lewis and Clark furnished a far more complete body of data than had ever before been recorded. They also sent back from Fort Mandan, in present North Dakota, or brought back to Washington, D.C. a number of ethnological specimens.

The final category of scientific knowledge that the exploration enriched was natural history. Usually based on their own observations but sometimes on Indian information, the two captains described hundreds of species of fishes, reptiles, amphibians, mammals, birds, plants, trees, and shrubs. Some were completely new to the world of science; others had never previously been encountered in North America; or earlier descriptions were sketchy and inadequate. In these categories, among mammals alone, are the pronghorn (antelope), bighorn sheep, mountain beaver, black-tailed prairie dog, white weasel, mountain goat, grizzly bear, coyote, and various species of deer, rabbit, squirrel, fox, and wolf. In addition to their descriptions, Lewis and Clark also sent back a large number of zoological specimens, including a few live ones, as well as skins, bones, skeletons, teeth, talons, and horns, and in addition a diversity of botanical items.

The Louisiana Territory

The French In North America

France, which originally settled Louisiana in the early 1700's, turned it over to Spain in 1762. In 1800, France and Spain signed the Treaty of San Ildefonso which 'retroceded' Louisiana back to France. At this time, exactly what comprised the Louisiana Territory was uncertain, as it was largely unexplored, but the 49th parallel (which today lies in Canada) was popularly thought to be the northern boundary; the western boundary was thought to be the continental divide (as yet unexplored and undiscovered), or possibly the Pacific coast.

French Goals in North America

As France prepared to again take possession of Louisiana in 1800, its leader, Napoleon, had aspirations for a strong French presence in North America. This provided a serious obstacle to President Jefferson's vision of the United States expanding west of the Mississippi, and Jefferson realized that he must act quickly. In 1802, the actual transfer of Louisiana from Spain to France had not yet officially transpired, and Jefferson began requesting that the still-reigning Spanish grant him permission to send an expedition through Louisiana, traveling up the Missouri strictly as an exploratory mission, and searching for a water route to the Pacific. He simultaneously directed the U.S. minister to France, Robert Livingston, to begin negotiating with France about a possible American purchase of Louisiana. At first, France showed no interest in selling Louisiana, and in fact Napoleon began amassing troops to be placed in Louisiana for the purpose of defending France's newly re-acquired territory.

France's Decision to Sell Louisiana

Napoleon's army, prior to its scheduled arrival in Louisiana, was first dispatched to the French-held Caribbean island of Santo Domingo, to suppress a revolution against France by the island's Negro inhabitants . To Napoleon's shock, fifty thousand of his troops were lost to a combination of guerrilla warfare and yellow fever; his strategy for a strong French presence in North America was in danger, since he could not provide the additional troops needed for occupying such a vast area, without seriously weakening his military strength in Europe. Sensing Napoleon's dire situation, Jefferson sent James Monroe to France to assist Livingston in his negotiations to purchase Louisiana. Napoleon realized that he was militarily powerless to stop the Americans from overrunning Louisiana, and decided to sell. In 1804, just before Lewis and Clark were to leave on their expedition, the U.S. took title to 830,000 square miles of territory - larger than the existing United States - for a sum of fifteen million dollars.

The British/Canadian Fur Trade

By the time the U.S. had purchased the Louisiana Territory, Canadian-based British fur companies, notably the Hudson's Bay Company, and more importantly, the North West Company, had already succeeded in establishing themselves in trade with Indian tribes in the Upper Missouri River valley in the Dakotas (the Mandans) and Montana (the Blackfeet). The activities of these British companies gave England the basis for a claim to the northern reaches of the Louisiana Territory, since at the time the northern boundary of the Louisiana Territory was uncertain, and unestablished. President Thomas Jefferson placed great importance on the establishment of a western fur trade that penetrated the northern plains from American territory, namely the mouth of the Missouri River at St. Louis, and which would compete directly with the British. One of the goals of the Lewis and Clark Expedition was to inventory the fur bearing animals of the country through which it passed. President Jefferson knew that a subsequent rush of American fur traders and trappers into the Upper Missouri would strengthen the United States' presence and claim to the area. The Lewis and Clark Expedition was also instructed by Jefferson to explore the northern tributaries of the Missouri, of which the Marias River - in Montana, was perhaps the most important, to help define the Louisiana Territory's northern boundary, and thus force the British northward.

Jefferson knew that a St. Louis-based, Missouri River fur trade could out-compete the British. The reason for this was the fact that the furs that the British were trading for in the Dakotas were transported via a complex and arduous system of rivers, lakes, and portages - eventually terminating in Montreal for shipment to England. This route was physically tedious and expensive. Jefferson knew that a water route which used the Missouri River would be more economical, and would thus be instrumental in helping the United States secure the Indian fur trade of the Dakotas, and in discouraging the British presence there.

The British Fur Trade in the Pacific Northwest

The British were also present in the Pacific northwest, in what is today Washington and Oregon. The British had firmly established themselves in the fur trade with the tribes along the Pacific coast and at the mouth of the Columbia River using ships which sailed from England, and Lewis and Clark had noted that as they began to get closer to the Pacific that the Columbia River Indians possessed increasing amounts of European-made trade items. Although the U.S. had a claim to the area based upon

Capt. Robert Gray's discovery of the mouth of the Columbia River in 1792, a British party, under the command of Captain Vancouver, had sent a boat one hundred miles up the Columbia in 1793, also giving the British a basis for a claim. By reaching the mouth of the Columbia by an overland route, Lewis and Clark would strengthen the U.S. claim to the Pacific Northwest.

Alexander MacKenzie's Explorations in the Northwest for Britain

Another factor which gave the British a claim in the Pacific northwest was the activities of Alexander McKenzie. In 1793, MacKenzie, a partner in the British North West Company of Montreal, and one of the great North American explorers, made a transcontinental crossing of Canada, which terminated when he descended the Bella Coola River and reached the Pacific Coast at Latitude 49°, just north of Vancouver Island, British Columbia. Before descending the Bella Coola River to the coast, he had been traveling towards the Pacific following the more southerly Tacoutche Tesse River, the major drainage in this region (later to be named Fraser River), but its canyons and rapids proved impassable, resulting in MacKenzie's detouring to the north, where he intersected the navigable Bella Coola, and followed it to the Pacific coast.

Upon his return, MacKenzie heard of the American, Robert Gray's 1792 discovery of a major river, located at Latitude 46 degrees - which Gray had named the Columbia. MacKenzie was convinced that this must be the same river that he had been descending (the Tacoutche Tesse, or Fraser), before being detoured northward to the Bella Coola. He now felt compelled to continue his exploration, being certain that Gray's Columbia and his Tacoutche Tesse (Fraser R.) were the same, thus giving Canada a claim to the mouth of the Columbia. To MacKenzie's great disappointment, Simon McTavish, head of the North West Company, would not fund additional exploration, and MacKenzie returned to Scotland and wrote of his travels and of their geo-political implications.

MacKenzie's book, published in 1801, and read by Thomas Jefferson, reasoned that his exploration - of what both he and Jefferson, at the time, thought was the Columbia - gave Canada a claim to the northwest. MacKenzie further reasoned in his writings that Canada possibly had a claim to lands west from Lake Superior extending along the 48th parallel to the continental divide - which would include portions of present-day North Dakota and Montana. Jefferson hoped that Lewis and Clark would make discoveries which would increase the knowledge of the course of the Columbia River, and establish an American claim to the Pacific Northwest.

The Fur Trade of the Upper Missouri

Introduction

The returning Lewis and Clark Expedition reported an abundance of fur bearing animals on the Missouri, and shortly after the expedition's return, fur trading interests based and financed out of St. Louis, began working their way up the Missouri to exploit this resource. The St. Louis fur companies were especially interested in beaver pelts which they shipped to Europe where beaver was in great demand for hats. Competing with the St. Louis companies were two Canadian-based British companies, operating out of Montreal, the Hudson's Bay Company and the North West Company, which had established a fur trade in the northern Great Plains and northern Rocky Mountains. By the 1830's the focus of the fur trade shifted from beaver pelts to buffalo robes.

Early Fur Trade of the Upper Missouri

The first significant incursion into the Upper Missouri by American fur traders, based out of St. Louis, was spearheaded by Manuel Lisa. In the period between 1807-1810 Lisa and his Missouri River Fur Co. sent two expeditions up the Missouri. The largest, comprised of 350 men, traveled up the Missouri to the mouth of the Yellowstone River, and then up the Yellowstone to the territory of the Crow Indians, in south-central Montana, where Fort Manuel was constructed. Lisa established a successful trade with the Crow, but this was not his main objective.

From the Crow country on the Yellowstone, Lisa sent a contingent of thirty-two men overland, following Captain William Clark's return route of 1806 over Bozeman Pass (the course of today's Interstate Highway 90). This group, led by John Colter, arrived near present day Three Forks, Montana, where the Gallatin, Madison, and Jefferson Rivers all join to form the headwaters of the Missouri River, an area which Lewis and Clark had reported as being fabulously rich in beaver. The men, several of whom had been members of the Lewis and Clark Expedition, built a fort - called Three Forks Post, and began trapping.

Three Forks Post was in Blackfeet country, and the Blackfeet were highly protective of their territory. The Blackfeet were already actively trading with the British to the north - but they refused to allow British trappers into their country - preferring to trap themselves, and to transport the beaver pelts to Canada for trade. The Blackfeet savagely repelled Lisa's men from the area. Twenty men, including George Drewyer and John Potts, both veterans of the Lewis and Clark Expedition, were killed. John Colter, also a Lewis and Clark Expedition member, was captured, but made his legendary escape. He challenged his captors to release him and to allow their fastest and bravest warriors to pursue him. The Blackfeet agreed, but first stripped Colter of his buckskins and moccasins. Running naked and barefoot through a prairie studded with prickly pear cactus, with Blackfeet warriors in hot pursuit, he succeeded in his escape, killing some Blackfeet in the process. Colter survived by jumping into the Jefferson River, and hiding for hours inside a beaver lodge, as the frustrated Indians scoured the area looking for him. Colter then hiked a few hundred miles back to Fort Manuel in Crow country. Further attempts to penetrate the Upper Missouri country were abandoned, and Lisa's company was ultimately dissolved.

The American Fur Company

Following Manuel Lisa's failure to penetrate Upper Missouri, St. Louis fur entrepreneurs were content to forget about trapping or trading in Montana. Instead they focused on the Missouri closer to St. Louis, and began developing a river-based fur trade, progressively establishing trading posts higher and higher up the Missouri above St. Louis. This strategy was helped by the development of the steamboat, which made it easier to haul trade goods upriver, and furs downriver. By 1819, for example, a steamboat had navigated the river to Council Bluffs, Iowa.

The most prominent of the St. Louis fur entrepreneurs was Pierre Chouteau, who in 1820, with a group of St. Louis businessmen, formed the French Fur Company. Although the company name and the partners would change many times (mostly referred to as Pierre Chouteau and Company), Chouteau succeeded in establishing a virtual monopoly which dominated the fur trade of the upper Missouri for the next five decades. Chouteau first focused on the beaver trade in the Dakota's, quickly dominating that area.

Unlike Manuel Lisa, Chouteau's strategy involved using the Indians - not white trappers - as the fur gatherers, and constructing trading posts where the Indians could exchange furs for manufactured goods. Chouteau's strategy for eliminating competitors was to either outprice them or to buy them out. Although many "opposition" companies entered the Upper Missouri fur trade, none of them achieved the size, longevity, or the success as did Chouteau's company.

In 1826, after Chouteau had been in business for six years, Ramsay Crooks, representing John Jacob Astor's New York City-based American Fur Company, bought out Chouteau's French Fur Company, leaving Chouteau in place as manager. At the same time, Crooks also acquired the Canadian-based Columbia Fur Company, which had been operating very successfully in the northern Great Plains for a number of years. Crooks merged these two acquisitions, and placed Chouteau in charge of the operations on the Missouri River. Thus, the Missouri River fur trade was now part of Astor's vast, monopolistic fur empire, which ultimately permitted Astor, a poor German immigrant, to retire with twenty million dollars.

Upper Missouri Fur Trade

During the 1820's the Missouri River fur trade settled into a pattern of operation - relying on both Indians and steamboats, which lasted through the end of the fur trade in the 1860's. At the heart of the American Fur Company's business strategy was using Indians as the gatherers of the furs, and providing trading posts where the Indians could exchange furs for manufactured goods; white trappers and "mountain men" were not of great importance in the Upper Missouri fur trade, as they were in the central Rocky Mountains. As steamboat technology advanced, the boats became more reliable, and were able to penetrate further upriver, thus providing a consistent means of moving trade goods into Indian country and furs back to St. Louis.

In 1829, Kenneth McKenzie, working for Chouteau, established and built Fort Union at the mouth of the Yellowstone River, close to the Montana border in North Dakota. This trading post quickly became the hub of the fur trade of the Upper Missouri. Initially Fort Union was accessed with man-powered keelboats, but in 1832, the first steamboat reached Ft. Union, further increasing its significance as the company's most important and profitable post. The American Fur Company created a subdivision named the "Upper Missouri Outfit", with Kenneth McKenzie at the helm, and he became known as the "king of the Upper Missouri" as he ruled the commerce of the vast Upper Missouri region from Fort Union.

Opening of Trade With the Blackfeet

As the American Fur Company progressively advanced its system of trading posts further up the Missouri, the old hostilities which the Blackfeet still held for Americans became a barrier which prevented the company from advancing into Montana. In 1830, one year after the construction of Ft. Union, the Blackfeet were still trading with the British in Canada, when McKenzie enlisted the aid of Jacob Berger in an attempt to persuade the Blackfeet to trade with the American Fur Company. Berger, in previous years, had been a trapper and trader with the Hudson's Bay Company at its Fort of the Prairie, in Canada, and had traded extensively with the Blackfeet, had a Blackfeet wife, and knew their language. Berger was successful in convincing the Piegan band of the Blackfeet, who inhabited the Marias River area of the Upper Missouri, to consider trading with the Americans, and he brought a large contingent of them to Fort Union to meet with McKenzie and receive presents. As a result, in the following year, 1831, McKenzie sent James Kipp, who had also been employed in the Canadian fur trade, to build a trading post in the heart of Blackfeet country. Kipp arrived with a party of men at the mouth of the Marias River (within the Upper Missouri River Breaks National Monument) and

The St. Louis levee in an undated photograph, probably between 1865 - 1880. The levee served the steamboat traffic on the Missouri and Missisippi Rivers. St. Louis was the final destination for the furs that were harvested by the Indians in Montana, and from there the furs entered a global trade market. The steamboats carried trade goods upriver to the trading posts on the Upper Missouri. Later the steamboats carried Army troops to subdue the Indians, as well as annuities for the tribes. When gold was discovered in Montana in the early 1860's, it kicked off a rush of white settlers; steamboats carried miners, merchants, and supplies upriver, and gold downriver. Montana Historical Society photograph.

built Fort Piegan (rm 22 L). The following year the fort was relocated seven miles upriver and renamed Fort McKenzie (rm 14 L). The trade with the Blackfeet was so lucrative that Fort McKenzie was regarded as the key to the American Fur Company's success. Other posts followed, such as Fort Chardon (rm 88 L), built in 1843 at the mouth of the Judith River, and Fort Benton (rm 1 L) in 1847.

Beaver, Silk, and Buffalo

By 1834 the beaver pelt trade was collapsing due to two circumstances: first, the demand for beaver hats in Europe was being replaced by the introduction of hats manufactured with Oriental silk, and secondly, the beaver populations were in a state of collapse due to over-harvesting (200,000 pelts exported annually to Europe). As a result, the fur trade adjusted by increasing its interest in buffalo robes, which were used to produce lap robes and overcoats. In 1840 the American Fur Company sent 67,000 buffalo robes down the Missouri, and in 1848, 110,000. As earlier, the suppliers of the robes were the Indians, with the men doing the hunting and the women dressing the skins. The buffalo robe trade continued through the 1860's until the demise of the great herds.

Bad Medicine On the Upper Missouri

Unfortunately for the Indians, one of the most important trade items was whiskey. Although the government banned the transport of whiskey into the Indian territory in 1832, the inspections of the steamboats were frequently incomplete due to bribery of the inspectors; whiskey was also shipped overland to avoid inspections, and Fort Union at one time even had its own still.

Another tragic result of the fur trade for the American Indians was the transmission of smallpox and the terrible toll which it took. A particularly serious outbreak occurred in 1837 when the American Fur Company steamboat, *St. Peter,* began to experience an outbreak of the disease while traveling upriver. As it stopped at the trading posts and delivered the infected trade goods, the disease shortly after began to break out in the native populations. At Fort Union, a party of white traders traveled upriver to the Blackfeet to warn them of the disease, but the Blackfeet insisted on receiving their trade goods, accusing the whites of trickery. In its wake, the 1837 smallpox epidemic is estimated to have killed 17,200 of the Mandan, Hidatsa, Arikara, Dakota, Assiniboine, and Blackfeet people.

The Waning Days of the Upper Missouri Fur Trade

By the mid-1860's a number of events were contributing to the decline of the fur trade on the Upper Missouri River. The movement of large numbers of whites into the west was resulting in the displacement of the Indian tribes, and this was causing many of the tribes to focus on warfare against the white invaders as they saw their way of life threatened. This resulted in the placement of army forts along the Upper Missouri, and the military campaigns against the Indians disrupted their fur trading activities. The government at the same time endorsed the annihilation of the great herds of buffalo as a means of cutting off the Indian's sustenance. The American Civil War was causing disruptions in both the national and international fur markets, and the Chouteau family was suspected of having ties with the Confederate government. Finally, the transcontinental railroad was about to be built through the heart of the Upper Missouri fur country, which also contributed to the decline of the buffalo herds. In 1865, Charles Chouteau dissolved the American Fur Company, closing this interesting and exciting chapter of the Upper Missouri's history.

History of Water Craft Used on the Missouri

Over the course of time humans used a variety of different boats on the Missouri River, ranging from the small Indian bullboat, used for local travel, to the technologically sophisticated steamboats, which originally served the fur trade, and later brought thousands of white settlers into Montana after the Bannack and Virginia City gold strikes of the early 1860's.

This Karl Bodmer painting is entitled, 'Bivouac on the Missouri'. The boat is called a Mackinaw. Before the days of the steamboats they were the primary means of transporting furs from the Upper Missouri fur trade to St. Louis. They were built at the upriver trading posts, loaded with furs, and launced into the current; they were sold for lumber upon reaching their destination. Courtesy Joslyn Art Museum, Omaha, Nebraska; gift of the Enron Foundation.

Non Powered Watercraft

Bullboats were an Indian invention made of hides from a buffalo bull (hence the name bullboat), and stretched over a frame of saplings. They were round and primarily used for local travel, with a capacity of one or two people. Bullboats were used by a small contingent of the Lewis and Clark Expedition as emergency transportation. Sergeant Nathaniel Pryor, under Captain Clark's command, was leading a four member contingent down the Yellowstone River Valley, traveling on horseback. The men's horses were stolen as they slept, presumably by Crow Indians. Alone in a wilderness, the men evaluated their situation, and in a demonstration of resourcefulness gained from more than two years of wilderness living, the party shot some buffalo and constructed bullboats, which they used to float down the Yellowstone for a considerable distance, until they rendezvoused with Captain Clark and the remainder of his command.

As the fur trade developed along the Upper Missouri, the fur men modified the bullboat for use in transporting furs out of Indian country. These modified bullboats, rather than being small and round, measured thirty feet in length and twelve feet in width, and after being loaded with six thousand pounds of furs, were poled downriver by two men. These boats were used on shallow tributaries of the Missouri, notable the Platte, Cheyenne, and Niobrara Rivers. Upon reaching the Missouri, their loads were transferred to larger boats for passage to St. Louis.

Dugout canoes were made by hollowing out a log of cottonwood, or sometimes walnut or cedar. Four men could build a dugout in four days, and they varied in length from fifteen feet to thirty feet. Occasionally a controlled fire would be used to soften the wood prior to its removal with axes, ultimately leaving a hull of about two inches thick. Strength-adding bulkheads were often created by

Karl Bodmer's rough sketch of Indian bullboats, used for local travel by Indians of the Upper Missouri. Courtesy Joslyn Art Museum, Omaha, Nebraska; gift of the Enron Foundation.

Four steamboats docked at the Bismark levee on the Missouri River in 1877 in present North Dakota. The boats are, from front to back, the Benton, the Western, the Nellie Peck, and the Far West. All of these boats saw service on the Upper Missouri as far as Fort Benton. Haynes Foundation Collection, Montana Historical Society.

leaving sections of wood, while in other cases strength was added by placing cross-braces across the width of the dugout. Dugouts were usually crewed by three men. Dugouts were used for local travel in the vicinity of fur trading posts, but were also used extensively to transport furs and other items all the way to St. Louis.

Pirogues were constructed of two canoes lashed parallel with each other and decked over with planks; this floor was then loaded with cargo. A steering rudder was fixed between the two canoe hulls. The "red pirogue" and the "white pirogue" of the Lewis and Clark Expedition were large pirogues which had seven or eight oars; specific details of their design is uncertain, but it is recorded in the captains' journals that one of the pirogues had a sheltered cabin in its rear. Because of their twin hull design pirogues could utilize a sail without danger of tipping over

The Mackinaw had origins in the eastern U.S. Mackinaws were a flat-bottomed craft designed for down river transport of furs, usually to a steamboat packet connection at St. Joseph, Missouri. The boats were built along the upper Missouri of hand-sawed lumber and held together with pins. Dimensionally they were as long as fifty feet, and up to twelve feet in length. They carried a crew of five - four oarsmen and a rudderman, and could hold fifteen to forty-five tons. Forts Union, Clark, Pierre, and Benton all had boatyards, called chantiers, for building mackinaws. Mackinaws traveled between seventy-five and one-hundred-fifty miles per day. At St. Joseph they were typically sold for lumber or firewood for $4-5 each. As steamboats began serving the Missouri, they occasionally would transport Mackinaws back upriver for re-use in the downriver transport of furs.

Keelboats were large boats, from fifty to seventy feet long and weighing ten tons. They were constructed of sawed lumber, and included a cabin and a mast. Most were built in Pittsburgh, and then floated down the Ohio River to St. Louis, where they were loaded with trade Indian goods for transport up the Missouri. When winds were favorable the keelboat utilized a sail for propulsion, however the main source of propulsion was manpower. Typically, a gang of twenty to forty men, known as voyageurs, would walk along shore and pull the boat with a one thousand foot long line, called a 'cordelle', while the boat was kept from the banks by a rudderman in the stern and a bowman who pushed the boat away from shore with a long pole. The cordelle was attached to the keelboat's mast so as to avoid snagging it on brush. In places where the nature of the banks prohibited cordelling, a technique called "warping" was employed - the cordelle was tied fast to a snag or a tree and the men on the keelboat would then haul the boat upstream by pulling on the anchored line. Oars, and probably more frequently poles, were also used for propulsion. A trip from St. Louis to the upper river would take an entire summer season. Upon reaching its destination the keelboat would be loaded with furs and then begin its return journey to St. Louis

Steamboats on the Upper Missouri

For many years the Missouri was considered unnavigable by steamboats in its upper reaches. However, as technology improved, the boats began to successfully penetrate the upper Missouri. Significantly, in 1832, the steamboat *Yellowstone*, owned by the American Fur Co., reached Fort Union at the confluence of the Missouri and Yellowstone Rivers, just across the North Dakota border. By 1840 the steamers were ascending the Missouri at a rate of fifty to one hundred miles per day. In 1843 the *Omega* made the trip to Ft. Union in fifty days, and returned to St. Louis in only two weeks. In succeeding years, as technology advanced, the steamers were able to penetrate further up the river, and finally in 1859, the *Chippewa*, piloted by Capt. LaBarge, reached the mouth of the Marias, just twenty-two river miles from Fort Benton. In 1860 the *Chippewa* and the *Key West* (Capt. LaBarge) both succeeded in reaching Fort Benton, which was to prove to be the head of navigation. By this time the boats were constructed with a wide beam, drew slightly more than two feet of water, and could carry 350 tons of freight.

The obvious advantages of the steamboats were their speed and their capacity for bulk carriage. The disadvantages were that they were expensive to build, their fuel demands were great, and if they wrecked, large quantities of goods were at risk. A steamboat burned from twenty-five to thirty cords of wood per day, leading to a rapid deforestation of the river's riparian cottonwood groves. At first the boats carried their own wood crews, but later, by the 1840's in Montana, "woodhawks", such as the famous John "Liver Eating" Johnson, settled along the river to supply the boats with fuelwood.

The boats hauled passengers and Indian trade goods up the river, and also government agents and government annuities for the Indians. Cabin rates, one way, from St. Louis to Ft. Benton was about $300; deck passage was $75; freight was ten to fifteen cents per pound.

The navigation season for the steamboats was limited. They primarily traveled during two periods of high water, which permitted the boats to travel over the shallow stretches of the river. The first of these high water periods was called the spring rise, which resulted from spring rains and lasted from March to May. This was followed by the more substantial summer rise, in early June, which resulted from melting of the snowpack in the mountains. By late June the river was usually unnavigable for the steamers.

Steamboats which navigated the Missouri needed more than their paddle wheel to negotiate the bars, rapids, and shallows of the Missouri. In ascending through a strong current a crew would often be sent ashore to place a "deadman". This was a large log which was buried in the soil on the bank of the river and to which a heavy rope, called a 'hawser', was attached. The hawser was then attached to the boat's steam powered capstan, permitting the steamboat to winch itself upstream.

If a steamboat became grounded on a gravel bar the boat would use a method called 'sparring' to free itself and continue advancing. Sparring involved the use of two long wooden poles, called 'spars', which were carried on the front of the boat and were rigged with an elaborate cabling system which enabled them to be used like a pair of crutches. The bottom tips of the spars were sheathed in iron and could be placed on the river bottom, angled toward the rear, and the boat's winch (the capstan) would drive the spars into the river bottom, and thus lift the bow of the boat off of the bar, while the paddle wheel nudged the boat a short distance forward. It was not uncommon for a boat to spend hours, and sometimes more than a day, sparring over a difficult section of river. Another method to deal with gravel bars involved having the crew, possibly assisted by passengers, wade into the river on each side of the boat and use a chain, pulled back and forth with a sawing action, in an attempt to disturb the gravel bar enough so that the river's current would erode the bar out from under the boat.

The steamboats were highly instrumental in the settling of Montana. Prior to the 1860's, there were no permanent white residents in Montana, only fur traders. This all changed with the discovery of gold in Montana throughout the 1860's, which precipitated a large influx of people, both miners and merchants. Fort Benton boomed, and earned its name as the "birthplace of Montana". Because of Indian troubles, the overland routes into Montana were hazardous, and the steamboats brought both people and supplies in and out of Montana. For example, in period from 1866-67 a total of seventy steamboats landed in Ft. Benton, delivering ten thousand passengers as well as twenty quartz mills which were used for crushing gold ore. In 1866 a single boat, the *Luella*, carried $1.25 million dollars in gold dust out of Montana, most of it in money belts worn by the passengers. One such heavily laden passenger fell overboard in two feet of water and was washed away by the current and drowned.

A photograph taken in June of 1877 at the Bismark levee showing the business end of two Missouri River steamboats, the Nellie Peck and the Far West. Although some side-wheelers saw service on the Upper Missouri, most were stern-wheelers. Haynes Foundation Collection, Montana Historical Society.

The steamboat John Chambers on the Missouri River at the Bismark levee, Dakota Territory in Spring 1877. This photo shows the spars - long, iron-tipped poles located on either side of the bow, and rigged with a complex cabling syestm. When a steamboat ran aground on a gravel bar it would lower the spars onto the river bottom and, using its winch, would lift itself on the spars, using them like a pair of crutches to inch its way forward. This technique became known as 'sparring' or 'grasshoppering'. It would sometimes take a steamboat a full day of sparring to get through a difficult rapid on the Upper Missouri. Haynes Foundation Collection, Montana Historical Society.

When the railroads arrived in Montana during the 1880's the steamboat rapidly lost its importance as a means of transportation; the last commercial steamboat to land in Ft. Benton was in 1890. For a few years thereafter, the U.S Army Corps of Engineers operated steamboats on the Upper Missouri for the purpose of maintaining the channel for navigation, until it was finally realized that the great boats would never again see service on the Missouri.

'Tourism' on the Upper Missouri

The inroads made by the fur traders, and the successful navigation of the Upper Missouri by steamboats, made it possible for individuals outside of the fur trade to travel into the wilderness of the Upper Missouri. In a number of cases these individuals were scientists and artists, and they became the first ethnographers to glimpse the Indians of the region before the rush of westward expansion decimated their numbers and their culture.

Such notables as George Catlin (1832), Prince Maximilian of Wied (1833), and John Audubon (1842), traveled by steamboat to study the natural history and the Indian tribes of various sections of the Upper Missouri. Of these, only Maximilian visited the section of the river preserved in today's monument.

Prince Maximilian of Wied was a German aristocrat, well educated, and possessing a keen interest in the native peoples of the Americas. In 1815-17 he visited Brazil and studied the native people there, publishing a book on his studies. The illustrations for this book were done back in Germany, based on the prince's field sketches, with help from a brother and sister. They urged him, as he planned for his trip to the west, that he engage a professional artist. For his trip to America he hired a well trained Swiss artist, Karl Bodmer, to render drawings of the expedition.

General William Clark (of the famous expedition), Superintendent of Indian Affairs in St. Louis, arranged for Maximilian and Bodmer to travel up the Missouri as guests of the American Fur Company. On April 10, 1833 the company's steamboat *Yellowstone* left St. Louis with Maximilian and Bodmer aboard, accompanied by Pierre Chouteau Jr., who was the head of the company's operations in St. Louis. In the Dakotas, Maximilian and Bodmer switched to a different steamboat, the *Assiniboin*, and arrived at Fort Union on June 24.

Fort Union was located at the confluence of the Missouri and Yellowstone Rivers, just east of the Montana-North Dakota border, and it was the headquarters of the American Fur Company on the upper river. The post was constructed in 1829, and was run by Kenneth McKenzie, who was known as "the king of the Upper Missouri". Despite the fort's remoteness, McKenzie had seen to it that the fort was stocked with fine china and silver, and an ample supply of fine wines. Maximilian and Bodmer were warmly welcomed by McKenzie, who undoubtedly enjoyed being visited by distinguished guests who were a welcome change from the American Fur Company employees that he supervised; largely of French descent, they were - in effect- poor, uneducated indentured servants whose wages largely went back to the company for lodging, food, and supplies.

After remaining two weeks at Fort Union to study the Indians and wildlife, and to permit Bodmer to sketch the country and the numerous Indians who frequented the post, they continued upriver aboard the keelboat *Flora,* sixty feet by sixteen feet, with fifty-two people aboard, and trade goods for the Indians. The primary means of propulsion for the *Flora* was the 'cordelle' - a rope which was pulled by a team of men walking up the river's banks. They were bound for the stretch of the Upper Missouri that today lies within the monument, with the destination being Fort McKenzie, located at the mouth

The Maximilian Expedition meeting Indians at Fort Clark, in present day North Dakota, in 1833. Maximilian is second from right, and Karl Bodmer, his hired artist, is on the right. Courtesy Joslyn Art Museum, Omaha, Nebraska; gift of the Enron Foundation.

of the Marias (river mile 14 L), and in the country of the Piegan Blackfeet. Fort McKenzie had been built in 1832, to replace Fort Piegan (1831; river mile 22 L), and it was the westernmost spearhead of the fur trade. While passing Arrow Creek (rm 79 R), the keelboat encountered a large encampment of Gros Ventre Indians, which unfolded into a rather tense situation for the travelers.

It was at Fort McKenzie that Maximilian and Bodmer had the unique opportunity to study and sketch the Indians of the upper reaches of the Missouri before they had been appreciably impacted by white culture. They remained at Fort McKenzie for five weeks, during which time Bodmer sketched prolifically. Piegan, Blood, Siksika, Gros Ventre des Prairie, and Kutenai Indians all sat for their portraits. Bodmer enjoyed a unique window of opportunity which no other artist ever experienced; his works captured the Plains Indian culture before it was appreciably changed by contact with whites. After Bodmer, life for these people changed rapidly, and today his drawings are a priceless window into the past.

While Bodmer sketched and painted, Maximilian prodigiously recorded his observations of plains Indian culture in his journals, which were later published, and rank with Bodmer's artwork for timeliness, accuracy, and thoroughness.

Bodmer and Maximilian witnessed numerous violent acts while at Fort McKenzie, and for safety reasons, abandoned plans to winter there. On September 14, 1833, they boarded a mackinaw, and left for Fort Clark in the Dakotas, where they wintered. As on the upriver journey, Bodmer made many sketches of the beautiful White Cliffs of the Missouri, within today's national monument, and present-day floaters who pass through this area are stricken by the accuracy of Karl Bodmer's sketches and the skill with which he captured the Upper Missouri's timeless beauty.

Discovery of Gold in Montana

Although the fur trade drastically changed life for the Indians on the Upper Missouri, it did not bring a large influx of whites into the territory, nor did it displace the Indians from their lands; they were still able to continue their traditional lifestyles, and roamed the plains at will. Gold - "the yellow metal that makes the white man crazy" - was responsible for the beginning of the end of the Plains Indian way of life.

The discovery of gold in Montana in the early 1860's, at locations such as Bannack, Virginia City, and Helena, encouraged large waves of whites to enter the state, many of whom stayed even when the gold played out. The gold discoveries were coincident with the successful navigation and conquest of the Missouri by steamboat, all the way to Fort Benton. Since travel overland was fraught with risk of attack by Indians, the steamboats provided a relatively safe means of travel into Montana from the east.

The gold discoveries prompted a boom in Fort Benton, and the small fur trading outpost became the "birthplace of Montana", with thousands of men arriving there each year. From Ft. Benton, the miners followed roads to the gold fields; these roads were also used by stagelines, bull trains, and mule trains which transported supplies to the mining communities. In Fort Benton, the firm of T.C. Power and Bros. formed to take advantage of the large profits to be reaped from the boom.

As Indian hostilities erupted in response to the overrunning of their lands, the white invaders demanded military protection. With the end of the Civil War, large numbers of troops, officers, and equipment became available; military forts were constructed and a series of campaigns begun against the Indians, eventually ending with the confinement of the tribes to reservations.

The steamboat Helena at Milk River Landing, Montana in 1880. Originally designed to bring trade goods into Indian country and furs back to St. Louis, the boats later carried thousands of white settlers into the Upper Missouri country. The large influx of white settlers was prompted by the discovery of gold in Montana in the early 1860's at Bannack and Virginia City. Haynes Foundation Collection, Montana Historical Society.

Native Peoples of the Upper Missouri

Introduction

In Montana, the Upper Missouri River area served as an environment for man from the paleo-Indian inhabitation of the North American continent, beginning at least fifteen thousand years ago, and perhaps extending to thirty thousand years ago. North American Indian people probably have their origin in Asia, having crossed the Bering Sea land bridge, and then proceeding southward along the Great North Trail into Montana. Though no intensive survey of the lands included in the Upper Missouri corridor has been made, some 173 known sites testify to extensive occupation of this wild and scenic area. These sites have provided evidence of temporary camping areas, an evolving stone age technology, sources of subsistence, ceremonial performance, and burial practices.

Early Pre-Historic Period

Within the monument, the earliest evidence of the presence of a paleo-Indian culture, sometimes referred to as Clovis man, is a Hell Gap projectile point, about ten thousand years old, found at a Missouri River site. These people were the early big-game hunters of the late Pleistocene period of geologic time, and they are classified as belonging to the Early Pre-Historic Period. The environment during this period of time was still being affected by the retreating Ice Age glaciers, and was cooler and wetter than the present-day climate. Lush grasslands, swamps, and lakes south of the continental glacial ice mass proved ideal habitat for herds of now extinct mammoth, mastodon, and giant bison. The paleo-Indian wandered in small groups pursuing these game herds, the major source of his subsistence. Always on the move, the early big game hunter left little evidence of his presence.

Middle Pre-Historic Period

Evidence of occupation of the Missouri breaks region during the Middle Prehistoric Period (between 7500 and 1800 years ago) is somewhat more abundant than that of the early period. The ending of the Ice Age led to an altithermal climate, trending towards warm and dry, which caused many of the large game species in Montana to become extinct, and the subsistence patterns of the wandering bands changed. In addition to bison, animals such as antelope, deer and elk, smaller mammals, reptiles, and birds fell prey to the hunter. Meals often included seeds, roots, and berries, indicating a hunter-gatherer society. The relative scarcity of food suggests a situation where small groups of people probably moved about regularly to find adequate means of subsistence.

Late Pre-Historic Period

During the Late Pre-Historic Period (between 1800 and 200 years ago), Indian people frequented the Missouri River area in a climate much like that of today. A major change in technology occurred, with the bow and arrow replacing the spear or lance. Around A.D. 1700, the introduction of the horse, which was introduced in the southwest by the Spanish, and found its way northward, proved to be a major advancement for the bison hunting culture. Bison, the basic food source, was generally plentiful and the herds permitted larger groups of people to subsist together, and required less time for the hunt.

In spite of a somewhat higher standard of living, there were still times of dire need. The Lost Terrace Site, an antelope butchering station along the Missouri, shows that the Indians used every possible bit of their prey.

Archeological investigations within the Upper Missouri have not been extensive, but some significant sites have been studied, for example at Lost Terrace, and in the vicinities of Hole-In-The-Wall (rm 64), and Thompson Bottoms (rm 46).

Life evolved but slowly for these Late Pre-Historic people until they were confronted by a transplanted European civilization, spearheaded by Lewis and Clark, that thirsted for a westward expansion across an uncharted land.

Upper Missouri Indian Tribes of Historic Times

At the time that Lewis and Clark arrived in Montana, in 1805, the Indian tribes that inhabited the Upper Missouri had already felt the effects of an expanding European-American population with its beginnings on the Atlantic coast. As white settlements pushed westward over the Appalachian Mountains, local tribes were displaced in a generally westward direction, creating a domino effect on other tribes who had not had direct contact with the whites. As a result, the tribes inhabiting Montana in the early 1800's were all relatively recent arrivals, who had in turn displaced other resident Indians. These people included the Blackfeet, Assiniboine, Gros Ventre, and Crow tribes, all of whom are presently represented on reservations in Montana.

Blackfeet

The Blackfeet were the dominant tribe along the Upper Missouri. By the time Lewis and Clark arrived, the Blackfeet had acquired horses from tribes to the west, and they were the only tribe to have acquired guns, which they got from the Hudson's Bay Company fur traders who had established trading posts north of the present day Montana-Canada border. The combination of guns and horses, combined with their aggressive demeanor, permitted the Blackfeet to dominate the northern plains.

It is believed that the Blackfeet migrated into Montana from the eastern woodlands of North America, after the arrival of whites. The Blackfeet were composed of three confederated tribes, the Piegan, the Bloods, and the Siksika (or Northern Blackfeet) , with the Piegan being most common in Montana, and the Bloods and Siksika occupying Canada.

The range of the Blackfeet was both north and south of the Missouri, from the Rocky Mountains to the central part of Montana.

Captain Meriwether Lewis, and three men from the expedition, traveled into the heart of Blackfeet country during a side excursion up the Marias River, and fell into a skirmish with a band of Blackfeet, killing two of the Indians. (See journal entry in the History Digest - rm 32).

As the St. Louis-based fur trade began developing, the Blackfeet, possibly due to the earlier encounter with Lewis, refused to trade with the Americans, and treated them with great hostility. It was not until 1832 that a successful trade with the Blackfeet was cultivated. Despite their acceptance of the Americans as trading partners, the Blackfeet resisted white incursions into their territory, and they defended their territory tenaciously, until they were finally overwhelmed by the white's military superiority. Today the Blackfeet Reservation is located along the east flanks of the northern Rockies.

Assiniboine

The Assiniboine are believed to have arrived in Montana in the mid-1700's, from north central Canada, and are thought to be an offshoot of the Sioux Indians. In the 1800's they allied themselves with the Cree, to help strengthen their position against their common enemy, the Blackfeet, who had become aligned with the Gros Ventre. The Assiniboine frequented the Missouri River valley in northeastern

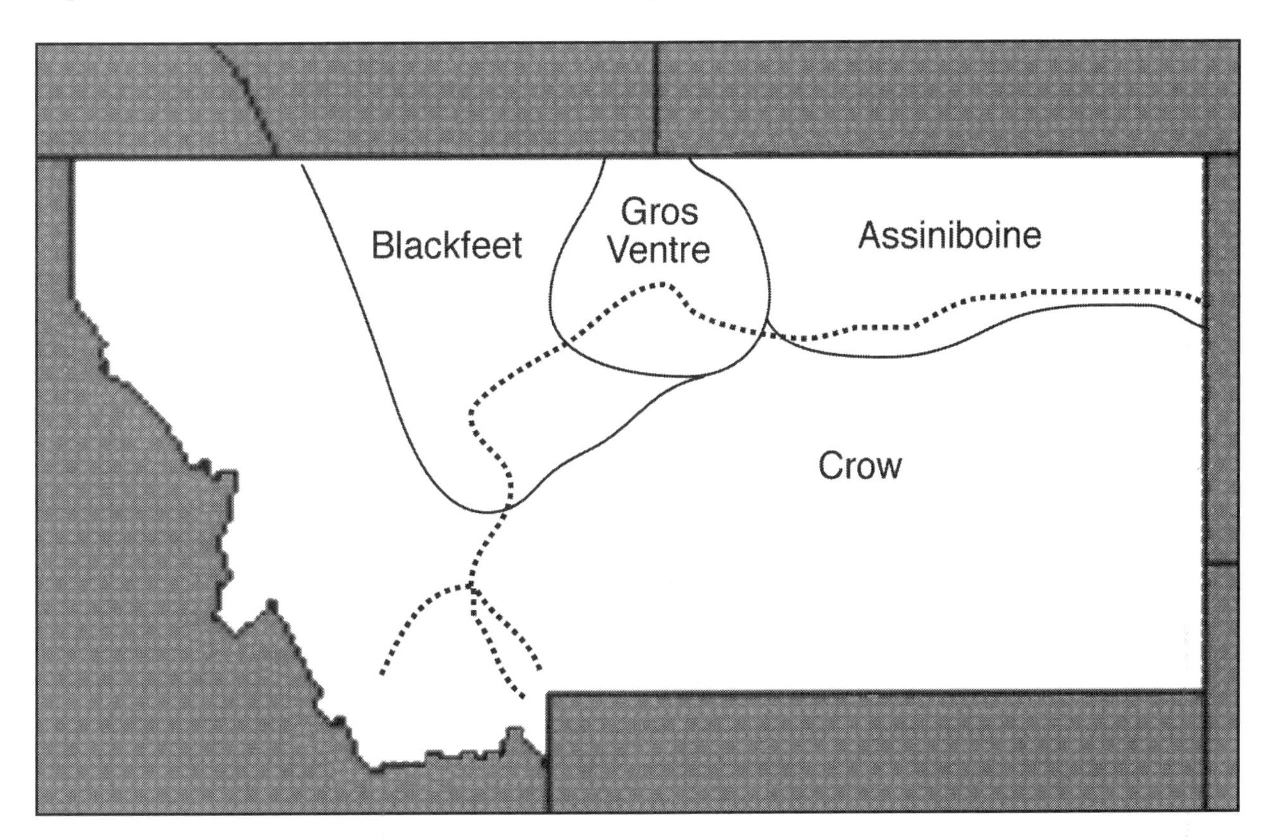

Map of Montana showing the approximate distribution of Indian tribes which inhabited the Upper Missouri area at the time of the arrival of whites. The dotted line is the Missouri River.

Stomick-Sosack, or Bull's Back Fat, was a chief of the Blood Blackfeet Indians, painted by Karl Bodmer in September, 1833 at Fort McKenzie. Courtesy Joslyn Art Museum, Omaha, Nebraska; gift of the Enron Foundation.

Mehkskehme-Sukahs, or Iron Shirt, was a chief of the Piegan Blackfeet Indians, painted by Karl Bodmer on August 11, 1833 at Fort McKenzie. Courtesy Joslyn Art Museum, Omaha, Nebraska; gift of the Enron Foundation

Ihkas-Kinne, Siksika Blackfeet chief, painted by Karl Bodmer at Fort McKenzie in 1833. Courtesy Joslyn Art Museum, Omaha, Nebraska; gift of the Enron Foundation

Pteh-Skah, Assiniboin chief, painted by Karl Bodmer at Fort Union in October, 1833. Courtesy Joslyn Art Museum, Omaha, Nebraska; gift of the Enron Foundation

Montana, and traded at Fort Union, at the confluence of the Missouri and Yellowstone Rivers. While Prince Maximilian and artist Karl Bodmer were at Fort McKenzie in 1833, they witnessed a raid by the Assiniboine on a group of Blackfeet who were camped outside the fort, and the scene was painted by Bodmer (see History Digest for river mile 14 L)

Gros Ventre

The Gros Ventre Indians, also known as the Atsina, were closely allied with the Blackfeet by the 1800's, and shared the eastern part of their territory. They are thought to have migrated to Montana from north central Canada, and their language has the same roots as the Blackfeet. The name Gros Ventre means "big belly", but it is not known what the origin of this name is. By the 1860's the Gros Ventre alliance with the Blackfeet unraveled and they moved further to the east. Karl Bodmer, in 1833, while traveling up the Missouri in a keelboat from Fort Union to Fort McKenzie, sketched a large Gros Ventre camp located at the mouth of Arrow Creek (rm 77 R)

Mexkemauastan, was a chief of the Atsina, or Gros Ventre Indians, painted by Karl Bodmer in 1833 at Fort McKenzie. Courtesy Joslyn Art Museum, Omaha, Nebraska; gift of the Enron Foundation.

Crow

The Crow have their origin in the headwaters area of the Mississippi River and are related to the Sioux Indians. They were among the earliest tribes to migrate to the Great Plains, probably arriving in the early 1600's. The Indian name for these people is "Absarokee", which means "children of the large beaked bird" - probably the raven or crow.

The territory occupied by the Crow centered along the Yellowstone River valley in central and eastern Montana, and they ranged north to the Missouri. They had a reputation as excellent horsemen. Although the Lewis and Clark Expedition did not have any direct contact with the Crow people, Captain William Clark, traveling by horse with his return contingent while exploring the Yellowstone River valley, was nagged by the loss of many of his horses, which disappeared at night while the men were sleeping. It is likely that the horses were taken by Crows.

Additional Information

Additional information about the history of the Upper Missouri may be obtained from the History Digest - Chapters Two, Three and Four; these chapters contain information about specific sites on the river, most of which are only accessible by boat, and the entries in these three chapters are keyed to the Bureau of Land Management's set of maps that are commonly used by floaters.

Also, the bibliography at the end of this book lists many excellent resources on the history of the Upper Missouri.

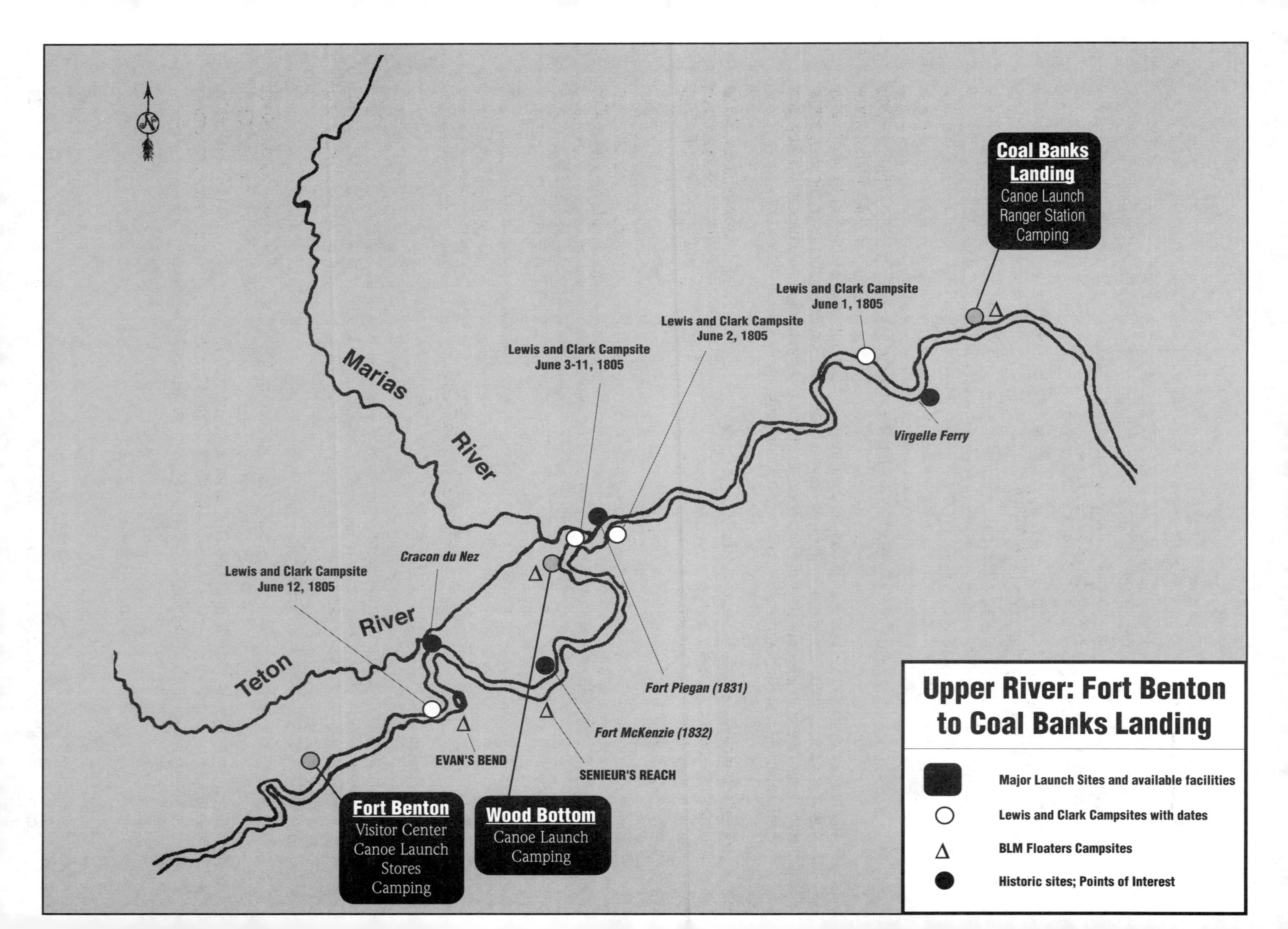
Upper River: Fort Benton to Coal Banks Landing
Major Launch Sites and available facilities
Lewis and Clark Campsites with dates
BLM Floaters Campsites
Historic sites; Points of Interest
Coal Banks Landing
Canoe Launch
Ranger Station
Camping
Lewis and Clark Campsite
June 1, 1805
Lewis and Clark Campsite
June 2, 1805
Lewis and Clark Campsite
June 3-11, 1805
Virgelle Ferry
Marias
River
Cracon du Nez
Lewis and Clark Campsite
June 12, 1805
River
Teton
Fort Piegan (1831)
Fort McKenzie (1832)
EVAN'S BEND
SENIEUR'S REACH
Fort Benton
Visitor Center
Canoe Launch
Stores
Camping
Wood Bottom
Canoe Launch
Camping

Chapter 2

History Digest: Fort Benton to Coal Banks Landing

Introduction

This chapter, and the following two, contain a history digest for the Upper Missouri National Wild and Scenic River. The digest is a mile-by-mile log of historic locations along the one hundred forty-nine mile stretch of the Upper Missouri, beginning at Fort Benton and continuing to James Kipp Recreation Area. The entries in the history digest begin at Fort Benton, which is given the designation of "river mile 0.0". Continuing downriver from Fort Benton subsequent entries are all listed by river mile, continuing to Kipp Recreation area at "river mile 149".

For floaters wishing to accurately pinpoint the locations of the history digest's entries, it should be used in conjunction with the detailed set of maps that is printed and sold by the Bureau of Land Management, entitled "Floaters Guide - Upper Missouri National Wild and Scenic River". See Chapter 7 for information about ordering these maps.

Chapter Two covers the stretch of river from Fort Benton to Coal Banks Landing; Chapter Three, from Coal Banks Landing to Judith Landing; and Chapter Four, from Judith Landing to James Kipp Recreation Area.

******

FORT BENTON

River Mile 0 to 1.6 Left

The return of the Lewis and Clark Expedition to St. Louis in 1806 brought with it tales of beaver and other fur bearers in large numbers along the Upper Missouri and its tributaries. These reports stimulated the development of the fur trade.

However, white activity did not develop easily in north-central Montana, largely because of hostilities with the Blackfeet Indians. These hostilities are believed to have begun with the Lewis and Clark Expedition at the Two Medicine River fight, along a tributary of the Marias, July 27, 1806 (see entry for river mile 22). A more substantial cause for the Blackfeet hostility may have been the appearance of white trappers in the ranks of their enemies, the Crows, in an 1807 battle.

Whatever the reason, no fur trade occurred in Blackfeet country until 1831 with the establishment of Fort Piegan (see river mile 22 left) at the mouth of the Marias River. Fort Piegan was replaced by Fort McKenzie (see river mile 14 left) the following year and McKenzie operated successfully until early in 1844 when two unscrupulous traders there killed a number of Blackfeet in revenge for an earlier altercation and hostilities with the Blackfeet were renewed.

In 1845 Alexander Culbertson was summoned from Fort Laramie by the American Fur Company to reestablish trading relations with the Blackfeet. Culbertson was married to a Blackfeet Indian woman, Natawista Iksana, the daughter of a Blood Chief, and was generally trusted by the Blackfeet.

Culbertson first established Fort Lewis on the south side of the Missouri three miles upriver from the present site of Fort Benton. That location soon proved to be unsatisfactory because winter ice jams and spring floods made it inaccessible to the Indians. Consequently, development at a new location began in 1846, and in the spring of 1847 the traders floated all moveable fixtures of Fort Lewis downriver to the present location of Fort Benton.

The new post was known as Fort Clay until Christmas of 1850, when it was renamed Fort Benton in honor of Senator Thomas Hart Benton of Missouri, a strong political supporter of the fur trade. The city of Fort Benton had its beginning during and through the fur trade era, and became the 'birthplace of Montana' - the stopping place of steamboats and the starting place of wagon trains.

A sketch of Fort Benton, built in 1846 by the American Fur Company, and named for Senator Thomas Hart Benton of Missouri, a friend of the fur trade. After the fur trade declined, the fort was used as a military post from 1869 to 1881. The fort was built of adobe bricks, and a small portion of the original fort still stands in the Fort Benton City Park. Montana Historical Society photograph.

The fur trade era stimulated the first extensive use of the Missouri River as an avenue of transportation. Keelboats, mackinaws, bullboats, and canoes plied the upper river bringing trade items and returning with a wealth of furs. At Fort Benton Indians and white fur traders alike exchanged their pelts and hides for clothing, arms, and other items. Liquor was used extensively as a means to separate Indians from their furs.

The vast amount of capital to be obtained encouraged steamboat captains to brave the treacherous Missouri. Steamboat navigation on the Missouri started in 1831 when a vessel named the *Yellowstone* arrived at Pierre, South Dakota, from St. Louis. The next year it got to Fort Union, on the present eastern boundary of Montana. Several other upstream efforts were made, and in 1859 Captain John LaBarge, accompanied by Charles Chouteau of the American Fur Company, attempted to reach Fort Benton. They fell only 12 $^1/_2$ miles short of their goal, unloading the *Chippewa* at the former site of Fort McKenzie (Brule Bottom).

Having learned much about the upper river the previous year, in 1860 the attempt was again made. On July 2,1860, the steamer *Chippewa,* followed closely by the *Key West,* reached Fort Benton and proved that the channel of the Missouri was navigable to that point. Navigability was established just in time to serve the gold camps which were about to open in southwestern Montana.

Fort Benton trading post, in ruins, photographed about 1896. Montana State Historical Society photograph.

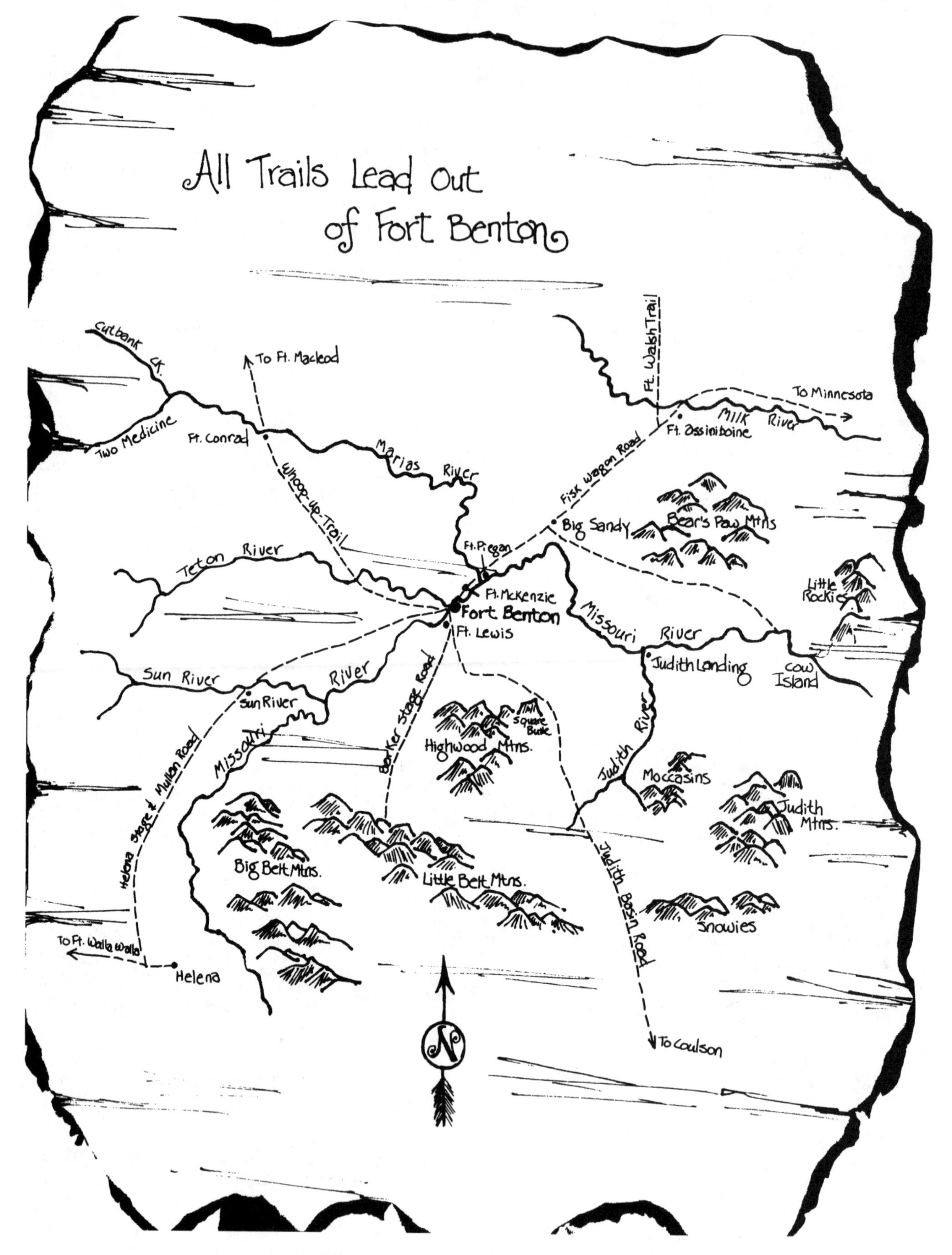

As the head of steamboat navigation on the Upper Missouri, Fort Benton became the jumping off point for a rush of incoming settlers, and the starting point for wagons that transported supplies throughout the newly populated Montana Territory. This map shows the many roads that left Fort Benton.

Another accomplishment in 1860 that enhanced the development of Fort Benton was the completion of a trail heading west to connect the heads of navigation on the Missouri and Columbia Rivers. In 1853 Lieutenant (later Captain) John Mullan began making surveys for a military road from Fort Benton to Walla Walla, Washington, although at that time no steamboat had yet arrived at Fort Benton. Mullan built the 624 mile road between 1859-60. He stayed with the project until 1862, making improvements and repairs. It crossed the Continental Divide near Helena.

Discoveries of gold in 1862 at Grasshopper Creek, in 1863 at Alder Gulch, and in 1864 at Last Chance Gulch put an entirely new picture on the development of Montana. The era of the fur trade was passing. The era of mining was beginning.

After 1865 it became obvious to the merchants of St. Louis that if they were to get the business that would develop from this new mining boom, they must modernize their transportation. They built vessels which could successfully negotiate the shifting channel of the Missouri during the few months each year that the river was passable.

Another factor favoring river traffic was that the Indian tribes virtually closed many of the overland trails, while the river route was faster and more comfortable and comparatively free of disturbance.

Traffic up the river became heavy in 1866. The steamboat business continued to grow to intercept shipments destined for the gold fields. Changes in the mining industry required changes in freight. In 1867 machinery for at least 35 quartz mills, for grinding gold ore, arrived in Fort Benton.

The editor of *The New Northwest,* at Deer Lodge, described the town as he saw it: "In the streets was a throng of varied and picturesque humanity; lumbermen from Minnesota and farmers from many parts of the great valley; Confederate sympathizers from Missouri and Union men from the Western Reserve; miners from the Pacific coast, and fur traders and hunters of the vanishing northwestern wilderness; Indians of many tribes, desperadoes and lovers of order, miners, traders, clergymen, speculators, land seekers, government officials - all the exuberant array of the American frontier."

The upriver trip from St. Louis to Fort Benton was usually made in sixty to sixty-five days. Passenger fare averaged $150. During the busy year of 1867 some fifteen hundred persons reached Montana on these vessels.

Steamboats returning to the east also carried freight. During the late summer of 1866 for example, Grant Marsh, master of the *Luella,* loaded $2^1/_2$ tons of Confederate Gulch gold dust on his boat. Valued at $1,250,000, it was the richest cargo ever to go down the Missouri. The *Luella* was also loaded with passengers at $300 for cabin passage (probably not single occupancy), a bit less for deck fares and rustle your own grub. For the trip, Grant Marsh drew $1,200 a month, and still made $25,000 for the owners of the *Luella.*

In the early 1870s, mining activities began to decline and the end of the river traffic was predicted. However, it spurted again later in the decade as the population grew in central Montana and Canada.

Historian Paul F. Sharp wrote, "As gold stampedes played out and as the whisky trade to the north vanished and the fur trade declined, Benton emerged as a commercial center of wholesalers and jobbers.... This transition to a commercial center changed Benton from a 'squaw town, a scalp market, the home of horse thieves, to a town of merchants' account books and manifest lists."

The all-time peak of river traffic was in 1879, with forty-seven boats carrying 9,444 tons up the river. In the 1880's traffic began to drop as the newly built railroads cut into the shipping market.

The steamboat DeSmet at the Fort Benton levee. Coincidental with the decline of the fur trade was the discovery of gold in Montana. The steamers were instrumental in shipping mining supplies and provisions for the miners into Montana. Montana Historical Society photograph.

Almost as exciting as the river traffic which brought commodities into Fort Benton was the transportation industry which carried the merchandise out. Stage lines, bull trains, mule trains, and similar methods of transportation were available for the commodities which reached Fort Benton destined for points beyond.

"All trails lead out of Benton" was a familiar statement. The community was the anchor of the Mullan Road to Walla Walla. The road to Helena and other gold mining towns branched off from the Mullan Road. The Whoop-Up Trail led into Canada and was an important factor in keeping Benton prosperous after the mining declined. The Fisk Wagon Road to St. Paul through northern Montana and North Dakota was another important road.

Again quoting Sharp, "The merchant princes of Fort Benton were the final agents for a vast system which provided Canadian and American ranchers, gold-seekers, treaty Indians, and government forces with the products of the looms of Manchester and Hartford, of the forges and furnaces of Sheffield and Pittsburgh, and of the distilleries of Boston and Louisville."

Fort Benton was never really a fort in the military sense. Its only military occupation was from October 1869 to June 1881. There never was more than one company of soldiers stationed at the post. Their chief military activity was tracking down illicit whiskey smugglers and deserters from their own ranks.

In the late 1870's river trade was at its peak. The influx of the Mounted Police into Canada brought law and order and this resulted in a lucrative trade for Fort Benton merchants. Until this time, the chief item of commerce exported to Canada had been whiskey. Fort Whoop-Up had been constructed as an outlet for the liquor trade originating in Fort Benton, but after the Mounties arrived it was soon closed. However, as the grasslands of Canada were settled, there was heavy demand for provisions and supplies which could not be freighted from Winnipeg. The only source of these supplies was Fort Benton.

The two principal businesses to supply these customers, as well as others in Montana, were the I.G. Baker Company and T.C. Powers and Brother. Both firms quickly prospered, building their businesses on the ruins left by the demise of the American Fur Company. Both the Baker and Power firms grew strong and wealthy through investments in such businesses as fur trading, mining, milling, banking, steamboats, freighting, and contracts with both the Canadian and American governments.

With the growth of merchandising came the related construction activities. For example, warehouses had to be built along Front Street to protect goods for trans-shipment. The building boom was on in earnest in 1882 when a total of three million bricks were turned out by the local foundry. The arrival of the railroad and accompanying decline in steamboat traffic signaled the need for expanded trading territory, so in 1888 Fort Benton merchants built a bridge over the Missouri to open up commerce with central Montana.

The most spectacular building project in Fort Benton was the Grand Union Hotel, finest in the northwest at the time. The three story Grand Union was the accomplishment of a hardware salesman, William H. Todd. He paid $10 for the land in 1867 and later obtained local financing of $30,000 for the building. Construction began early in 1881 and required 15 months to complete. The formal opening was November 2,1882. It took 500,000 red and yellow bricks from the local kiln. The final construction cost was $50,000, plus $150,000 for furnishings. The grand opening was the most elaborate social affair in the history of Fort Benton.

The steamboat Josephine at the Fort Benton levee, in the 1880's. As Montana became more settled, the steamboats were modified from freight carrying vessels to passenger vessels. Before the railroads arrived in Montana in the late 1880's, steamboats were the primary means of trensportation into and out of the area. Haynes Foundation Collection, Montana Historical Society photograph.

An ox team pulling three freight wagons in Fort Benton. The men who drove these wagons were called 'bullwhackers'. Goods that were shipped to Fort Benton by steamboat were shipped to their destinations by these freighters. During low water years when steamboats could not reach Fort Benton, they would unload their freight at Cow Island, where ox teams would freight it to Fort Benton.

The arrival of the railroad not only impacted Fort Benton's steamboat industry, but the area of commerce served by the community was also reduced. Mrs. James J. Hill, wife of the president of the Manitoba (later the Great Northern) Railroad, drove the silver spike at Fort Benton on September 29, 1887, and the era of the great river trade came to an end. The last private boat to come upriver was the *O.K.* It burned on the levee in 1908 after damaging its superstructure on the drawbridge at Fort Benton. The *Baby Rose,* locally built, served local commerce, mostly agricultural, between 1909 and 1916. The *Josephine* and the *Mandan,* both government snag boats, made trips up the river to Fort Benton into the 1920's. The growth of Great Falls further shrank the sphere of commercial activity of Fort Benton. However, the town held on and adjusted to a new economic opportunity. The arrival of trail herds of cattle from Texas signaled the beginning of the livestock industry in the late 1870's and early 1880's.

By 1885 Chouteau County's livestock industry had assumed large proportions. Its ranges supported 100,000 cattle, 60,000 sheep and 10,000 horses.

Then came the disastrous winter of 1886-87. It followed a summer of extraordinary drought when springs and streams dried up and ranchers searched frantically for feed. The severe winter wiped out many ranches. Cattle drifted with the blizzards and were buried in snow-filled coulees or froze to death piled against newly constructed wire fences. Losses for some of the ranches in the region ranged from sixty-five to ninety percent.

The result was the end of the open range. Montana livestock became largely home-owned and ranch units were much smaller. Cowboys had to learn to be hay hands, as it was recognized that winter feed was necessary. Hayfields had to be protected, and so ranches were fenced.

Fort Benton evolved to serve the early livestock industry, as it would the farmers who came largely as a result of the Homestead Act of 1909. It continues to be the economic hub of Chouteau County.

FORT LA BARGE

River Mile 0.3 Left

In 1862 another attempt was made to loosen the monopoly held by the American Fur Company on the Upper Missouri. Fort LaBarge was built about seven hundred yards above Fort Campbell, which by this time was quite dilapidated. LaBarge consisted of a substantial warehouse and other structures but was not palisaded and was within plain sight of Fort Benton, which lay just a mile downriver.

The fort was named LaBarge in honor of the senior member of the firm of LaBarge, Harkness & Company that established it. The firm was formed when Joseph LaBarge and four others put in $10,000 each for the *Shreveport,* a small, light draft boat, and the larger *Emilie.*

Joseph LaBarge entered service with the American Fur Company in 1832, later learned piloting on the Missouri, and became one of the most highly respected of pilots and captains. He operated boats for the American Fur Company and for opposition companies for many years. It was his brother, John, who brought the *Chippewa* into Fort Benton in 1860, proving the river navigable to that point.

The *Shreveport* and *Emilie* arrived at Fort Benton June 17, 1862, the first boats except those of the American Fur Company to ever reach this point. The *Emilie* had brought 350 tons of freight and 250 passengers. The smaller *Shreveport* had done proportionately as well. To this point in time the venture could have been assumed a success. The enterprise was, however, destined to be short-lived.

James Harkness was in charge of the firm's business at the upper end of the river. Among his responsibilities was the job of securing contracts for hauling freight to the mining settlements near Deer Lodge. Harkness was irresolute in both his business efforts and his ability to cope with wilderness life. Instead of remaining at Fort LaBarge and honoring the freight contracts, he returned to St. Louis.

Then in 1863 the river was unusually low and the *Shreveport* could get no further west than Cow Island, 128 miles downriver in the heart of the badlands. The LaBarge, Harkness & Company was unable to deliver goods which they had contracted to bring upriver for parties living at Bannack.

The entire venture dissolved in a series of lawsuits and a dispute with the American Fur Company over goods the firm left in storage at Cow Island.

These lawsuits led to the eventual sale of the buildings at Fort LaBarge, Harkness & Company. The sheriff's sale list of October 10, 1866, listed a store room, dining room, blacksmithy, carpenter shop, dwelling room, steam sawmill, grist mill, an office, an icehouse, and eleven log cabins for sale.

Joseph LaBarge calculated that the two year venture cost him $100,000.

FORT CAMPBELL

River Mile 0.6 Left

In 1847 Alexander Harvey, a vengeful former employee of the American Fur Company, relocated Fort Campbell to this location. The original Fort Campbell was built in 1846 on the right hand side of the Missouri a short way up from Cracon du Nez (the narrow ridge of land between the Teton and Missouri Rivers at river mile 9). The history of this fort is given at its original location at river mile 8.5 right.

Harvey had been fired by the American Fur Company for his role in the massacre of Blackfeet Indians at Fort McKenzie in 1844, the event which led to that post's demise. He then relocated Fort Campbell purposely to oppose the American Fur Company at Fort Benton.

Smarting from his dismissal and mad about an alleged plot to assassinate him, Harvey enlisted the powerful financial backing of the famous Robert Campbell of St. Louis. He also induced three dissatisfied American Fur Company clerks, Charles Primeau, Antoine R. Bouis and Joseph Picotte (nephew of Honore Picotte, General Agent for the American Fur Company), to join him in establishing an opposition firm. It became known as Harvey, Primeau, and Company.

The new post was built of adobe, the first such construction in the Blackfeet country. The principal customers were Piegan because Harvey had taken a Piegan wife. Fort Campbell did a fair trade, but did not seriously rival Fort Benton. One reason for the success of the business may have been that Harvey's tigerish ferocity appealed to the Blackfeet. For example, one day when Mountain Chief, a great Piegan warrior, was boasting from atop a building about his white scalps, Harvey climbed up and knocked Mountain Chief off with a club. Harvey was a man of relentless energy and a top flight trader.

After Harvey died on July 20,1854, Harvey, Primeau and Company gradually changed hands and a new enterprise, Frost, Todd, and Company took over the opposition. In 1857, the company in charge of Fort Campbell changed again and became known as Clark, Primeau, and Company. Then in 1860, the American Fur Company bought out this company.

In 1861 the American Fur Company offered Fort Campbell to the Jesuit missionaries for use until permanent quarters could be found. In October, Fathers Imoda and Giorda established a mission, Saint Peter's, at Fort Campbell. This was probably the last use of Fort Campbell.

In February 1862, Saint Peter's was relocated to the north bank of the Missouri six miles above the mouth of the Sun River (south of Great Falls).

(also see FORT CAMPBELL - River Mile 8.5 Right)

FORT BENTON LAUNCH

River Mile 1.2 Left

Floating on the Missouri

James Willard Schultz was born in New York. As a youth he developed a fondness for the outdoors, but was rebellious and troublesome for his parents. They sent him to military school, which he never took much liking to and was eventually expelled. His parents permitted him to visit relatives in St. Louis, where he was able to hear many tales of the west from the continuous stream of people who were heading up the river from St. Louis, as well as from those returning. The lure was irrrestible for the seventeen-year old lad.

Schultz boarded the steamboat *Benton*, arriving in Fort Benton in 1877. There he made the aquaintance of the aging James Kipp, the famous fur trader, who helped Schultz develop an interest in and friendship with the Blackfeet Indian tribe. This interest eventually led to Schultz marrying a Blackfeet woman, named Natahki, or Fine-Shield-Woman, and he essentially became a part of the tribe. This occurrred just before the extermination of the great buffalo herd at the hands of the white man, and Schultz had an opportunity to observe the last days of the Plains Indian buffalo culture, before the Blackfeet were confined to their reservation and became largely dependent upon the white conquerors. Schultz and his wife settled on a ranch on the reservation. His Indian name was Apikuni, or Far-Off-White-Robe.

Schultz and his wife floated the Upper Missouri in 1901, beginning at Fort Benton, at a time when the "breaks" was still a rather untamed place. Schultz's journals from the trip were used as material for a series of articles which he submitted to *Forest and Stream Magazine*, and which were published as installments the following year.

Schultz had a delightful writing style and provided some unique insights into the history of the river. Excerpts from *Floating on the Missouri* are included throughout the three history digest chapters at the appropriate locations.

The boat we had named the "Good Shield", which is the English of our better half's Indian name, was just a plain sharp-bowed, flat-bottomed skiff, some nineteen-feet long and five-feet beam. Not exactly a thing of beauty, but staunch, light of draft, and serviceable ...

The swift current was gently tossing and swaying our craft as if to say: "Come, why tarry? Cast loose and I will bear you swiftly into the land of your dreams." Well, then, the river should have its way.

"Get aboard and take the stern seat," I said to Sah-ne-to (Schultz's wife, Natahki, also known as Fine Shield Woman), and as soon as she had done so, I pushed out into the stream. Splash! Sah-ne-to dropped a little beaded buckskin sack into the water. What it contained I know not, nor did I ask. But I heard her low prayer: "Spirits of the water, people of the depths, accept my poor sacrifice. Pity us, I entreat you; draw us not down to our death in your cold, dark realm; cast us not upon the rock hidden by the foaming current. Pity, pity. Accept my offering, I pray you, and harm us not."

Sah-ne-to has not forgotten the gods and devils of her people if she has been married to a pale-face these twenty years and more. Missionaries and their creeds are as nothing to her; the sun, the glorious, dazzling, resplendent orb, is the kind and living ruler of the world . By his aid, and through sacrifice, the evil spirits may be kept from working harm."

SHONKIN CREEK BOAT YARD

RIVER MILE 4.8 RIGHT

The mouth of Shonkin Creek was the location of a construction yard where mackinaws were constructed for the trading post at Ft. Benton. Mackinaws were made of hand sawed lumber and were fastened together by wooden pins. (A drawing of a Mackinaw appears in Chapter 1). They were flat bottomed crafts and usually carried five men, four at the oars and one at the rudder. The unique, high ended boats were used for downriver trips only and carried about fifteen tons of freight, though loads as large as forty-five tons are recorded.

The name Shonkin is probably derived from "Chantier," French for "yard of a ship."

Lewis and Clark referred to Shonkin Creek as Snow River in their journals.

LEWIS CAMP OF JUNE 11, 1805, AND CLARK CAMP OF JUNE 12, 1805

RIVER MILE 8.2 LEFT

Lewis and Clark separated briefly at the mouth of the Marias River (some 14 miles below). Lewis set out overland with four men to locate the Great Falls and to prove that their crucial decision to follow the left-hand or south river was correct. Clark stayed at the Marias one more day to finish repairs to equipment and to complete their cache there. Lewis at this time had a bad case of "disentary."

[Lewis - Tuesday, June 11th - on the Missouri River]

This morning I felt much better, but somewhat w[e]akened by my disorder. at 8 A.M. I swung my pack, and set forward with my little party. proceeded to the point where Rose River (today's Teton River) a branch of Maria's River approaches the Missouri so nearly. from this hight we discovered a herd of Elk on the Missouri just above us to which we desended and soon killed four of them. we butchered them and hung up the meat and skins in view of the river in order that the party might get them. I determined to take dinner here, but before the meal was prepared I was taken with such violent pain in the intestens that I was unable to partake of the feast of marrowbones ... having brought no medecine with me I resolved to try an experiment with some simples; and the Choke cherry which grew abundantly in the bottom first struck my attention; I directed a parsel of the small twigs to be geathered striped of their leaves, cut into pieces of about 2 Inches in length and boiled in water untill a strong black decoction of an astringent bitter tast was produced; at sunset I took a point [pint] of this decoction and about an hour after repeated the doze. by 10 in the evening I was entirely releived from pain and in fact every symptom of the disorder forsook me; my fever abated, a gentle perspiration was produced and I had a comfortable and refreshing nights rest. Goodrich who is remarkably fond of fishing caught several douzen fish of two different species ... the white cat(fish) continue as high as the entrance of Marias River, but those we have caught above Mandans never excede 6 lbs. I believe there are but few in this part of the Missouri. saw an abundance of game today even in our short march of 9 miles.

[Lewis - Wednesday, June 12th]

This morning I felt myself quite revived, took another portion of my decoction and set out at sunrise. I now boar out from the river in order to avoid the steep ravines of the river which usually make out in the plain to the distance of one or two miles....having traveled 12 miles by 9 in the morning, the sun became warm, and I boar a little to the south in order to gain the river as well to obtain water to allay my thirst as to kill something for breakfast ... we arrived at the river about 10 A.M. having traveled about 15 m. at this place there is a handsome open bottom with some cottonwood timber, here we met with two large bear, and killed them boath at the first fire, a circumstance I beleive has never happened with the party in killing the brown bear before. we dressed the bear, breakfasted on a part of one of them and hung the meat and skins on the trees out of the reach of the wolves ... after refreshing ourselves abut (about) 2 hours we again ascended the bluffs and gained the high plain; saw a great number of burrowing squirrels in the plain today. also wolves Antelopes mule deer and immence herds of buffaloe ... we had a most beatifull and picturesk view of the Rocky mountains which were perfectly covered with snow ... they appear to be formed of several ranges each succeeding range rising higher than the pre-

ceding one untill the most distant appear to loose (lose) their snowy tops in the clouds (from this location Lewis was probably seeing the Highwoods, Little Belts, Big Belts, and the Lewis Range); this was an august spectacle and still rendered more formidable by the recollection that we had them to pass ... we traveled about twelve miles when we again struck the Missouri ... and determined to remain here during the balance of the day and night, having marched about 27 miles today ... on our way in the evening we had killed a buffaloe, an Antelope and three mule deer ... This evening I ate very heartily and after pening the transactions of the day amused myself catching those white fish mentioned yesterday; they are here in great abundance I caught upwards of a dozen in a few minutes...

The Lewis contingent made about twenty-seven miles on this day, and on the next they discovered the Great Falls.

Cascade Falls, one of the 'Great Falls of the Missouri'. Shortly after leaving the expedition's Marias River camp, Meriwether Lewis, on June 13, 1805, became the first white man to view the Great Falls, which over a ten mile section of river consists of 5 major falls, and numerous cascades. Unfortunately, almost all of the falls are now impacted by hydroelectric development. Haynes Foundation Collection, Montana Historical Society.

[Clark - Wednesday, June 12th - on the Marias River]

...last night was clear and cold, this morning fair we set out at 8 oClock & proceeded on verry well wind from the S.W. The interpreters wife verry sick so much so that I move her into the back part of our covered part of the Perogue which is cool, her own situation being a verry hot one in the bottom of the Perogue exposed to the Sun ... saw emence No. of swallows ... the bluff are blackish Clay & Coal for about 80 feet. the earth above that for

Another of the falls which make up the 'Great Falls of the Missouri', discovered by Meriwether Lewis, and photographed before being destroyed by hydroelectric damming. Haynes Foundation Collection, Montana Historical Society.

30 or 40 feet is a brownish yellow ... Saw a number of rattle Snakes today one of the men cought one by the head ... three canoes were in great danger today one diped water, another was near truning over & c ... the Interpreters woman verry Sick worse than She has been. I give her medison ... one man have a fellon riseing on his hand one other with the Tooth ake has taken cold in the Jaw &c.

The following morning, June 13th, Clark continued upriver, passing "Snow River" (today's Shonkin Creek) early in the day. Having discovered the Great Falls, Lewis dispatched Joseph Fields to inform Clark (June 14th), then went on to explore the many pitches and rapids that make up the falls. The area thrilled him and he described the first major cataract as "sublimely grand," the second as "pleasingly beautiful," etc. The captains were reunited at the mouth of Portage Creek (today's Belt Creek) on Sunday, June 16th. This location became the expedition's 'Lower Portage Camp', the staging area for the month long portage around the Great Falls of the Missouri.

FORT CAMPBELL

RIVER MILE 8.5 RIGHT

Fort Campbell was originally built at this location in 1846 by Alexander Harvey. This small log fort was located about one hundred yards from the river on the first bottom opposite and a little above Cracon du Nez (the narrow ridge of land between the Teton and Missouri Rivers at river mile 9). The following events led to the establishment of Fort Campbell and its opposition to the American Fur Company forts.

The massacre of a peaceful Blackfeet trading party at Fort McKenzie (see river mile 14 left) in February 1844, by Francois A. Chardon and Alexander Harvey led to the abandonment and destruction of that post.

By April the pair had relocated and built a new fort opposite the mouth of the Judith River. This new post was called Fort Chardon or Fort FAC. Fort Chardon was situated directly on a main war trail between the Blackfeet and Crow nations and was thus an unsafe area for trading parties. This coupled with the loss of trading relations with the Blackfeet caused a severe business setback for the American Fur Company.

Honore Picotte, General Agent for the American Fur Company, in an attempt to correct the situation instructed Alexander Culbertson to return to the Upper Missouri and build a new post, regain the Blackfeet business and close Fort Chardon. Culbertson established Fort Lewis then closed and burned Fort Chardon in the spring of 1846.

Picotte was troubled by Harvey, the experienced but violent employee and decided to have him come to Fort Pierre where he could keep a personal eye on him.

At Fort Union, enroute to Fort Pierre, Harvey found three company men plotting to assassinate him. On reaching Fort Pierre early in December 1845, he threatened to prefer charges against the three men. Rejecting Picotte's best efforts to placate him, Harvey stormed down to St. Louis to carry out his threats. Honore feared that the vengeful employee might even organize an opposition company.

At St. Louis Harvey not only pressed charges against the company men, but reported Chardon, his old cohort, for selling liquor to the Indians. Although the cases never reached court, the four accused were banished from the Indian country for a year and the company's reputation was impaired.

Picotte's fears were realized when Harvey secured financial backing from Robert Campbell and formed the Harvey, Primeau and Company. On July 17, 1846, this new opposition company left St. Louis aboard the *Clermont No. 2.* Later that year this company built Fort Campbell at this location. Under Harvey's vengeful drive the company eventually established posts to compete successfully with every one of the American Fur Company posts.

Alexander Harvey moved Fort Campbell upstream in 1847 to better compete with Fort Lewis which had moved to the present site of Fort Benton. The new location offered Fort Campbell a better site in relation to timber supplies and trade opportunities. The history of Fort Campbell at the new location was previously given at river mile 0.6 left.

CRACON du NEZ

River Mile 9 Left

The Cracon du Nez, also called Gros Condunez, is derived from the French and translates to "the bridge of the nose", and was probably named by the French boatmen who commonly comprised keelboat crews. It is a very narrow ridge, apparently resembling the bridge the nose.

Geographically, Cracon du Nez seperates two parallel flowing rivers - the Missouri and the Teton, by a mere one-half mile. The Missouri at this location takes a sharp right-hand turn, causing the current to be forcefully directed against the north bank, resulting in aggressive undercutting and eroding. As a consequence, the entire hillside below the main ridge of Cracon du Nez is undergoing massive slumping (a type of landslide). Unless the river's course changes, the Missouri will relentlessley wear away at Cracon du Nez, reducing it to river level, and at that point the Teton River will be diverted into the Missouri at this location. This process is called "stream capture", or "stream piracy" by geologists. Presently the Teton River flows to the east, and enters the Marias River at Loma, about six miles from here.

From *Floating on the Missouri;* refer to narrative at river mile 1.2 left for background:

A little farther down we passed the "Groscondunez". Here the Teton River makes an elbow to the south at the apex of which it is divided from the Missouri only by a narrow, sharp, high ridge. Along its crest runs an old Indian trail, a short cut from the fort to the mouth of the Marias. It was here, in 1865, that the Piegan chief, Little Dog, met his death, murdered by his own people.

The Piegans then were bitter enemies of the whites. They would come to the fort professing peace and trade their robes but parties of the warriors were out at all times of the year traveling even as far south as the California Overland Trail in search of scalps and plunder. Of the whole tribe Little Dog alone was the white man's friend, and by every means in his power he tried to keep his people at peace with them, even shooting one or two of the most obstinate and bloodthirsty. He was the especial favorite of the factor of the American Fur Company, Major Andrew Dawson, who gave him many valuable presents from time to

time, and often sent him down the Missouri on the company's boats that he might see something of the world. His warriors feared him, for he ruled them with an iron hand, and they were jealous of the favors showered on him. No one had such fine guns, such brilliantly colored blankets, such durable saddles and bridles as he.

One day four or five of the more hot-headed warriors held a secret council and determined that, if the tribe was to keep up its record of scalps and plunder taken, their chief must die. The camp was then at the mouth of the Marias, some twelve miles below the fort, and they knew that Little Dog was up there visiting the factor, and would return home that afternoon. So they went up to the Groscondunez and lay in wait for him. At dusk he came riding leisurely along, humming his favorite war song. As one man they leveled their rifles and fired at him, and he fell from his horse without a cry or groan, stone dead.

Strange to relate, every one of his murderers died within a year; some in battle, some by disease, and one by a fall while running buffalo. The people said it was because the sun was angry at their foul deed and had forsaken them. It was an unlucky day for the tribe when their chief was killed. Relieved from the restraint his unbending will had imposed, the braves began a systematic warfare against whites. Lone trappers and hunters - "woodhawks " - along the river, travelers on the Oregon Trail, and the trail between Fort Benton and the mines to the west were waylaid and murdered by scores and scores. And then came that January morning in '70 when Colonel [E.M., Baker and his two companies of infantry crept up the edge of the bluff on the Marias overlooking a part of the Piegan camp, some eighty lodges.

There was a massacre! There the whites avenged the death of many an unfortunate pioneer, of many a helpless wife and child. Of all the inmates of those eighty lodges, but three escaped. Men, women, and children were indiscriminately shot and then burned in piles of their lodges and household effects. It was a severe lesson, but in no other way could the Piegans have been taught to cease their murderous ways; from that day they took no more white scalps.

Little Dog was Sah-ne-to's uncle. No wonder, then, that as we passed the scene of his untimely death, she was for a time somewhat depressed in spirits. But on such a lovely morning no one could long have sad thoughts.

CORPS OF ENGINEERS

River Mile 9.3

In the 1870's as the intensifying Indian warfare along the Upper Missouri made dependable delivery of army supplies by steamboat more important than ever, the Federal government now felt compelled to reduce the river's perils to navigation.

The job of improving "Old Misery", as the river was ruefully known, was entrusted mainly to the Army's Corps of Engineers. The steamboats themselves played an important role, often serving as working platforms for labor crews. These crews either lived aboard when onshore accommodations were not available or in barracks-like scows towed behind the steamers.

The U.S. Army Corps of Engineers engaged in channel management below Fort Benton. The large boat is probably the Josephine. The boat on the left bank is a barracks boat, which housed the work crew; the boat in the channel is a miniature snag boat, probably the Baby Josephine, designed for removing snags from shallow parts of the channel. Montana Historical Society photograph.

The improvement program consisted of clearing the streambed of dead trees and other obstructions as well as altering sections of the river itself. Surveys conducted by the Corps of Engineers pinpointed the specific danger spots; among them rapids through which safe passageways had to be blasted and stretches where bank erosion, especially in the flood season, sometimes choked the river channel with sediment overnight. The Missouri silted in so bad at Sioux City in 1879 that wags told the story of a woman who attempted to commit suicide by jumping into the river, only to find herself stuck in two feet of mud.

The Engineers relied on a number of techniques to keep the river open and to check bank erosion. One of the most effective was to build "training structures" - dikes and piers angled into the river to divert the current away from an eroding shoreline. These structures also increased the river's velocity, thus loosening sediment on the bottom and deepening the channel for steamboats.

The importance of the Army Corps of Engineers' efforts in removing hazards from the Missouri's channel can be assessed by a look at the record of the wrecks that occurred on the river. In an 1897 report to the War Department, Capt. H.M. Chittenden, then Secretary of the Missouri River Commission, analyzed steamboat wrecks on the Missouri for the period from the beginning of navigation to that year. A passage from his analysis follows:

The total number of wrecks embraced in the list is 295*, distributed according to cause of wreck as follows:

Cause of Wreck	Number of boats wrecked	Cause of Wreck	Number boats wrecked
Snags	193	Ran into the bank	1
Fire	25	Storm and wind	2
Ice	26	Collisions	1
Rocks	11	Overloading	1
Bridges	10	Swamping in violent eddy	1
Explosion of boiler	6	Unknown	14
		Sand bars & falling river	4
			Total 295

*This includes 6 boats wrecked twice and finally lost, 1 boat wrecked three times and finally lost, 12 boats wrecked once and save, and 1 boat wrecked twice and saved. This reduces the actual number of boats lost to 273.

FORT FOX AND LIVINGSTON

River Mile est. 11 Right

Fort Fox and Livingston was established sometime around 1842 by Fox, Livingston, and Company. A Fort Fox and Livingston, located between Fort Lewis and Fort Piegan, was noted and sketched by Father Nicolas Point (*Wilderness Kingdom)* on March 21, 1847, but its exact location is unknown.

During the fur trade era (1830s - late 1850s) competition was keen, with rival companies challenging each other for dominance in different regions of the country. The following realignments in the fur trade business led to the establishment of Fort Fox and Livingston.

A number of the better known men associated with the fur trade along the Upper Missouri emigrated to the United States from Canada in 1822. Among them were Honore Picotte, Kenneth McKenzie and James Kipp. These men had been displaced by trading company mergers in Canada.

These three and five others (three fellow emigrants and two U.S. citizens) formed the Columbia Fur Company. In July 1822, they secured a trading license in Saint Louis from Indian Superintendent William Clark (of the famous expedition) to trade with the Mandans and others on the Missouri. Under the drive and genius of McKenzie the new firm flourished for 6 years, challenging all rival firms on the lower Missouri.

The year 1827 brought a major reorganization of the fur companies. In response to this reorganization three of Columbia's founders, including McKenzie, contracted with Astor's Western Department of the American Fur Company to manage a new division called the Upper Missouri Outfit. This action was devastating to the original Columbia Fur Company, and by December of 1827 the company was finished.

As general agent for the Upper Missouri Outfit, the aggressive McKenzie soon established his headquarters at a new post at the mouth of the Yellowstone, which became known as Fort Union.

McKenzie was the general agent for the Upper Missouri Outfit until 1838 when he made his farewell voyage downriver, turning over control to Honore Picotte, his successor as general agent. The firm went on to dominate the trade for the next 27 years.

However, in 1842 Fox, Livingston and Company established Fort Fox and Livingston and did provide some serious business competition. The two companies competed for several years then Picotte succeeded in buying out Fox, Livingston and Company in May 1845.

ROWE ISLAND GOVERNMENT SHIPYARD

River Mile 13 Left

Among the Army Corps of Engineers steamboats that worked to keep the Upper Missouri open to navigation were the *Josephine,* the *City of Fort Benton* (a dredge) and the *Baby Josephine,* a pint sized work boat. All were built either in Fort Benton or at the government shipyard located at Rowe Island.

The *Josephine* made two trips to Fort Benton in 1885 - May 12th with five hundred tons and July 6th with two hundred tons. The bulk of her cargo was construction materials for the *City of Fort Benton.*

The *City of Fort Benton* was launched on July 22,1885. After setting and adjusting her boiler, the dredge got a trial run August 15. It worked the river channel at the old ford at Fort Benton on September 9, but the government funds were soon gone. It sat out the winter behind an ice break at Fort Benton.

In 1887 the Corps of Engineers mothballed the *City of Fort Benton* and *Baby Josephine* until 1891 at Rowe Island.

After receiving more funds in 1891 the *City of Fort Benton* did some work near the Marias and as far downriver as Wolf Point. In 1892 she was destroyed by fire near the mouth of Eagle Creek.

The Josephine was destroyed by ice in South Dakota in 1907.

FORT MCKENZIE

River Mile 14 Left

Fort McKenzie was built late in 1832 to trade with the three tribes of the Blackfeet Nation - the Piegan, Bloods, and Siksika (also know as the Blackfeet proper) and with several neighboring nations such as the Gros Ventre, Sarcee and Kutenai.

Because of the success of Fort Piegan (river mile 22), Kenneth McKenzie sent David D. Mitchell back upriver in the fall of 1832 to reestablish trade with the Blackfeet. On the way upriver the party was caught in a violent storm. Their keelboat was dragged from her moorings, tossed and battered by wind and waves and then hurled against a sandbar. The keelboat sunk with two of her crew and $30,000 worth of merchandise and gifts for the Indians. Mitchell returned to Fort Union (at the mouth of the Yellowstone) for a fresh supply of goods. This trip typically took about thirty-four days.

Unbeknown to Mitchell and his crew, Fort Piegan had been burned during the winter by a party of Blood Indians who apparently weren't aware of the intentions of the builders to return and continue trading in the spring. When Mitchell and his men finally arrived at the site of Fort Piegan, they found the ashes of the ruined post and several thousand hostile Indians waiting to receive them. Because of the delays caused by the loss of the first keelboat the Indians felt they had been duped by the traders.

Rather than rebuild Fort Piegan, Mitchell decided to relocate to a site eight miles further upriver. At the new site the men worked like beavers, for the peril of the situation was apparent to all. The Indians could easily have annihilated the traders and helped themselves to the trade goods. But by cajolery and an unbelievable exercise of tact and wisdom, Mitchell kept them placated until a new stockade was erected and the men were safely inside.

Mitchell first named the new post Fort Piekann, but then renamed it Fort McKenzie in honor of Kenneth McKenzie, the head of the Upper Missouri Outfit. The successful establishment of Fort McKenzie marked a permanent foothold in Blackfeet country.

The Piegans were the most important beaver hunters, while the Bloods and Siksika dealt more in the trade with buffalo robes. At first, trade in this area was mainly in beaver pelts, which were used to make hats in Europe, but when the silk hat came into vogue, the trade shifted to buffalo robes.

In 1833, Alexander Culbertson replaced David Mitchell as chief trader and served there until 1842. In 1842 Culbertson was reassigned to Fort Laramie in Wyoming, and was replaced by Francois A. Chardon.

Karl Bodmer drew this sketch of Fort McKenzie in 1833, its second year of existence. Bodmer was a Swiss artist, twenty-three years old, who had been hired by Prince Maximilian of Wied, a German aristocrat and scientist who traveled up the Upper Missouri to study the native peoples and the natural history of the area. Courtesy of Joslyn Art, Omaha, Nebraska; Gift of the Enron Art Foundation.

Trading was carried on in a room between inner and outer gates. Only a small number of Indians from outside the fort were allowed in this room at one time. After the Indians were primed generously with whiskey, trading was carried on through a window that opened into an adjoining room that contained the trade goods. Trade whiskey usually consisted of watered down alcohol that contained chewing tobacco and a generous amount of red pepper. Trading ordinarily commenced in the morning, at which time the American flag was raised and a salute fired from the cannon. The chiefs then entered the fort bearing gifts and, in turn, received presents from the officials of the fort. After the necessary formalities had been observed, and trading with the chiefs was concluded, business was carried on with the rest of the tribe.

Alexander Philip Maximilian, Prince of Wied-Neuwied, a noted German scientist and explorer, visited Fort McKenzie in 1833 while he studied the local Indians and collected floral and faunal specimens. He was accompanied by Charles (Karl) Bodmer, an accomplished artist, who sketched and made paintings of the Indians and scenes in the surrounding countryside. They were an ideal team. Maximilian was an experienced naturalist, one of the "whole men" of nineteenth century Europe with deep interest in the natural and social sciences - and the money and position to indulge it. The young Bodmer, only twenty-three years old, had been superbly trained in Zurich and Paris, and his artist's eye was a perfect complement to his patron's scientific view. Bodmer's vivid sketches and watercolors depicted not only Indians at peace and war, but also the sweeping vistas of the Upper Missouri and the wildlife that abounded there. The year before, artist George Catlin had ventured up the Missouri as far as the mouth of the Yellowstone at Fort Union, but he stopped short of the spectacular country of the upper river. Bodmer sketched furiously during their upriver trip, and once made twenty drawings in less than three miles. Bodmer's work was to give the outside world its first look at what would be Montana and at the fabled river that led there. Today Bodmer's paintings and sketches of the Upper Missouri Indians are recognized as priceless snapshots which captured these native peoples' culture prior to its being diluted by extensive contact with whites.

Maximilian described Fort McKenzie as being similar to others of the American Fur Company's posts on the river:

... it forms a quadrangel, the sides of which are forty-five to forty seven paces (roughly 140 feet) in length, and is defended by two blockhouses, with some pieces of cannon. It is much smaller than Fort Union and worse and more slightly built. The dwellings are of one story, and low: the rooms small, generally without flooring, with a chimney, a door, a flat roof covered with green sods ... The flagstaff stands in the center of the courtyard. The gate is strong, double, and well protected; when the trade with the Indians is going on the inner gate is closed: the entrance to the Indian store, between the two gates is then free, a strong guard being stationed at the store. (Thwaites: 1906)

Alexander Culbertson's journal provides further description and indicates the possibility of some improvements in the years after Maximilian was a guest at the fort:

Three sides of the fort are built of pickets of hewn cottonwood, eighteen feet long, planted three feet deep in the earth ... The fort is 200 feet square, ranging north and south and facing south. On the northeast and southwest corners are bastions built of cottonwood timbers.

The tranquil appearance of Fort Mckdnzie in the previous Karl Bodmer drawing contrasts sharply with this drawing, also by Bodmer. It depicts a raid by a group of Assiniboin Indians on a group of Piegan Blackfeet who were camped on the grounds outside the fort. Courtesy of Joslyn Art, Omaha, Nebraska; Gift of the Enron Art Foundation.

While at Fort McKenzie, Maximilian and Bodmer observed an Indian battle right in front of the fort. Bodmer painted the fort the next day leaving us the only known picture of Fort McKenzie drawn while the fort was in existence. Bodmer probably added the battle to the picture upon returning to Germany. Major Alexander Culbertson gave the following account of the battle to John James Audubon when Audubon was visiting Fort Union in 1843:

August 23, 1833. At the break of day we were aroused from our beds by the report of an enemy being in sight. This unexpected news created naturally a confusion among us all; never was a set of unfortunate beings so surprised as we were. By the time that the alarm had spread through the fort, we were surrounded by the enemy, who proved to be Assiniboins. The number, as near as we could judge, was about four hundred. Their first attack was upon a few lodges, Piegans, who were encamped at the fort. We exerted ourselves however, to save as many as we could, by getting them into the fort. But the foolish squaws, when they started from their lodges, each took a load of old saddles and skins, that they threw in the door, and stopped it so completely that they could not get in, and there the enemy massacred several. In the mean time our men were firing with muskets and shotguns. Unfortunately for us, we could not use our cannon, as there were a great many Piegans standing between us and the enemy; this prevented us from a telling shot on them at once. The engagement continued for nearly an hour, when the enemy finding their men drop very fast, retreated to the bluffs a half a mile distant. After the arrival of our reinforcements, which consisted of one hundred and fifty mounted Piegans, we charged and fought again for another two hours, and drove them back across the Maria's River some six miles distant, where they took another stand.

The battle ended when the sun went down.

The next year, 1834, the fort was besieged by a Crow band, who did not appreciate the American Fur Company selling guns to their enemies, the Blackfeet. The siege lasted nearly a month. It may have been considerably less as the records are not clear, but it ended quickly. Supplies were getting short at the fort and Culbertson was determined to attack the Crows as a last desperate act. The morning before the planned attack, the whites observed a general commotion in the Indian camp. The whole camp began taking down lodges, packing their lodges in great haste and before the afternoon was out, the whole Crow camp moved across the river and were out of sight. That same evening a group of Blackfeet arrived at the fort bringing plenty of meat.

The trading post became an important part of life for the Indians. It served as an Indian recreation center and as a health and welfare center. Post records tell of Indians coming in for the treatment of wounds and illnesses. Indians also customarily brought the bodies of dead leaders to the post for burial. The Piegans were more than happy for the whites to be responsible for the spirits of their dead, something the Indians greatly feared. News of other tribes was also obtained at the trading post. Trade goods were not the only thing transmitted at the post from white to Indian. Indians must have learned a great deal about the strange customs of the whites.

The smallpox was introduced to the Blackfeet in 1837 at Fort McKenzie. The epidemic originated in infected clothing placed aboard an American Fur Company's steamer in St. Louis. A Blackfeet Indian boarded the steamer at the mouth of the Little Missouri and changed to a keelboat at Fort Union bound for Fort McKenzie. On this stretch of the river, this Indian and two others broke out with the disease. Culbertson, was worried about the affliction and ordered the keelboat to stop at the mouth of the Judith until freezing weather set in. A large camp of some five hundred lodges of Piegan and Blood did not believe the devastating manner of the disease and threatened to go get the keelboat themselves if Culbertson would not bring it up. Culbertson ordered the boat to proceed to Fort

McKenzie where two of the passengers shortly died, but the Indians insisted on trade as usual, then departed. Twenty-six Indian women and a white man died as the disease swept the fort. Nearly six-thousand, or two-thirds of the entire Blackfeet population were estimated to have been killed by the disease.

The year 1837 had been a year of financial panic in the eastern United States, but David Mitchell was able to convince the company to buy more robes and thus sell more robes to buyers by saying the Indians are dead and dying, and there won't be any next year (1838). His strategy worked as these numbers show. The winter after the smallpox epidemic ten thousand robes were traded; robes belonging to victims of the epidemic were probably included in this number. The trade increased, until twenty-one thousand robes were traded at Fort McKenzie in 1841.

The life of Fort McKenzie was cut short in January of 1844. A party of young Blackfeet warriors returning from the Crow country asked admittance to the fort and were refused. Francois A. Chardon, a hotheaded Frenchman (chief trader since 1842) and his lieutenant, Alexander Harvey, refused to admit the Blackfeet, for reasons now forgotten. The warriors retaliated by stealing or killing some of the fort's livestock, either a pig or a milk cow; the story was told both ways. Harvey, Chardon, and others pursued them with a well armed party. One member of the party, Tom Reese, Chardon's Negro slave, was killed and scalped, enraging Chardon and Harvey. Vowing revenge, Harvey and Chardon loaded the fort's cannon with 150 or so lead bullets, aimed it at the approach to the main gate and waited for the next Indian trading party.

In February, a small band of either Piegans or Bloods arrived at the fort to trade. When they approached, Harvey took his position by the cannon while Chardon, armed with a rifle, lay in wait for the chiefs. Chardon was too quick on the trigger and fired before Harvey was ready. Chardon killed one chief at the first shot, but before Harvey could put fire to the touch hole, the Indians at the gate had scattered. Only five were hit and only two were killed (although some stories say as many as thirty were killed instantly). Harvey finished the wounded braves with his knife and compelled the Blackfeet squaws of the fort to dance the scalp dance around the bodies of the fallen Indians, whose scalps he himself had taken.

This action made further trading at the fort impossible. Chardon and company moved downriver to the mouth of the Judith about April 5, 1844. Fort McKenzie was then burned by either whites or Indians, and to this day the site is known as Brule' (burned) Bottom.

Brule' Bottom became the head of navigation for a short time in 1859. The American Fur Company commissioned a small boat called the *Chippewa* that year. She was the first stern-wheeler to navigate the upper Missouri, and was better adapted to the river than any of her predecessors. She was accompanied by the *Spread Eagle* as far as Fort Union, and then pressed forward alone, passing the Milk River, the highest point reached by the *El Paso* in 1850, and reached Brule' Bottom on June 17, 1859. Short on fuel, concerned by a falling river and being only twelve miles from Fort Benton, Charles P. Chouteau, who was in charge, decided to unload freight the at this point. He visited Fort Benton, and the next day, after completing the unloading of supplies, he had Captain John LaBarge point the *Chippewa* downstream for the return trip.

The following year the *Chippewa* did reach Fort Benton on July 2, 1860, becoming the first steamboat to ever reach the present head of navigation. She was followed closely by the *Key West.* Not long after, her services to the American Fur Company were terminated when, at the mouth of the Poplar River, deckhands set the *Chippewa* afire while stealing liquor. The boat, which carried gun powder among her cargo, was abandoned and shortly blew up.

LEWIS AND CLARK AT THE MOUTH OF THE MARIAS

RIVER MILE 22 LEFT

The Marias River was named by Captain Lewis for a cousin, Maria Wood. It was originally spelled "Maria's", but over time the apostrophe was dropped and the pronunciation was changed. It was at Marias River that, as one historian so aptly put it, Lewis and Clark entered the "where the hell are we" phase of their expedition. It was here also that Lewis rejoined the rest of his contingent after exploring the headwaters of the Marias during the return trip in 1806. In 1831, the first trading post on the Missouri above Fort Union, called Ft. Piegan, was located here, and in 1864 the townsite of Ophir, its developers hoping to rival Fort Benton for the steamboat business, was started here. The events will be traced chronologically.

Lewis and Clark Campsite of June 2-10, and Clark Campsite of June 11, 1805

Lewis and Clark traveled some fifteen miles upriver June 2, 1805, to reach this point. Excerpts from the journals of that day, and the next ten days follow.

[Lewis - Sunday, June 2nd]

The wind blew violently last night and was attended by a slight shower of rain; the morning was fair and we set out at an early hour ... The river bluffs still continue to get lower and the plains leveler and more extensive; the timber on the river increases in quantity ... Game becomeing more abundant this morning and I thought it best now to loose no time or suffer an opportunity to excape in providing the necessary quantity of Elk's skins to cover my leather boat which I now expect I shall be obliged to use shortly. Accordingly I walked on shore most of the day with some of the hunters for that purpose and killed 6 elk 2 buffal[o]e 2 Mule deer and a bear, these anamals were all in good order we therefore took as much of the meat as our canoes and perogues could conveniently carry. the bear was very near catching Drewyer; it also pursued Charbono who fired his gun in the air as he ran but fortunately eluded the vigilence of the bear by secreting himself very securely in the bushes untill Drewyer finally killed it by a shot in the head; the (only) shot indeed that will conquer the farocity of those tremendious anamals ... we came too on the Lard. side in a handsome bottom of small cottonwood timber opposite to the entrance of a very considerable river (today's Marias River).

[Lewis - Monday, June 3rd]

This morning early we passed over and formed a camp on the point formed by the junction of the two large rivers ... An interesting question was now to be determined; which of these rivers was the Missouri, or that river which the Minnetares call Amahte Arz zha or Missouri, and which they had discribed to us as approaching very near to the Columbia river. to mistake the stream at this period of the season, two months of the traveling season having now elapsed, and to ascend such stream to the rocky Mountain or perhaps much further before we could inform ourselves whether it did approach the Columbia or not, and then be obliged to return and take the other stream would not only loose us the whole of this season but would probably so dishearten the party that it might defeat the expedition altogether. convinced we were that the utmost circumspection and caution was necessary in deciding on the stream to be taken. to this end an investigation of both streams was the first thing to be done ...

... accordingly we dispatched two light canoes with three men in each up those streams; we also sent out several small parties by land with instructions to penetrate the country as far as they conveniently can permitting themselves time to return this evening and indeavour if possible to discover the distant bearing of those rivers by ascending the rising grounds ... Capt. C. & myself stroled out to the top of the hights in the fork of these rivers from whence we had an extensive and most enchanting view; the country in every derection around us was one vast plain in which innumerable herds of Buffalow were seen attended by their shepperds the wolves; the solatary antelope which now had their young were distributed over it's face; some herds of Elk were also seen; the verdure perfectly cloathed the ground, the weather was pleasent and fair; to the South we saw a range of lofty mountains (probably today's Highwoods) which we supposed to be a continuation of the S. Mountains (Judith Mtns.) ... behind these Mountains and at a great distance, a second and more lofty range of mountains appeared to stretch across the country in the same direction with the others, reaching from West, to the N of N. W., where their snowey tops lost themselves beneath the horizon. this last range (probably the Little Belts and Big Belts) was perfectly covered with snow. the direction of the rivers could be seen but little way, soon loosing the break of their channels, to our view, in common plain. on our return to camp ... we diacovered a handsome little river (today's Teton River) falling into the N. fork on the Lard. side about one and one half ms. above our camp ... this little river has as much timber in its bottoms as either of the larger streams ... the wild rose which grows here in great abundance in the bottoms of all these rivers is now in full bloom, and ads not a little to the beaty (beauty) of the cenery (scenery)

we took the width of the two rivers, found the left hand or S. fork 372 yards and the N. fork 200. The north fork is deeper than the other but it's courant not so swift; it's waters run in the same boiling and roling manner which has uniformly characterized the Missouri throughout it's whole course so far; it's waters are of a whitish brown colour very thick and terbid, also characteristic of the Missouri; while the South fork is perfectly transparent runds very rappid but with a smoth unriffled surface it's bottom composed of round and flat smooth stones like most rivers issuing from a mountainous country. the bed of the N. fork composed of some gravel but principally mud; in short the air & character of this river is so precisely that of the missouri below that the party with very few exceptions have already pronounced the N. fork to be the Missouri; myself and Capt. C. not quite so precipitate have not yet decided but if we were to give our opinions I believe we should be in the minority ...

Lewis goes on to express confusion about information that they had received from various Indians at their winter camp at Ft. Mandan. They aren't sure if the Milk River, which they passed on May 8th, was "the river that scolds at all others" which the Indians told them to expect, or if they are just encountering it now. They are also dismayed that the Indian information did not include any mention of another major river entering on the larboard (right) side at this location.

... what astonishes us a little is that the Indians who appeared to be so well acquainted with the geography of this country should not have mentioned this river on wright (right) hand if it be not the Missouri; "the river that scolds at all others", as they call it if there is in reallity such an one, ought agreeably to their account, to have fallen in a considerable distance below , and on the other hand if this right hand or N. fork be the Missouri I am equally astonished at their not mentioning the S. fork which they must have passed in order to get to those large falls which they mention on the Missouri. thus have our cogitating faculties been busily employed all day.

Those who have remained at camp today have been busily engaged in dressing skins for cloathing, notwithstanding that many of them have their feet so mangled and bruised with the stones and rough ground over which they passed barefoot, that they can scarcely walk or stand; at least it is with great pain they do either. for some days past they were unable to wear their mockersons; they have fallen off considerably, but notwithstanding the difficulties past, or those which seem to mennace us, they still remain perfectly cheerful.

In the evening the parties whom we had sent out returned agreeably to instructions ... Their accounts were by no means satisfactory nor did the information we acquired bring us nigher to the decision of our question or determine us which stream to take ... Capt. C. and myself concluded to set out early the next morning with a small party each, and ascend these rivers untill we could perfectly satisfy ourselves of the one, which it would be most expedient for us to take on our main journey to the Pacific. accordingly it was agreed that I should ascend the right hand fork and he the left. I gave orders to Sergt. Pryor Drewyer, Shields, Windsor, Cruzatte and La Page to hold themselves in readiness to accompany me in the morning. Capt. Clark also selected Reubin & Joseph Fields, Sergt. Gass, Shannon and his black man York, to accompany him. we agreed to go up those rivers one day and a halfs march or further if it should appear necessary to satisfy us more fully of the point in question ... we took a drink of grog this this evening and gave the men a dram, and made all matters ready for an early departure.

The next morning the captains, with their contingents, depart; Lewis heads up the Marias River, while Clark is exploring the Missouri. Lewis is particularly interested in the Marias, because he was instructed by Jefferson to gather information about northerly tributaries of the Missouri, which could be significant in determining the northern boundary of the Louisiana Teritory and the position of the U.S. - Canadian border. On the expedition's return journey in 1806, Lewis, having the advantage of possessing horses, conducted a more extensive exploration the Marias River, at which time he determined that it had its source in the Rockies much further south than he had hoped.

[Lewis - Tuesday, June 4th - On the Marias River]

This morning early Capt. C. departed, and at the same time I passed the wright hand fork opposite to our camp below a small Island ... The north fork which I am now ascending lies to my left and appears to make a considerable bend to the N. W ... I now directed my course through a high level dry open plain. the whole country in fact appears to be one continued plain to the foot of the mountains or as far as the eye can reach; the soil appears dark rich and fertile yet the grass is by no means as high nor does it look so luxurient as I should have expected, it is short just sufficient to conceal the ground. great abundance of prickly pears which are extreemly troublesome; as the thorns very readily perce the foot through the Mockerson; they are so numerous that it requires one half of the traveler's attention to avoid them.

... after walking about eight miles I grew thisty (thirsty) and there being no water in the plains I changed my direction and boar obliquely in towards the river, on my arrival at which about 3 mls. below the point of observation, we discovered two deer at feed at some distance near the river: I here halted the party and sent Drewyer to kill one of them for breakfast; this excellent hunter soon exceded his orders by killing of them both ... we soon kindled a fire cooked and made a hearty meal .... after refreshing ourselves we proceded up the river (for about 16 miles) ...... we ascended the hills which are about 200 feet high, and passed through the plains about 3 M. but finding the dry ravenes so steep and numer-

ous we determined to return to the river and travel through it's bottoms and along the foot and sides of the bluffs, accordingly we again reached the river about 4 Miles from the commencement of the last course and encamped ... in rained this evening and wet us to the skin; the air was extremely could ... we saw a great number of Buffaloe, Elk, wolves and foxes today ... the river bottoms form one emence garden of roses, now in full bloe (bloom).

[Clark - Tuesday, June 4th - On the Missouri River]

Capt. Lewis & my self each with a small party of men set out early ... our first course was S. 25. W. seven miles to the S. fork (Missouri) at a Spring at which place the little river (Teton) which falls into the N. fork (Marias) is 100 yards distant only Seperated from the South fork by a narrow ridge (today this narrow ridge is called Cracon du Nez), our course from thence S. 20 degrees W. eight miles to the river at an Island where we dined below a small river that falls in on the SE side (today's Shonkin Creek) which heads in a mountain to the S.E about 20 miles (the Highwoods) ... after eating we proceeded on N. 45 degrees W. Struck the river at 3 miles 5, 9 & 13 miles at which place we encamped in an old Indian lodge made of Stiks and bark at the river near our camp we saw two white Bear, one of them was nearly catching Joseph Field - Joseph Fields could not fire, as his gun was wet, the bear was so near that it struck his foot, and we were not in a situation to give him assistance, a clift of rocks seperate us the bear got allarmed at our Shot & yells & took to the river. Some rain all the afternoon Saw several Gangues of Buffalow at a distance in the open plains on each side, Saw Mule deer antilopes & wolves ...

One of the marvels of the expedition is that no one was killed by a grizzly bear. They had many close encounters. The Lewis and Clark Journals document that at least forty-three grizzlies were killed by expedition members, most of them in Montana, and it appears that the reasons for shooting bears included thrill-seeking as well as safety. When the expedition began to first encounter grizzly bear, the challenge of hunting them was undoubtedly the primary motivation for the men shooting at them. Although there are journal entries that mention the men eating grizzly bear meat, as well as them rendering bear oil from grizzly carcasses, it is doubtful that they killed bears primarily for either of these purposes. The journals make it clear that Plains Grizzly appeared to be very inquisitive, if not downright aggressive, evidenced by a number of cases where the journals describe grizzlies coming into their camp. Certainly a grizzly in close proximity to camp posed a real threat and warranted action.

[Lewis - Wednesday, June 5th - On the Marias River]

This morning was cloudy and so could that I was obleged to have recourse to a blanket coat in order to keep myself comfortable altho' walking. the rain continued during the greater part of the night. the wind hard from the NW. we set out at sunrise and proceded up the river eight miles on the course last taken yesterday evening, at the extremity of which a large creek falls in on the Stard ... at the entrance of this creek (Black Coulee) the bluffs were very steep and approached the river so near on the Stard. side that we assended the hills and passed through the plains; at the extremity of this course we returned to the river which then boar North ...I discovered a lofty single mountain which appeared to be at a great distance, perhaps 80 or more miles ... from its conic figure I called it tower Mountain (today's Sweegrass Hills) ... we now passed through the river bottoms (for about six miles) ... at the extremity of which I again ascended the bluffs ... on this course we passed through the plains found the plains as yesterday extreemly leavel and beautifull, great quantities of Buffaloe, some wolves foxes and Antelopes seen... near the river the plain is cut by deep ravenes ...

... we saw the largest collection of the burrowing or barking squirrels (prairie dogs) that we had ever yet seen; we passed through a skirt of the territory of this community for about 7 miles ... as we had not killed or eat anything today we each killed a burrowing squirrel as we passed them in order to make shure of our suppers. we again intersepted the river ... we killed five Elk and a blacktailed or mule deer and encamped on Stard. side of the river in a handsome well timbered bottom where there were several old stick lodges ... I had the burrowing squirrels roasted by way of experiment and found the flesh well flavored and tender; some of them were very fat.

[Clark - Wednesday, June 5th - On the Missouri River]

Some little rain & snow last night the mountains to our S.E. covered with snow this morning - air verry cold & raining a little ... about the time we were setting out three white bear approached our camp - we killed the three & eate part of one & set out & proceeded on N. 20 degrees W. eleven miles struck the river at maney places in this distance ... From the ridge at which place I struck the river last, I could discover that the river run west of south a long distance, and has a strong rapid current, as this river continued its width debth & rapidity and the course west of south, going up further would be useless, I deturmined to return ... struck the little river (the Teton River) ... proceeded a few miles & camped ... I saw great numbers of Elk & white tale deer, Some beaver, antelope mule deer & wolves& on bear on this little river marked my name in a tree ...

[Lewis - Thursday, June 6th - On the Marias River]

I now became well convinced that this branch of the Missouri had it's direction too much to North for our rout to the Pacific, and therefore determined to return the next day ... I had sent Sergt. Pryor and Windsor early this morning with orders to procede up the river to some commanding eminence and take it's bearing as far as possible. in the mean time the four others and myself were busily engaged in making two rafts on which we purposed descending the river (they were about 8 miles - 15 river miles - below today's Tiber Dam); we had just completed this work when Sergt. Pryor and Windsor returned, it being about noon ...we now took dinner and embarcked with our plunder and five Elk's skins on the rafts but were soon convinced that this mode of navigation was hazerdous particularly with those rafts they being too small and slender. we wet part of our baggage and were near loosing one of our guns; I therefore determined to abandon the rafts and return as we had come, by land ... we again swung our packs and took our way through the open plains for about 12 Mls. when we struck the river ... continued our rout down the river only a few miles before the abbruptness of the clifts and their near approach to the river compelled us take the plains and once more face the storm; here we boar reather too much to the North and it was late in the evening before we reached the river ... we encamped a little below the entrance of the large dry Creek called Lark C. (Black Coulee) having traveled abut 25 Mls. since noon. it continues to rain and we have no shelter an uncomfortable nights rest is the natural consequence.

[Clark - Thursday, June 6th - On the Teton River]

a Cloudy Cold raw day wind hard from the N.E. we set out early & traveled down the little river which was imedeately in our course ... at 5 oClock we arrived at our camp on the point, where I expected to meet Capt Lewis he did not return this evening. My self and party much fatigued haveing walked constantly as hard as we could march over a Dry hard plain, decending & assending the steep river hills & gullies.

[Lewis - Friday, June, 7th - On the Marias River]

It continued to rain almost without intermission last night and as I expected we had a most disagreable and wrestless night. our camp possessing no allurements, we left our watery beads at an early hour and continued our rout down the river. it still continues to rain the wind hard from N.E. and could. the grownd remarkably slipry, insomuch that we were unable to walk on the sides of the bluffs where we had passes as we aascended the river. notwithstanding the rain that has now fallen the earth of these bluffs is not wet to a greater debth than 2 inches; in its present state it is precisely like walking over frozan grownd which is thawed to small debth and slips equally as bad. this clay not only appears to require more water to saturate it as I before observed than any earth I ever observed but when saturated it appears on the other hand to yeald it's moisture with equal difficulty. In passing along the face of one of these bluffs today I sliped at a narrow pass of about 30 yards in length and but for a quick and fortunate recovery by means of my espontoon (a short staff with a pike point at one end) I should been precipitated into the river down a craggy pricipice of about ninety feet. I had scarcely reached a place on which I could stand with tolerable safety even with the assistance of my espontoon before I heard a voice behind me cry out god god Capt. what shall I do on turning about I found it was Windsor who had sliped and fallen about the center of this narrow pass and was lying prostrate on his belley, with his wright hand arm and leg over the precipice while he was holding on with the left arm and foot as well a he could which appeared to be with much difficulty.

... altho' much allarmed at his situation I disguised my feelings and spoke very calmly to him and assured him that he was in no kind of danger, to take the knife out of his belt behind him with his wright hand and dig a hold with it in the face of the bank to receive his wright foot which he did and then raised himself to his knees; I then directed him to take off his mockersons and come forward on his hands and knees holding the knife in one hand and the gun in the other this he happily effected and escaped.

... it was useless we knew to attempt the plains on this part of the river in consequence of the numerous steep ravines which intersected and which were quite as bad as the river bluffs. we therefore continued our rout down the river sometimes in the mud and water of the bottom lands, at others in the river to our breasts and when the water became so deep that we could not wade we cut footsteps in the face of the steep bluffs with our knives and proceded. we continued our disagreeable march through the rain mud and water untill late in the evening having traveled only about 18 miles, and encamped in an old Indian stick lodge which afforded us a dry and comfortable shelter.

... we roasted and eat a hearty supper of our venison not having taisted a morsel before during the day; I now laid myself down on some willow boughs to a comfortable nights rest, and felt indeed as if I was fully repaid for the toil and pain of the day, so much will a good shelter, a dry bed, and comfortable supper revive the sperits of the waryed (wearied), wet and hungry traveler.

[Clark - Friday, June 7th - At Base Camp on the Missouri]

rained moderately all last night and Continus this morning, the wind from the S.W. off the mountains, The Thermometer Stood at 40 ° ... I allow several men to hunt a short time to day, the rain continue moderately all day the bottom verry muddy ... Capt. Lewis not returned yet. river falling

[Lewis - Saturday, June 8th - On the Marias River]

It continued to rain moderately all last night this morning was cloudy untill about ten oClock when it cleared off and became a fine day. we breakfasted and set out about sunrise and continued our rout down the river bottoms through the mud and water as yesterday, tho' the road was somewhat better than yesterday and we were not so often compelled to wade in the river. we passed some dangerous and difficult bluffs The river bottoms affording all the timber which is to be seen in the country they are filled with innumerable litle birds that resort thither either for shelter or to build their nests. when the sun began to shine today these birds appeared to be very gay and sung inchantingly ... The whole of my party to a man except myself were fully persuaided that this river was the Missouri, but being fully of opinion that it was neither the main stream or that which it would be advisable for us to take, I determined to give it a name and in honour of Miss Maria Wood. (a cousin of Captain Lewis) called it Maria's River. it is true that the hue of the waters of this turbulent and troubled stream but illy comport with the pure celestial virtues and amiable qualifications of that lovely fair one; but on the other hand it is a noble river; one destined to become in my opinion an object of contention between the two great powers of America and Great Britin with rispect to the adjustment of the North westwardly boundary of the former ... it abounds with animals of the fur kind ... in addition to which it passes through a rich fertile and one of the most beatiflly picteresque countries that I ever beheld, through the wide expance of which, innumerable herds of living anamals are seen, it's borders garnished with one continued garden of roses, whilc it's lofty and open forests, are the habitation of miriads of the feathered tribes who salute the ear of the passing treveler with their wild and simple, yet sweet and cheerfull melody.

I arrived at camp about 5 OClock in the evening much fatiegued, where I found Capt. Clark and the ballance of the party waiting our return with some anxiety for our safety having been absent near two days longer than we had engaged to return ...... I now gave myself this evening to rest from my labours, took a drink of grog and gave the men who had accompanyed me each a dram ...

[Clark - Saturday, June 8th - At Base Camp on the Missouri]

rained moderately all the last night & Some this morning untill 10 oClock, I am some what uneasy for Capt. Lewis & party as days has now passed the time he was to have returned, I had all the arms put in order and permited several men to hunt, aired and dried our stores &c ... about 5 oClock Capt. Lewis arrived with the party much fatigued, and inform'd me that he had assended the river about 60 miles by Land (the actual distance was 77 1/2 miles).

[Lewis - Sunday, June 9th - At Base Camp on the Missouri]

We determined to deposite at this place the large red perogue (the larger of their two pirogues - they also had six dugout canoes) all the heavy baggage which we could possibly do without and some provision, salt, tools powder and Lead &c with a view to lighten our vessels and at the same time to strengthen their crews by means of the seven hands who have been heretofore employd in navigating the red perogue; accordingly we set some hands to diging a hole or cellar for the reception of our stores. these holes in the ground or deposits are called by the engages cashes.

... today we examined our maps, and compared the information derived as well from them as from the Indians and fully settled in our minds the propryety of addopting the South fork for the Missouri, as that which it would be most expedient for us to take ... we therefore cannot hope by going Northwardly of this place being already in Latitude 47° 24" to find a stream between this place and the Saskashawan which dose penetrate the Rocky mountains, and which agreeably to the information of the Indians with rispect to the Missouri, dose possess a navigable curent some distance in those mountains. The Indian information also argued strongly in favour of the South fork ...

... Those ideas as they occurred to me I indevoured to impress on the minds of the party all of whom except Capt. C. being still firm in their belief that the N. Fork was the Missouri and that which we ought to take; they said very cheerfully that they were ready to follow us any where we thought proper to direct but that they still thought that the other was the river and that they were affraid that the South fork would soon termineate in the mountains and leave us at a great distance from the Columbia ... finding them so determined in this beleif, and wishing that if we were in an error to be able to detect it and rectify it as soon as possible it was agreed between Capt. C. and myself that one of us should set out with a small party by land up the South fork and continue our rout up it untill we found the falls or reached the snowy mountains by which means we should be enabled to determine this question prety accurately. this expedition I prefered undertaking as Capt. C. is the best waterman &c. and determined to set out the day after tomorrow ...

[Clark - Sunday, June 9th - at Base Camp on the Missouri]

... the men all engaged dressing Skins for their clothes, in the evening the party amused themselves danceing and Singing Songs in the most Social manner.

[Lewis - Monday, June 10th - at Base Camp on the Missouri]

The day being fair and fine we dryed all our baggage and merchandize. Shields renewed the main-spring of my air-gun we have been much indebted to the ingenuity of this man on many occasions; without having served any regular apprenticeship to any trade, he makes his own tools principally and works extreemly well in either wood or metal, and in this way has been extreemly servicable to us, as well as being a good hunter and an excellent waterman.

... we now scelected the articles to be deposited in this cash which consisted of 2 best falling axes, one auger, a set of plains [planes], some files, blacksmiths bellowses and hammers Stake tongs &c. 1 Keg of flour, 2 Kegs of parched meal, 2 Kegs of Pork, 1 Keg of salt, some chissels, a cooper's Howel, some tin cups, 2 Musquets, 3 brown bear skins, beaver skins, horns of the bighorned anamal, a part of the men's robes clothing and all

their superfluous baggage of every discription, and beaver traps. (As a precaution, they also made three small caches in different locations of powder, lead and an ax) we drew up the red perogue into the middle of a small Island at the entrance of Maria's river, and secured and made her fast to the trees to prevent the high floods from carrying her off. put my brand on several trees standing near her, and covered her with brush to shelter her from the effects of the sun.

... we drew out our canoes, corked, repared and loaded them. I still feel myself somewhat unwell with the disentary, but determined to set out in the morning up the South fork or Missouri leaving Capt. Clark to compleat the deposit and follow me by water with the party; accordingly gave orders to Drewyer, Joseph Fields, Gibson and Goodrich to hold themselves in readiness to accompany me in the morning ... Sah-cah-gah, wea, our Indian woman is very sick this evening; Capt. C. blead her. the night was cloudy with some rain.

THE FUR TRADE AT THE MOUTH OF THE MARIAS

RIVER MILE 22 LEFT

FORT PIEGAN

The confluence of the Missouri and Marias Rivers was the site of the first fur trade post built on the Missouri in Montana. Fort Piegan was built in 1831 to trade primarily with the Blackfeet, and it gave the American Fur Company presence in the Upper Missouri county that proved highly profitable for three decades.

Following the passage of the Lewis and Clark Expedition, the Blackfeet Indians showed such an uncompromising hatred for Americans that they kept their country closed to trappers. This hostility was attributed to an unfortunate collision between a band of Blackfeet and Captain Lewis with his return trip contingent along the Two Medicine River (a tributary of the Marias) on July 27, 1806. During the skirmish two Blackfeet were killed while trying to steal rifles and horses from the Lewis party. A more substantial cause of the Blackfeet animosity may have been the appearance of white trappers in the ranks of their enemies, the Crows, in a battle which occurred in 1807. Whatever the reason, the country of the Upper Missouri was closed to whites until 1830.

In 1827 Kenneth McKenzie had contracted with Astor's Western Department of the American Fur Company to manage a new division called the Upper Missouri Outfit. As general agent for the Upper Missouri Outfit, the aggressive McKenzie soon established his headquarters at a new post at the mouth of the Yellowstone, which became known as Fort Union. Fort Union was the best built and most spacious and well equipped post west of the Mississippi. McKenzie was declared by Chittenden to have been the most able trader the American Fur Company ever had in its employ. Before long Fort Union was the center of a large and successful operation. McKenzie then began to look with a covetous eye toward the northwest - the region of the dreaded Blackfeet.

In the winter of 1830, McKenzie sent a four-man party, headed by Jacob Berger, to the upper river in an attempt to capture some of the rich beaver trade of the Blackfeet for the American Fur Company. Berger had served with the Hudson's Bay Company at posts frequented by the Blackfeet on the South Saskatchewan River. Berger spoke the Blackfeet language, understood their characteristics and was well qualified to accomplish McKenzie's goal.

The emissaries followed the course of the Missouri to the mouth of the Marias River where they discovered a band of Piegan, a branch of the Blackfeet Indians. Fortunately, they saw the Indians first and through a brilliant but desperate maneuver saved themselves from the butcher shop. At the sight of these Indians, about whom so fearful a tradition had developed, the men only thought of running away. But Berger, unfurling a large American flag, commanded them to fall in behind him and pluckily advanced. The boldness of the maneuver, with the fact that Berger was recognized by some of the tribesmen, resulted in successful negotiations.

Berger persuaded a party of forty of the tribe to accompany him to Fort Union and arrange with McKenzie for a trading post to be established among them. The distance was greater than the Indians expected and they became suspicious and possibly bored. In any event the monotony of the journey was varied by their daily threats to kill and scalp every white man of the party and return to their own lands. At last, when within a day's march of Fort Union, they seemed about to fulfill their painful threats. Berger, however, made one last bargain with them; if the fort should not be reached the following day the white men would forfeit their lives without further protest.

The great stockade and floating flag of the trading post must have been a poignantly welcome spectacle to the little band of trappers. Its magnificence greatly impressed the Indians and Berger led them in triumph to McKenzie. At Fort Union they were lavishly courted for their goodwill and promised that a trading post would be established the following season at the mouth of the Marias.

Accordingly, James Kipp, a Canadian of German descent and a veteran of the fur trade upon the lower Missouri River, left Fort Union in July 1831, with seventy men and an outfit of Indian goods to build Fort Piegan. After a tedious, upriver voyage the party arrived at the mouth of the Marias River and selected the point of land between the two streams for the proposed establishment. They arrived about the middle of October.

The day after the arrival of the white men at this place, hordes of Piegans appeared. They seemed friendly enough, but the presence of a tumultuous mob of curious, capricious, and always uncertain-tempered Indians would have made the building of the post very difficult. Kipp smoked with the chiefs, made presents to them and courteously requested them to withdraw their people for seventy-five days, at the end of which time, he said, the post would be completed and open for trade.

The Indians complied, and returned promptly on the appointed day. They were astonished to find the buildings finished. During the first ten days after the post was built 2,400 beaver skins were traded. The Piegans would not permit a white man to set a trap in their country. They were, however, good beaver hunters themselves and the post, Fort Piegan as it came to be called, prospered. The post soon obtained over four thousand beaver pelts, as well as many other smaller furs.

The winter of 1831-32 was severe and the Indians were somewhat unfriendly. One time during the winter the fort was attacked by Blood Indians, who were supposedly influenced to do so by the rival British fur traders in Canada. When spring came Kipp could not convince his men to remain in Blackfeet country. All but three returned to Fort Union with the pelts; three Frenchmen had married into a local Piegan band. After it was abandoned Fort Piegan was burned.

There are two stories with regard to the destruction of Fort Piegan. One says the Indians were annoyed because the trading station was closed and burned it after the departure of the traders. The other says that David Mitchell, who replaced Kipp on the upper river the following year, found Fort Piegan's location unsatisfactory, and burned it after he completed Fort McKenzie (see river mile 14 left).

EARLY SETTLEMENTS AT THE MOUTH OF THE MARIAS

River Mile 22 Left

OPHIR TOWNSITE

Ophir City, the paper metropolis of 1864, was to be built where the Missouri, Marias, and Teton Rivers all come together. It had several things in its favor. It was twenty-two miles downriver from Fort Benton; during the low water season of the Missouri, steamboats had difficulty getting above the bad shoals in the river above Brule' Bottom (the former site of Fort McKenzie) and occasionally had to unload at Rowe's landing for trans-shipment by freight wagon to Fort Benton. There was timber for building purposes along the banks of the three rivers, and the townsite offered plenty of level ground along the river banks for wharves, warehouses, and dwellings.

The dream of a great tri-river city in Montana was the brainchild of several men who had supporters in high places of the territorial government. Stock in the company was issued on March 24, 1864. On February 2, 1865, eleven months after the stock was issued, a charter for incorporation was obtained from the Bannack Legislature.

The charter granted a townsite to be known as Ophir at the junction of Marias and Missouri Rivers, along the south bank of the Marias River to the mouth of the Teton, then down the Teton for six hundred yards and thence to the Missouri, containing 320 acres. A second charter was also granted for a town along the north side of Marias River which also contained 320 acres; this area was to be called North Ophir.

The corporation was to have all rights to the river fronts for docks, wharves, and warehouses. A dozen companies in all were formed including the East Ophir Townsite and the Missouri River Portage and Railroad Company, formed to build a wagon road and later a railroad around the Great Falls of the Missouri. Two ferry companies were set up to transport freight across the rivers. The Upper Missouri Steamboat Navigation Company was to build steamboats for transporting goods above the Great Falls to Gallatin City at the three forks of the Missouri. Also included in the grandiose plans were wagon roads across the mountains into the Flathead Valley, across Lewis and Clark Pass to the Mullan Road, and to Fort Walla Walla in Washington.

The field manager hired to build this town in the wilderness was N.W. Burris. He built a cabin along the river and engaged the steamboat *Cutter* to transport materials for the company. Burris then employed several men the spring of 1865 to build the town and set up a sawmill. Four hundred lots were laid out and a few log cabins were built. All went well until late May.

The cause of what happened next is the subject of a couple of stories. The first is that nine Blood Indians were killed on the streets of Fort Benton by two men named Spearson and Bostwick. The bodies were thrown into the Missouri. The second story is that during the winter, Charley Carson, cousin of the renowned Kit Carson, was trapping along the Missouri with two comrades, when three Bloods stole their horses. Charley and his comrades pursued them, caught them cooking, shot them, and regained their horses.

Whichever the cause, a war party of 180 Blood Indians under Calf Shirt was proceeding to Fort Benton for vengeance when they encountered Burris and his work party of nine men three miles up the Marias cutting timber. On May 25, 1865, the Indians attacked the men, surrounding them and cutting off their retreat to the river. As oxen were killed, the men used them for breastworks. Soon they were overrun and killed by the Indians. Four of the ten men were massacred were scalped. The following day the sternwheeler *Cutter,* which had been hauling building materials from Fort Benton, picked up the bodies and brought them back to a grove of boxelders at the townsite for burial.

This event ended the dream of Ophir. The Indians made a hasty retreat and crossed the line into British territory. The sawmill was moved and the only evidence remaining was a few log cabins from a metropolis dreamed of on paper by some early Montana pioneers. The cabins eventually ended up feeding the fires of steamboat boilers.

The Steamboat Helena, at the mouth of the Marias River in 1878. Montana Historical Society photograph.

ARCHER'S ISLAND

River Mile 24.5 Left

This large island is now attached to the north shore, yet as late as 1909 it presented an obstacle to navigation known as "Archer's Bar. "It is one of the places where Neihardt came to grief in his boat *Atom II* during the trip immortalized in the book *The River and I.*

David R. Archer says his dad homesteaded near the mouth of the Marias on the south side in 1883, and raised cattle. He busted during the bad winter of 1886 and finally moved to Fort Benton in 1903. These landmarks may be named after his father, as they are slightly northeast of the mouth of the Marias, in the general area his father homesteaded.

LEWIS RETURN CONTINGENT CAMP of JULY 28,1806

River Mile 32 Right

After a separation of nearly two weeks, all factions of the Lewis party were reunited, and their first campsite together below the Great Falls portage was in this vicinity.

During the return trip back to the States in 1806, the two captains separated near present Lolo, Montana, each taking a detachment to investigate new lands. Captain Clark headed for the Yellowstone River country, while Captain Lewis was going to explore the headwaters of the Marias River.

Upon reaching the Great Falls of the Missouri, Lewis split his party, leaving the bulk of the men to make the portage and to recover the caches at Portage [Belt] Creek and Marias River. On Wednesday, July 16, 1806, Captain Lewis headed out with Drewyer and the Fields brothers for the Marias. Their goal was to see if this tributary of the Missouri would reach far enough north to satisfy the northern boundary agreement of the 1783 Paris Treaty between the U.S. and Great Britain.

The 1783 Treaty of Paris, which ended the American Revolution, stated that the northwestern boundary of the Northwest Territory would be determined by a line drawn from the northwestern most point of Lake of the Woods (latitude 49° 37' North) to the Mississippi River. It was later discovered that the Mississippi River did not reach far enough north to satisfy that article of the Treaty. After the Louisiana Purchase was finalized, one of the purposes of the Lewis and Clark Expedition was to find a tributary to satisfy the treaty. Captain Lewis found that the Marias River did not reach far enough north and consequently he named his last camp on that river "Camp Disappointment."

They reached "Camp Disappointment" on Tuesday, July 22. After discovering that the river, actually today's Cut Bank Creek, came out of the mountains south of west, they stayed at the campsite in an attempt to determine the exact location. Bad weather prevented use of their sextant. They left on Saturday, July 26, and headed south to rejoin the rest of the party. That evening they were compelled to camp with a party of eight Blackfeet along the Two Medicine River.

[Lewis - Sunday, July 27th]

This morning at daylight the indians got up and crouded around the fire, J. Fields who was on post had carelessly laid his gun down behind him near where his brother was sleeping. one of the indians the fellow to whom I had given the medal last evening sliped behind him and took his gun and that of his brother unperceived by him, at the same instant two others advanced and seized the guns of Drewyer and myself, J. Fields seeing this turned about to look for his gun and saw the fellow just running off with her and his brother's - he called to his brother who instantly jumped up and pursued the indian with him whom they overtook at the distance of 50 to 60 paces from the camp seized their guns and rested them from him and R. Fields as he seized his gun stabed the indian to the heart with his knife - the fellow ran about 15 steps and fell dead ...

... having recovered their guns they ran back instantly to the camp; Drewyer who was awake saw the indian take hold of his gun and instantly jumped up and seized her and rested her from him but the indian still retained his pouch, his jumping up and crying damn you let go my gun awakened me I jumped up and asked what was the matter which I quickly learned when I saw drewyer in a scuffle with the indian for his gun. I reached to seize my gun but found her gone, I then drew a pistol from my holster and terning myself about saw the indian making off with my gun. I ran at him with my pistol and bid him lay down my gun which he was in the act of doing when the Fieldses returned and drew up their guns to shoot him which I forbid as he did not appear to be about to make any resistance or commit any offensive act he dropped the gun and walked slowly off, I picked her up instantly, Drewyer having about this time recovered his gun and pouch asked me if he might not kill the fellow which I also forbid as the indian did not appear to wish to kill us, as soon as they found us all in possession of our arms they ran and indeavored to drive off all the horses ...

... I now hollowed to the men and told them to fire on them if they attempted to drive off our horses, they accordingly pursued the main party who were dr[i]ving the horses up the river and I pursued the man who had taken my gun who with another was driving off a part of the horses which were to the left of the camp. I pursued them so closely that they could not take twelve of their own horses but continued to drive one of mine with some others; at the distance of three hundred paces they entered one of those steep nitches in the bluff with the horses before them, being nearly out of breath I could pursue no further, I called to them as I had done several times before that I would shoot them if they did not give me my horses and raised my gun, one of them jumped behind a rock and spoke to the other who turned around and stoped at the distance of 30 steps from me and I shot him through the belly, he fell to his knees and on his wright elbow from which position he partly raised himself up and fired at me, and turning himself about crawled in behind a rock which was a few feet from him. he overshot me, being bearheaded I felt the wind of his bullet very distinctly. not having my shotpouch I could not reload my peice and as there were two of them behind good shelters from me I did not think it prudent to rush on them with my pistol which had I discharge I had not the means of reloading untill I reached camp; I therefore returned leasurely towards camp, on my way I met with Drewyer who having heared the report of the guns had returned in surch of me and left the Fieldes to pursue the indians.

... we reached the camp and began to catch the horses and saddle them and put on the packs ... we had caught and saddled the horses and began to arrange the packs when the Fieldses returned with four of our horses; we left one of our horses and took four of the best of those of the indian's; while the men were preparing the horses I put four sheilds and two bows and quivers of arrows which had been left on the fire, with sundry other articles; they left all their baggage at our mercy. they had but 2 guns and one of them they left the others were armed with bows and arows ... the gun we took with us ... we took some of their buffaloe meat and set out ascending the bluffs by the same rout we had decended last evening leaving the ballance of nine of their horses which we did not want ... having ascended the hill we took our course through a beautiful level plain a little to the S. of East. my design was to hasten to the entrance of Maria's river as quick as possible in the hope of meeting with the canoes and party at that place having no doubt but that they (the Indians) would pursue us with a large party and as there was a band near the broken mountains or probably between them and the mouth of that river we might expect them to receive inteligence from us and arrive at that place nearly as soon as we could, no time was therefore to be lost and we pushed our horses as hard as they would bear ... at 3 P.M. arrived at Rose River (today's Teton River) ... having traveled ... 63 ms. ...we halted an hour and a half took some refreshment and suffered our horses to graize ... took to the open plains; by dark we had traveled about 17 miles further, we now halted to rest ourselves and horses about 2 hours ... set out by moon light and traveled leasurley ... we continue to pass immence herds of buffaloe all night as we had done in the latter part of the day

we traveled untill 2 OCk in the morning having come by my estimate after dark about 20 ms. we now turned out our horses and laid much fatiegued as may be readily conceived. my indian horse carried me very well in short much better than my own would have done and leaves me with but little reason to complain of the robery.

After resting a few hours Lewis, Drewyer, and the Shields brothers continued their flight to the Missouri River. They were keenly aware that the Indians would pursue them and seek revenge. Complicating this already tense situation was the fact that, while Lewis was exploring the Marias, there were three seperate factions of the expedition all scattered in the general vicinity, and all of whom were to meet Lewis at the mouth of the Marias. These factions included the remainder of Lewis' contingent, three of whom were uncovering the pirogue and cached items that were deposited at the base of the Great Fall, at Portage Creek; three others, also part of Lewis' contingent, had been left at the head of the Great Falls, where they were to rendezvous with a portion of Captain Clark's contingent who were boating there from the Dillon, Montana area., approximately two hundred river miles away. This combined group would portage equipment and boats to Portage Creek, thus uniting all three seperate factions of the expedition, and then travel to the mouth of the Marias to wait for Lewis. Lewis had no idea how far any of the three factions had progressed, or if they were even reunited; in short he had ample reason to be gravely concerned.

In what is perhaps the most fortunate - or lucky - event of the entire expedition, just as Lewis, Drewyer, and the Shields brothers reached the Missouri, they sighted the entire reunited party just approaching the meeting place at the mouth of the Marias in their dugout canoes and a pirogue.

[Lewis - Monday, July 28th]

The morning proved fair. I slept sound but fortunately awoke as day appeared I awaked the men and directed the horses to be saddled, I was so soar from my ride yesterday that I could scarcely stand, and the men complained of being in a similiar situation however I encouraged them by telling them that our own lives as well as those of our friends and fellow travelers depended on our exertions at this moment ... I told them that we owed much to the safety of our friends and that we must wrisk our lives on this occasion ... I now told them that it was my determination that if we were attacked in the plains on our way to the point (mouth of the Marias) that the bridles of the horses should be tied together and we would stand and defend them, or sell our lives as dear we could.

We had proceeded about 12 miles on an East course when we found ourselves near the missouri; we heard a report which we took to be that of a gun but were not certain; still continuing down the N. E. bank of the missouri about 8 miles further, being then within five miles of the grog spring (Cracon du Nez, river mile 9 left) we heared the report of several rifles very distinctly on the river to our right, we quickly repared to this joyfull sound and on arriving at the bank of the river had the unspeakable satisfaction to see our canoes coming down. we hurried down from the bluff on which we were and joined them striped our horses and gave them a final discharge imbarking without loss of time with our baggage ... we decended the river opposite to our principal cash which we proceeded to open after reconnoitering the adjacent country. we found that the cash had caved in and most of the articles burried therin were injured.

... having now nothing to detain us we passed over immediately to the island in the entrance of Maria's river to launch the red perogue, but found her so much decayed that it was impossible with the means we had to repare her and therefore mearly took the nails and other ironworks about her which might be of service to us and left her. we now reimbarked on board the white perog[u]e and five small canoes and decended the river about 15 ms. and encamped on the S. W. side near a few cottonwood trees.

[Lewis - Tuesday, July 29th]

Shortly after dark last evening a violent storm came on from N. W. attended with rain hail Thunder and lightning which continued the greater part of the night. no[t] having the means of making shelter I lay in the water all night. the rain continued with but little intermission all day.

LEWIS AND CLARK CAMPSITE OF JUNE 1, 1805

River Mile 37 Left

The Corps of Discovery camped in this vicinity the evening of June 1, 1805, after making nearly nineteen miles - twenty-three miles by their estimate - during the day. They camped on an island along the left hand side, the last in a series of four between here and the Virgelle Ferry crossing. The river shifts a great deal in this area, as the number of gravel bars will attest to, so the exact site is difficult to fix. They left Stonewall (Eagle) Creek (river mile 55.7 left) that morning.

[Lewis - Saturday, June 1st]

The morning was cloudy and a few drops of rain. Set out at an early hour and proceeded as usual by the help of our chords. the river Clifts and bluffs not so high as yesterday and the country becomes more level ... Capt. C. who walked on shore today informed me that the river hills were much lower than usual and that from the tops of those hills he had a delightfull view of rich level and extensive plains on both sides of the river ... the plains are more fertile at some distance from the river than near the bluffs where the surface of the earth is very generally covered with small smothe pebbles which have the appearance of having been woarn by the agitation of the waters in which they were no doubt once immerced. A range of high Mountains (probably today's Highwoods) appear to the S. W. at a considerable distance covered with snow; they appear to run Westerly. no timber appears on the highlands; but much more than yesterday on the river and Islands ... game is by no means as abundant as below; we killed one male bighorn and a mule deer today; saw buffalow at a distance in the plains particularly near a small Lake on Lard. side about 8 Ms. distant ... we passed six Islands and encamped on the 7th ... the wind has been against us all day ... saw some Indian Lodges of sticks today which did not appear to have been long evacuated.

COAL BANKS LANDING RECREATION SITE

RIVER MILE 41.7 LEFT

This site is reminiscent of one of the major problems of the steamboat era - fuel. Since the average boat burned about twenty-five cords of hardwood or thirty cords of cottonwood in twenty-four hours of steaming, the timber along the bottoms soon became scarce. Hence, efforts were made to utilize the bituminous coal so common along the Upper Missouri. According to Captain Grant Marsh, neither he nor any of the steamboat men were able to make any use of the native coal deposits. When added to the boiler fireboxes, the coal would redden around the edges without burning.

The Virgelle Ferry, located at river mile 41. The ferry, operated by Chouteau County, travels across the river utilizing two cables, the lower of which warrants caution by floaters during high river levels; the docked ferry should always be given a wide berth.

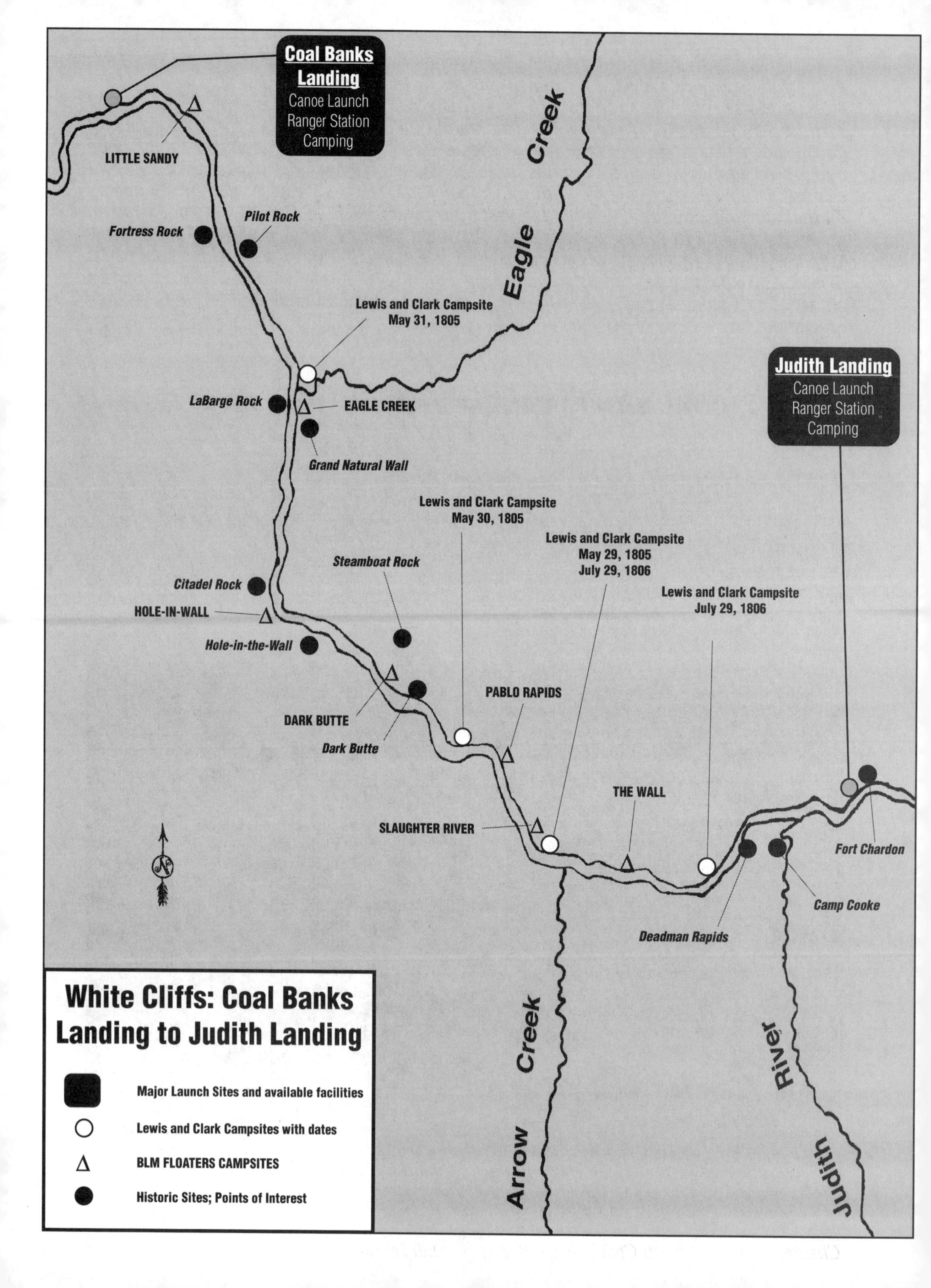

Coal Banks Landing
Canoe Launch
Ranger Station
Camping
LITTLE SANDY
Eagle Creek
Pilot Rock
Fortress Rock
Lewis and Clark Campsite
May 31, 1805
LaBarge Rock
EAGLE CREEK
Grand Natural Wall
Judith Landing
Canoe Launch
Ranger Station
Camping
Lewis and Clark Campsite
May 30, 1805
Lewis and Clark Campsite
May 29, 1805
July 29, 1806
Steamboat Rock
Lewis and Clark Campsite
July 29, 1806
Citadel Rock
HOLE-IN-WALL
Hole-in-the-Wall
PABLO RAPIDS
DARK BUTTE
Dark Butte
THE WALL
SLAUGHTER RIVER
Fort Chardon
Camp Cooke
Deadman Rapids
Arrow Creek
Judith River
White Cliffs: Coal Banks Landing to Judith Landing
Major Launch Sites and available facilities
Lewis and Clark Campsites with dates
BLM FLOATERS CAMPSITES
Historic Sites; Points of Interest

Chapter 3

History Digest: Coal Banks Landing to Judith Landing

COAL BANKS LANDING and CAMP OTIS

River Mile 43 Left

In 1886 Camp Otis, a summer camp and steamboat off-loading area, reportedly consisted of an officers quarters, telegraph office, barracks, messroom, warehouse, and a stable. At one time the settlement even had a post office called Ruger, perhaps for the commandant.

Camp Otis was the off-loading area for steamboats bringing most of the materials for the construction, furnishing and operation of Fort Assiniboine. After being unloaded at Camp Otis the materials were taken by freight outfits north the last 45 miles to Fort Assiniboine.

Fort Assiniboine was necessary because settlers in the Montana Territory demanded greater protection from Indians, even though most tribes were losing their capacity to make war. Montanans worried especially about the Sioux under Sitting Bull who numbered over four thousand, but generally remained in Canada. Fugitive Nez Perces and other Indians joined them. Sitting Bull's people generally behaved peacefully, but they perplexed both the Canadians and the Americans. As the buffalo herds began to thin out in Canada, Sioux bands roamed south of the border to hunt on the reservation lands in northern Montana.

Amidst the tensions caused by the Sioux's wanderings, the Army built Fort Assiniboine in 1879 on the northwestern slopes of the Bears Paw Mountains (near Havre). This million-dollar installation grew to become one of the major military bases in the West. As earlier posts like Forts Shaw and Ellis were closed down, Fort Assiniboine's handsome brick buildings became the Army's nucleus for all regional operations.

The completion of the railroad in 1887 eliminated the need for Camp Otis as a supply depot and it was abandoned. Fort Assiniboine was abandoned as a military establishment in 1911, and eventually became an agricultural experiment station.

HOMESTEADING HISTORY

River Mile 45

In 1929 the editor of the *Havre Daily News* wrote, "... There is something attractive to some of us in the pioneer spirit and atmosphere, something fascinating in the nature that could take the raw material of a state and shape it into a living commonwealth. The men who trod the paths that are already beaten and blazed have their great virtues and necessary place. The progressive unfolding of a community gives honorable work for generation after generation. But the tale of the man or woman who pushed into unmarked placed and tramped the first trails across the virgin land is one we never weary of hearing. They were the salt of the earth, the men and woman who were here for the first beginnings and who found the way which we have later followed ..."

Agriculture is the mainstay of the economy of central Montana. The pioneers in this industry were the cattle and sheep ranchers and the homesteaders. First on the scene was the open range cattle industry. Among those running cattle in the Breaks were many miners who left the gold camps when placer mining gave way to more expensive quartz (hard rock) operations. The Great Northern crossed the continent in the late 1880s and with the railroad came the homesteaders. Along the river, bottom land farmers fenced the open range cattle country and attempted to cultivate the sage-covered river terraces.

The original Homestead Act of 1862 allowed the homesteader to file on one hundred-sixty acres. The Enlarged Homestead Act of 1909 doubled that acreage. In 1912 the proving-up time requirement was reduced from five to three years. Prior to 1914, land with mineral potential could not be homesteaded; in that year, however, this land was opened to entry with the minerals reserved to the United States. The Stock Raising Homestead Act in 1916 increased the allowable acreage for the homesteader to 640 acres per entry.

Because of this favorable legislation and heavy promotion, the region vastly increased in population. Those who came invested heavily in time, sweat, tears, and money for their homesteads. However. there was little homesteading success along the Missouri. The river valley proved too harsh an environment for the small plot farmer. Drought, grasshoppers and the unsuitability of the land for cultivation combined to drive many a homesteader from his claim. Isolation sometimes became overwhelming, and it often contributed to the decision to relinquish a homestead or sell out. The great depression also had a major impact, driving even more settlers from the Breaks.

The river corridor is lined with reminders of the early settlers. In some places only the outline of a foundation remains. In others, rustic frame and log structures still stand. Today's river traveler can visit these sites and try to visualize what it might have been like to struggle for a living and to imagine the realization of dreams that were not to be.

For the next few miles, floaters pass the first of the many homestead sites that were located along the Missouri. There are many interesting stories about the people who settled along the river - who they were and where they came from, when they came and what they endured. Some of the more interesting highlights are included among the pages that follow.

LOWER THOMPSON BOTTOM

River Miles 45.4 - 46 Right

Robert L .Thompson purchased 37.12 acres here for $185.60 in 1914 ($5 per acre). There were no trees in the area at the time of the purchase. Thompson got tired of walking down to the river to get drinking water and decided to dig a well. He dug several holes, the deepest being eighty feet. However, he decided the distance down to water was greater than the walk to the river, so he continued to carry his water the remainder of his time there.

EDGAR McGUFFIN HOMESTEAD

River Miles 47 - 47.5 Left

Missouri-born Edgar McGuffin established himself here on January 1, 1911, and filed final proof on the one hundred fifty-two acre homestead on June 11, 1913, at age sixty-four.

A single man, McGuffin had earlier filed on 160 acres approximately fifteen miles northwest of here in 1905. The earlier choice of land was based on the government sponsored Marias (irrigation) Project. However, the irrigation project never materialized, so McGuffin built a reservoir and dug a three-quarter mile ditch to provide his own source of water. His efforts were a failure and unable to make a living off the land, he was forced to become a sheepherder. The homestead was relinquished back to the government.

This homestead had an estimated fifty acres of cultivable land on top, and the rest was to be used for grazing. In 1911, McGuffin broke five acres of sod and sowed "alfalfia" - the hay crop was poor. In 1912, he broke an additional five acres of sod and sowed wheat - the crop was cut for hay and yielded about one-half ton per acre. In 1913, ten more acres of sod were broken and the twenty acres sowed to wheat - again the crop was cut for hay and yielded an estimated one ton per acre.

ISAACSON BOTTOM

River Miles 47.8 - 48.8 Right

John T. Isaacson, a Norwegian with a wife and two children, homesteaded here in 1901. One of his little sons was sickly and couldn't be much help with the farming. The youngster planted cottonwoods along the riverbank in an effort to make the area look as it did before the woodhawks cut everything to sell to the steamboats. He reportedly carried a bucket of water to each tree every day.

In the flood of 1908, Isaacson lost everything but a saddle horse, team and wagon, and a red rooster. He moved to higher ground to the southwest up the Sag.

THE SAG (RATTLESNAKE COULEE)

River Mile 48.8 Right

Old-timers call this coulee The Sag. Two miles up The Sag, Rattlesnake Coulee joins. At this junction two stone cabins were built offset so that gun portals from each protected the door of the other. Mr. Black lived there. He contracted with Jim Hill to supply beef for the Great Northern Railway construction crew. Mr. Black never owned a cow, so to appear credible, he contracted with John Isaacson to purchase cattle for the crew. Black never bought any cattle, but was never short on a shipment to Hill.

STEVE HARRIS BOTTOM

River Miles 50 - 51 Right

Harris was a Greek who settled here early in the 1900s. He lived here until 1933, when he died.

FORTRESS ROCK

River Mile 50.5 Right

About a three-fourths of a mile back from the river is the rocky prominence of Fortress Rock, which is easily identified by its rusty-brown color, in sharp contrast to the surrounding white sandstone and grey shale. Fortress Rock marks the first outcrop of igneous rock along the river - rock formed by molten magma. Outcrops of igneous rock continue downriver for many miles past this point. (Refer to the Geology chapter for detailed information.)

PILOT ROCK

River Mile 51 Left

This ranch has been known as Pilot Rock Ranch, and the Jappey Ranch, which is the name of the family that settled this area. After the flood of 1908 when Hauser Dam broke, Mr. Jappey marked the high waterline and built his barn just above it. He was sure that the water would never be higher. The barn is still there.

The rocky prominence in the ranch's yard is composed of an igneous rock called shonkinite, and is commonly known as Pilot Rock; it. However, the historical location of "Pilot Rock" is somewhat in dispute.

Regardless of the historically correct location of "Pilot Rock", the name is reminiscent of the steamboat pilots. In addition to a captain, most boats also carried one or more pilots. The river pilots were a haughty, independent breed, so given to independent decision that many captains were unwilling to leave the pilot house until forced to by utter exhaustion. Captains who were also capable pilots, such as Joseph LaBarge and Grant Marsh, considered themselves fortunate.

Though captains appeared to hate the river pilots with passion because of their independence, Chittenden gave them an important place in his writings. He stated, "The Missouri River pilot was beyond question the most skillful representative of his profession. In no other kind of navigation were the qualities of quick perception, intuitive grasp of a situation, nerve to act boldly and promptly, coolness and judgment in times of danger, so important and so constantly in demand."

THE WHITE CLIFFS OF THE MISSOURI

River Mile 53

This is the beginning of the White Cliffs of the Missouri, an area of stunning beauty that has been admired and written about by travelers through this area beginning with Lewis and Clark. The White Cliffs continue for a distance of about twenty-five river miles. The cliffs are made of a formation called the Eagle Sandstone. See the Geology Chapter for more detailed information.

EBERSOLE BOTTOM

River Miles 52.2 - 53 Right

Jake Ebersole lived here long before the turn of the century in an old wolfer or woodhawk dugout. The area was used early in the 1860s as a wood supply yard for steamboats. Ebersole irrigated the bottom from a spring. After he died, George Allen settled here in 1898 and received a homestead patent in 1910 at the age of seventy-two.

The remains of several structures line the riverbanks (this is private land). The building furthest upriver was probably built by a later settler in the 1930s. Just in front of that structure is George Allen's home, which has been reduced to a mere cottonwood foundation. The next structure downriver is a dugout, probably the home of a woodhawk during the steamboat era. A fourth structure in the group is also very old.

The coulee mouth in the middle of the sandstone cliff on the north bank is known as The Cove, a popular lunch stop for river boaters.

HORSE RUSTLER'S CABIN

River Mile 53.5 Right

Jimmy or Jack Munro, a squatter in the latter half of the 19th century, built this house of field stone and cut sandstone. Munro was a stone mason by trade, but made his living in horses. He never bought or corralled a horse; instead, he let them run wild in the Breaks by the hundreds. He would just "rustle" up a herd and run them to Miles City to sell them. It is said that no one could handle a horse like Munro.

He reportedly built several of the stone cabins along the river.

At river mile 53, floaters begin to enter the area known as the "White Cliffs", whose beauty has awed many a traveler. This sketch, 'View of the Stone Walls', was done by Karl Bodmer in 1833, and is a view upriver from river mile 57.2. LaBarge Rock is the dark rock on the left bank, and Grand Natural Wall is on the point on the right bank. (Courtesy Joslyn Art Museum, Omaha, Nebraska; Gift of the Enron Art Foundation.)

LEWIS & CLARK CAMP OF MAY 31,1805

RIVER MILE 55.7 LEFT

The Corps of Discovery camped at, "... the upper part of a timbered bottom on the Stard. side ... just above the mouth of ... a stone wall creek ..." on May 31, 1805. The "Stone Wall Creek" is today's Eagle Creek. The day proved to be quite memorable for the explorers.

[Lewis - Friday, May 31st]

soon after we got under way it began to rain and continued until meridian when it ceased but still remained cloudy through the ballance of the day. The obstructions of rocky points and riffles still continue as yesterday; at those places the men are compelled to be in the water even to their armpits, and the water is yet very could, and so frequent are those point[s] that they are one fourth of their time in the water, added to this the banks and bluffs along which they are obliged to pass are so slippery and the mud so tenacious that they are unable to wear their mockersons, and in that situation draging the heavy burthen of a canoe and walking acasionally for several hundred yards over the sharp fragments of rocks which tumble from the clifts and garnish the borders of the river; in short their labour is incredibly painfull and great, yet those faithful fellows bear it without a murmur

The toe (tow) rope of the white perogue, the only one indeed of hemp, and that on which we most depended, gave way today at a bad point, the perogue swung and but slightly touched a rock, yet was very near overseting ... Capt. C. walked on shore this morning but found it so excessively bad that he shortly returned. at 12 OCk. we came too for refreshment and gave the men a dram which they received with much cheerfullness, and well deserved.

The hills and river Clifts which we passed today exhibit a most romantic appearance. The bluffs of the river rise to the hight of from 2 to 300 feet and in most places nearly perpendicular; they are formed of remarkable white sandstone which is sufficiently soft to give way readily to the impression of water; two or thre thin horizontal stratas of white freestone, on which the rains or water make no impression, lie imbeded in these clifts of soft stone near the upper part of them ...

... The water in the course of time in decending from those hills and plains on either side of the river has trickled down the soft sand clifts and woarn it into a thousand grotesque figures, which with the help of a little immagination and an oblique view, at a distance are made to represent eligant ranges of lofty freestone buildings, having their parapets well stocked with statuary; collumns of various sculpture both grooved and plain, are also seen supporting long galleries in front of those buildings; in other places on a much nearer approach and with the help of less immagination we see the remains or ruins of eligant buildings; some collumns standing and almost entire with their pedestals and capitals; others retaining their pedestals but deprived by time or accident of their capitals, some

lying prostrate an broken othe[r]s in the form of vast pyramids of connic structure bearing a serees of other pyramids on their tops becoming less as they ascend and finally terminating in a sharp point. nitches and alcoves of various forms and sizes are seen at different hights as we pass ...

... a number of the small martin which build their nests with clay in a globular form attatched to the wall within those nitches, and which were seen hovering about the tops of the collumns did not the less remind us of some of those large stone buildings in the U. States. the thin stratas of hard freestone intermixed with the soft sandstone seems to have aided the water in forming this curious scenery. As we passed on it seemed as if those seens of visionary inchantment would never have and can, end; for here it is too that nature presents to the view of the traveler vast ranges of walls of tolerable workmanship, so perfect indeed are those walls that I should have thought that nature had attempted here to rival the human art of masonry had I not recollected that she had first began her work. These wall rise to the hight in many places of 100 feet, are perpendicular, with two regular faces and are from one to 12 feet thick, each wall retains the same thickness at top which it possesses at bottom. The stone of which these walls are formed is black, dence and dureable ... these stones are almost invariably regular parallelepipeds, of unequal sizes in the walls, but equal in their horizontal ranges, at least as to debth. these are laid regularly in ranges on each other like bricks, each breaking or covering the interstice of the two on which it rests. thus the purpendicular interstices are broken, and the horizontal ones extend entire throughout the whole extent of the walls.

Paddling through the White Cliffs; view upriver from below Eagle Creek.

... These walls pass the river in several places, rising from the water's edge much above the sandstone bluffs, which they seem to penetrate; thence continuing their course on a streight line on either side of the river through the gradually ascending plains, over which they tower to the hight of from ten to seventy feet untill they reach the hills, which they finally enter and conceal themselves. these walls sometimes run parallel to each other, with several ranges near each other, and at other times interscecting each other at right angles, having the appearance of the walls of ancient houses or gardens. I walked on shore this evening and examined these walls minutely and preserved a specimine of the stone ...

... on these clifts I met with a species of pine which I had never seen, it differs from the pitch-pine in the particular of it's leaf and cone, the first being vastly shorter, and the latter considerably longer and more pointed (Lewis is describing the Limber Pine). I saw near those bluffs the most beautifull fox that I ever beheld, the colours appeared to me to be a fine orrange yellow, white and black ... it appeared to me to be about the size of the common red fox of the Atlantic states, or reather smaller than the large fox common to this country.

EAGLE CREEK

River Mile 55.7 Left

In addition to being one of the most scenic locations along the river, Eagle Creek is among the more historically significant areas.

As with most of the major side drainages intersecting the river, Eagle Creek was frequented by early residents. Remnants of drive lines, processing stations, tipi rings, rock cairns and flint knapping workshops are reminders of their presence. If you happen across one of these features, remember that they are keys to the past - for archeologists to be able to accurately interpret them, they must be left undisturbed and enjoyed in place. Lewis and Clark were, of course, the first white men to see the area when they camped here during their exploration to the Pacific.

In the 1870s Congress appropriated funds to clear the Missouri channel. Accordingly the *City of Fort Benton,* a government dredge built in Fort Benton in 1885, was commissioned to work on the Fort Benton ford and shallow spots downriver. She burned at Eagle Creek in either 1891 or 1892.

In 1890, New York born John Murray settled along the Missouri on the bottom lands below Eagle Creek. He was forty-six years old at the time and had a wife and five children. He built a 22' x 24' house and later added a 24' x 16' wing. Murray cultivated thirty-five to forty acres of the bottom land and had a stable, corral, fencing, chicken house and shed.

In 1892, Michigan born James Conley settled along the Missouri on the bottom land above Eagle Creek. He is believed to have been a crew member on *City of Fort Benton* which burned in 1891 or 1892. He was twenty-six years old at the time and had a wife and three children. He built a 28' x 28' house, stable, corral, corn crib, blacksmith shop and considerable fence. He cultivated thirty acres of bottom land and ran cattle and horses on the range.

The area was surveyed in 1896 by the General Land Office, and both Murray and Conley filed "settlement prior to survey" homestead applications that November. They witnessed each others applications and a John Lehfeldt provided the second testimony on each. Both men received their patents on July 3, 1901, Murray to one hundred seventy-two acres and Conley to one hundred forty-five acres.

In 1906, Conley established a post office at Eagle Creek which lasted only fifteen months.

In 1914, after crop failures, Murray irrigated his bottom land by means of a twenty horsepower steam engine. He boosted his harvest to one and one-half tons of hay per acre.

Another government steamboat to frequent the Eagle Creek area was the *USS Mandan.* She was a snagboat 124 feet long with a steel hull and was built in 1891. She saw service on the upper river from 1908 to 1921. This was the last steamboat to arrive at Fort Benton - June 20, 1921 - and her departure marked the end of an era. The *Mandan* swamped at Eagle Creek in 1910 when the crew failed to get her ashore before ice locked her in.

The crew of the *Mandan* was fond of leaving behind reminders of their passing. Graffiti making reference to the *Mandan* can still be seen on the river cliffs in several places.

LaBarge Rock, viewed from Eagle Creek. It is composed of igneous rock that formed as molten magma intruded into the white-colored Eagle Sandstone that surrounds it.

LABARGE ROCK

River Mile 56 Right

This large igneous formation across the river from Eagle Creek was probably named for Captain Joseph LaBarge, the more important of two noted brothers who captained Missouri River steamboats.

Captain John LaBarge was master of the *Chippewa* when she reached Brule' Bottom (river mile 14 left) on June 17, 1859, proving the river navigable to that point. But Captain Joseph LaBarge was the better known of the two brothers. He was the principal informant of Hiram M. Chittenden during the compilation of his notable work on steamboat history. The two volumes are virtually a biography of Captain Joseph LaBarge, who ranked with Captain Grant Marsh among the most capable and fearless navigators of the upper river. In addition to being a capable captain, LaBarge was also an able pilot.

A number of landmarks up and down the river served as sign posts for captains and pilots of river boats. Consequently, some of the islands and formations were named after well known river travelers and events arising from boating.

Captain Joseph LaBarge, pictured in his later years. LaBarge was one of the most highly regarded steamboat pilots on the Missouri. His long carreer started with the American Fur Company, and later he owned a number of different steamboats, whose services he contracted to various parties. He also was involved as a partner in LaBarge, Harkness, and Co., an unsuccessful opposition fur company that constructed Fort LaBarge in the town of Fort Benton. His biography, "History of Early Steamboat Navigation on the Missouri River", was written by Hiram Chittenden. Montana Historical Society photograph.

The Grand Natural Wall, river mile 56.9 left, is an outstanding example of a geologic feature called a dike. It formed about 5
million years ago as molten magma intruded into the surrounding rock, which at the time was deep underground. The dike is more
resistant to erosion than the surrounding rock and thus towers above it.

GRAND NATURAL WALL

River Mile 56.9 Left

Grand Natural Wall is an outstanding example of a dike. It formed as hot magma from great depths pushed its way into a crack in the white-colored Eagle sandstone which surrounds it, and then cooled and hardened. This occured about 55 million years ago, at a time when all of these rocks were still covered by thousands of feet of overlying rock. The dike is much more resistant to erosion than the surrounding sandstone. Rain water has, over time, eroded the sandstone much faster than the igneous rock, stripping it from the sides of the dike, and resulting in this impressive prominence.

From *Floating on the Missouri,* Schultz; refer to narrative at river mile 1.2 left for background.

Along through the canyon, as it may aptly be termed, the river flows very swiftly. In a short time we arrived at the mouth of Eagle Creek, fourteen miles from our starting point in the morning. Just below here stands a thin wall of rock, rising from the water's edge straight up for several hundred feet and running back northward until merged in sandstone bluff. The wall is built up, layer upon layer, of blocks of the stone of unvarying width and thickness, but of different lengths, which, singularly enough, always overlap, so that no interstice is more than the height of the block. On the opposite side of the river the continuation of the wall can be seen, jutting from the southern bluff. How long has it taken the old river to tear the half-mile gap in it?

Sah-ne-to said that this great wall was built by Old Man when he made the world. I objected to her theory on the ground that no man could have lifted the massive blocks.

"Just by jumping," she replied, "he made the backbone of the world (the Rockies). Why, then, had he not the power to lift those rocks?"

I answered not. Surely it was no more of a fable than certain others we wot of; the rock, for instance, that gushed water upon the blow of a certain ancient individual s staff.

GAGE CLARK HOMESTEAD

River Mile 57 Right

At the age of fifty-six, Gage Clark left New York to start a new life with his wife and child along the banks of the Missouri River. He settled here in September of 1900 and built the five room, two story frame house whose remains still occupies the bottom land. The house is rather unique in that the walls are of large, heavy plank - speculation is that the plank was salvaged from a steamboat wreck. Despite the age of the house, most of the deterioration has been from vandals in need of firewood.

Clark also built outbuildings and fence. He cultivated five to six acres the first couple years, then he increased that to twenty to twenty-five acres. He grazed the rest of his one hundred seventy-five acre tract. He received patent to the land in April of 1908 at age sixty-two. In about 1930, the outbuildings were dismantled and floated downriver to Johnson Bottom (river mile 64.7 right).

The stone house across the coulee was reportedly built long before Clark's arrival for a Mr. and Mrs. Creighton by Jack Munro (horse rustler at river mile 53.5 right). It is constructed of hand cut, native sandstone with squared sides and ashlar (quarry-faced or rough) faces. The cornerstones are rusticated (recessed along the edges to make the corner square and the joints conspicuous) and there were voussoir (tapering or wedge-shaped) stones forming an arch over wooded window lintels. The window sills were one solid stone, notched to appear as three stones. All in all, quite a structure for the remote, rugged Breaks of the nineteenth century.

MATCHETT RANCH

River Miles 58.8 - 59.5 Left

During the second wave of homesteading in Montana, around 1929, Leo F. Matchett, his wife and daughter filed a stock raising homestead entry and began running cattle in the Breaks. Among the improvements on his 647 acres spread was a stock watering reservoir on top for his seventeen head of cattle.

The Stock Raising Homestead Act of 1916, which permitted filing on the larger 640 acre tracts, did much to return the Breaks country back to its best use, grazing livestock.

RITLAND BOTTOM

River Miles 59.5 - 60.7 Left

"Perseverance" is almost synonymous with "successful homesteading", and in that context, Thor Ritland epitomizes the description. He came to the United States from Norway in 1902, and filed a Homestead Entry that same year. He was unable to meet the requirements for the land and so was forced to relinquish his claim. He kept trying though, first under a Desert Land Entry, then under another Homestead Entry and finally under a Stock Raising Homestead Entry. His determination paid off and he finally acquired title to the land in 1935.

Ritland's first house was lost in the flood of 1908. Using a rowboat, he gathered timbers floating downriver from Hauser Dam, and he built the "best dam_ house on the river!"

KIPPS RAPIDS

River Mile 59.7

This rapid is named for James Kipp, who built the first trading post of the American Fur Company in the Blackfeet country (Port Piegan at river mile 22 left) in 1831. In 1847 he was described as "a hardy veteran upward of sixty-five years old, who for many years had a farm near Independence, Missouri, and had made the journey to the Yellowstone and back about twenty times."

This shoal or "rapid" is also known as the Eagle Rapids from the spire-like rock near the east shore. John G. Neihardt *(The River and I,* 1910) said that this rapid can be identified from a considerable distance upstream by "a sibilant, metallic note as of a tense sheet of silk drawn over a thin steel edge," and he added that it made other rapids they passed through look like mere ripples on the surface.

CITADEL ROCK

River Mile 62 Right

Citadel Rock has been a landmark and inspiration to travelers on the Upper Missouri River since 1805. The rock was used to plot the course of the Lewis and Clark Expedition and was noted by Captain Clark as being "... a high steep black rock riseing from the waters edge." The rock was named by early fur traders who used it as a river landmark.

Citadel Rock, river mile 62 right, view from downriver. This important landmark is another of the igneous intrusions that contribute to the beauty of the landscape in the White Cliffs. Citadel Rock is directly across the river from an area that was intensely affected by intruding magma, and is undoubtedly connected to it.

Citadel Rock is another feature formed by intruding magma, similar to Grand Natural Wall, and LaBarge Rock. Just across the river from Citadel Rock, the canyon walls are riddled with veins and masses of this same igneous rock, in some cases making up the major portion of the rock outcropping in this vicinity, and extending for at least a mile back from the river. Obviously this area was the focus of a large intrusion by the hot magma, which formed the rusty brown-colored rock as it cooled. It appears that this locale was a center of igneous activity from which magma spread laterally in all directions, thus forming many of the dikes, sills and plugs for many miles both up and down river.

In his epic voyage to Fort McKenzie in 1833, Prince Maximilian noted this site on August 6th of that year. Citadel Rock was immortalized that day in a now famous sketch by Maximilian's fellow traveler, Karl Bodmer. Bodmer's sketch (the view is to the northwest or upriver) has been reprinted many times and Citadel Rock today serves to emphasize the accuracy and detail which made him famous.

The rock inspired Maximilian to write of it again on his downriver voyage of September 16, 1833, when he, "... passed the Citadel Rock, to which we bid adieu for ever, not without regret."

Citadel Rock was also a landmark to steamboat travelers on the Upper Missouri and is noted on most river maps of that era.

In 1967, it was declared a State Monument, and in 1974, was placed on the National Register of Historic Places.

BRIDGEFORD HOMESTEAD

River Miles 62.1 - 62.3 Right

In 1913, during the peak of Montana's homestead boom, Iowa-born William L. Bridgeford settled here with his wife and two children. Most of his "filing" was up on top. As with so many new settlers, he had a hard time.

In 1914, he broke ten acres and sowed six acres to rye and one-half acre to potatoes. He cut the rye for hay and harvested one hundred bushels of potatoes.

Then in 1915, he broke twelve more acres of sod and planted all twenty acres to oats. He was hailed out.

The year 1916 is remembered in the area as the year of the big wheat crop as virgin soil and good weather combined to produce good grain crops. Bridgeford had broken another twenty acres of sod and sowed forty-two acres of wheat. He froze out. He re-sowed the ground to oats and rye, and managed to thresh fifty bushels of each and cut the rest for hay.

In 1917, the land became his and he had earned all 317 acres of it.

SEXTON HOMESTEAD

River Miles 63 - 63.7 Right

Kentucky born Arch H. Sexton homesteaded here on April 10, 1914. He was a single man thirty years old.

In 1915, he broke five acres of sod, sowed oats and cut the crop for hay.

In 1916, he broke five more acres of sod and sowed five acres to oats and five acres to wheat. His crop was hailed out.

In 1917, he broke fifteen more acres of sod and sowed twenty acres to oats.

In proving-up his homestead, he built a 12' x 16' house, 12' x 24' barn and $1^{3}/_{4}$ miles of fence.

MUD SPRING COULEE

River Mile 63 Right

Probably the best map of the Lewis and Clark Expedition was made by Samuel Lewis in 1814 from the original drawings by Captain Clark. Reprints of the map vary in some of the finer details. For example, the Philadelphia Edition published with Elliott Coues, *The History of the Lewis and Clark Expedition (1893),* shows a "Crevice Creek "entering the Missouri from the south between Stone Wall Creek (Eagle Creek) and Slaughter River (Arrow Creek). This must be Mud Spring Coulee which enters the Missouri just upriver from Hole In The Wall.

HOLE IN THE WALL

River Mile 63.8 Right

High above the river is a thin spine of rock with a large hole, about twenty feet in diameter, known as Hole-In-The-Wall, which has long been a prominent landmark along the river. Father Nicolas Point (Wilderness Kingdom, "Fort Lewis and a Barge Down the Missouri") referred to Hole-In-The-Wall as "Pierced Rock" when he passed it on May 22, 1847.

Close examination of the rock spine that contains Hole-In-The-Wall reveals that it is composed of two different kinds of rock which interact with one another to produce this impressive feature. The most obvious of the two types of rock is the white Eagle Sandstone, in which the 'hole' is located. Less obvious, but perhaps more instrumental is a core of igneous rock that provides the structural integrity integrity to the narrow spine which contains Hole-In-The-Wall. This igneous rock is the same rock - shonkinite - that makes up the other intrusions in the White Cliffs. Because the ingnous rock is so much more resistant to erosion than the sandstone, it provides the structure for Hole-In-The-Wall. The rusty-brown colored igneous rock can been seen from the river while floating past the spine, but can be best seen by hiking up to the ridge above the Hole-In-The-Wall. The hole itself formed as a small crack initially formed in the wall, which allowed wind to pass through the hole; as the wind accelerates through the hole its erosive power is increased, allowing it to be quite effective in removing sand grains from the hole, continuously enlarging it.

ELBOW RAPIDS

River Mile 64

John G. Neihardt (*The River and I,* 1910) described Elbow Rapids, at the base of Hole In The Wall, as "deep and safe - much like an exaggerated mill-race." However, Lt. August V. Kautz, noted on June 30, 1860, "We passed the Hole in the Wall. We were unable to get up with the *Chippewa."*

Elbow Rapids was one of the places the *Chippewa* had to resort to the practice of "warping." Men were put ashore to carry a heavy tow-line to a suitable point above the rapids. There the tow-line was attached to a "deadman" - a tree trunk buried crossways on the beach, and the boat was hauled up the rapids by winching in the line with a capstan or "steam nigger."

JOHNSON BOTTOMS

River Miles 63.7 - 66 Right

This area was an especially coveted piece of ground. The first settler filed claim in 1903, but remained only three and one-half years. The second, Christen R. Christensen arrived here in 1917 and stayed through three drought stricken years. The third, Percy Brown, also hung on three years. The fourth settler, Jesse Greenwell (see the autobiography that follows) spent three and one-half years, leaving in 1928. Following the 1929 stock market crash, John Johnson filed claim here.

Hole-in-the-Wall, river mile 64 right. The Missouri river is below in this photograph looking upriver. The rock that the hole occurs in is a slab of Eagle Sandstone that is cored with an intrusion of igneous rock, which provides strength and support for the weak sandstone. Haynes Foundation Collection, Montana Historical Society

Johnson was born in Skien, Norway, in 1881 and came to the United States in 1901. At the age of forty, he settled here in October of 1929. Johnson successfully proved-up on the homestead, and received patent to the land on November 10, 1936.

A couple of factors contributed to Johnson's success. First, and this was true in many cases in the Breaks, he was a bachelor, so he had no other mouths to feed and could avoid some of the fineries. Second, although he cultivated sixteen acres for a short time, he used the land wisely for grazing, the purpose for which it was best suited. Johnson built a 14' x 16' house, a 16' x 26' barn, a 7' x 16' feed house and four miles of fencing. Much of the lumber used in his outbuildings was dismantled from the Gage Clark place (river mile 57 right) and floated downriver in the form of rafts.

The following passage gives a glimpse of what life was like in Montana for people living on and near the river. From *Splkes, Spurs, and Cockleburs,* Geraldine History Committee, Fort Benton: The River Press Publishing Company, 1976, pp. 226-227.

"Ruby Brown Greenwell History" by Ruby Greenwell

I went to Missouri to visit my sister Josie Gilmore and family. While there I met and married Jesse Greenwell in 1917. He went to the army and I ran the farm and took care of the stock. Mother Greenwell stayed with me at this time. Jesse came home, quite ill. He had a bad heart condition, so I still did the farm work.

The next year his condition had improved. We sawed trees, Jesse hewed square sides, eight feet long and sold them for ties. The smaller part was cut eight feet long and I barked them and sold them to mine props. We also had stock. We sold this farm in 1923 and headed for Montana, landing in Geraldine in January, where we stayed with the Gilmores for a month before going to my mother's homestead on the Arrow Creek. We remained there until April, then went to work for Joe Jones on the Creek for three summers. Later we went to his place on the Everson bench, helping harvest his crop and cooking for him.

Jesse and I then began working with a threshing rig outfit. Jesse hauled bundles, receiving $5.00 per day for himself and the team and bundle rack. I got $1.00 per day cooking for seventeen men, sometimes having to cut my own wood for the fire. I did all the bread baking, everything was cooked fresh as there weren't any cans to open then. After the cook-car pulled home, Jesse still followed the threshing machine with Sam Colter, while I stayed with Mary Colter, helping her with the stock. After Jesse drew his pay he put it in the Denton bank. One morning we heard the bank had gone broke, we figured a year's salary was gone, but we were lucky, we had our money in the bank that hadn't closed . We drew the money and bought cattle and horses with it. After that the banks carried insurance.

We moved to the Dave Wilson place, near Denton, my brother, Ralph stayed with us so he and Jesse started breaking horses. After the boys got the rough off the horses, I took one, Ralph the next one and Jesse would take a green bronc and we would ride to mother's in Geraldine. By the time we rode back home all the horses were pretty well broke. We received $10.00 a head for this but they had to be "lady" broke. We were also looking after Dave's cattle and feeding them.

In the spring of 1924, we moved to the Field 's place. My brother, Bill stayed with us. The boys put in the crops on Bill's homestead, the Field's place, which is just east of Chris Molines and mother's place. We had good crops this year. I raised turkeys for sale. We homesteaded on the Missouri River this summer and this was the last homestead to be taken. We later relinquished this place but lived there from 1925 until 1928. We built a 12' by 14' shack with boards and dirt roof, dirt floor, wrapped with tarpaper, and papered with newspapers inside for more warmth, also cleaner. After moving there in April we built more buildings. We milked cows and sold cream, carrying five gallon cans of cream on our leg, horseback for seven miles to the Ramsey place. Our mail carrier, Clarence Clark, took the cream to Geraldine and shipped it to Lewistown for us. He brought our groceries to us. We went to town only four or five times a year as it was twenty-six miles. We had quite a herd of stock by now. I raised turkeys for market. We rented the Wademan place to grow crops, also had crops on the river. We had the best garden and raised real big watermelons. Mrs. Pelifky passed away, so Louie hired Jesse and I to work for him. I cooked and Jesse did the field work. We took our turkeys, chickens and milk cows along, staying there until Louie harvested his crop, had a sale and rented his place. We returned to our home. We mined our coal from the breaks, this was hard work but it kept us warm. A lot of wood was also burned.

In 1928, we moved to the place where Lennie Duvall now lives, about twenty miles from town. We rented this place, farming it and renting more land west of us. We bought a Hart Parr tractor and a Ford coupe. We were moving along faster. In 1930 we moved to the Bronson place, eleven miles from Geraldine, living there until 1937. We bought the Bill Hines homestead, which he filed on in 1910. We lived in Bill's homestead shack, later using it for a garage after we moved a larger house on the place. We also bought some land from Evers and farmed and raised stock.

Jesse passed away in August 1957 and I have farmed since, doing my own farm work except combining. I also run cattle part time so I guess I can rate as a pioneer as I have helped prove up on three homesteads. I have traveled nearly every winter, since Jesse has been gone. I have been in every state but two, also flew to Hawaii. Three ladies and I drove to Alaska, two ladies and I drove to Old Mexico. I rode on the local wagon train last year (1975) and expect to do so this summer. I have a home in Geraldine, where I live in the winter but can hardly wait until spring comes to go out to the farm.

I owe all to the most wonderful mother any kid ever had. Some of these have been hard times but I have enjoyed most of it very much. I am so thankful the Lord has been so good to me

STEAMBOAT ROCK

River Mile 69 Left

Steamboat Rock is the large columnar sandstone formation on the bluff about one-half mile northeast of the river. It is located 2,215 river miles from St. Louis according to the combined reckoning of the Mississippi and Missouri River Commission.

Geologically, the area around Steamboat Rock and Dark Butte is a good place to view the effects of faulting on the rocks. Generally, in this area, and particularly on the left side of the river, there appears to be two distinct layers of Eagle sandstone, the white, cliff forming rock that makes up the White Cliffs. One of the layers makes up Steamboat Rock, several hundred feet higher than the river; the second layer is only a couple of hundred feet above the river. These two layers of sandstone were at one time connected, but have been broken and separated by faulting, in this case a type of fault called a thrust fault. The two sandstone layers are separated by dark shale, probably the Marias River Formation.

The Corps of Engineers attempted to complete a survey of the Upper Missouri from its mouth to Fort Benton in the 1880's. The basic purpose of the survey was to measure river distances, map the river completely, install bench marks and study the major trouble spots. The survey had been made to Fort Pierre by 1884, the same year in which the Missouri River Commission was established. The commission completed the survey in 1887. The shoreline and topographic details were completed by 1890 and a map was published in 1893.

The first significant result of the survey was a new set of official distances. Before the survey, steamboat men depended on rough measurements of the river which always considered the river meanderings. Thus steamboat owners called the distance from St. Louis to Fort Benton about three thousand miles. However, since the engineers did not measure the stream curves but simply measured across them the official distance from the mouth of the Missouri to Fort Benton was only two thousand-two hundred seventy-four miles. These official distances were quickly adopted by the army and Indian Bureau, since the government awarded its contracts on the basis of rates per one hundred miles. The surveying and mapping done during the 1880's was basic to all engineering work done after that time, whether it pertained to navigation or flood control.

It may be timely at this point to explain more about the boats that were used on the Upper Missouri, lest one be led to think that the steamers had the market cornered. Other important boats on the Missouri included canoes, pirogues, mackinaws, bullboats and keelboats.

Canoes were a shell generally hewn from a large cottonwood tree. They ranged from fifteen to twenty feet long. Their hull was strengthened by partitions left crosswise in the shell. Dugout canoes were used mostly for short, local trips and were floated individually or in pairs joined by a platform which was then floored over. Sails could be used on the craft.

The name pirogue was applied to various river crafts but seems to have most commonly referred to dugouts or two dugouts fastened together. When a square end was left on a canoe it was called a pirogue.

Between Fort Mandan and the Great Falls, Lewis and Clark had six dugout canoes and two pirogues. The smaller of their pirogues, the infamous "White Pirogue," was of sturdy, hardwood (poplar) construction and some thirty-five feet in length and perhaps seven feet wide at the bow. Two oarlocks were mounted toward the stern and four mounted toward her rounded bow. She gradually tapered to the stern, which was not square but somewhat pointed. At the stern was a curved tiller, used to operate the rudder. A convertible awning was fitted over the area in the stern. A mast with a square sail and a spiritsail along with a halyard for lowering these sails and the U.S. colors stood high to the front of center. At the bow was a hemp rope (called a cord) for cordelling when the river was too much for the six oars. There were also setting poles. Captain Clark planned on loading her with eight tons of provisions according to his field notes of April 13,1804.

Mackinaws were made of hand sawed lumber and were fastened together by wooden pins. They were flat bottomed crafts and usually carried five men; four at the oars and one at the rudder. The unique, high ended boats were used for downriver trips only and normally carried about fifteen tons of freight. Two with forty-five ton capacities accompanied the Chippewa during her return down river in 1859. There was a yard for making mackinaws just below Fort Benton and the mouth of Shonkin Creek.

Bullboats were shaped much like inverted mushrooms. They were made of willow framework covered by bull buffalo hides.

Keelboats were sixty to seventy foot long wooden crafts with about a thirty foot mast and a keel from bow to stern. Most of these were built in Pittsburgh. They were propelled by a number of systems. Sometimes they were pulled by a long line (cordella) attached to the top of the mast. Sometimes oars were used, or long poles were used to push them along. When the wind was right, a square sail was rigged. In rapid water, a long line was sometimes tied upstream and then the boat was pulled along by men taking line in on the deck. This last means was another method of "warping."

View of Dark Butte, looking downriver. The butte is composed mostly of an igneous rock called shonkinite. Of interest in this photo is the presence of two seperate layers of white Eagle Sandstone, caused by a thrust fault which has broken the layer of Eagle Sandstone and forced one segment to be lifted, or thrust, above the other.

DARK BUTTE

River Mile 69.5 Left

Dark Butte, a prominent historic landmark on the Upper Missouri, is a plug - a large mass of igneous rock, called shonkinite, that was injected into the Eagle Formation and which cooled at depth. As with all of the intrusions in the White Cliffs area, it is characterised by a rusty-brown color, and by its resistance to erosion - it thus forms a high prominence towering above the more easily eroded sedimentary rocks.

Incorporated within the shonkinite can be seen blobs of white Eagle Sandstone, which were mixed into the molten magma when it was being emplaced.

The thrust faults which occur in this area (see Steamboat Rock, river mile 69) are well displayed at Dark Butte, where two distinct layers of white Eagle Sandstone are visible, the first just above the level of the river, and the second near the top of Dark Butte, these two layers were once a single contiguous layer that has been offset by thrust faulting. The igneous mass of Dark Butte is positioned between the two sandstone layers, suggesting the possibility that the fault also acted as a conduit for the hot magma.

SLUGGETT HOMESTEAD

River Miles 69.2 - 70.3 Left

Twenty-four year old Lester Sluggett settled here in 1924 with his wife and two daughters. In proving-up his homestead he built a 14' x 20' and 14' x 12' house, chicken coop, 18' x 20' barn, reservoir, well, and four miles of three-wire fence. He also broke eighty acres of sod. In 1929 he harvested three hundred bushels of wheat from his cultivated land. This might seem a small yield from eighty acres, but from 1930 through 1932, his crops failed entirely. In 1933 he cut twenty-five tons of oat and wheat hay and afterwards he shifted to livestock as the means to earn a living. Sluggett earned the patent to his land in September of 1936.

This was Sluggett's second attempt at homesteading along the river. In 1920 he settled on land at river miles 81 to 82.5 left. He built a 12' x 24' house and a mile of fence, but then stayed only about two weeks. In relinquishing the homestead entry in October of 1924 Sluggett stated, "I abandoned the land about three years ago, and I am relinquishing it today at the Havre Land Office, the land is not very much good, and I found that you could not get in and out of the place, as any road built to the place would wash right out ... with the first rain or snow melt." A neighbor, Arthur Lohse, corroborated the statement by saying that only a saddle horse could be used to get in and out.

DIMITROFF HOMESTEAD - SHEEP SHED COULEE BOTTOM

River Miles 69.9 - 71.2 Right

George Dimitroff was born in Salo Chuprena, Bulgaria, in 1891. He immigrated to Baltimore, Maryland, on October 20, 1910. He settled in the central Montana area and was living in Lewistown on October 4, 1917, when he was inducted into the U.S. Army. During World War I he was a corporal and served with Company A, 362nd Infantry, 91st Division and saw action at St. Mihiel, Meuse Argonne and Lys-Scheldt, Belgium. After the war he returned to the Lewistown area. For his military service he was made a naturalized citizen.

In 1921 he contested the homestead entry of Mary Roberts Blanchard for 165 acres at this location. Though the records don't show exactly why, he was granted a preferred right on October 14, 1921, and filed his entry a week later. He established residence here on April 22 the following year. There was already a 14' x 16' house on the bottom and he built a 12' x 14' barn, a 6' x 8' log chicken coop, two miles of three wire fence, and improved a spring. He broke ten acres of sod and sowed spring wheat the spring of 1922, but lost the crop to grasshoppers. That fall he broke an additional ten acres of sod and sowed winter wheat. The original ten acres was again sowed to wheat the spring of 1923. In July, both crops looked good, but grasshoppers were again a concern.

On July 17, 1923, Dimitroff attempted to file final proof on the homestead, but had to ask for a postponement because his discharge and naturalization papers weren't accessible. "...... my discharge papers were put in a large safe at Kotkin's store (grocery "cash & carry") here in Lewistown, Montana, several months ago, and when I went for them on the morning of July 17th last, to use in evidence at proof, it was found that the safe could not be opened, and thus far has defied all efforts at opening; for this reason I am unable at this time to furnish same; hence I am compelled to ask that *further action on my final proof be suspended* till I can obtain the original "discharge" and furnish a certified copy thereof; ... " The extension was granted, and by October 22, 1923, the War Department had supplied the necessary documents and his final proof was completed.

On January 29, 1924, thirty-three year old George Dimitroff, a single man, received his Final Certificate for patent.

LIDSTONE FERRY

River Mile 71

Ruby Lidstone grew up with her family in Spokane. Her father had a brother who was homesteading in this vicinity, and after a visit here decided to file a homestead claim on this land on the north side of the river. The "squatters-rights" that he applied for required that someone live on the land full-time. His wife however wanted no part of the challenge of living in such a remote area, but Ruby thought it would be just fine living here, and volunteered to do so, arriving October 13, 1913. Initially she spent a lot of time at her uncle's place, six mile away, but eventually moved into anexisting one-room log shack with a heating stove and a kerosene oven; drinking water was hauled from the river in buckets. Choteau County provided for a free ferry to be built here to serve the local farmers and ranchers, providing a crossing for travel between Big Sandy and Geraldine. The ferry operated at this location from 1917 to 1925, when service was discontinued.

The ferry was quite popular with bootleggers who transported whiskey through the breaks at night, bound for Canada, and there were many nights when Ruby was awakened by their activities. She frequently slept with a loaded rifle in her bed.

Ruby was very resourceful, making all of her own clothes from fabric ordered from the Montgomery Ward catalog, and she made her underwear from cotton flour sacks. She married and raised her family in this area.

Ruby's son Elmer tells of a story in the early fall of 1918 when Jeanette Rankin, the first woman to serve in the United States Congress, was descending the south side of the breaks towards the ferry, bound for Big Sandy on a campaign tour. Her car had run low on oil. Elmer rode his horse back to the homestead, but the only thing on hand was linseed oil. He rode back with it and the car ran fine, but smoked quite a bit. Rankin stopped to have lunch with the Lidstones before continuing on to Big Sandy, where she promptly got an oil change.

LEWIS & CLARK CAMP OF MAY 30, 1805

RIVER MILE 71.2 LEFT

The Corps of Discovery camped here after a miserable day after making only 5.4 miles.

[Lewis - Thursday, May 30th]

The rain which commenced last evening continued with little intermission untill 11 this morning when we set out; the high wind which accompanied the rain rendered it impracticable to procede earlyer. more rain has now fallen than we have experienced since the 15th. of September last. many circumstances indicate our near approach to a country whos climate differs considerably from that in which we have been for many months. the air of the open country is asstonishingly dry as well as pure. I found by several experiments that a table spoon full of water exposed to the air in a saucer would evaporate in 36 hours when the murcury did not stand higher than the temperate point at the greatest heat of the day; my inkstand so frequently becoming dry put me on this experiment. I also observed the well seasoned case of my sextant shrunk considerably and the joints opened.

... this day we proceded with more labour and difficulty than we have yet experienced; in addition to the imbarrasments of the rappid courant, riffles, & rockey points, which were as bad if not worse than yesterday, the banks and sides of the bluff were more steep than usual and were now rendered so slippery by the late rain that the men could scarcely walk. the chord is our only dependance for the courant is too rappid to be resisted with the oar and the river too deep in most places for the pole. the earth and stone also falling from these immence high bluffs render it dangerous to pass under them. the wind was also hard and against us. our chords broke several times today but but happily without injury to the vessels

... in the course of the day we passed several old encampment of Indians, from the apparent dates of which we conceived that they were the several encampments of a band of about 100 lodges who were progressing slowly up the river; the most recent appeared to have been excavated about 5 weeks since. these we supposed to be the Minetares or black foot Indians who inhabit the country watered by the Suskashawan and who resort to the establishment of Fort de Prarie (Lewis is referring to the North West Company's fort, on the present site of Edmonton, Alberta).

MICKLUS HOMESTEAD

River Miles 72.7 - 73.7 Right

This is another piece of land that was filed on several times before it went to patent. A homestead entry was filed on the bottom lands in October of 1906, but was canceled in April of 1914. Another claimant filed on the land in May of 1915, enlarged the claim to include some of the steeper surrounding country in August of the same year, then relinquished the land in December of 1915.

Mike Micklus settled on this three hundred fifteen acre site in 1916. Before he could prove-up on the land, he was inducted into the service. However, the law provided that the land remain in his name while he served in World War I. Micklus returned with a bride and cultivated feed crops for cattle and a few potatoes for his own use. An error in the legal description resulted in several letters to Senator Henry Lee Myers before the claim could be patented. Patent to the land was issued on May 14,1920, but soon after Micklus moved to Holdingford, Minnesota.

PABLO RAPIDS

River Mile 73.2

The treacherous nature of the Upper Missouri was shown when the *Marion,* commanded by Captain Abe Wolf, went hopelessly aground here in 1866. The bartender appeared to be the only employee working while the steamboat was inoperative, and he should have gotten double time-and-a-half. The entire crew and passengers remained in such a drunken state that they were unable to help the boat over the rapids.

Captain Grant Marsh was summoned with the *Luella* to salvage the *Marion's* freight. His first act upon taking command was to close the bar, then to sober up the crew and put them to work transferring freight. The *Marion* was finally freed, but the constant pounding of the rapid waves damaged her beyond repair. Her machinery was salvaged and sold in Fort Benton.

Wolf Island, one mile below the top of the rapids, may have been named for the unfortunate Captain Wolf.

BAIN DESERT LAND ENTRY

River Miles 73.3 - 74.5 Left

Luther and Martha Bain came to the river in 1908. They first settled on land downriver (river miles 75.6 - 76.9 left) on what is now known as Sneath Bottom. In 1910 they took possession of the land at this location. Neither area had been surveyed when they settled.

General Land Office surveys covering both properties were approved on February 19, 1916. Luther filed a desert land entry claim on 148 acres at the downriver location and Martha filed a desert land entry claim on 165 acres at this location.

Shortly after they settled at this location, they began an extensive irrigation project and completed yearly proofs as required. They received patent to Luther's tract on March 1, 1918, but ended up having a tough time making final proof on this land. By 1921, post war inflation made it impossible for them to purchase the pump they planned to raise the water fifty-five feet from the Missouri to Martha's plowed fields. Rather than cause Martha to lose the land on which they had toiled for eighteen years, the General Land Office allowed them to purchase the land and Martha received her Desert Land Entry Patent on September 5, 1928.

LARSON BOTTOM

River Miles 75.3 - 75.8 Right

Andrew Larson of Sweden filed on this bottom land in 1905. He proved according to the requirement of the Desert Land Law, but had to wait until 1916 for the land to be surveyed before receiving patent. It was then found that he had 175 acres, rather than the allowed 160 acres, and that the state had reserved the coal rights. It took until July 3, 1918, to get through the tangle of red tape for him to acquire ownership.

LEWIS & CLARK CAMP OF MAY 29,1805
LEWIS CAMP OF JULY 29, 1806

River Mile 76.6 Left

The Corps of Discovery camped here after traveling upriver from the Judith Landing area, a distance of 12.2 miles. The party discovered a major tributary, which Clark named the Judieth River, for Julia (Judith) Hancock, whom he married in 1808.

The name "Slaughter River", was given to this camp because of the large concentration of dead buffalo that the expedition observed just a short distance downriver, leading Lewis to conclude that they had happened upon the site of a buffalo jump, or 'pishkun'. Archeological investigations have failed to substantiate the presence of a pishkun in this area, so the source of the buffalo carcasses that the expedition observed remains unknown.

[Lewis, - Wednesday, May 29th, 1805]

This morning we set out at an early hour and proceded as usual by the Chord. at the distance of two and one-half miles passed a handsome river which discharged itself on the Lard. side, I walked on shore and acended this river about a mile and a half in order to examine it...great abundance of the Argalia or Bighorned animals in the high country through which this river passes.

Cap. C who assended this river much higher than I did has thought proper to call it Judieths River ...

... I counted the ramains of the fires of 126 Indian lodges which appeared to be of very recent date perhaps 12 to 15 days. Capt. Clark also saw a large encampment just above the entrance of this river on the Stard. side of rather older date...

... today we passed on the Stard. side the remains of a vast many mangled carcases of Buffalow which had been driven over a precipice of 120 feet by the Indians and perished; the water appeared to have washed away a part of this immence pile of slaughter and still their remained the fragments of at least a hundred carcases they created a most horrid stench. in this manner the Indians of the Missouri distroy vast herds of buffaloe at a stroke; for this purpose one of the most active and fleet young men is scelected and disguised in a robe of buffaloe skin, having also the skin of the buffaloe 's head with the years and horns fastened on his head in form of a cap, thus caparisoned he places himself at a convenient distance between a herd of buffaloe and a precipice proper for the purpose, which happens in many places on this river for miles together; the other indians now surround the herd on the back and flanks and at a signal agreed on all shew themselves at the same time moving forward towards the buffaloe; the disguised indian or decoy has taken care to place himself sufficiently nigh the buffaloe to be noticed by them when they take flight and runing before them they follow him in full speede to the precipice, the cattle behind driving those in front over and seeing them go do not look or hesitate about following untill the whole are precipitated down the precepice forming one common mass of dead an[d], mangled carcases: the decoy in the mean time has taken care to secure himself in some cranney or crivice of the clift which he had previously prepared for that purpose. the part of the decoy I am informed is extreamly dangerous, if they are not very fleet runers the buffaloe tread them under foot and crush them to death, and sometimes drive them over the precipice also, where they perish in common with the buffaloe.

we saw a great many wolves in the neighbourhood of these mangled carcases they were fat and extreemly gentle, Captain C. who was on shore killed one of them with his espontoon. just above this place we came too for dinner opposite the entrance of a bold running river 40 Yds. wide which falls in on Lard. side. this stream we called Slaughter river (Arrow Creek). it's bottoms are but narrow and contain scarcely any timber. our situation was a narrow bottom on the Stard. possesing some cottonwood. soon after we landed it began to blow & rain, and as there was no appearance of even wood enough to make our fires for some distance above we determined to remain here untill the next morning, and accordingly fixed our camp and gave each man a small dram. notwithstanding the allowance of sperits we issued did not exceed 1/2 gill (about 2 ounces) per man several of them were considerably effected by it; such is the effects of abstaining for some time from the uce of sperituous liquors; they were all very merry.

This was one of the few campsites used by the Corps of Discovery on both their outbound and return journeys. Captain Lewis camped here in 1806 with his party after traveling forty-four one-half miles downriver. The previous day Lewis had rejoined the rest of his party near the mouth of the Marias after the wild flight from the Blackfeet.

[Lewis - Tuesday, July 29th, 1806]

Shortly after dark last evening a violent storm came on from N. W. attended with rain hail Thunder and lightning which continued the greater part of the night. not having the means of making a shelter I lay in the water all night. the rain continued with but little intermission all day ... at 11 A. M. we passed that very interesting part of the Missouri where the natural walls appear, particularly discribed in my outward bound journey. we continued our rout untill late in the evening and encamped on the N. E. side of the river at the same place we had encamped on the 29th. of May 1805 ... the river is now nearly as high as it has been this season and is so thick with mud and sand that it is with difficulty I can drink it. every little rivulet now discharges a torrant of water bringing down immence boddies of mud sand and filth from the plains and broken bluffs.

ARROW CREEK (Lewis & Clark's Slaughter River)

River Mile 77.4 Right

Arrow Creek is a major drainage flowing from the south into the Missouri. The rich bottomland, with an abundnce of timber and game contributed to its usefulness to native peoples as a habitation site.

From *Floating on the Missouri,* Schultz; refer to narrative at river mile 1.2 left for background:

Dinner was over, the dishes washed, a quantity of dry wood piled behind the stove. Sah-n'e-to lit the lantern and resumed work on a pair of moccasins she was embroidering with a vine-like pattern of various colored cut beads. "Tell me," I said, "why this stream is named Ap-si-sak-ta - the Arrow River?"

"It was given that name long ago," she replied, "by the ancient ones, on account of a strange, a very strange, thing which took place":

One time in that long ago there was a beautiful young girl named Ah-we-kas - the Antelope - the daughter of a chief. She was as good as she was handsome, and very industrious. No one tanned whiter buckskin, softer robes than she. No wonder, then. that all the young men were her slaves, and longed to make her their wife. But to all of them she replied, 'No,' and remained with her parents, doing all she could for their welfare and happiness. One after another the great men, the rich men of the camp, made offers to the old people for her, offers of horses and other wealth, but always her parents would ask her if she was willing, and when she replied, 'Nay,' they did not urge her. So the girl grew up, year by year more and more beautiful, and reached womanhood. 'Tis said that her hair when unbraided almost swept the ground; that her large, soft eyes were like those of a fawn, deep and clear, with an expression in them - I cannot say just what - that made the heart of man beat furiously in his bosom. She was tall and slender, yet of a rounded and graceful figure. She could run like a deer, and swim with the speed of an otter.

One spring the people were camping for a time somewhere on this river. One day there came from the camp of the Blackfeet, far to the north, a young man to visit his Piegan relatives, and that very evening he was invited by the father of Ah-we-kas to come to his lodge and feast. The young woman set some food before him, took one look at his face and hurriedly returned to her seat. He had one glimpse into her lovely eyes and was so distraught that he could not eat. In that one glance both knew that they were made for each other. After that the young Blackfoot came to her lodge every day and talked long with her father of the north country. of the doings of his people - of their wars, their hunts and adventures. But he never spoke to her, nor she to him; but if they gazed at one another shyly, bashfully, as lovers will - well, what harm?

At last, one day, the young man informed the chief that on the morrow he would return to his people, "But," he continued, "I shall soon return, driving many horses before me."

As he passed out of the lodge somehow his hand met that of the girl, and he gave it a gentle squeeze; she in turn pressed his, and then covered her head with her robe in shame of her boldness.

"I wonder, now," the old man mused, "what he meant by that - that he would soon return driving many horses before him?"

Ah-we-kas was sure she knew, but made no reply.

Most importunate of all her suitors was Black Bull, a man of savage temper and a great warrior. He was tall, and broad, and heavy, of great strength, and as homely as he was strong. By his success in war he had become very rich; no one owned more horses, no one had a greater store of weapons, fine garments, robes and furs, than he. Two wives he had already, women whom he forced to toil incessantly, and whom he cruelly beat when anything went wrong. And now he wanted Ah-we-kas for his third wife. Almost daily he sent word to her father, offering this and that for her, until finally the messenger carried this: "Thus says the Black Bull: Take my whole herd and the rest of my property what you will, and give me your daughter in return."

But, as before, the answer went back: "No, she refuses you."

Then Black Bull became angry, beat his wives, and rushed madly out of his lodge and away he knew not where. Passing the trail to the river he met Ah-we-kas and raised his hand to strike her, a fearful scowl on his face. Then he changed his mind and cried out: "And so you refuse me; know, then, that you shall yet become my wife, or die."

Twas but a few days after this that the young Blackfoot returned, driving before him, as he had said he would, a band of fine horses, red and white, yellow and white, black and white; all of them spotted horses. And his relatives took the horses and tied them up about the lodge of the father of Ah-we-kas, and gave him the young man's message.

"What say you now?" the old man asked his daughter. "What word have you for this new suitor?"

Burning with shame, her head bent low, she pressed his wrinkled hand and whispered: "You may keep the horses."

So they were married. When Black Bull heard the news he cursed them and his unpropitious gods, and swore to have revenge. A day or two later Ah-we-kas went to the river for water, and as she stooped down at the shore Black Bull sprung upon her, bore her to the ground, and lifted his knife to stab her in the side. But even as the blow was descending the knife dropped from his hand, and with a groan he fell quivering on her senseless form, an arrow buried in his back. And there he died. The girl, recovering from her faint, shrieked long and loud, and people came running to her aid. They drew the dead man away, and noticing the arrow sticking in his back, withdrew it. No one had seen its like before; the polished shaft was black and heavy, the tip was long and broad, and made of some white substance neither bone nor stone, but most resembling bone; the feathers, stiff and well rapped on were from some unknown bird, and had all the colors of the rainbow. The warriors looked long and curiously at it as 'twas passed from hand to hand, and then be thought them to search for the one who had owned and shot it. But Mik-sik-um, wisest of medicine men, stopped them. 'Search not, 'he cried, 'for 'twill be of no avail; the owner of this arrow is not visible to mortal eyes. This man lies dead, the victim of his own bad heart and passions. 'Tis a judgment of the gods. Let his women bury him at once and get him from our sight.

"And so," Sah-n'e-to concluded, "this river got its name." "And the arrow?" I asked. "Whence came it? Who shot it?"

"How stupid you are," she replied. "For her goodness and virtue Ah-we-kas was favored by the sun. In her time of need he aided her. He shot the arrow, of course. Mik-sik-um, the medicine man, knew that as soon as he saw it, for he was wise in the mysteries of his craft."

"Well, anyhow, Sah-n'e-to," I said, "tis a good story, and we will not question the truth of it. Put another stick in the stove for the night is chilly."

I lit a smoke and after a little continued: "But, say, Sah-n'e-to, don't you think the young Blackfoot might have shot that arrow? It was of strange material and make, but he might have obtained it from some far northern tribe, people whom the Piegans had never heard of."

"No."

"Why ?"

"Because."

I had no more to say, and smoked in silence. When a woman says "because," a man is up against it.

HILDIA NOTTINGHAM

RIVER MILE 77.4 RIGHT

One of the first white settlers in the Arrow Creek area was a woodhawker named Hildia Anderson Nottingham. Several years after he started his steamboat fuel supply business he formed a partnership with two other men. They would go up Arrow Creek when the water was high, cut down trees and float the logs to the Missouri. At the river the logs were cut into cord wood and piled ready for the steamboats. He claimed that the partners were always well paid for their labor when the wood was sold to the river steamers.

Shortly after the woodhawking partnership dissolved, Nottingham established a trading post near the mouth of Arrow Creek. He traded in beads, flour, bacon, tobacco, sugar, blankets and calico with the Indians for buffalo and deer hides and some beaver pelts. Nottingham made friends with many of the Indian parties who came to the post to trade.

At one time he had a young Indian boy, the son of a chief, to help with the chores. He was a venturesome lad and often got himself into difficulty. One day he was bringing the horses in to the post from a picket line. Evidently thinking that it would look more businesslike, he tied one of the halter ropes around his waist. On the way to the buildings, the horse became frightened and dragged the lad quite a distance before he could be stopped. Luckily the boy was not seriously injured, or his father might have taken a dim view of the white man's medicine. Another time the boy got too close to a wounded buffalo and was in great danger of being killed. Nottingham shot the animal and the Chief, having witnessed the incident, was very grateful to him for saving his son.

The trading business came to an end when the Indians were put on reservations. At the turn of the century, Arrow Creek changed its wild and romantic role to play host to homesteader Peter Tillman.

UPPER ROLF BOTTOMS

RIVER MILES 78.2 - 79.3 LEFT

Ferdinand Rolf settled here some time before the spring of 1905 when the township was surveyed. His name appears on the General Land Office map. He filed a homestead entry in June of 1907, almost a year after the survey was approved. He did not prove-up and in October of 1913 the homestead was relinquished. Only a tumbled down shack remains to tell us of his efforts.

Fredrick Rolf settled on the next bottom downriver. It is not known if the two were related, but with the proximity of the properties, in all likelihood they were.

GROS VENTRE INDIAN CAMP

RIVER MILE 78.6 LEFT

It was from about this vantage point, looking diagonally across the Missouri up Arrow Creek. that Karl Bodmer painted the junction of Arrow Creek and the Missouri in 1833, showing over tow hundred lodges of Gros Ventre Indians camped there. Prince Maximillian and Karl Bodmer had traveled by steamboat to Fort Union, at the confluence of the Yellowstone and Missouri. From Ft. Union they boarded a keelboat, the *Flora*, destined for Fort Mckenzie (river mile 14 left). Bodmer's painting captures the tension of the incident, as Indians swam to the keelboat, almost swamping it. The incident is herein described in an excerpt taken from Prince Maximillian's journal.

[Prince Maximilian - August 5th, 1833]

Being detained by a violent thunder-storm, it was one o'clock before we reached the place where the Missouri flows through a rather narrow gorge, from the remarkable sand-stone valley, called the Stone Walls; a white sand-stone hill appeared before us on the north bank, as the first specimen of that formation; and on the left was the mouth of Bighorn River , between considerable hills, on which numbers of Indians had collected. (Arrow Creek/Slaughter River - Maximilian had a set of Captain Clark's maps. The Captains first called the Judith River the Bighorn River. and in the process of duplication, some map makers showed two drainages rather than making the name change) In the front of the eminences the prairie declined gently towards the river where above 260 leather tents of the Indians were set up; the tent of the principal chief was in the fore-ground, and, near it, a high pole with the American flag. The whole prairie was covered with Indians, in various groups, and with numerous dogs; horses of every colour were grazing round, and horsemen galloping backwards and forwards, among whom was a celebrated chief, who made a good figure on his light bay horse. While this was passing, several Indians had been on board, many of whom swam across to us; among them, a tall man came on board in this manner, shook off the water, and went without ceremony into the cabin, but Mr. Mitchell (David Mitchell, founder of Fort McKenzie) drove him out, and gave him to understand that none but the chiefs could be admitted there; he then had the Indians told to go back to their camp where he would visit them.

While the camp was saluted at intervals with cannon shot, and the Indians answered with their guns, the keel-boat, which had hoisted its flag, was anchored on the north bank, opposite to the tents, a very necessary precaution to prevent our coming directly into contact with all the Indians at the same time. About forty Indian warriors, drawn up on the bank, having made a running fire, and our cannon again saluted, Mr. Mitchell, with the interpreter, Doucette, took the boat and rowed across. He alone had pistols, the others were unarmed. On the summit of the bank, all the Indians formed a long red line, and immediately below, on the water's edge, sat the chiefs, in a detached small body. After Mr. Mitchell had seated himself by them, and had some conversation with them, he invited them to accompany him on board, and brought us eight of these chiefs, who sat down in the cabin to smoke their pipes. Among them were several men of a good open character; but one was a very bad man, Mexkemauastan (the iron which moves), who Mr. Mitchell had turned out of doors the year before, at Fort McKenzie, on account of his bad conduct. We were now entirely in the power of these people, and had every reason to fear the vengeance of this man. Prompted, doubtless, by his own interests, he behaved, to our astonishment, in a most friendly manner; shook hands with us, and, like his comrades,

Karl Bodmer's rendition of the American Fur Company's keelboat 'Flora' being 'greeted' by Gros Ventre Indians from a large encampment on Arrow Creek. This rather tense situation occurred as Prince Maximilian and Karl Bodmer were traveling to Fort McKenzie as guests of the company. Maximilian recorded that more than "260 leather tents" comprised the camp. (Courtesy Joslyn Art Museum, Omaha, Nebraska, gift of the Enron Foundation.)

gratefully accepted the presents which were made him. He wore his hair in a thick knot on the forehead, and had a deceitful, fawning countenance. While we were engaged with these chiefs ,we saw a number of men and women, from all parts of the bank, swim through the river, or cross over to us in their round boats, made of buffalo skin, and our keel-boat was suddenly entered on every side and crowded with them. Tall, slender men covered the deck, thrust themselves into the apartments, and we were really overwhelmed with them. They all demanded brandy, powder and ball, and brought to exchange with us, skins, leather, and dried and fresh meat. The leather boats, laden with their articles for barter, were brought alongside the keel-boat, drawn by one swimmer, and pushed by another, and in this manner we were soon hemmed in, so that it was necessary to ask the chiefs to clear the vessel; they indeed, induced the greater part of the young men to leap into the water, though only to enter the boat soon after on the other side.

Our situation was everything but agreeable, for these same Indians had entirely demolished a fort, on the frontiers of Canada, two years before, killed a clerk, and eighteen other persons, besides murdering several other white people in those parts; they had, in addition to this, had a quarrel with Lewis and Clarke, and no confidence could we therefore place in them, though Mr. Mitchell affirmed that he always transacted business with them with pleasure, and had never had any proofs of the treachery imputed to them. If it was their intention to treat us in a hostile manner, there was no way for us to escape; and how easily might the most trifling dispute with these rude men lead to a breach, by which fifty whites, in the power of eight or nine hundred Indians, would have had no chance. They were therefore treated with much apparent confidence and familiarity, and everything went off very well. A favourable wind for using our sail was very welcome, in assisting us to escape from this perilous situation. Doucette had been sent on shore with some goods, and instructions to barter with the Indians, and thus, in some measure, to satisfy their desires. We on board saw our people on shore closely surrounded by a great mass of Indians; the noisy traffic was long continued, though Mr. Mitchell had repeatedly given orders for the return of the boat. We were obliged to wait a long time, and already began to be apprehensive for the safety of our dealers, when we at length saw the boat, overloaded with Indians, put off from the bank, on which orders were given to proceed immediately on our voyage. About fifty robust Indians joined our men in towing, and we were drawn along very rapidly; our keel-boat was so crammed with people, that it drew much water. In this singular company we began to pass through the most interesting part of the whole course of the Missouri, namely, the Stone Walls; but we could not breathe freely enough duly to appreciate the surrounding scenery, before we were quit of our troublesome visitors. The chiefs were repeatedly informed that the boat was ready to carry them on shore, and they had all received presents, with which, however, some of them were not satisfied; at length they were all sent off, with an intimation that they might go to Fort McKenzie, to their allies, the Blackfeet, where the goods would be landed, and the barter conducted as they desired. We lay to for the night, on the right bank, at the fore part of the Stone Walls, and a number of Indians, especially women, who were found concealed in the vessel, and turned out, kindled fires near us. Many articles were missing, and we had given much more than we received, yet we were truly glad at having come off as well as we did. A strong watch, with an officer, was set for the night.

LOWER ROLF BOTTOMS

River Miles 79.3 - 80.4 Left

Not much is known about Fredrick Rolf, but some of the features of the property indicate an interesting, possibly tragic story remains to be told. In this remote, seemingly inaccessible location he built one of the most sophisticated sandstone houses along the river. However, it appears that the roof may never have been finished, the house might not have been lived in. Rolf filed on this 179 acres of land on February 17,1909, only two days before the Enlarged Homestead Bill became law. Three log foundations suggest that Rolfs lived in a cabin while building the stone house. He successfully proved-up, receiving patent to the land in August 21, 1914.

Rolf's house featured a field stone facade on an interior wooden frame. The sandstone was ashlar (quarry or rough faced) and not coursed. The corner-stones were squared and rusticated (recessed along the edges to make the corner and the joints more conspicuous). The lintels over the doors and windows were three-stone jack arch (flat arch with a keystone), while the window sills were smooth, one-piece cut sandstone. The doors and windows had wooden framing. The interior walls were lathed and plastered. Near the south wall was an unusual triangular chimney that served two rooms. The west half of the house had a stone walled basement. The roof consisted of four gables joined about 8 feet from the south end. The house probably had four main floor rooms and two or three basement rooms. All in all, a unique structure that demonstrated expert craftsmanship in the use of native sandstone.

The Fredrick Rolf homestead building as it appeared before its collapse during the winter of 1980-81.

Why or when Rolf left is not known. Lacking a weather tight roof, the abandoned structure deteriorated bit by bit, until during the winter of 1980-81, snow and wind brought down the final remnants of the house.

SLUGGETT HOMESTEAD

RIVER MILES 81 - 82.5 LEFT

This bottom is the location of Lester Sluggett's first attempt at homesteading (refer to river miles 69.2 - 70.3 left). He came here in 1920, built a 12' x 24' house and stretched a mile of fence. He stayed here only a couple of weeks, because when it rained he found that he couldn't get out. As soon as the weather cleared, Sluggett got out - for good. All that remains is a deteriorated cottonwood log foundation.

NAT CRABTREE'S WOODYARD

RIVER MILE 83.7 RIGHT

Nat Crabtree was a 'woodhawk', one of a hardy breed who lived along the Missouri and earned a living by stocking firewood for sale to the passing steamboats, which consumed about twenty-five chords per day. These men worked hard, lived an isolated and humble existence, and were often plagued by hostile Indians, who were justifiably resentful of the hordes of whites that were coming into Montana in the 1860's.

From *Floating on the Missouri,* Schultz; refer to narrative at river mile 1.2 left for background. We join Schultz as he's searching for the grave of Nat Crabtree so he can re-mark it if necessary.

We landed at the mouth of the coulee and looked long and carefully for the wooden cross which had marked it, but could not find even a grass-grown mound. Time and the constant wash from the hills had obliterated all traces of it. So all trace of the last resting place of Nathaniel Crabtree, one of the bravest and most careless of men, is lost. It was here he met his fate. He and George Croff had long been partners in the woodyard business, in trapping, hunting and trading.

George told me, just before I left home for this trip: "In 1865, we had a woodyard at the Coal Banks. Winter and summer buffalo were always in sight of our cabin, but just for a change and a little sport we used to go out to the Bear Paw Mountains once in a while and kill a wagonload of elk, deer, sheep, antelope and bear, using the fat of the latter in lieu of lard. The Indians were always prowling around in those days in search of the white man's scalp and horses, and one never knew when a war party might jump him. So on these hunts, after supper was over, we used to go some distance from the fire and make our beds in a dark piece of woods or brush. On such occasions I would always ask Nat where he had placed his rifle, and nine times out of ten he would reply: "Oh, I don 't know; it's lying somewhere over there by the fire."

Well, I'd lecture him about his carelessness, but he always laughed and declared there was no danger, and I usually had to hunt the weapon up and lay it by his side. He was as good a friend and comrade as a man could wish for, - honest, brave, good natured, a tireless worker. But he was careless; your good-natured, easy-going men generally are careless.

In the fall of '67 we moved down to the mouth of the Judith and started to get out wood for the steamboats there, having cut and sold all there was in the vicinity of the Coal Banks. We built a good-sized cabin on the flat about two miles west of the creek's junction with the Missouri. Camp Cook, a temporary post of three or four companies of mounted infantry, was located on this stream, and some four miles from us, so we felt pretty secure from Indian raids. Still, they used to bother us some, and the soldiers, too. One night a guard saw what he took to be an Indian sneaking up to the tarpaulin-covered supplies he was watching, and called out "Halt!" a number of times. But the Indian never stopped, and when he got up as close as he wanted to, he leveled his old fuke and gave the soldier a mortal wound. Of course, the whole camp rushed out then, and what do you suppose the officers did? They ordered their men to light a lot of lanterns and search the timber and brush for the Indians! They were a pretty green outfit, both officers and men.

We had six men in our employ cutting pine up in the breaks and in the hills, but one of them was always on the lookout for any sneaking war party, while the rest worked. Nat and I hauled the wood to the river with three yokes of bulls (oxen). We had no horses, and we took turns going after the cattle in the morning. On the 5th of April, '68, I remember the date well, it was Nat's turn. I got up before daylight to prepare breakfast, and soon afterward he started out, leaving his rifle, as usual. I never went away from the cabin without mine.

Well, daylight came, and at sunup we had breakfast, but Nat did not return. The men shouldered their axes and rifles and were just starting to their work when we saw the soldiers' herd of horses, some four or five hundred head, running up the long, sloping hill on the west side of the valley of the Judith. And behind them, whooping, yelling and lashing, rode a lot of Indians, urging them on. If felt at once that something had happened to Nat, and we started out to look for him. After going half a mile out on the flat I saw the bulls and turned toward them, and when near the coulee they were feeding in I saw my partner rise up out of the sagebrush, stagger a few steps toward the cabin, and then fall. I hurried to where he had disappeared and found him lying face down in the brush, three arrows sticking in his back. He had fainted. I called the men, and sending one of them for the doctor at Camp Cook, had the rest help me get Nat to the cabin.

I pulled out two of the arrows, but the third one, which had struck him in the lower part of the back, and was pressing against the lower part of the abdomen, I dared not touch. In a little while Nat recovered from his faint, and after drinking a glass of whisky and water, seemed his old cheerful self again. He had found the bulls, he said, and was going around behind them to drive them in, when five Indians rose up out of the sagebrush only a few yards behind him and fired five arrows into his back. He got hold of the upper ones and pulled them out, and then looked around for a club or a rock with which to defend himself. But there was nothing of the kind in sight, and then the pain became so acute that he grew dizzy, reeled and fell. The Indians started off toward the hills, but after going a short distance one of them turned back, drawing his knife, evidently with the intention of taking his scalp. But Nat's hat had fallen off, exposing his partially bald head, and when the Indian saw the fringe of thin locks he turned and hurried to rejoin his companions.

The Steamboat 'Rosebud' with a full head of steam, traveling upriver through Deadman Rapids. The cable, extending from the front of the boat, is anchored to a 'deadman' on the shore, and the boat is pulling itself through the rapids by winching the cable with its steam driven capstan. Montana Historical Society photograph.

The doctor came after awhile and extracted the remaining arrow. "Poor fellow," he said, "I fear you're done for," and leaving a little medicine of some kind to ease the pain, he went away.

"Of course I'm done for," Nat told me. "I knew that as soon as I was shot. But cheer up, old boy, and don't take it so hard; it can't be helped, and we've just got to make the best of it. Yes, I know I ought to have taken my rifle; if I had they would never have molested me. Well, old pard, give me your hand and let me go to sleep; if I never wake, good-bye and good luck."

Those were the last words he ever spoke. He dozed away into a deep sleep, from that into a stupor, quietly breathed his last soon after midnight, and I lost the best friend I ever had. I felt so badly about it that I couldn't bear to stay there any longer, and leaving everything in charge of one of the men, took the first boat for Fort Benton."

DEADMAN RAPIDS

River Mile 84.5

Through the years this stretch of river was known by several names, as the following information suggests.

Lewis and Clark deemed this area "Ash Rapids" probably for the few ash trees in the area at the time of their expedition. They said of these trees they were "... the first we have seen for a great distance..." These trees eventually fell to the ax of an Englishman named Courtney who ran a woodyard at the head of the rapids.

In later years the rapids took on a more sinister name. In 1860 these rapids were commonly called "Drowned Men Rapid," while in 1876 they were referred to as "Drowned Man's Rapids".

The origin of the name is not certain, however a popular account for the name says it honors the men of Alexander Harvey's crew who traveled from the Judith River to Fort McKenzie in 1837, to warn Alexander Culbertson that smallpox had broken out on the American Fur Company boat bringing up trading goods. The Blackfeet refused to believe the men and demanded the goods he brought upriver. On their return to Harvey at the Judith, one canoe capsized in the rapids and all four men aboard were lost. Their heroic mission was in vain, for within a short time smallpox ravaged the Blackfeet camps.

In Neihardt's *The River and I* (1910), this area was referred to as Dead Man's Rapids, a very turbulent stretch of water."

Regardless of whether the tragedy was plural or singular, it seems likely the name harkens to some water-accident of the days before the steamboat. Very likely, the unfortunates were voyageurs of low estate - unworthy of specific remembrance in a time when life was held so cheaply.

The strong current here was troublesome for steamboats, and they often had to resort to warping to get above the rapids.

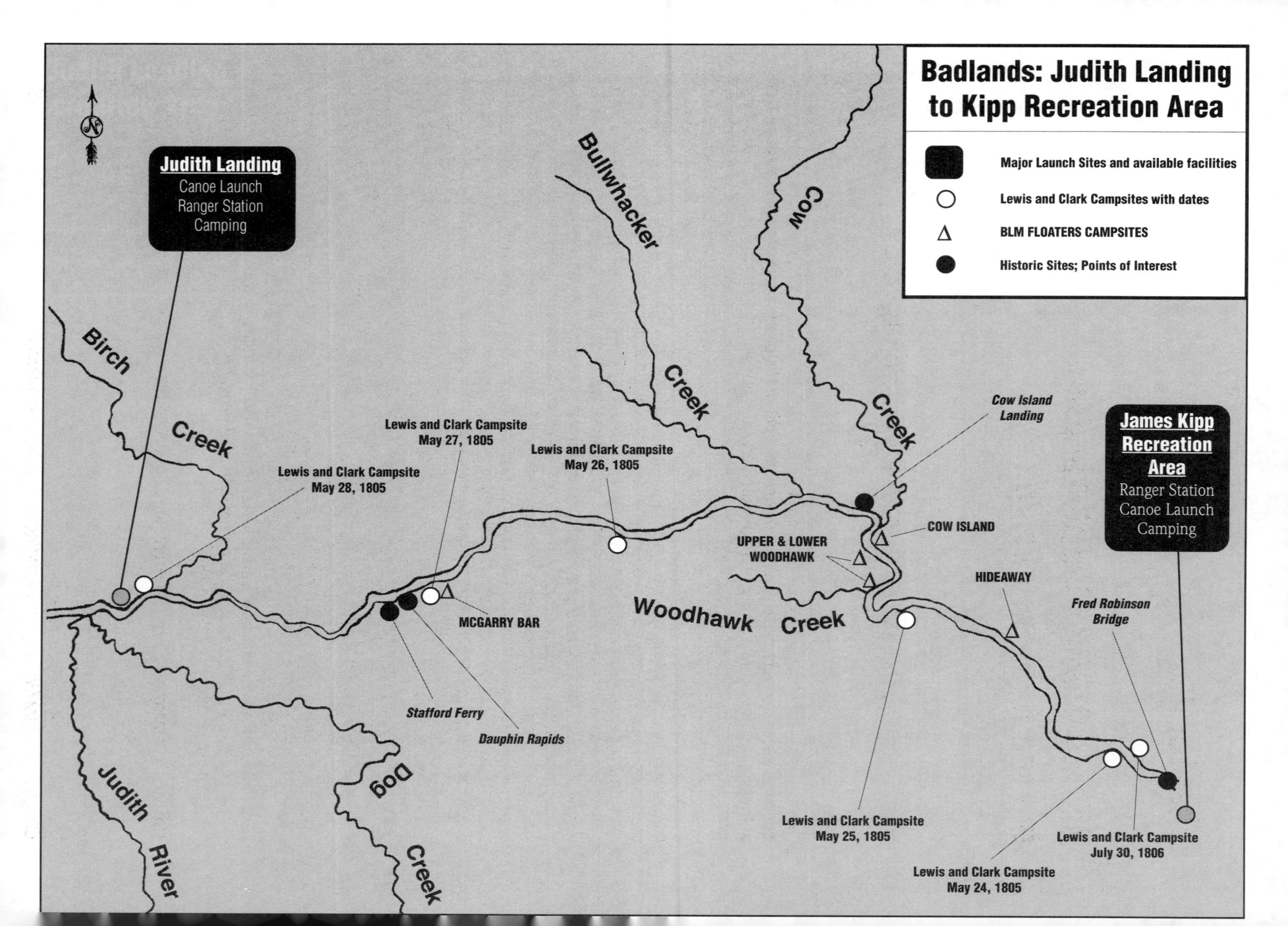

Badlands: Judith Landing to Kipp Recreation Area
Major Launch Sites and available facilities
Lewis and Clark Campsites with dates
BLM FLOATERS CAMPSITES
Historic Sites; Points of Interest
Judith Landing
Canoe Launch
Ranger Station
Camping
Birch Creek
Bullwhacker Creek
Cow Creek
Lewis and Clark Campsite May 28, 1805
Lewis and Clark Campsite May 27, 1805
Lewis and Clark Campsite May 26, 1805
Cow Island Landing
James Kipp Recreation Area
Ranger Station
Canoe Launch
Camping
COW ISLAND
UPPER & LOWER WOODHAWK
HIDEAWAY
MCGARRY BAR
Woodhawk Creek
Fred Robinson Bridge
Stafford Ferry
Dauphin Rapids
Judith River
Dog Creek
Lewis and Clark Campsite May 25, 1805
Lewis and Clark Campsite July 30, 1806
Lewis and Clark Campsite May 24, 1805

Chapter 4

History Digest: Judith Landing to Fred Robinson Bridge

JUDITH LANDING HISTORIC DISTRICT

River Miles 84.5 - 92.8

On December 6, 1975 the river from above Deadman Rapids to below Holmes Council Islands and lands on either side were placed on the National Register of Historic Places as a Historic District. In addressing the significance of the Judith Landing area the nomination stated, "The Judith Landing Historic District is one of the few areas that encompass all the threads of the major themes of man's history on the plains of Montana - the prehistoric and historic aboriginal cultures, whiteman's exploration, the fur trade, the steamboat era on the river highways, the collision of white expansion with the Indian's last stronghold and the resultant military occupation, and finally, the establishment of permanent white settlements, the range-cattle industry and farming."

Among the features identified within the Historic District are:

- Indian trails, lookouts, occupation sites and burial grounds
- Lewis & Clark Expedition campsite of May 28, 1805, and related landmarks
- Deadman Rapids, 1837(?) water accident site
- Ship Creek, fur trade era location for building barges (rafts, mackinaws, etc.)
- Fort (Francois A.) Chardon, 1844-1845 trading post
- Father Pierre Jean DeSmet Flathead-Blackfeet 1846 negotiation site
- Issac Stevens 1855 Treaty site
- Stumps, remnants of woodhawking activity
- Camp Cooke and Military Reservation (first military post in Montana) 1866-1870
- Clagett Hill Road, military and freight road of the late 1860's
- Fort Clagett, 1867 commissary for Camp Cooke that evolved into a trading post and eventually into the base for the PN (Powers-Norris) operation
- PN cable ferry, 1880-1908
- Mat Duncan's grave, a "dude" killed by Indians in 1881
- Various structures associated with the PN operation, 1882-forward
- Stage pasture for replacement horses for the Judith Landing Stage
- Todd/Baker homesteads and irrigation development of around the 1890's
- Lohse cable ferry, 1923-1982.

The details of many of the above features are discussed in the entries which follow.

FORT CLAGETT

RIVER MILE 86.3 RIGHT

Fort Clagett began as a commissary at Camp Cooke, a U.S. Military post (see River Mile 86.8 R), in either 1867 or 1868 with Thomas J. Bogy as the chief trader. The commissary was a branch of the Fort Benton-based T.C. Power & Bros. operations that supplied merchandise, delivered hay to the Camp, kept troops and animals enroute between Camp Cooke and Fort Shaw (near Great Falls), and traded in hides and robes.

The military post was abandoned on March 31, 1870, but continued correspondence and accounts with "Camp Cooke" well into 1872 indicate that T.C. Powers & Bros. maintained an establishment in that location. The last entry in the company journals concerning the enterprise at Camp Cooke is dated April 30, 1872. Thereafter, the Power interests at the Judith River were referred to as Fort Clagett.

It is probable that T.C. Power, a Republican, changed the name of the trading post from Camp Cooke to Fort Clagett in order to honor William Clagett who, in 1872, was running for the office of Territorial Delegate to the U.S. Congress. Clagett lost the election, but Fort Clagett kept its name.

About the time of the name change, Bogy was replaced as Power's trader at Fort Clagett by James A. Wells. Wells stayed with the operation for nearly a decade.

There is quite a debate today about whether Fort Clagett occupied the abandoned buildings of old Camp Cooke. One line of thought holds that Fort Clagett did occupy these buildings, another holds that the Camp Cooke buildings were dismantled and reassembled slightly to the northwest of the original site and used as Fort Clagett and still another line of thought holds that Fort Clagett simply stayed where it was while Camp Cooke's buildings were demolished and sold as fuel.

The General Land Office map of 1884 shows Fort Clagett one to two miles northwest of Camp Cooke, and field investigations confirm the location.

Lt. R.E. Thompson, on a reconnaissance to Judith Basin, wrote in his diary on September 14, 1875: "... visited Fort Claggett, a small Indian trading post on the Missouri, a short distance above the Judith. It consists of two log buildings facing each other; their ends joined by a stockade with a small flanking arrangement at the alternate angles ..."

Paleontologist Edward Drinker Cope visited Fort Clagett in the summer of 1876 and noted in a letter written to his wife on August 27, '... I hope to cross the Missouri River to the trading post called Claggett which is where old camp or Fort Cooke used to be ..."

Correspondence between Wells and Power in 1875 and 1876 shows that Wells was trading with the Mountain Crows for otter skins. Also in 1876 Wells was instructed not to offer for sale or trade any arms or ammunition to Indians, a prelude to the Nez Perce Indian scare one year later.

In 1877, the Nez Perces, rather than remain confined on a reservation, trekked from Northern Idaho across Montana in an attempt to reach Canada. As the fleeing tribe drew near the Missouri River, Wells notified Power & Bros. in Fort Benton that he feared the Indians would cross the river at or near Fort Clagett.

Upon receipt of Well's news in Fort Benton, Major Ilges dispatched Lt. Harden and sixteen enlisted men of Company F, 7th. Infantry, and a mountain howitzer to Fort Clagett by mackinaw, while Ilges and twenty volunteers set off overland to augment the Fort's defenses. Two days after their arrival, it was learned that the Nez Perces were headed for Cow Island and the Ilges command promptly headed downriver in an attempt to intercept them.

Correspondence between Wells and Power from 1878 to 1880 is primarily concerned with business matters. It is evident that they were beginning to run cattle for there are references to cattle arriving and Wells was urged to build a corral for them. An inventory for 1878 shows that the trading post was well stocked with a variety of items, ranging from shawls and drawers to bridles, cornmeal and brass nails.

Competition for the Indian trade must have been fierce, for a letter to Wells from Power in 1880 urges him to: "... fix up an Indian house and have it comfortable...this must be done to assure trade...you must remember that you are not the only trader in the field. Kipp and others above you are trying to draw the trade to them ..."

For the next few years, it appears there was some indecision as to what to call Wells' trading post; letters are addressed to Fort Clagett and Clagett City as well as to Judith Landing and Judith River. The implication is that at some time between 1876 and 1881 Wells had moved his post from the old Camp Cooke location to a new spot on the east (downriver) bank of the Judith River, perhaps to take advantage of proximity to a ford across the Missouri River located there.

In any event, by 1882 construction of a stone warehouse began below the mouth of the Judith and the old Fort Clagett near Camp Cooke had been abandoned, Henry B. Davis, a surveyor, wrote its epitaph in 1884: "Old Fort Clagett ... one cabin standing."

CAMP COOKE

River Mile 86.8 Right

Following the Civil War, the operations of the U.S. Army focused on the western frontier. As gold was discovered in the Rocky Mountains and as public lands were opened to homesteaders in the 1860's, immigrants moved west in ever-increasing numbers, intruding more and more on Indian territory.

Reacting to the white invasion of their lands, Indians retaliated by mounting small-scale, scattered, guerrilla-type attacks along the immigrant trails. White settlers turned to the army for protection. Regular army units were assigned to guard large, well-organized emigrant parties and forts were established along major overland routes and along the Missouri River. Camp Cooke was the north westernmost outpost of a sequence of military forts along the major trade and travel artery into the northern Rockies.

Exactly why Camp Cooke was located at this junction of the Judith and Missouri Rivers remains unclear. Logic dictated its placement at Fort Benton (the burgeoning community at the head of navigation) or at Cow Island or the mouth of the Musselshell (often-used points for the transfer of steamer freight and passengers to overland transportation when the upper river was too low to navigate).

Inspector-General D.B. Sackett was sent to Montana Territory to select a site for the military outpost. He decided against Fort Benton, which was of a size to be able to defend itself and which lacked sufficient materials for the construction of a post and the maintenance of its livestock. Instead, he recommended a site at the mouth of the Musselshell. The War Department, however, selected a site at the Judith-Missouri junction.

Camp Cooke, the first military outpost in Montana, was named in honor of Brig. Gen. Phillip St. George Cooke, then in command of the Department of the Platte. It was established on July 11, 1866. Its location was not entirely without justification as it was three miles upstream to Deadman Rapids and fifteen miles downstream to Dauphin Rapids; both treacherous waters which gave steamboat captains considerable difficulty and were likely points of Indian attack.

The post was originally garrisoned by Companies B, D, E and F of the 13th. Infantry under the command of Major William Clinton. In 1867 they were reinforced by a group of one-hundred soldiers, bringing strength at Camp Cooke to approximately four-hundred men.

The 1867 reinforcements, under Lt. Horrigan, arrived on the steamer *Octavia.* That same summer the *Luella* brought Mrs. Sarah Elizabeth Canfield to Camp Cooke.

An officer's wife, Sarah Canfield found the post better than some, for she "had the companionship of four other officers' wives." She wrote the following description: "The fort is built in design like all I have seen with bastions Stockade moat etc. but there is considerable timber on the river bottoms and So there is a sawmill here and the rows of houses were framed of wood and filled in with 'adobe' bricks ... The roofs of these houses are made of poles laid at intervals coming to a peak in the centre then brush laid over the poles and a foot or more of earth spread over all - as it seldom rains in this country this makes a very good dwelling. The walls of the room were whitewashed and the floors of rough board. When carpeted they make nice cozy homes."

However substantial the Camp might have appeared, defects in the cottonwood logs used in its construction soon appeared as Mrs. Canfield discovered: "We had a hard rain today. Some of our roofs leaked a little. Mrs. Nugent found her three months baby lying in its crib with muddy water dripping in its face ..."

Once the fort was constructed, the men had little to do as there were no other white settlements near the Judith. According to Mrs. Canfield there were hardly any Indians either: "We have only seen a few Indians, who were friendly and came in to trade ...." The situation changed over the next 3 years, however, for the Surgeon's report documents the arrival and departure of many Indian groups. The following is a sample for February 1869: "Feb. 14, twenty Crow arrived; Feb. 16, thirty-one Crow arrived and twenty-five left post; and Feb. 18, one hundred-four lodges of Crow Indians arrived and encamped on the east bank of the Judith."

Although Camp Cooke is often portrayed as existing in desolate isolation, this picture is not quite true. On March 31st, 1868, the camp clerk recorded eighteen "civilians, citizens, attaches, Camp followers, traders and others" living in the vicinity of the military post. Except for the high water months of May, June and July, steamboat traffic on the river was virtually nil. Throughout 1866 and 1867 indications are that the hastily-constructed fort began to deteriorate rapidly, along with the soldiers' morale. The post experienced an invasion of rats and numerous desertions by soldiers for the gold fields.

Camp Cooke's only "major" engagement with the Indians occurred in 1868. In April a small party of Sioux attacked the camp's horse herd, capturing thirty-four horses and mules and fatally wounding Nat Crabtree, a woodhawker living near the camp (see river mile 83.7 right). The following month a war party of Sioux launched an assault against the fort itself. Camp Cooke was undermanned at the time since one hundred troops had been dispatched to the mouth of the Musselshell. About twenty-five hundred Indians lay siege to the fort between 1 p.m. and 7 p.m. on May 21st. The report of Major Clinton declared that: "It is almost impossible to tell their numbers as they were scattered all over the hills surrounding the fort. It was the boldest attack I ever saw made by Indians. I went out with a party of six men but was driven in. I am sorry to report that Lieut. Aumian was wounded in the foot by the accidental discharge of a carbine in his own hands during the attack. Three rounds were fired from the Cannons."

By 1869 moves were afoot to abandon Camp Cooke. Other forts in more favorable locations - notably Fort Shaw between Helena and Fort Benton - had been constructed and much of the Cooke garrison was transferred there, leaving only three officers and twenty-seven enlisted men at Camp Cooke. The public had begun to ridicule Camp Cooke's rather inactive history, the attack of 1868 notwithstanding. Several articles appeared in the Helena Herald, of which the following is an example: "Looking to the front ... the eye is greeted with the view of a long range of low bluffs; to the rear is visible a long range of high bluffs; to the right ... medium size bluffs ... to the left ... assorted bluffs. But the largest 'bluff' of all was by the Government when it located this post in such an out of the way place, and tried to make sensible people believe that it was for the protection of the people of Montana." About the rats: "Great feature is rats. They have taken possession of everything and every place of importance, the whole site undermined by them, resembles a great honeycomb. Quarters are full of rats, all ages, kinds, sizes and shapes. Becoming very insolent and overbearing toward whites. Foutreen hundred killed in a four day engagement. The government feeds them on oats. corn, flour and bacon." Also: "The old and sensible rats, who have sown their wild oats, make their headquarters in the warehouses, while the more youthful ... frequent the store, where they hold high carnival ... hurdy gurdies, prized fights, etc ..."

In July of 1869. Major General W.S. Hancock and his chiefs of staff arrived at Camp Cooke on the steamer *Ackley* to conduct an inspection. They were not impressed, as the report by Lt. Col. Samuel D. Holabird indicates: "This unfortunate post ... is entirely overrun with rats, and may be said to be in process of demolition by them. The storehouses are in ruins ... Everything eatable in the storehouses is gnawed and destroyed ... The rats seem conscious of having the upper hand at Camp Cooke, and their audacity is something that must be seen to be believed. Little idea can be formed of what it costs the Government yearly to occupy this post and feed these rats: it would build a new post every two years ... General neglect and indifference characterize this post. The small garrison merely holds on in spite of the rats. The Indians have moved away and left it alone."

After this assessment of Camp Cooke's effectiveness, it is not surprising that the fort was abandoned by the Army on March 31, 1870.

BLACKFEET-FLATHEAD COUNCIL OF 1846

RIVER MILE 87.6 LEFT (?)

The buffalo of the eastern Montana plains were a staple for not only the plains Indians, but for many tribes living in the mountains to the west, such as the Flatheads, who would make annual buffalo hunting trips to the Missouri River Basin. The majority of the Blackfeet regarded this region as their own preserve and frequently attacked the mountain tribes, whom they regarded as intruders. Missionaries who worked among Monatana Indians made efforts at establishing inter-tribal peace. Jesuit Fathers DeSmet and Point arranged for a council at the mouth of the Judith in 1846.

Fathers DeSmet and Point left the Flathead mission of St. Mary's on August 16, 1846, and traveled to Fort Lewis, at the site of present day Fort Benton. There they met with many of the Blackfeet and Father Point would end up staying the fall and winter, evangelizing the Blackfeet as well as the personnel of the post.

The missionaries accompanied the Blackfeet on their autumn hunt. In the company of the Small Robe, an isolated band of Piegan Blackfeet, they were camped near the Judith on the morning of September 14th when they were joined by the "populous tribe of the Piegans." There were also a number of Gros Ventres and Bloods. No sooner had the greetings been completed and the Blackfeet camp settled down then the Flatheads arrived. Father Point reports: "Never had these gallant warriors of the great wilderness appeared more noble than on that day. While the body of the army, ranged in several frontal lines, advanced with a measured gait, singing their old chants, one of the chiefs, who was numbered among the bravest, circled about at the head in a truly knightly fashion. They were accompanied by the Pend d'Oreilles and the Nez Perces ... Soon the frank manner of the Flatheads communicated itself from person to person and all fraternized as if they had never been enemies." The Nez Perces, however, were described by Father Point as "troublesome" and "quarrelsome."

Father DeSmet wrote in his diary: "The wonderful success of the Flat-Heads in the different wars they have been compelled to wage has confirmed their enemies in the persuasion entertained for some years that the medicine of the Black-gowns (Blackrobes) is stronger than their own ... Tomorrow will be the feast of the Exaltation of the Cross. The Chief, enquires, if it would please us to see the Black-Feet manifest their joy in their own way ... the answer was, 'Do the best you can to show your friends that you are pleased."

The meeting consisted of pipe smoking among the Blackfeet of Chief Big Lake (or Great Lake - grand chief of the Piegan), the Flatheads of Chief Victor, and the missionaries, a dance, and other celebrations. This peaceful intercourse between the previously hostile Blackfeet nation and the western Flatheads is considered to be the first "peace negotiation" arranged by a white man in the Montana region. An additional plus for the new allies was that they could now present a united front against the Crow.

Of the location of this historic gathering, DeSmet says only: "... we encamp for the night in a beautiful cotton grove on the margin of the Judith River." There is some support for the notion that it was on the north side of the Missouri nearly opposite the mouth of the Judith.

A major factor in the success of the treaty council was the medicine of the Blackrobes. As Father DeSmet noted in his diary, the Blackfeet were impressed by the success of the Flathead, who had been Christianized, in different wars. One such demonstration occurred during a summer buffalo hunt, when a band of Flatheads, from west of the continental divide, was joined by a friendly band of un-Christianized Piegans, called the Small Robes, to help in the hunt. Set upon by a larger band of Crows, the combined Flatheads and Small Robes tribes managed to repulse the attackers. Father Nicolas Point, who along with Father Pierre Jean DeSmet were with the hunt, described the event this way: "Indian fights are very similar to a 'jeu de barres', and for this reason last a long time without spilling much blood. Thus, instead of saying 'we shall fight,' they say, 'We shall have sport.' In this fight, which lasted nine hours, there were only ten killed and fourteen wounded, all on the side of the Crows, with the single exception of a Nez Perce. Why had this one man been killed? "Having witnessed the Flathead praying before battle, the people of the Small Robe reasoned that it was "because he had not made the sign of the cross before going into battle." The Little Robe were so impressed that seventy-six of them accepted Christianity before they left the site of the battle.

JUDITH LANDING

River Mile 88 Right

Sometime between 1876 and 1881, Fort Clagett (see River Mile 86.3 L) was moved east to the downriver side of the Judith. By the end of 1882, James A. Wells, the chief trader, was ready to move into a new large stone store. The 30' x 100' structure (x 12' high) would become the center of a small but active community. At different times there was even a post office in the settlement, with Wells bidding successfully for the mail delivery job for the period of April to November 1880, and October 1882 to June 1883.

Late in 1883, Wells' health failed and he was bought out by thirty-five year old Major Gilman R. "Bill" Norris. Norris arrived in November, and soon added a house, stable and various other outbuildings to the site. Norris successfully bid for the mail handling job in June of 1884, and retained the Judith to Maiden (a gold mining camp near Lewistown) mail route through 1919.

Shortly after Norris became manager of the T.C. Power & Bros. interests at the Judith, the operation really began to grow. Eventually they would incorporate with Norris as a partner, and the operation would become known as the Judith Mercantile and Cattle Company. The Powers-Norris brand (P-Lazy N) would become synonymous with the Judith Landing area.

A major concern of the Power-Norris interests became freighting and shipping the wool sheared by the area ranchers. Norris met with the Wool Growers Association on March 2, 1884, and as an enticement, he agreed to erect sheep sheds capable of handling 20,000 sheep. In correspondence with Power, he estimated that this would insure the Block-P steamboats 150,000 pounds of wool freight each year. In addition, they received a penny a head for all sheep sheared.

That same year Norris also built a 26' x 60' warehouse. It was located between the stone store and the river and has since fallen victim to a southwardly meandering Missouri.

In 1885, Norris filed a homestead entry on the 164 acres encompassing the Judith Landing operations. During this year the developments included a saloon, hotel, blacksmith shop, and a 30' x 50' stable. The records also show that Norris was grazing livestock (with or without the Indian's permission) north of the river on Blackfeet Indian Reservation land.

During the spring of 1887, massive floods raised havoc at Judith Landing. Freight destined for Lewistown and Maiden was stacked on scaffolds two and a half feet above the warehouse floor, and it still lay in two feet of water. Norris reported to Power: "Besides goods in warehouse, we had 20 sax wool, 10000# sheep pelts and lot of Hides on the bank. They were under water for 4 days and now smell so that it is hard to get near to handle them ..."

Norris' wool shipping business was severely damaged by the flood. A ferry helped somewhat by making the operation more accessible to growers on the north side of the river. Then the arrival of the railroad, a more reliable form of freight transportation than the steamboats, at Big Sandy pretty much finished the wool operation.

As early as 1884, Norris was encouraging Power to install a ferry at Judith Landing. He even had the support of General Forsythe from Fort Maginnis (on the north side of the Judith Mountains). In 1887 the ferry became a reality through the efforts of C.W. Rochester. On August 2nd, the steamer *Helena* brought the cable, and on the 16th Norris informed Power that, "...Rochester brothers have the Ferry in. Good boat, 70 feet long, can cross largest teams or any kind of stock ..." The ferry saw immediate service with Norris noting on the 24th of August that over 5,000 head of sheep were going to cross the river. The following May Norris complained to T.C. Power, "We should have had it (the ferry)."

An interesting side note to the ferry business was that each time a steamboat passed, the ferry cable had to be dropped. After the *F. Y. Batchelor* passed on June 11, 1890 (with the last commercial cargo to Fort Benton), the windlass broke while raising the ferry cable and one man was killed.

On May 1, 1888, seventeen million acres of the Blackfeet Indian Reservation north of the river was opened for settlement. Stockmen flocked to this prime rangeland north of the river. Most of their original range was depleted from overgrazing and the drought of 1886. Many stockmen were also looking for a new start after the disastrous winter of 1886-87. More than 2,400 head of livestock crossed the ferry that year.

In 1888 a new blacksmith shop was built at Judith Landing.

In 1889 Norris received a Cash Entry Patent to the land he filed on in 1885. He also received a Desert Land Entry Patent for an additional 400 acres. Developments at Judith Landing now included a school which was a strong attraction for additional settlers.

In 1890 Norris got control of the ferry. On February 14th he wrote to Power in Fort Benton: "We have been compelled to buy the Rochester Ferry boat ... got it for nothing, $400 ... Mr. Rochester is leaving the country and had to dispose of his boat here - It is absolutely necessary that we control this boat on account of biz on the north side of the river. If we had not bought the Boat it would have been taken by Broadwater & Co. which would have made it bad for us here ... The Boat is high and dry & perfectly Safe from Ice. The receipts of the Boat last season was over $1200..."

On July 2, 1980, the River Press in Fort Benton reported: "We learn that Major G.R. Norris, of Judith, has the ferry across the Missouri ... in first class condition for handling livestock. Corrals and chutes have been built for the convenience of drives, on both banks of the river, and the ferry is capable of handling two thousand head of range cattle per day, without danger of loss. Judith Landing Ferry, situated at the town of Judith, during the four closing days of last week transported fourteen thousand head of sheep and four thousand head of cattle from the south to the north side of the Missouri. These drives are on the way to ranges around the foot of the Bear Paw and Little Rocky Mountains and in Milk River valley, which sections are rapidly filling up from older ranges in Fergus and Yellowstone and other counties in the state."

The Judith Landing Ferry crossed the Missouri at river mile 87.4. In 1897, a cabin and pasture were developed on the north bank to supply remounts for the Maiden-Judith-Big Sandy stage.

In 1901 Norris was visited by James Willard Schultz during his river float (see river mile 1.2 left for background). Schultz recorded the visit:

... came to the mouth of the Judith, where our friend, Wm. Norris, has a large ranch, ferry and general store. We had not met since the buffalo days, and of course began to talk of old times at once. Norris waters several hundred acres of land back from the river with a ditch from the Judith, and some immense stacks of alfalfa showed what irrigation will do in this dry region. Beside hay, he has succeeded every year in raising field corn, tomatoes, tobacco, melons and sweet potatoes, to say nothing of the commoner vegetables. Looking over the place and talking of other days, the time passed all too quickly, and 'twas sundown before we knew it; so leaving the Good Shield tied to the ferryboat, we camped where we were, and were well cared for.

One measure of Norris' success at Judith Landing might be the elegant two-story, fifteen-room house built for him by William Lutge in 1904. Still usable, it was Norris' third house here.

The devastating flood of 1908 took its toll at Judith Landing. Among the losses was the ferry. Local tradition maintains that was the end of the Judith Landing Ferry service until 1923. However the General Land Office survey crews in the area in 1912-13 documented a ferry and landings owned and operated by the Judith Mercantile and Cattle Co.

After the 1908 flood, and in response to the lack of ferry service, Hartwig Lohse, a German who settled along the river in the 1890's, is credited with building a rough bridge of willows across the river at PN Island. He provided guide service across this structure, which is supposed to have been an exciting experience.

In 1923 Hartwig Lohse installed a new cable ferry that landed on the north bank at the location of today's boat ramp. The log cabin on the west side of the approach road was the ferry operator's cabin.

Judith Landing had its share of "wild west" incidents. On the south side of the river, in the shadow of Clagett Hill, lies Mat Duncan. He was killed by Indians on April 2nd, 1881, and was buried where he fell. Duncan was a twenty-one year old boy from New York City who was working at the site of Fort Clagett. A band of renegade Indians were up on the bluffs, daring the white settlers, and this young city boy - against the advice of his elders - approached them and was shot and killed.

Another story involves Bill Norris. Rustlers ran off one night with a bunch of the ranch's horses. Norris and some other men managed to catch the villains and shackled them to a post in Norris' cabin. The rustlers got loose and, taking their revenge, firmly chained Norris and his men to the same post. They took the horses again and disappeared.

Another time, a stage driver absconded with $400.

One of the more famous people to visit the Judith Landing area was the preeminent paleontologist Edward Drinker Cope. F.V. Hayden, a geologist, had visited the general area in 1854-55 and 1859-60. He had identified some dinosaur bones near the Judith Landing. Cope came in 1876 specifically to search for additional fossils. In the Judith area, Cope found the remains and fossils of many reptiles and fishes, including Laelaps, Hadrosaurus, and Elasmosaurus platyurus.

Today's bridge was started in 1980, and after more than two years of battling ice jams and floods, it was opened for service the fall of 1982.

FORT CHARDON

River Mile 88.6 Left

Fort Francois A. Chardon (Fort F.A.C.) was the third in a series of fur trade posts established by the American Fur Company along the Upper Missouri. The first was Fort Piegan (see River Mile 22 L), established by James Kipp in 1831. The second was Fort McKenzie (see River Mile 14 L), established by David Mitchell in 1832. Alexander Culbertson replaced Mitchell as factor at McKenzie in 1833, and retained the position of chief trader until 1842. Over the years, McKenzie enjoyed a very profitable trade. Then came the new factor, a hotheaded Frenchman by the name of Francois A. Chardon.

Chardon arrived at Fort McKenzie from Fort Union on June 22,1843, heading a complement of thirty men. Unfortunately, Chardon was a heavy drinker and was frequently influenced by his deputy, the volatile Alexander Harvey (refer to Fort Campbell - river mile 0.6 left). Affairs at the post went well until January 1844, when a Blackfeet war party sought admittance to the post. They were refused for reasons now forgotten and, in retaliation, killed livestock as they departed. Harvey, Chardon, and others pursued them with a well armed party. One member of the party, Tom Reese, Chardon's Negro slave, was killed and scalped, enraging Chardon and Harvey.

On February 19, 1844, Harvey and Chardon found an opportunity to even the score with the Blackfeet when a small band consisting of men, women and children arrived at Fort McKenzie with robes for trade. As they clustered about the main gate, Harvey fired a small cannon loaded with half-ounce lead balls into the group. Six individuals were killed outright, others were wounded and soon killed. Two children were captured and the remainder escaped. Other versions of this slaughter were recorded at a later date; some put the number of the slain Blackfeet at thirty.

This ill-advised massacre had a disastrous effect on relations between whites and the Blackfeet. Even at the time, many fur trade employees deplored the action of Harvey and Chardon. As a result of this skirmish, the site of Fort McKenzie became untenable and was soon abandoned.

This abandonment may have also been influenced by a quarrel between Harvey and Chardon. Harvey left the fort, traveled to St. Louis, and filed charges with the Superintendent of Indian Affairs that Chardon had sold liquor from May 1,1843 to March 31,1844.

Soon after the massacre and before their split, Chardon and Harvey sent a party to establish a fort on the north bank of the Missouri, opposite the mouth of the Judith River. The fort, named Fort Francois A. Chardon (Fort F.A.C.), was built in great haste and secrecy. There is evidence that this new post was in operation by April 5, 1844. Fort McKenzie was later burned by either the traders or Indians and to this day the site is known as Brule' (burned) Bottom.

The Blackfeet were enraged at construction of the new post and harassed the people living there, killing horses, cattle and perhaps its employees. In addition, the fort was situated directly on a main war trail between the Blackfeet and Crow nations and thus was an unsafe area for trading parties. Few robes and furs were traded at this site and there are indications that the employees spent much of their time in idleness and semi-starvation.

The drop in Blackfeet trade was strongly felt by the American Fur Company, which was at the center of a public controversy over an attempt to reenter the whiskey trade. In 1845, Alexander Culbertson was summoned from Fort Laramie to re-establish trading relations with the Blackfeet. From his service at Fort McKenzie and his marriage to a Blackfeet woman, Natawista Iksana, daughter of a Blood Chief, he was trusted by the tribes.

Because of its poor location, Culbertson decided to abandon Fort F.A.C. Chardon and the other employees were sent downriver to other posts. Culbertson gathered up the goods and supplies from Fort F.A.C. and used them to establish a new post, Fort Lewis, on the south shore of the river just above modern Fort Benton. Construction began about September 1, 1845 and was completed by the end of the year. He also took pains to make peace with the Blackfeet and to induce them to trade at his new post.

In May 1846, Culbertson went downriver to Fort Union with the robes and furs from Fort Lewis. While passing Fort Francois A. Chardon, now vacant, Culbertson ordered it burned to demonstrate to the Indians his contempt for the Fort McKenzie massacre.

The exact location of Fort F.A.C. has been debated over the years, with a lot of speculation but little proof. Then, during the construction of the bridge in 1980, earth moving equipment working on the periphery of the highway right-of-way nicked the corner of a site which turned out to be the elusive Fort Chardon.

EARLY IRRIGATION

River Mile 88.6 Left

From *Floating on the Missouri,* Schultz; refer to narrative at river mile 1.2 left for background.

After an early breakfast we boarded the Good Shield and resumed our voyage. A mile below Norris' place we passed a ranch on the opposite side of the river, which depended upon a wheel for irrigation. It was an immense affair of wood and steel rods, sixty feet in diameter, and revolving by the force of the current against its broad blades. Large, deep troughs, or buckets, took up the water and poured it into a long flume extending to the irrigation land. It kept up a constant stream of more than one hundred inches, and that quantity will water a very large acreage.

The land to the north once had an elaborate system of irrigation dikes. There is some confusion as to who built them. They are on land settled on by Joseph Baker prior to the 1912-13 General Land Office surveys, and the dikes were there at that time. An old buffalo hunter by the name of Tom Todd was also in the area at the time and he eventually turned his land over to Baker. There is reason to believe that Todd was in Baker's employ. In any event, by the time of the survey, Baker was using a Fairbanks-Morse pump, probably fired by a coal/steam generator, to move water into a redwood or cedar flume. Schultz is the only one to ever mention the large water wheel. It probably fell victim to ice or to the 1908 flood.

Baker didn't file for the land until the 1920's. His wife, Sara, filed for Desert Land Entry on October 8, 1920, and Joseph filed for additional acreage on February 18, 1921.

STEVENS TREATY COUNCIL OF 1855

River Mile 88.7 Left

The Judith Landing area was the site of a treaty council between Isaac Stevens, Governor of Washington Territory, and representatives of most of the major Indian tribes in the region in 1855.

Much of the groundwork for the council was accomplished in 1853 when Stevens was commanding an expedition for the Federal government to investigate a northern railroad route across the plains and Rocky Mountains to the west coast. Having traveled cross-country from Saint Paul, he arrived at Fort Union on August 1, 1853. There he met Alexander Culbertson, and in conversations that followed, Stevens determined that Fort Benton was the pivotal point in his plans.

Culbertson accompanied the Stevens party west to Fort Benton, guiding them along a route he had pioneered with a wagon in 1851. With Culbertson's aid, Stevens talked with Indians along the way. He then spent three weeks in Fort Benton talking with chiefs of the various branches of the Blackfeet, arranging for a great peace council at Fort Benton at a later date. He also talked with the Flatheads and Pend d'Oreilles west of the Continental Divide during his return to the coast.

Stevens returned to Fort Benton on July 26, 1855, to initiate the peace council. One of the first jobs was to contact the various tribes and get them to Fort Benton. Key to the success of the talks were gifts from the government for the Indians. These gifts were being shipped upriver by keelboat.

Word was received on September 1st that the boats with their supplies and gifts still hadn't reached the Judith River. Five weeks later, the keelboats still hadn't reached the Judith River. Stevens decided to shift his council to the Judith River area, and messengers were sent to inform the tribesmen, many of whom were then around Fort Benton. It was apparent that the boats would not reach Fort Benton for many days after the date set for the council, so it was logical to move to a location that the boats could reach sooner. Also, it seems that Stevens may have been worried that latent hostility between the Blackfeet and other tribes might flare up if they had to wait too long.

The boats finally reached the Judith on October 10th. Several reasons are given for the delayed arrival. Mismanagement by Alfred Cummings, a commissioner involved in the talks, is an often related reason. In later years, the American Fur Company was accused of purposely causing the delay. However, the records show that it was a low water year.

The delay meant that hundreds, perhaps thousands, of warriors simply drifted away in disgust or from hunger. Stevens had hoped for ten thousand Indians, which could have been the grandest council ever on the plains, but got twenty-five hundred instead. There were Blackfeet (including the Blood and Piegan branches), Gros Ventres, Flathead, Pend d'Oreilles, Nez Perces, Crees and Snakes. The Crow had been invited, but did not attend. Most of the tribes were looking for assurances from the Blackfeet that would allow them to hunt buffalo on the plains without fear of attack.

The negotiations took place between October 13th and 16th. Stevens' son, Hazard (who had accompanied his father), described the setting: ... a wide, level plain covered with a noble grove of huge cottonwoods. It was on the left bank of the Missouri, nearly opposite but below the mouth of the Judith ... The Governor's camp was pitched under the lofty cottonwoods, and lower down was the camp of the crew of men who had dragged the boats up the river. They were a hundred strong, mostly Germans, having many fine voices among them, and were fond of spending the evenings in singing."

By the terms of the Treaty, the land to the north of the Missouri from the Bears Paw Mountains to the Continental Divide and to the south between the Musselshell and the mouth of the Milk River would be the home of the Blackfeet nation. The U.S. Government would be allowed to build roads, military posts and telegraph lines within Blackfeet territory, and to navigate the river in return for annual annuities. A couple of years later, Edwin Hatch, Indian agent, reported issuing annuities to about eight thousand Indians at the Judith.

Chittenden (*History of Steamboat Navigation on the Missouri River*, (1903) says of the Stevens Treaty Council: "The Indians departed with their lavish presents. The era of the fur trader had ended and that of the Indian Agent had come."

LEWIS & CLARK CAMP OF MAY 28,1805

River Mile 88.8 Left

The Corps of Discovery camped here, opposite the mouth of today's Dog Creek, after traveling 14.5 miles, during which they encountered a succession of challenging rapids.

[Lewis - Tuesday, May 28th]

The weather dark and cloudy, the air smokey, had a few drops of rain; we employed the chord generally to which we also gave the assistance of the pole at the riffles, and rocky points; these are as numerous and many of them much worse than those we passed yesterday; arround those points the water drives with great force, and we are obliged in many instances to steer our vessels through the appertures formed by the points of large sharp rocks which reach a few inches above the surface of the water, here should our chord give way the bough is instantly drivin outwards by the stream and the vessel thrown with her side on the rocks where she must inevitably overset or perhaps be dashed to peices; our ropes are but slender, all of them except one being made of Elk's skin and much woarn, frequently wet and exposed to the heat of the weather are weak and rotten; they have given way several times in the course of the day but happily at such places that the vessel had room to wheel free of the rocks and therefore escaped injury; with every precaution we can take it is with much labour and inflnite risk that we are enabled to get around these points ... the river country &c continued much as yesterday untill late in the evening when we arrived at the entrance of a large Creek which discharges itself on the Star side is 35 Yds wide and contains running water; this we called Thompson's C. (after one of the party - today's Birch Creek at mile 91.3 left) here the hills recede from the river on both sides, the bottoms extensive particularly on the Stard side where the hills are comparitively low and open into three large vallies which extend for a considerable distance in a Northwardly direction; here also the river spread s to more than 3 times it's former width and is filled with a number of small and handsome Islands covered with cottonwood some timber also in the bottoms, the land again fertile. these appearances were quite reviving after the drairy country through which we had been passing. Capt. C. walked on shore in the early part of the day and killed a big horned anamal; he saw a great number of them ... This evening we encamped on Stard opposite to the entrance of a small Creek (today's Dog Creek).

Lewis and Clark camped here on the north bank opposite the mouth of Dog Creek, which they named Bull Creek, the evening of May 28,1805. After turning in for the night the expedition had a harrowing experience with a buffalo bull, which prompted them to name this location 'Bull Creek'. The following entry records the events of the next day, but is incluced here because it recounts the expedition's experience with the buffalo.

[Lewis - Wednesday, May 29th]

Last night we were all allarmed by a large buffaloe Bull, which swam over from the opposite shore and coming along side of the white perogue, climbed over it to land, he then allarmed ran up the bank in full speed directly towards the fires, and was within 18 inches of the heads of some of the men who lay sleeping before the centinel could allarm him or make him change his course, still more alarmed, he now took his direction immediately towards our lodge, passing between 4 fires and within a few inches of the heads of one range of the men as they yet lay sleeping, when he came near the tent, my dog (a Newfoundland named Seaman) saved us by causing him to change his course a second time, which he did by turning a little to the right, and was quickly out of sight, leaving us by this time all in an uproar with our guns in our hands, enquiring of each other the cause of the alarm, which after a few moments was explained by the centinel: we were happy to find no one hirt. The next morning we found that the buffaloe in passing the perogue had trodden on a rifle, which belonged to Capt. Clark's black man (York), who had negligently left her in the perogue, the rifle was much bent, he had also broken the spindle; pivit, and shattered the stock of one of the blunderbushes on board, with this damage I felt well content, happey indeed, that we had sustaned no further injury.

... This morning we set out at an early hour and proceded as usual by the Chord. at the distance of 2 $^{1}/_{2}$ Miles passed a handsome river which discharged itself on the Lard. side, I walked on shore and acended this river about a mile and a half in order to examine it ... it appeared to contain much more water as the Muscle-Shell river, was more rappid but equally navigable ... the water of this River is clearer much than any we have met with great abundance of the Argalia or Bighorned animals in the high country through which this river passes. Cap. C. who assended this R. much higher than I did has thought proper to call it Judieths River. the bottoms of this stream as far as I could see were wider and contained more timber than the Missouri ... on the Missouri just above the entrance of the Big Horn (Judith) River I counted the remains of the fires of 126 Indian lodges which appeared to be of very recent date perhaps 12 or 15 days. Capt. Clark also saw a large encampment just above the entrance of this river on the Stard. side of reather older date, probably they were the same Indians.

The Judith River, at first named "Bighorn" by Lewis, was afterwards renamed by Clark in honor of Miss Julia Hancock of Fincastle, Va., who later became his wife. She was but thirteen years of age at this time, and by her friends was nicknamed "Judy." They were married in 1808, and she bore him five children. She died in 1820 at the age of twenty-nine.

IRON CITY ISLANDS

River Mile 94

The name recalls the steamboat *Iron City*, which on its downriver journey, was attacked by Indians while grounded at these islands. The event is undoubtedly one of those typified by this bit of doggerel:

"So there we stuck on that doggone bar
And in some two minutes found
There was other folks in that neck o' woods
That knew we were aground."

What is known of the Iron City's adventure is contained in Larpenteur's brief entries at Fort Union. "July 3, 1866. *Rubicon* arr. from above ... brought news of the killing of mate of the *Iron City* by Indians: her whereabouts uncertain," and, "July 14, 1866. *Iron City* arr. from above."

During those troubled years when the Sioux were harassing the Missouri River steamboats, the pilot houses of upper-river boats were sheathed in boiler plate which gave master and pilot adequate protection. The passengers were relatively safe behind the boxes, sacks and bails of cargo piled along the bulwarks and railings, but the crew, when working a grounded vessel off a shoal, was always very much exposed.

THE HAGADONE HOMESTEAD

Frank - River Miles 95.3 to 97.7 Right
Family - River Miles 98 to 99.3 Right

Just beyond the edge of the high bank at River Mile 97 on the right, is the homestead of Frank Hagadone. Among the features at this site is an exceptional collection of horse-drawn farm implements. The Hagadone story has several chapters, beginning with an adventuresome couple, proceeding through judicious use of the various land laws to acquire property, and ending, in this accounting, with a sixty-three year old man living alone on the banks of the Missouri River.

Francis M. "Frank" Hagadone was born on May 18, 1870, in Denton, Texas. By 1904, he had made his way to South Dakota, where in March, he filed on a 160 acre homestead some fourteen miles northeast of Kadoka, in the southwest part of the state.

A few years later, the lure of the West was felt by Helena A. "Lena" Orth in Kenosha, Wisconsin. She joined other prospective homesteaders, boarded a "Migrant Train," and traveled to Kadoka. There she took up a one hundred fifty-seven acre homestead six miles south of Frank's.

About the time that Lena filed final proof on her homestead (November of 1913) the couple was married. Five months after filing final proof she received patent to her land.

The couple had one daughter, Agnes, while living in South Dakota. After her birth, the homesteads were sold and the family moved to Montana. Eventually they settled along the south side of the Missouri River between River Miles 98 and 99.3.

The Hagadone move to the river took place in 1917. The family now included two more daughters, Mary and Myrtle. They lived in a house typical of most homestead houses of that time - two rooms, tar papered on the outside, a dirt covered roof and dirt banked on three sides. They didn't get the floor completed the first year, and the dirt floor was covered with tarps and cow hides.

One day Lena noticed Mary, who was not yet two years old, and her puppy playing and patting something under one of the tarps. She investigated and discovered a rattlesnake who was not in a playful mood. Mary was bitten. Every method known was used to save her life - applying a tourniquet, gashing with a razor, sucking the wound, trussing her leg into the body of a freshly killed chicken, and poultices of bread and milk. She was a desperately ill little girl, but she survived.

Winter came early and hit hard that first year on the river. One evening there was a frantic pounding at the door. Frank opened the door to a man whose clothing was ice-crusted. While getting him into dry clothing and warming him with hot coffee, he told of his plight.

He was a member of a crew bringing two store-barges down river from Fort Benton. Their destination was Charlie Kendall's headquarters (see River Mile 142.5 L). The early on-set of winter caught them enroute and they were frozen into the ice in the river just above the Hagadone homestead. In his attempt to go for help, he had broken through the ice and was a very much chilled man by the time he reached the house.

The next day Frank helped the crew remove the cargo from the barges. All the food stuffs were stored in the Hagadone root cellar. The barges were then torn apart and the lumber piled along the river bank, far enough back to be safe from flooding and ice during the spring break-up. After the ice froze more solid, the supplies were taken down river to Kendall's by bobsled. For his help, Frank was given lumber for the badly needed floor. The remaining lumber from the barges was rafted down river to Kendall's place in the spring.

The two store-barges caught in the ice just above the Hagadone place in 1917 were probably very similar to those in the accompanying illustration. Charlie Kendall also built these, shown being loaded in Fort Benton, but the year was 1912. Ungainly craft, they were constructed of building materials needed down river, and they literally dismantled as they traveled downriver and their components and cargo were purchased by homesteaders along the river.

This township had been surveyed in 1916, but it was 1918 before the plat map was approved. In December of 1918, Lena filed for a water right on the Missouri River. She documented appropriating water from the river with a centrifugal pump into a 12" x 30" ditch on June 15, 1918.

In January of 1919, Lena filed a Desert Land Entry on the bottom lands immediately adjacent to the river. The following March, she filed an Additional Homestead Entry (additional to her original entry in South Dakota) on the lands beyond those which could be irrigated, mostly to the south along the toe of the valley slope. Together, these lands brought the Hagadone spread to 290 acres.

The first couple of years were mostly spent clearing sage and other brush from the land, and in surveying, then developing the irrigation system. By 1920 they had twenty-two acres in corn, five acres in garden, thirty-five acres broken, and an additional one hundred acres cleared. Their harvest that year included four hundred pounds of potatoes, one hundred-fifty bushels of corn and ten tons of feed. Improvements on the land included the 12' x 24' frame house, a 20' x 26' log barn, an 8' x 10' log granary, and one-half mile of fence.

Produce from the large Hagadone garden included watermelons, cantaloupes, squash, tomatoes, peanuts, sorghum cane, and mangels (a type of beet). Much of it was taken by boat or pack horse to McClellands, twenty miles down river, where it was loaded on a buckboard, hauled sixteen miles south to Winifred, and sold. There was no road to the homestead.

The corn crop included certified seed corn, Minnesota #13, which was sold to various seed nurseries.

Frank built a small sorghum mill. Agnes remembers that after the extracted syrup was cooked down it tasted "Something like a combination of Karo and molasses."

The homesteading statutes required that one-sixteenth of the land be in cultivation by the second year, with one-eighth additional acreage each year after. Because of drought, sickness, and the time needed to clear the land of sage and other brush, the Hagadone's fell behind on the required acreage, and their homesteading attempt was jeopardized for awhile. However, they were successful, and on May 11, 1922, they received final certificate to the homestead portion of the spread.

Domestic problems developed and late in 1923, Frank moved out. He settled in a cabin owned by Herbert Cameron some 2 miles up river (at the river mile 97 location). This bottom land had originally been homesteaded by George Clyborne, Cameron's brother-in-law.

Clyborne had been the foreman at the Bill Fergus Ranch, a large sheep operation west of Winifred. He quit his job to have a go on his own here in the Breaks. He filed a homestead entry on 146 acres in December of 1918. However, he relinquished the homestead in February of 1924.

Frank bought the cabin from Cameron, and in April of 1924, filed an Enlarged (to his South Dakota homestead) Homestead Entry on the same land that Clyborne had previously claimed.

After the divorce, Lena stayed on for four more years managing the place. In May of 1925, forty-three year old Lena Hagadone filed final proof on the Desert Land Entry portion of the spread. In witnessing Lena's final proof, William Hellar, a neighboring rancher from up on the bench, stated, "She grew some very good corn and the best garden in the whole country. The land will grow most any kind of a crop planted."

Charlie Peterson of Winifred bought the place from Lena. Then in 1941, the government purchased the spread under the Bankhead-Jones Farm Tenant Act; a program developed to retire sub marginal farm lands from agricultural production. In the meantime, Frank was developing his additional homestead. The first year he had a garden with melons, potatoes and vegetables. Over the next several years he broke land until he eventually had fifty-five acres in corn and millet.

Lewistown, 042676
D.L.A. of R. McClelland
report by
F. Erickson, S.A.
FD 23898

NOV 15 1919

DEPARTMENT OF THE INTERIOR,

GENERAL LAND OFFICE.

Helena, Montana, November 12, 1919

The Commissioner,
General Land Office,
Washington, D. C.

Approved: NOV 14 1919
Nathan Gammon
Chief of Field Division.

Sir:

On January 14, 1919, Rena McClelland, of Winifred, Montana, filed in the U. S. Land Office, Lewistown, Montana, desert-land application 042676 for Lots 8, 9, Sec 27, Lots 1, 2, 4, NW¼NE¼, SE¼NW¼, Sec 34, T. 23 N., R. 18 E., M. P. M.

On September 10, 1919, I made field investigation and have to report as follows:

IRRIGABLE LAND:

There are approximately 96 acres irrigable as follows:

Lot 9,	-	8.9 acres,
Lot 8,	-	9.8 acres,
Lot 1,	-	24.7 acres,
Lot 2,	-	15.3 acres,
Lot 4,	-	32.5 acres,
SE¼NW¼	-	5 acres.

The NW¼NE¼ has no irrigable land under the proposed system and will therefore have to be withdrawn.

CHARACTER OF LAND:

The land is desert in character, lying on the Missouri River bottom thirty miles north of Winifred, Montana.

FD 23898

The soil is partly gumbo and partly a good sandy loam. No timber.

IMPROVEMENTS:

Frame house, 24x36, with cellar under house,	$500.00
Log barn, 16 x 20 ft.	150.00
Log chickenhouse,	50.00
Log blacksmith shop,	50.00
Small shed,	20.00
Good cave,	75.00
Small frame cabin,	75.00
1 mile of woven wire fence	240.00
2 flumes,	60.00
3/4 mile of ditch and laterals	50.00
1¼ miles of 3 wire fence,	150.00
Pumping plant, consisting of No. 5 Gould's Centrifugal Pump and Frost Engine, with pipes, etc.	2500.00
41 acres in cultivation,	205.00
Total	$4125.00

IRRIGATION SYSTEM:

Part of the irrigation system has been installed and has been in operation for two or three years. Ditch has not been completed on Lot 1, Sec 34 and Lots 8, 9, Sec. 27.

DITCH:

The ditch is already completed from the pumping plant to the north line of the SE¼NW¼, as shown by the accompanying plat. Three laterals have also been made to carry the water to and upon the cultivated land. Survey has been made for a ditch to extend to a coulee near the east line of Lot 9, which is as far as it is possible to take the water.

T.23N.
R.18E.

D.L.A. 042676.
Rena McClelland

FD23898.

PUMPING PLANT:

A pumping plant consisting of a Gould's No. 5 centrifugal pump, having a six inch intake and a five inch discharge with a capacity of 750 G.P.M., and a Frost horizontal steam engine has been installed near the quarter corner between Sections 33 and 34 and has been in operation for two or three years. Coal is used as fuel as it can be mined within four miles of this land and is hauled across the river in the winter on the ice. The plant is of sufficient size for the proper irrigation of all the land under the constructed and proposed ditch, as one acre foot to the acre is sufficient.

RECOMMENDATION:

I respectfully recommend that this application be allowed as to Lots 8,9, Sec.27, Lots 1, 2, 4, SE¼NW¼; Sec. 34, and a withdrawal has been filed for the balance.

Very respectfully,
Fred Erickson
Special Agent, G. L. O.

Papers filed in 1919 to give title to the McLellands for the lands they homesteaded at river mile 101.

In May of 1927, he filed an additional stock raising homestead entry on one hundred seventy-six acres of bottom land immediately up river from the new spread. This brought the place up to 322 acres. However, the furthest up river portion of this latest filing was in conflict with a minerals permit for oil and gas held by James F. Early of San Francisco. It took more than a year to clear up the situation - Hagadone documenting that he wouldn't care if Early developed the minerals, and Early documenting that he didn't care if Hagadone developed the land for livestock use.

Frank made final proof on the enlarged homestead in October of 1929. He'd lived there mostly alone since before the divorce. Improvements at the time included a 14' x 16' frame house, a 14' x 18' barn, a 10' x 20' log chicken house, a 10' x 12' tool house, a 12' x 12' ice house, two corrals and one and one-half miles of fence.

On January 29, 1934, sixty-three year old Francis M. (Frank) Hagadone filed final proof on the stock-raising homestead entry. He'd broken about sixty acres and seeded it to "tame hay" (crested wheat grass and yellow clover) for pasture. He usually grazed about fifteen head of livestock.

In June of 1980, the Bureau of Land Management purchased Frank's two homesteads from Art Osburnsen as part of the management program for the Upper Missouri National Wild and Scenic River.

MCCLELLAND DESERT LAND ENTRY

River Miles 100.5-101.5 Right

John A. (Jack) McClelland was a Canadian of Irish descent. He immigrated to Montana and the United States in 1886, and proceeded by riverboat to Cow Island Landing. He first freighted with oxen between there and the Chinook area. Later he acquired a cattle ranch and a sawmill in the Bears Paw Mountains.

He became a naturalized citizen of the United States in October of 1894. In 1902, Rena Shinn of Lucas County, Iowa, became his bride. The marriage produced a daughter in 1904 and another in 1906.

During the spring of 1906, McClelland sold all of his holdings in the Bears Paw and moved his family to the bottom land on the south side of the Missouri. By July of that same year they had a thirty-five horsepower steam engine hooked up to a Gould's No. 5 centrifugal pump and were irrigating portions of their newly acquired land.

In the spring of 1908, the flooding waters of the Missouri washed away all of the buildings of the McClelland family. Jack proceeded to "Start all over again." He bought and hauled lumber from the sawmill in the Bears Paw to build a new two-story home on higher land along the river. This sturdy, comfortable and attractive home was constructed of 2x4s, put together one on top of the other, like bricks.

This township wasn't surveyed until 1916, and it was 1918 before the plat map was approved. In preparation for the applications which would make the land legally theirs, Rena McClelland filed for and received a "water right" to draw irrigation water from the Missouri River in June of 1917.

In January of 1919, Rena McClelland filed for a desert land entry on the property with the General Land Office. Among the witnesses was James Stafford, a merchant from Winifred who nine years later would buy the property from the McClellands. The original filing was for 230.24 acres, but the acreage was reduced twice - first because not all of it was irrigable, then because some of it was found to contain coal which couldn't be transferred out of public ownership.

Rena filed final proof on the remaining 143.03 acres in April of 1920. Since they'd been developing their irrigation system since 1906, little effort was required to satisfy the legal requirements. However, the McClellands had failed to file annual proofs that they had irrigated during the intervening years, so the final certification was delayed a full year. At the time of final proof, Rena was living in Lewistown so that the McClelland girls could attend school.

Jack McClelland was quite an industrious man. The steam engine from his irrigation system saw double duty as the power supply for a sawmill that he operated. He used coal to fire the steam engine. The coal was hauled about four miles from a mine north of the river. It was mined in the winter when the river crossing could be made on the ice.

About the time that they acquired legal title to their lands, Jack built and operated a small cable-guided wood-plank ferry.

The ferry landing was just down river from the new house. Access from the north was down a steep road constructed by the Army in 1869, when they were salvaging materials from the steamboat *Peter Balen* which burned at the head of Dauphin Rapids. Access from the south followed an old woodhawk skid trail. McClelland often had to hitch up his sturdy team of horses to rescue motorists who braved the primitive roads.

Although the steamboat era had passed, the *Josephine* and *Mandan* government snag boats made trips on the river into the 1920s. The sound of a steamboat whistle meant McClelland had to lower his ferry cable to allow them passage.

The original ferry washed out in the flood of 1927. It was replaced by another wooden ferry by the county in 1931. In 1939, Blaine County constructed a new road to the present ferry site, and replaced the old wooden ferry with a steel one in 1947.

The McClellands sold the place to James Stafford in 1928 and moved to Jardine, Montana. There they worked in mining and timbering interests. Jack died there at the age of eighty. Rena lived to see more than ninety years of Montana's growth from pioneer homesteading to the Montana of today.

DAUPHIN RAPIDS

River Mile 102

From *Floating on the Missouri,* Schultz; refer to narrative at river mile 1.2 left for background.

The swiftest part of the navigable Missouri is a twenty-six mile stretch east from the Judith; the water is all swift, and there are thirteen rapids in the course. We found well defined channels of deep water through the Birch, Holmes, McKeevers, Gallatin, Bear and Little Dog rapids, and then drew near the Dauphin Rapids, which I had been worrying

about ever since our start from Fort Benton. Years before the Government engineers had run a long wing dam out from the south shore at this point, throwing all the water into one narrow, deep channel. But the ice had battered it season after season, wearing it away, and as I looked now I could see only a line of white foam where it had once stood . The roar of the water was sullen and menacing. On the flat nearby some men were building a cabin, and rowing ashore I walked over to them. "Are you building a sheep ranch?" I asked.

"Not on your life!" one of them replied. "We've got a little bunch of cattle; the sheep men run us out where we were located over on the railroad, and we've found a good range here. The first blankety-blank sheep man that shows up in this vicinity with his flocks had better come heeled, for we'll sure fight."

I sympathized with them. The sheep men are, without doubt, "killing the golden goose;" the luxuriant range which would have lasted forever if stocked with cattle only, is being rapidly ruined by them. And then, what will our children do? There is no great West for them to explore and exploit.

The cattlemen were very sociable. They pointed to a cellar they had dug, about five feet in depth, and said that at the bottom of it their shovels had uncovered the remains of a fire, some 44-caliber cartridge shells and some human bones. There were no cartridges of that kind used in this country until 1866, so in thirty-five years or less the wash from the hills had deposited five feet of soil upon the bottom. How I wished I could know the tragedy which had here taken place. Most likely the bones were the remains of some white men, surprised and murdered by Indians.

"Game, especially mule deer", the cattlemen said, was fairly abundant. The day before one of them had seen two good-sized bunches of mountain sheep back in the hills. "But," he continued, with a sly wink, "of course I didn't shoot at them, as the game law prohibits the killing of them at any season of the year."

I asked about the rapids, and was informed that the main channel was full of boulders, two boats having been wrecked on them that season. This was not encouraging, so I decided to investigate a gap I had seen in the wing dam near the south shore. Crossing over, I put on the waders, and staff in hand, ventured out step by step to the center of the opening, finding eighteen inches of water in the shallowest place. Below the gap that part of the stream narrowed considerably, and while it was too swift to be sounded afoot, it looked to have plenty of depth, so I waded back to the boat and determined to try it. We started slowly, with just enough speed to afford steering way. Sah-ne-to was frightened and confused by the leaping, foaming, roaring water off to the left, so I bade her let go of the tiller, and steered with the oars. We glided over the shallow place and through the gap without a bump or scrape, and then into the narrow channel; here I could not touch bottom with oars, and felt sure I had solved the problem of the dreaded rapids. And so I had, for a minute or two we ran safely into the main channel at the foot of them.

I have been unable to learn much about "old man" Dauphin, for whom these rapids were named . He was a French Creole, born in St. Charles, Missouri, and was long an employee of the American Fur Company. In 1857 he resigned from their service and became a "freeman", or free trapper. Employees were known as "company men". In the winter of l857-58, Dauphin made his headquarters at the mouth of Milk River, trapping for some distance up that stream and on the Missouri. When spring came he made four large, long dugouts, lashed them together, and then piling his beaver skins on them drifted down to St. Louis with the current, 1,950 miles by the channel of the river. What a large number of flat-tails he must have had.

Louis Dauphin, for whom the rapids is named, was a respected hunter and scout on the Upper Missouri. For a time he was a hunter on the steamboats, whose job was to provide fresh meat for the crew and pasengers. Typically the hunter would leave the docked steamer at midnight, and walk ahead, hunting the banks. Any game that he killed would be hung on a tree on the riverbank, to be picked up by the passing steamboat. Dauphin was the favorite hunter of Captain Joseph LaBarge, who described him as seeming to delight in danger, and having no fear of Indians. His lack of prudence led to his death at the hands of the Sioux in 1865 at the mouth of Milk River.

DAUPHIN RAPIDS

River Mile 102.1

Steamboat navigation on the Upper Missouri was often difficult, even under the best of conditions. Key to successful passage up the river was the amount of water in the river. During high water the heavily laden steamboats had to lay line to a deadman buried along the bank and warp (winch) their way through the rapids with a capstan. During low water snags, shoals, and rocks created other problems.

Dauphin Rapids was the worst barrier to navigation on the upper river. As a result, the area was often a beehive of activity as boats unloaded and reloaded freight, freight was transported overland around the rapids, and fuel wood was acquired.

During low water, shoals at Grand Island (river mile 139) and Cow Island (river mile 128) meant that steamboats had to be lightened to gain clearance. They would unload about half their freight at Grand Island and then fight their way to the bottom of Dauphin Rapids. Here they would unload, and then return to Grand Island for the rest of their freight. Passage over Dauphin Rapids frequently required that the steamboats carry no freight, and only enough fuel for the passage.

When the water level at Dauphin Rapids became so low that passage was impossible, the steamboats had to resort to a couple of other options. If there were boats on the river above, contracts would be negotiated with them for hauling the freight to upriver ports from above the rapids. Steamboats that worked the circuit between Dauphin Rapids and Fort Benton became known as "double-trippers". Among them were the *Cora, Silver Bow, North Alabama, Big Horn, Only Chance, Fanny Barker, Violla Belle, Peninah, Andrew Ackley, Huntsville, Miner, Silver Lake* and *Peter Balen.*

When Dauphin Rapids became impassable, the other option was to off-load freight at Cow Island Landing for overland transportation to Fort Benton, using horse, mule, and ox teams.

Though many boats were severely damaged by the treacherous currents and shallow boulders of Dauphin Rapids, there are no documented steamboat wrecks in the area caused by the rapids. The only steamboat lost here was the *Peter Balen,* and she was destroyed by fire in July of 1869 while tied up at the head of the rapids. One story says the *Peter Balen's* boiler blew, while another says a crew member heating wash water was to blame.

One of the best ways to get a feel for the activities surrounding, and the difficulties encountered by steamboats at Dauphin Rapids is to review steamboat logs. Excerpts from a selected few follow:

LOG OF THE *LILLIE MARTIN* in 1865

FRIDAY JUNE 23d at Grand Island. This morning at 4 oClk got up and commenced discharging freight in order to lighten this took us until $1^{1}/_{2}$ *o Clk Pm then started and made fair headway, found current very strong We lightened up to 3 feet and found 3 feet. Weather clear and cool Lay all night at 9 oClock.*

SATURDAY, JUNE 24th. Left this morning at daylight and made very fair headway, wooded twice during the day, found the river becoming more narrow and water very strong Succeeded in getting along until we reached "Daufin Rapids" having arrived there at 4 oClock Pm here the Twilight tried to make the riffle but could not afterwards we tried and met with some success, opinions varied as to our ability to get over. Today we saw and killed a "Mountain Sheep" this is the first seen yet though they are said to be very abundant. Weather clear and cool, lay all night below "Daufins Rapids."

SUNDAY, JUNE 25th. This morning at daylight tried to get over Daufins Rapids, but failed, had to drop back and lighten this took us until dinner time, after dinner the passengers (excepting ladies) all went ashore and spent the afternoon there, awaiting the "Lillies" getting over, after a lengthey trial She failed the hawser having broken which caused her to drop back very fast, and gave those who remained aboard a good fright. after dropping She landed on the bar, and remained all night here the passenger who were ashore were ferried over to the boat and had to wade some distance in the water before getting on board, this created a good deal of amusement to those who were lucky enough to have remained aboard though it made some of them think d_ _n even if they didn't say it. Weather clear and pleasant. River 3 feet and falling.

MONDAY JUNE 26th. Still at "Daufins Rapids" started at 6 oClk to try again and see if we can get over, after some time and constant perseverance we finally succeeded in getting over, which caused great rejoicing, the balance of the day was consumed in reloading the freight lightened, this took us until $7^{1}/_{2}$ *oClk Pm which made* $51^{1}/_{2}$ *hours at "Daufins Rapids" the "Twilight" commenced at* $8^{1}/_{2}$ *oClk Pm. Started at* $7^{1}/_{2}$ *oClk Pm and went about 5 miles above the Rapids where we lay all night. Weather clear and warm. River 3 feet and falling (*$^{1}/_{2}$ *inch).*

On Thursday, June 29th, the *Lillie Martin* made it to the mouth of the Marias River, her up-river port that year. The boat turned down river on July 1, and upon reaching Grand Island on July 2nd, the cargo left there, plus some of the *Twilight's*, was reloaded. Faced with a falling river, and having run aground a couple of times, the freight of the *Lillie Martin* was off-loaded at Cow Island Landing. While at Cow Island the steamers *Deer Lodge* and *Roanoke*, having attempted to go further, returned to Cow Island Landing and also unloaded there. The *Lillie Martin* was pointed toward home on July 4th.

The following year (1866) the *Lillie Martin* made it to Fort Benton on June 29th. This was a much better "water year," and she only had to resort to cordelling to get past Dauphin Rapids.

LOG OF STEAMER *BERTHA* FROM SIOUX CITY, IOWA, TO FORT BENTON, MONTANA in 1868 - John P. Arnold, master.

The *Bertha* was nicknamed "Scarred Wolf." She was a 180 feet long side-wheeler, and made four trips to Fort Benton between 1868-70.

Friday, July 31, 1868 - Twenty-four days out. Departed at peep of day. Ran up to Bird's rapids (river mile 115), struck rocks, finally got over. Next bluff is a huge rock above the coolie that usually makes a break. now it is four or five feet out of water. We do not run any distance without striking rocks. Weather cool. River stationary. Have had no mosquitoes for several nights. Got on a rock at the foot of Bear's rapids. Captain went contrary to advice of pilots and laid line to right shore, after sparring over some huge rocks she started for the right shore and brought up on some large rocks, got off and sounded. Came over, rubbed and bumped around terribly, got over at dinner time. We strike rocks at nearly every boat's length we go. Arrived at Dauphin's 6 p.m., sounded and put out warp, found thirty inches, went into it, but she did not get to the shoal water. In sparring her about a rock came through, water was over her timbers two or three times.

Saturday, August 1, 1868 - About 2 a.m. we got into the left shore and began putting out freight. About 6 a.m. the Leoni Leoti came down, put out a line and dropped through. She says the Success was at Drowned Man's rapids, thirty-four miles (River Mile 84.5 - in fact only 18 miles from here) above at dark last night, and the Leoni Leoti reports only twenty-two inches here at Dauphin's. Her pilot, Mr. Jacobs, says the Success found thirty inches, same as we did. We put out nearly all of our freight (three or four yawl loads) on left shore and cordeled it up to left point above the rapids. We succeeded in getting her a little further up than she was last night, but rubbed very hard on the rocks, broke our wheel badly, dead man pulled up or broke in two and we were compelled to drop into shore. Sounded left chute, two feet, laid up.

Sunday, August 2, 1868 - Weather beautiful. River fell one inch last night. We are still at the bank. Cleaned our boilers last night. Andrew Ackley came down about 9:30 a.m. and landed on left shore above rapids. Her passengers walked down to the Leoni Leoti, she left as soon as all were on board. We made arrangements with the Ackley to take our freight to Benton for l 1/4 cents per lb. She came down over the rapids about 10:30 a.m., got the freight on board, also the passengers, and started up about 6 p.m., went up without a line, struck some rocks. Atkins and Sims went up to the freight pile above rapids. We bade all our friends adieu and returned to our boat after dark. Ackley leaves at daylight for Benton and we for Sioux City. God speed both.

The *Bertha* hit a bridge at St. Joseph, Missouri, on June 25, 1873 and sank.

THE LOG OF THE *HENRY M. SHREVE* FROM ST. LOUIS, MISSOURI, TO FORT BENTON in 1869 - Henry S. Carter, Captain

This was the *Henry M. Shreve's* only trip to Fort Benton.

WEDNESDAY JUNE 2nd. Left as usual at 3 oclk A.M. & arrived at Cow Island 6 oclk with Str. Viola Belle close behind. Found Str. Mountaineer aground with her Wheel Broken & apart of her Cargo on Shore. Peninah laying to the Shore Repairing her wheel and Str. Lacon just got over the Shoal Rapids. 10 oclk Str. Big Horn came up. 11 oclk Peninah over & gone. 12 oclk Str. Importer Passed down from Benton & with a good trip of Passengers in

Sight, Reporting only 30 Inches at Dauphan Rapids. This is truly Discouraging as we Draw 3 feet with a part of our Cargo on Board. 1 oclk P.M. we are now 57 Days out from St. Louis & have a tremendious Strain on our Hauser on Shore pulling over the Rapids at Cow Island. Passed Str. Lacon Hard aground at Birds Rapids. 9 oclk P.M. Str. Peninah & Shreve arrived at a good Pine Wood 6 miles below Dauphins Rapids at the Salty Price of $15 per Cord. Str. Shreve took 20 Cords & Gave Due Bill for $350. The Str. Peninah took 8 Cords only. Laid up here for the night. The Importer Reported today that there was only 30 inches Water on Dauphins Rapids. (Saw 10 Mountain Sheep this Evening)

THURSDAY JUNE 3rd Left as usual 3 oclk A.M. This morning cloudy and indications of Rain. Arrived at Dopans [Dauphin] Rapids with the Peninah. Found the Str. Only Chance aground & working hard on the Rapids. The Shreve is drawing 3 feet & we find only 30 Inches in the Rapids. The Peninah is Lightering up again. We have laid a line ahead & now expect to pull over a Point by main Strength. 11 oclk Str. Shreve now commenced lightering up to 30 Inches with the 2 Yawls & Str. Viola Belle on the opposite side of the River Lightering up & Hauling her freight around the Shoal Water with Teams. 1 oclk Peninah Lightered up to 27 Inches & now hard aground on the Rapids. Knocked off Lightering at 8 oclk but rolling all our barrels on Shore to commence early in the morning. 9 oclk Str. Big Horn arrived up. Only Chance still aground in the Channel. Our only prospects is in the Antisipated Rise tonight & tomorrow as the River Raised $^{1}/_{2}$ inch today on the Rapids & the prospects flattering for a continuance. Men down today from Camp Cook reports the Judeth - a considerable little Stream as Running out very freely. The Weather is Cool & Cloudy all day & Strong indications of Rain. Laid up now for the night & today at 1 oclk was 58 days out from Saint Louis.

FRIDAY JUNE 4th Dauphins Rapids is a Very hard Road to Travel. The Strs. Peninah & Only Chance Drawing only 2 feet both hard aground on the Rapids & Completely blocking up the Channel. The River fell last night one Inch which is truly discouraging. Str. Viola Belle Left this morning bound down for her freight Pile Stored on Grand Island, after putting out her entire Cargo & leaving men with it to haul it to the head of the rapids in her absence. There is no other alternative for the Shreve but to follow the Same Course. Str. Big Horn is lightning whare the Viola Belle Left. The Weather this morning is Clear, pleasant & delightful. I oclk P.M. The Boats all hold their Respective Positions as above described & We are now 59 Days out from St. Louis (Str. Mountaineer just arrived).

SATURDAY JUNE 5th This morning is Bright, Clear & pleasant & Dauphan Rapids Still holds the Fleet in the following order - Peninah & Andy Eckley over & at the Head - Shreve & the Mountaineer at the foot & Big Horn Still aground in the middle Shoal Water. Mountaineer Putting her Cargo off & Lightering over with 2 Yawls with Mules to tow & will Return to Cow Island for Balance of her Cargo. 11 oclk A.M. Str. Shreve Reshipped all of her passengers on the Penina at $15 ea. for Cabin & $3 for Deckers to Benton, all left Satisfyed & in a good humour. The Mountaineer would Ship her Passengers on the Big Horn & Left the foot of the Rapids bound down to Grand Island to bring up the Balance of our Cargo. Left 8 M[en ,& 2 Clerks with our frght Pile at the foot of the Rapids to get it over with our Big Yawl in our absence. The River in a Stand today & last night. 12 oclk M Met Strs. Sallie & Huntsville 6 & 8 miles below the Rapids. 1 oclk P.M. We are now 60 Days out from St. Louis & 10 Miles above Cow Island. Met Str. Viola Belle Returning with the Balance of her Cargo. Str. Lacon still hard aground head down & in a bad predicament - out of

Wood & Sawing both Guards off for Fuel. Arrived at our freight Pile on Grand Island at 4 oclk P.M. Got all our freight on Board at 8 oclk & Arrived at Wood Yard 7 miles above at 9 oclk & took on 20 Cords Green Cotton Wood at $7 Cord. This was a fast Job & quick time with 3/4 crew Since 11 oclk. Lay up here for the Night at Cow Island Wood Yard.

SUNDAY JUNE 6th Left at 3 Oclk A.M. Stopped at Ice House one mile above & got 779 lbs Ice at $1^{1}/_{2}$¢ lb. - $11.68 & Gave Due Bill for the Wood $140.00 & Ice $11.68 - makeing $151.68. Hailed by a Yawl with the Pilot & 4 Men of the Str. Sallies. Crew came down for a Capston Wheel at this WYd Put out by Str. Peninah. They got it & we took them all on Board. Mr. Richeson the Pilot in Charge had a large & fine Mountain Goat that he had killed on the trip down in his yawl. Arrived at Cow Island Shoals at $8^{1}/_{2}$ oclk A.M. & Got over with a Line & Hard Sparring at $10^{1}/_{2}$ oclk - 2 Hours which was a very Quick & Successful Job. 1 oclk P.M. We are now at Sturgeon Island & 61 Days out from St. Louis. Passed Str. Lacon Still hard aground at Sturgeon Island, Head down & Still at Work. Arrived at Dauphans Rapids Pine WYard 6 miles below the foot at 4 oclk - took on 10 Cords Pine Wood at $15.00 Cord & Gave Due Bill for $150.00. Left at 6 oclk - 2 Hours takeing on this wooding. It is now very Cloudy & Raining & every appearance of having a Big & Heavy Rain tonight. The River Reported to have Risen $1^{1}/_{2}$ Inches at the Rapids Since we left yesterday. We feel much apprehension for our freight Pile at the Rapids as it is not tarpaulined & we are makeing all posible Speed up this 6 miles to get our Tarpaulian over it, but Trust that Capt. Wray of the Silver Bow will protect it with his as we here [sic] that she has Returned & takeing on her Cargo Laying along side of our Freight Pile (This is our hope & Salvation). Arrived at Dauphans Rapids at 7 oclk & was gratifyed to Learn that our Freight had been protected & did not get Damaged by the heavy Shower of Rain Found all of our freight had been Lightered over to the head in our absence. Silver Bow & North Alabama at the head of the Rapids Down from Benton. Silver Bow finished takeing on her Cargo & Left tonight for Benton & North Alabama loading with the Mountaineers Cargo what She brought up to leave in the morning. Raining & Indications of Rain tonight, which we ll pray for (Laid up all Quiet for the night.)

MONDAY JUNE 7th This day Cloudy & Rain in Showers Interfearing with our lightering. Str. Mountaineer left at 9 oclk for Cow Island for the Balance of her Cargo. Str. Viola Belle & Huntsville got over the Rapids. North Alabama Left for Benton. We Succeeded in makeing a Written Contract with her to take 100 Tons of our Cargo to Benton on this her return trip at $1^{1}/_{2}$¢ per Pound, the best that we could do. The River has risen 3 Inches today & the Prospects [are good] that there will be water enoughf for us to try it in the morning & to go on to Benton. If So, we have a prospect of geting all of our Cargo through to Benton in the next 8 or 10 days, which is a very important consumation, at the Same time Very expensive. But we hope our actions in this uncertain position - how to act may turn out for the Best - 10 oclk P.M. Str. Mountaineer has returned from Cow Island with the Balance of her Cargo - Str. Sallie Still laying at the foot of the Rapids - will be ready to try it tomorrow. At I oclk today we are 62 Days out from St. Louis.

TUESDAY JUNE 8th. The River very unexpectedly fell 3 Inches last night. Notwithstanding the Str. Shreve & Sallie Raised Steam & both Boats went over & to the Shoal Water on the Rapids. The Sallie got over the first difficult part & at the 2nd Stuck. The Shreve got her Yawl & Hawser out way up the Bank & was abought to bring it on Board in order to haul over. Just at that time Capt. Carter Concluded that it was going to be an all day Job with a falling River - that it was not best to get the Shreve over this Rapids. 8 Oclk A.M. We are now landed at our old Landing & now finishing to day to lighten every pound to the head & for the Shreve to return to St. Louis $8^{1}/_{2}$ oclk Str. Cora passed over & down to St. Louis,

Reporting the River above to be very low & but little rise antisipated. We learn that She is very much Broken up & in a bad condition by hard Work on Shoal Water - $9^{1}/_{2}$ oclk. Str. Sallie has got over Drawing only [?] Inches. The Shreve & Mountaineer the only & last 2 boats at the foot & both trying to get ready to head down for St. Louis as being the most advisable under all the difficult Surrounding Circumstances. 12 oclk. Str. Shreve again left her Landing for 2nd time to cross the Rapids. 1 oclk P.M. We are now 63 Days out from St. Louis & Hauling over Dauphan Rapids. $4^{1}/_{2}$ oclk P.M. The Bulley Shreve is now over & is laying along Side of her Freight Pile with her entire Cargo & will Soon Commence takeing it on. The Shreve was only $4^{1}/_{2}$ Hours geting over this difficult & trying Spot. Having Passed the light Stearn Wheel Str. Sallie aground on the Rapids. This has been the quickest trip from the foot to the Head of any Boats, Since our first arrival here. 5 oclk P.M. Str. Sallie is now over & Along Side of her freight Pile. Mountaineer just Started to come over. Str. Lacon is laying at the Foot of the Rapids - 9 oclk P.M. Str. Mountaineer over & at her freight Pile - 4 hours geting over, beating us $^{1}/_{2}$ Hour and the Quickest Trip over that has been made. Both Boats Worked hard until 2 oclk A.M. takeing on Cargo. The Shreve Left one $^{1}/_{2}$ of her Pile Supposed to be 100 Tons for the Str. North Alabama to take up as per contract.

WEDNESDAY JUNE 9th. This day is Clear Bright & pleasant & we now have a good prospect of Geting the Shreve & her entire Cargo up to Benton in the next 7 or 8 days. River fell last night $^{1}/_{2}$ Inch. Str. Sallie left at 11 oclk last night. The Str. Lacon Still at foot of the Rapids. $8^{1}/_{2}$ oclk A.M. Shreve & Mountaineer both now underway & bound for Benton.

The *Henry M. Shreve* reached Fort Benton on Saturday, June 12th, sixty-seven days out of St. Louis. During the up-river haul she burned 1,051 cords of wood at a cost of $6,048.70.

She was pointed back down river on June 15th. The *North Alabama, Miner, Viola Belle, Lacon* and *Peninah* were still tied up at the Fort Benton levee. The return to St. Louis took seventeen days. The *St. Louis Dispatch* of July 1 records her arrival that day and notes that she immediately dropped down to the docks for repairs. The *St. Louis Missouri Democrat* of July 2 states the *Shreve,* "had enough of the mountain trade this year."

The Missouri River steamboats were powered by wood-burning engines. A boat could go through as many as thirty cords of wood in one twenty-four hour period, and steamboat captains resorted to many expedients, to replenish their supply. Often they used "reck-heaps" and piles of driftwood, while at other times crew members would be set ashore to cut timber. The latter method required a great deal of time, however, and exposed the boat and crew to Indian attacks. The standard method was to purchase wood from "Woodhawks" - men who set up woodyards along the river, cutting and selling wood at the sometimes exorbitant cost of $15 per cord. Rapids were favored spots for the woodhawks since the steamboats usually slowed or stopped at these points and often had to take on extra wood to get up enough steam to pass them. Since Dauphin Rapids was one of the major double-tripper ports as well, woodhawking became a major "industry" in this area.

The woodhawks cut timber both on the hillsides and on top of the bluffs. Oftentimes, they would work through the winter to garner a large enough supply to last through spring and summer; in this area many of the old stumps are cut off 4 and 5 feet high, evidence that they were timbered during winter snows. The cut timber was dropped off the top of the bluffs, then skidded on trails across the flats to the river's edge. Forgotten piles of stacked wood and old skid trails are still visible throughout much of the area. Also visible are the remains of small log or stone dug-outs and cabins used by the woodhawks.

The major hazard of the woodhawk's life seemed to be the Indians. Seven woodhawks came up the river on the *Peninah* in 1867 from Pennsylvania, and built a dug-out on a flat on the north bank at the foot of the rapids. A year later, in August of 1868, the crew of the *Bertha* coming downriver from Fort Benton found their bodies at their dug-out, some in their bunks and the rest at the doorway. The crew from the boat buried them near where they fell in shallow, rock-covered graves.

In addition to commerce, the Upper Missouri was an important avenue of transportation for the military. Major Howell recommended in 1867 that work should be done at the Cow Island Shoal and at Dauphin Rapids. The major improvements recommended at the rapids were the removal of the large boulders and blasting a direct channel through the "reef." After years of delays, Congress finally appropriated $1,383,000 for needed improvements in the Missouri's channel.

The report of the Secretary of War to the two houses of Congress in 1877 contains the following report of Lieutenant Edward McGuire, First Lieutenant of Engineers:

IMPROVEMENT OF MISSOURI RIVER ABOVE THE MOUTH OF THE YELLOWSTONE

A letter from the office of the Chief of Engineers dated March 21, 1877, informed me that, in addition to my other duties, I was placed in charge of the work of improving the Missouri River above the mouth of the Yellowstone."

Upon investigation I found that there were three reports upon this subject: One by Maj. Charles R. Suter, Corps of Engineers (Report of the Chief of Engineers, 1875), one by Capt. C.W. Howell, Corps of Engineers (Report of the Chief of Engineers, 1868), and one by Thomas P. Roberts, published by the War Department in 1875. Each of these reports recommended improvements in but general terms. As no detailed surveys have ever been made, it was impossible for them to do otherwise. Still they are definite enough to show that the work should be commenced in the upper portion of the river within the first 300 miles from Fort Benton, where the obstructions to navigation consist of a series of rapids difficult of passage in consequence of the slight depth at low-water stage and the rapidity of the current. Of these rapids Dauphin's, Cow Island, and Two-Calf Island are mentioned in the reports as demanding the first attention, and the opinions of steamboatmen, as expressed to me, coincide with that conclusion. Of these three, Dauphin's Rapids present the greatest difficulties.

In view of the above a party, consisting of one assistant engineer, one recorder, one overseer, and twenty-three men, was organized in this city and started for Dauphin's Rapids on the 11th instant.

The remoteness of the scene of operations from all depots of supplies and the uncertainty of the time of arrival and departure of the steamboats necessitated the purchase at once of material of such a nature and in such quantities as to supply all needs in any contingency which may arise.

An escort of one company of the Seventh Infantry was requested, and it was ordered to meet the working party at Dauphin's Rapids not later than the 25th instant. In addition I obtained, upon requisition on the chief ordnance officer of the Department of Dakota, 24 rifles and 3,000 rounds of ammunition for use by the party in an emergency.

Permission was obtained for the purchase of the rations from the subsistence depot at Fort Buford, and the rations will be drawn for sixty days at a time.

Water-gauges will be established and a detailed survey of the immediate locality of the work will be made directly after the arrival of the party. Gauges will also be established at Carroll and Fort Buford, if any one can be found at those points who will, for a reasonable compensation, keep a record of the stage of water. The assistant engineer was furnished with a thermometer and an aneroid barometer, and it is hoped that it may be possible to run a line of levels between the points. By the above means it is thought that information more detailed than that which we now possess of the nature and habits of the river will be obtained.

The main work will consist in procuring a channel of a width of 300 feet, if practicable, and of a depth of 4 feet at low-water stage. This will necessitate the removal of reefs, bars, and bowlders by "grabbing" or blasting, and the construction of wing-dams of brush or stone so disposed as to obtain a sufficient amount of water and diminish the velocity of the current, if found to be necessary. For the work there will be used one scow rigged with a derrick and "stone-grab," one dwelling-boat, one working-boat, and one yawl, or "batteau", as it is termed by the lumbermen in this section of the country.

The party will move the escort and itself from point to point by means of these boats. It is expected that at least the work on the three points mentioned above will be completed during the coming season.

At the close of operations the material will be stored at Carroll, in order to be at hand, and to save the expense and trouble of transportation in case there should be an appropriation to continue the work another year.

In a *Supplementary Report,* submitted 2½ months later, Lieutenant Maguire reports:

I have visited the party at work at Dauphin's Rapids, and have found that the work is not only more difficult, but far more extensive than was to be expected. The bed of the stream is almost literally paved with bowlders for a distance of at least half a mile. I was led to believe, from Roberts's report, that there were but few boulders scattered here and there through the channel.

I have also learned that there are other points above Dauphin's which must be improved before the river will be navigable in low-water. There are seventeen places above Dauphin's which should be attended to. In view of this, I would request permission to change the recommendation (contained in my annual report) for an appropriation of $30,000 to one of $75,000.

With this amount three parties can be worked to good advantage, and there can be purchased for each party a small engine, a thing that is very much needed for working the rakes and facilitating the operations in other ways.

I have been unable to send this letter earlier, on account of the want of any means by which to do so.

Very respectfully, your obedient servant
Edwd. Maguire ....Lieutenant of Engineers, U.S.A.

In the *Annual Report of the Secretary of War for the Year 1878,* Lieutenant Maguire reported:

At Dauphin's Rapids a channel 100 feet wide and 1,800 feet long was cleared of rocks. Several bunches of rocks were also taken out below the foot of this channel. The number of rocks removed was 2,400, measuring 286.5 cubic yards, and requiring for their removal 128 dynamite blasts, in addition to the ordinary grappling. A dam to close the right chute was carried out to a distance of 130 feet. The work on this dam was discontinued because it was found to be throwing water into the channel and interfering with the removal of the rocks. It has a crest of 6 feet, an upstream slope of 1:2, and a downstream slope of 1:1. It contains 200 cubic yards of stone. The upstream slope is covered with a layer of gravel, 50 cubic yards having been used for this purpose. In addition, about 1,000 cubic yards of stone were collected on the banks. This amount will suffice for the completion of the above-mentioned dam and for the construction of the proposed one above it. Three other short dams (containing about 60 cubic yards of stone) were constructed near the left bank.

In 1879, he reported:

At Dauphin's Rapids the 100 feet channel was cleared for a further distance of 1,600 feet, requiring the removal of 675 cubic yards of stone and the use of 226 blasts. The total length of channel attained during the two seasons was 3,400 feet, with a minimum depth in places of 30 inches, the remainder varying in depth from 3 to 5 feet.

The dam to close the right chute was finished. This dam has a length of 530 feet, and contains 791 cubic yards of stone.

JOHN MAGDALL HOMESTEAD

River Mile 103 Left

Homesteading often required more than the skill to carve a farm or ranch out of the wilderness, the tenacity to cope with the often hostile environment, or the ability to survive the disappointment and economic loss of a hail storm or grasshopper invasion. The red tape of the bureaucracy, jockeying for the better lands still open to homesteading, and competition for access to scarce water sources taxed even the most patient of men. John Magdall is an excellent example.

Magdall came to the Breaks around 1915, selecting a 320 acre homestead on top, some $3^1/_2$ miles northwest of here. The township wasn't surveyed until 1916, and it was 1918 before the plat map was approved, so Magdall did not file on his homestead until 1919. Among his improvements was a small spring developed from a seep a half mile southeast of his house. It was marginal water at best, but it was the closest available.

Magdall received patent to his three hundred-twenty acre tract on August 3, 1921. Two days later he filed on a second 320 acres of adjacent land. The additional entry was made possible by the Stock-Raising Homestead Act of 1916 which increased the allowable acreage to six hundred-forty acres. The additional entry was ill conceived, and the filing eventually raised issues that would haunt Magdall for the next eighteen years.

Applications for homestead entries had to be made in "good faith" for the purposes intended by the legislation. Among other things, this usually meant that the lands were expected to be contiguous. Magdall's additional entry was for the only vacant lands (public lands still available for homesteading) adjacent to his original place. Unfortunately, except for two forty acre parcels (one of which contained Magdall's spring) the lands were rough "Breaks." In later years he would describe most of the land as, "wholly worthless and unfit for grazing livestock, being eroded badlands bearing little or no vegetation."

It must not have been too long before Magdall started having second thoughts about his additional entry. One of his first steps toward correcting the situation was to divest himself of interest in the original homestead. In December of 1925 he sold half of the place to a neighbor. In July of 1926 he conveyed title for the remaining acreage to his wife, Mary.

Magdall made little effort to make the required improvements on his additional entry, and in February of 1927 the General Land Office canceled his application.

In July of 1930 Magdall made a second additional stock-raising homestead entry. This application was for the two good forty acre plots adjacent to the original place and for 242 acres along the north side of the Missouri River. Then the frustrations began.

Shortly after its receipt, the General Land Office suspended action on the additional entry. Magdall was $2.25 short on his filing fee. In the meantime, while fencing the land Magdall discovered that eighty acres of the land he'd described in his application were steep side slopes and not the bottom land he wanted

Magdall sent in the $2.25, along with a map showing the location of the lands he really wanted, and requested that his application be changed. The General Land Office responded by informing him that he would have to completely re-file with the correct legal descriptions - the plat map was not adequate to initiate the requested changes.

Magdall refiled his application. Unfortunately, this time he erred and included a small piece of land on the south side of the river in the legal description. He'd been dealing with the Great Falls General Land Office, but lands south of the river were the responsibility of the Billings General Land Office. Action on his application was again suspended.

Magdall refiled his application. By now it was the end of August.

The following spring Magdall found the section corners that applied to the legal descriptions of his land, and discovered that the map he'd been using showed the Missouri River in the wrong location. In June of 1931 he again refiled his application, finally with the correct legal descriptions for the lands that he wanted.

The second round of Magdall's frustrations involved water. Lands that contained springs or water holes, which were needed for public watering purposes, were not available for homesteading. In 1916 Magdall had developed a small spring from a seep adjacent to his original homestead, and the forty acre tract containing the spring was included in his most recent filing.

Nine days after Magdall submitted the final correction on his additional stock-raising homestead entry, the neighbor who had purchased half of Magdall's original homestead contacted the Helena General Land Office and claimed that the additional entry was invalid because it contained a spring needed for public watering purposes. Taking matters into his own hands, this same neighbor fenced the spring, cut Magdall's fences, and turned sixty head of cattle loose on the tract.

In July the Blaine County Attorney wrote the General Land Office and informed them that he and the Sheriff had met with Magdall and visited the spring. He went on to say that they, "did not feel that the water would have been there had Magdall not developed the well," and described other water sources that the neighbor had available for his cattle.

In August the General Land Office notified Magdall that everything in his filing appeared in order, except that he had failed to "make a showing" that there were no public waters on the lands added during the latest shuffle of legal descriptions.

An apparently confused Magdall responded in September, "if there are any forms please send it to me and I'll do the rest." He went on to admonish them that the Missouri River was, "certainly bigger than a spring or water hole and the lots (irregular shaped tracts of land smaller or larger than the normal legal subdivision) of my filing cannot control the using of it by the public. There are hundreds of farms along side and yet I don't know a case where a restriction was used." Regarding the spring, he pointed out that he'd developed it sixteen years previously, and that the one neighbor was the only one in all those years to question the public's right to use it. He went on to say that the neighbor had, "become of my enemy trying under false intentions yet malicious egotism claiming it for "open hole" but keeping it for himself."

In October Magdall satisfied the deficiency in his filing by providing the General Land Office with a notarized affidavit that stated, "That there are no springs or water holes," or, "hot springs or springs the waters of which possess curative properties," on the most recently described entry.

In February of 1932, the neighbor must have decided that his protest wasn't receiving enough attention, because he wrote the Washington headquarters of the General Land Office questioning the validity of Magdall's entry since the spring was needed for public watering purposes.

The Washington General Land Office responded that an investigation had been ordered, but that no results had been received.

In March the neighbor again wrote Washington, this time alleging that the spring had been available for public use for seventeen years. He also stated that what the Blaine County Attorney and others said in support of Magdall was "untrue." In this correspondence, however, the neighbor revealed what was at the root of his protest. He wrote "For past three years Montana was very dry and our Community reservoir dried out. Some of the stockmen been hauling water for their stock. My reservoir dried out in June. The only water I could have is that spring. So instead to see my cattle dying from want of water, I turned them on Government land that adjoined the land ... So my cattle got drinking water at the spring." The neighbor went on to claim that there was enough water at the spring for one hundred head of cattle. He concluded the letter, "I am hauling my drinking water twenty-two miles both way just because this man won't let me go to this spring."

In April the General Land Office requested the U.S. Geological Survey to examine the spring and the surrounding country and to provide an opinion on the nature of the spring that Magdall had developed.

In July another cloud appeared on Magdall's horizon. Eight of his neighbors petitioned the General Land Office to designate a half-mile wide stock-driveway down Coal Coulee (which drains into the Missouri at river mile 104.2 left). They claimed that they needed access to water and to a ford at the mouth of Coal Coulee. They needed access to the ford so that they could get their livestock south to the town of Winifred and the Milwaukee Railroad. In order to make the stock-driveway possible, they wanted Magdall to be denied the opportunity to perfect his additional stock-raising homestead entry along the river bottom lands. This should have involved only a half-mile of Magdall's river frontage, but in legal descriptions accompanying the petition 1.5 miles of the 2.1 miles of river frontage embraced by Magdall's entry would be affected.

In August the General Land Office approved a report that discounted the claims that Magdall's spring qualified as public water. It documented that Magdall had developed it from a seep, that there wasn't much water, and that what water there was poor quality. However, the report went on to give credence to the stock-driveway petition, and it raised the question of whether Magdall used "fraud and deception" in filing on the river lands rather than on available public lands contiguous to his original homestead.

In responding to the allegations, Magdall again stated that the available lands contiguous to his original homestead were worthless. With regard to the stock-driveway, he testified that there was a road to a ford $2^1/_2$ miles above (at river mile 100.5) his stock-raising homestead, that there was a ferry at the Judith Landing area, and that the Ragland Bench community had built a road to the Judith Ferry. He also pointed out that he wasn't aware of any cattle ever having been driven down Coal Coulee.

In September, the Washington Office of the U.S. Geological Survey recommended that the spring protest be dismissed.

Soon after, the Commissioner of the General Land Office forwarded the stock-driveway petition to the Secretary of the Interior with a favorable recommendation.

In October, the Chief of the Field Division of the Helena General Land Office was ordered to investigate the lands contiguous to Magdall's original homestead. The propriety of the river-side entry was still in question. On the bright side, the spring protest was officially dismissed.

Shortly thereafter, the field examiner submitted a report to the Commissioner that supported Magdall. It said that the contiguous lands were indeed useless, that the river bottom was capable of supporting livestock or growing crops like corn, and that Magdall had made a number of improvements on the additional stock-raising homestead entry. This report also recommended the stock-driveway, but went on to suggest that Magdall be allowed to select additional bottom lands down river from the withdrawn corridor as a sort of reimbursement for his loss.

Near the end of December of 1932, the case involving the allegations against Magdall was closed. Furthermore, since his additional stock-raising homestead entry was valid and made in good faith, he would not have to modify the selection.

The neighbor who'd raised the issue about the spring continued to cause Magdall problems. In September of 1934, a frustrated Magdall wrote Senator Burton K. Wheeler and charged that the man's cattle kept breaking down his fences and eating his pasture. "What's a man to do?" he asked. However, since trespass actions fell under State law, neither Senator Wheeler nor the General Land Office could help. In January of 1936 drought conditions and a poor financial situation caused Magdall to petition the General Land Office for an eighteen month extension to make final proof. A July response was that there was no law providing for extensions, and that he had thirty days to file final proof or risk having his homestead entry canceled.

In September of 1936, Magdall managed to file his final proof. Four days afterwards he was informed that the special agent of the General Land Office Division of Investigations had protested the final proof because, "it being alleged that said entry has not been initiated, or maintained, in accordance with the law authorizing such entries."

Two years later the investigation was complete and Magdall received his final certificate. Then on May 24, 1939, he received patent to the 320 acres he'd struggled so long for.

John Magdall was sixty-three years old the year he received final patent to his river bottom lands. He was also troubled by rheumatism. Improvements at the time included eighteen acres cleared of sagebrush and rocks, broken, and planted to corn and oats. The year he filed final proof (1936) grasshoppers got the entire crop.

In 1931 he'd built a 12' x 12' log dugout cabin. In 1932 he'd added a 20' x 20' log barn and about two miles of barbed wire fence. In 1935 he'd built an 18' x 24' log house, added an 8' high by 30' in diameter pole corral to the barn, and dug a 16' deep well. When his final proof was investigated in 1938, the well had been deepened to thirty feet.

LEWIS & CLARK CAMP OF MAY 27, 1805

RIVER MILE 103.3 RIGHT

The Corps of Discovery camped here after making 10.9 miles during the day.

[Lewis - Monday, May 27th]

We employed the chord most of the day; the river becomes more rappid and is intercepted by shoals and a greater number of rocky points at the mouths of the little gulies than we experienced yesterday. the bluffs are very high steep rugged, containing considerable quantities of stone and border the river closely on both sides; once perhaps in the course of several miles there will be a few acres of tolerably level land in which two or thre impoverished cottonwood trees will be seen. great quantities of stone also lye in the river and garnish it's borders, which appears to have tumbled from the bluffs where the rains had washed away the sand and clay in which they were imbeded. the bluffs are composed of irregular tho' horizontal stratas of yellow and brown or black clay, brown and yellowish white sand, of soft yellowish white sandstone and a hard dark brown freestone, also of large round kidney formed and irregular seperate masses of a hard black Iron stone, which is imbeded in the Clay and sand. some little pine spruce and dwarf cedar on the hills. some coal or carbonated wood still makes it's appearance in these bluffs, pumicestone and birnt hills it's concommutants also are seen. the salts and quarts are seen but not in such abundance. the country more broken and barren than yesterday if possible. about midday it was warm to this the high bluffs and narrow channel of the river no doubt contributed greatly.

This evening we encamped, for the benefit of wood, near two dead toped cottonwood trees on the Lard side; the dead limbs which had fallen from these trees furnished us with a scanty supply only, and more was not to be obtained in the neighbourhood.

CHIMNEY BEND

RIVER MILE 108 RIGHT

The area around Chimney Bend is beautiful badlands topography, the rocks being the Claggett Formation and the Judith River Formation. On the right side of the river the normally horizontal sedimentary rocks have been folded and faulted, adding to the complexity of the geology of this area.

In February 1980, twenty-seven Rocky Mountain Bighorn Sheep were introduced into this area to replace the indigenous Audubon Bighorn Sheep that were hunted to extinction early in the twentieth century. The introduction has been successful and today Bighorns are commonly seen in this area.

From *Floating on the Missouri*, Schultz; refer to narrative at river mile 1.2 Left for background.

The Missouri River badlands, viewed from river mile 103 right, about two miles below the Stafford Ferry, and a mile below Dauphin Rapids. During the steamboat years, this area would have been a beehive of activity, as boats lined up to fight their was through Dauphin Rapids.

Below these rapids (Dauphin) the hills are lower, the valley wider, the pine groves on the slopes more frequent. Five miles farther down we passed a rock chimney, sole remnant of a once-comfortable woodhawk's cabin. I remembered taking refuge in it once, on a trip up the river on the ice. It was bitterly cold, night was coming on, the horses were tired, and we were looking for a sheltered place to camp when we sighted the cabin. No one was at home, but the latch string hung out, and we took possession of it after unharnessing the horses and picketing them. My half-blood companion built a roaring fire in the broad fireplace and we had some meat roasting, the coffee pot boiling, in short order. Many and many a time since I have thought of the unique chair which stood in front of the hearth. The framework was of large pine poles, over which had been stretched a green buffalo hide, dark and glossy, and heavy furred, the head, where the hair was longest and thickest, forming the seat, the rest of it the long, sloping back. Used day after day as the hide dried, it had shrunk here and given away there, until when it finally set, it fitted every curve of one's body. It was the most comfortable chair I ever sat in, and I determined to make one like it as soon as I got back to our trading post. But one thing or another always prevented, and at last the buffalo were exterminated, and then there was no more of the required material to be had.

WILSON HOMESTEAD

RIVER MILES 109.8 TO 111.2 LEFT

A stone-faced dugout at the base of the river bluff documents the former presence of a woodhawk or other long forgotten early pioneer. But it was 1923 before the bottom was homesteaded.

In January of 1923, twenty-one year old Major B. Wilson filed on 156 acres here. Prior to filing, he and his brothers visited the bottom and searched for survey markers to help them describe the land. Snow hampered their efforts and when they did find a "section corner," they misinterpreted it. When he moved to the bottom the following May, he discovered his error. He had to file an amendment to his homestead entry.

That first year he built a house, barn, corral and two miles of fence. He also planted twenty-five acres of corn and twenty-three acres of oats. Over the next three years he continued to plant between twenty-five and thirty acres of corn yearly for fodder.

In 1926, Mary Robertson Hagood filed an application for oil and gas exploration on lands that included Wilson's homestead. This application brought to light the fact that Wilson had been allowed to make his homestead entry without reserving the minerals to the United States.

In November of 1926, Wilson was supposedly served notice that he had thirty days to submit an oil and gas waiver or have his homestead entry canceled. He failed to do so, and in January of 1927 his homestead entry was canceled.

Apparently, the first Wilson knew of the oil and gas conflict was when he received notice of the homestead entry cancellation.

In March he signed the required waiver and submitted testimony, corroborated by the local postmaster, that he had never received the original notice. Since his homestead entry had been canceled, he also filed an additional homestead entry on the same lands.

In November of 1928, the General Land Office accepted Wilson's testimony and reinstated his original homestead entry. However, in the same correspondence, they gave him thirty days to file notice of his intention to submit final proof, or again have his entry canceled.

Wilson complied, and by June of 1929 he had patent to the land.

By the time of final proof, Wilson had a wife and child. In 1927 he'd switched from raising corn to raising rye, which he used for horse pasture. In 1928 he ran one hundred head of sheep on the pasture.

CABIN RAPIDS

River Mile 113.5 Right

From *Floating on the Missouri,* Schultz; refer to narrative at river mile 1.2 left for background.

Just above them (Bird Rapids) on the south side there is a fine grove of cottonwoods, and as the wind was blowing unpleasantly hard, bringing with it occasional squalls of rain, we decided to camp in their shelter.

We tied up, and digging a trail to the top of the bank with a pickax, set out to find a clear place among the willows and buck brush for the tent. Not twenty yards from the shore five whitetail deer broke cover and ran for the hills, on their way starting four more, which ran up the valley. There was no grassy place in the timber, and upon coming to its outer edge we saw something which made us think that we did not care to camp there after all. In the center of the wide flat just above was a deserted woodhawk's cabin, windowless and doorless, and in front of it stood two men watching the deer which had run up that way. Then they turned and looked in our direction long and carefully. With my glass I could see that their faces were covered with beard and that beside their rifles, they each had two revolvers at their belts.

Before leaving Fort Benton I had heard that a certain desperado named Larson, who had escaped from the Canadian mounted police and from the Montana authorities, was in hiding somewhere on the river. At the Judith it was claimed that he had been seen near Cow Island. Also, it was surmised that the Kid Curry gang, murderers and robbers of the Great Northern express car, were still hiding somewhere in these badlands.

Now Sah-ne-to knew nothing of this, as she does not understand English, and I had thought best to say nothing about it; but as soon as she saw the men near the deserted cabin, their horses picketed nearby, her suspicions were aroused. "Surely," she said, "these men are not of good heart; let us go on."

And we went. They saw us and hurried toward their horses; we rushed to the boat and pulled across to the north side, where the channel is, and shot down through the rapids. Just below them, at the bend, cut coulees and a high bluff precluded any possibility of their following us on horseback if they felt so inclined, but we saw no more of them. Likely they had been badly scared. I hoisted a part of the sail and we fairly flew for about four miles before the fierce wind, landing finally on Sturgeon Island for the night.

It's not known when the deserted woodhawk's cabin that Schultz refers to was built. It appears on Missouri River Commission maps that were drawn from 1890 surveys. The name "Cabin Rapids" probably resulted from its presence, which would date it well back into the steamboat era. The existing buildings, however, do not date to that period, although one barn appears to have been built with some used logs.

The land finally became the homestead of Ervin L. Smith. He filed on 149 acres here in July of 1922. By mid-August he had established his residence. The records indicate that his brother, Arnold, lived here with him. Ervin was native born, and at the time of entry he was twenty-five years old and a bachelor.

In 1923 the Smiths planted twenty acres of corn that yielded six hundred bushels. They doubled the acreage in 1924, and harvested two hundred bushels. By 1925 they had fifty acres in corn, but got only 150 bushels. In 1926 they converted the cultivated ground to alfalfa and pastured hogs on it.

Ervin Smith filed proof and received final certificate in December of 1927. At the time he had a 20' x 30' house, a 100' x 100' cattle shed, and two log barns, one 16' x 20' and the other 18' x 20'. In addition, he had a couple of root cellars, an ice house, and a half mile of three wire fence. At some point in time he added a unique willow corral or windbreak to the cattle shed.

The General Land Office had allowed Smith to file his entry without reserving the oil and gas to the United States as required by a law of July 17, 1914. They also issued him final certificate with the same error. This conflict, plus the fact that he filed final proof two years late, delayed his receiving patent to the land. He finally signed a waiver on the minerals, and they issued him patent on June 27, 1929.

It's not known when the deserted woodhawk's cabin that Schultz refers to was built. It appears on Missouri River Commission maps that were drawn from 1890 surveys. The name "Cabin Rapids" probably resulted from its presence, which would date it to the steamboat era. The existing buildings, however, do not date to that period, although one barn appears to have been built with some used logs. The remaining structures include a very unique willow corral or wind-break.

Several attempts were made to settle this bottom. A homestead entry was made in June of 1919, only to be relinquished in May of 1920. Walter Heldt made a desert land entry here in March of 1921, but it was relinquished in July of 1922. Ervin L. Smith purchased the relinquishment. Smith credits Heldt with building the cabins.

When asked why he thought Heldt sold out, Smith replied that times were hard. You'd put in a little garden and eat a lot of jack rabbits and sage hens. People along the river always had a fishing set line in the water. You couldn't sell any-thing, so there was no way to make a buck.

Ervin Smith was raised in the Ozarks in the Little Osage River country. At the age of eleven, he frequently played hooky from school. His teacher reacted by saying, "If I wasn't interested in books any more than you are, I think I'd just stay home." He replied, "I think I will!" His dad responded by putting him to work picking corn and "working the heck out of me."

It wasn't long before Ervin thought, "To heck with this." One night after the family had fallen to sleep, he slipped out of the house, walked eleven miles to the railroad siding at Osceola, Missouri, waited in a box car, hopped the first freight past, and ended up in Kansas City some eighty miles later.

Ervin recalls being amazed by all the lights of Kansas City - he'd never seen such a thing. He was penniless, but he shortly encountered a lady who got him a job as a well diggers assistant and put him up in a spare room.

Ervin Smith arrived in the Central Montana area around 1917. When he filed on the 149 acre river side homestead in August of 1922, he was twenty-five years old and a bachelor.

One of the first things he did was plow up twenty acres of sage brush. The following spring the broken ground was planted with corn. He didn't stick around to watch the crop because he had a job on a ranch up on top. When he did return, he was amazed at the crop, which proved to be about 600 bushel. He picked the corn and stored it in the cabins, which he converted to feeders. He bought some sows, and turned them loose on the place. Then he went back to his job as a ranch hand.

When he returned to the river later that fall, the sows had produced pigs that would probably make up two train car loads. Not having seen anyone for most of the summer, they were wild as could be. Ervin recalls one old sow jumping in the river and swimming to the other side. He hid, and as soon as she thought he was gone, she swam back. He gathered the pigs and trailed them on horse back to a farm up on top, turning them loose on some uncut wheat. When asked about trailing pigs on horse back, Ervin laughingly recalls that if you snapped them with your rope they'd jump about twenty feet.

A buyer contacted Ervin about the pigs, and they weighed several of them before negotiating the price. Ervin delivered them to the rail head at Winifred, arriving just at dark. The pigs were a tall breed, but lean. A fellow approached Ervin and asked what they would weigh. Ervin told him and the guy bet Ervin $10 he was wrong. Another fellow chimed in that he'd take $10 of that bet. Ervin of course took their money - when dealing with Ervin Smith, gambler beware.

The following year, twice the amount of acreage was planted to corn, but the yield was only a third of the previous year. In 1925, fifty acres was planted, but the yield was down even more to 150 bushels. In 1926, the cultivated ground was converted to alfalfa.

Ervin filed final proof and received final certificate in December of 1927. However, the General Land Office had allowed him to file his entry without reserving the oil and gas to the United States as required by a law of July 17, 1914. They also issued him final certificate with the same error. This conflict delayed his receiving patent until he signed a waiver on the minerals. He finally did, and he received patent on June 27, 1929. The delay taught Ervin Smith a lesson - in later years, he bought, sold or traded a lot of land, and he usually ended up with the mineral rights. Leases on those mineral rights have served him well during his retirement.

Ervin never planned to "camp" along the river, "it just wasn't the place to be in those days." He sold out to a neighbor, Glenn Allison, who had homesteaded over on Woodhawk and had an "additional" up on the hill nearby.

After leaving the river, Ervin tried wheat farming. The first year he got hailed out, the second year he "dried out." He told his wife he'd never set himself on a tractor again, and he never did. This was cattle country.

Over the years, Ervin would do a lot of horse trading, and his dealings took him over quite a bit of the Breaks country. As a result, he knew a lot of the people covered in this History Digest. When asked if the river presented a barrier to north/south travel, he replied that people knew where the fords were. However, he recalled one time helping the Sanfords gather horses north of the river. When he crossed, the water wasn't even to his horses shoulders. After a rather unsuccessful and somewhat brutal day of running horses, Ervin returned to the river crossing and spurred his horse in. "Gee whiz! The horse hit the water and he tipped over backwards walking on his hind legs." George Middleton lived on the other side, and Ervin hollered to get his attention. George appeared with a lantern, and Ervin asked what was wrong with the river, was he on the crossing? Middleton replied that he was right close to it, but that they had turned water loose at the dam in Great Falls and the river had raised about three feet.

One time Ervin accompanied a couple loads of horses to Des Moines, Iowa. After he had them delivered he decided, "I'm going to see a little of this old world." He hopped a freight (his favorite means of travel) to Oklahoma City, bummed around there for awhile, and then got a job driving a car to Los Angeles. In Los Angeles, he got a job as a movie extra. This line of work eventually brought him to the Jackson Hole, Wyoming area with a movie about the Oregon Trail.

One scene in the movie called for circled wagons under Indian attack. Several retakes were required, and apparently Ervin and a buddy got tired of it. They loaded sand and dirt in front of their blank cartridges and waited for the action. The Indians were wearing only breechcloths, and the stunt stung their legs so bad that they quit. The director was furious. Ervin had been a big winner in a poker game (one of his favorite forms of entertainment), so he drew his wages, hopped a freight to Great Falls, bought a Model A Ford, and returned home.

Ervin Smith believed in growing grass. Sagebrush was something that should be plowed, burned or sprayed. Where only one cow could survive in sagebrush, four could live when it was gone. He was also a terror on the coulees, and a lot of pine and juniper thickets were converted to grass with a match from his hands.

His exploits were many, and included, in addition to all of the foregoing, making whiskey and producing rodeos. One time he was thrown when his horse tripped on a badger hole. He broke his shoulder blade, collar bone and nose. The injuries were so severe that when he tried to remount he "faded away." His brother, Arnold, started to take him to Lewistown some seventy-five miles away in a Model T, but the road was so rutted and the jarring so bad that he could feel the broken bones grating against one another. Returning home, he had his wife get down the "doctor book." She made bandages from bed sheets, and bound him up proper. He never did go to a doctor because she did a good job. He healed up quickly.

During one of his trips into the Breaks, Ervin was visiting with Jim Kipp, who confided in him that someday they'd make a park "out of this whole country down here."

LEWIS & CLARK CAMP OF MAY 26,1805

RIVER MILE 114.2 RIGHT

The Corps of Discovery made 18.7 miles before they camped just above the head of today's Bird Rapids.

[Lewis - Sunday, May 26th]

Set out at an early hour and proceeded principally by the toe line, using the oars mearly to pass the river in order to take advantage of the shores. scarcely any bottoms to the river; the hills high and juting in on both sides, to the river in many places. the stone tumbleing from these clifts and brought down by the rivulets as mentioned yesterday became more troublesome today ... Capt. Clark walked on shore this morning and ascended to the summit of the river hills he informed me on his return that he had seen mountains on both sides of the river runing nearly parralel with it and at no great distance; also an irregular range of mountains on lard about 50 Mls distant; the extremities of which boar W. and N. W. from his station.

... scarcely any timber to be seen except the few scattering pine and spruce which crown the high hills, or in some instances grow along their sides. In the after part of the day I also walked out and ascended the river hills which I found sufficiently fortiegueing ... on my return to the river I passed a creek about 20 yds wide (today's Bullwhacker Creek) near it's entrance it had a handsome little stream of runing water; in this creek I saw several softshelled Turtles which were the first that have been seen this season; this I believe proceeded reather from the season than from their non existence in the portion of the river from the Mandans hither. on the Stard shore I killed a fat buffaloe which was very acceptable to us at this moment; the party came up to me later in the evening and encamped for the night on the Lard side; it was after Dark before we finished butchering the buffaloe, and on my return to camp I trod within [a] few inches of a rattle snake but being in motion I passed before he could probably put himself in a striking attitude and fortunately escaped his bite, I struck about with my espontoon being directed in some measure by his nois untill I killed him.

Our hunters had killed two of the Bighorned Anamals since I had left them. we also passed another creek (today's Cow Creek) a few miles from Turtle Creek on the Stard 30 Yds in width which also had runing water bed rockey. (we called it Windsor Cr.) late this evening we passed a very bad rappid which reached quite across the river, (water deep channel narrow graves &c on each side); the party had considerable difficulty in ascending it altho' they doubled their crews and used both the rope and pole. while they were passing this rappid a female Elk and it's fawn swam down through the waves which ran very high, hence the name of Elk rappids which they instantly gave this place, these are the most considerable rappids which we have yet seen on the missouri and in short the only place there has appeared to be a suddon decent. opposite to these rappids there is a high bluff and a little above on Lard a small cottonwood bottom in which we found sufficient timber for our fires and encampment ... This is truly a desert barren country ... we have continued every day to pass more or less old stick lodges of the Indians in the timbered points, there are two even in this little bottom where we lye.

This proved to be a memorable day for the Captains. During the morning Captain Clark climbed to a high point along the bluffs to the left and saw the Rocky Mountains for the first time. Refer to river mile 122.3 left for his record of this experience.

MIDDLETON HOMESTEAD

RIVER MILES 116.0 TO 116.8 RIGHT

George Middleton was born in Lead, South Dakota, sometime around 1880. While still quite young, the family was attacked by Indians. The parents hid George and his older brother in a wood box behind their stove. Both parents were killed in the ensuing fight, but the Indians didn't find the two boys. George remembered staying in the house several days before someone found them.

The older brother remembered the name of a relative that lived in the Bears Paw Mountains in Montana, and the boys were sent there. The relative turned out to be quite a harsh man who worked the boys very hard. As soon as he was able, the older brother left, never to be heard of by George again. Still a youth, George had to stay with this relative. He remembered being required to ride every day, regardless of the weather. In later years, he attributed a severe case of arthritis to this treatment.

As soon as he was old enough, George struck out on his own. He came to the Breaks during the fall of 1913, pitched a tent on the north side of the river, and waited for winter. As soon as the river froze solid enough, he crossed on the ice and established himself at this location. A single man, he lived in a dug-out until August of 1918 when he completed a 15' x 16' log house.

Friends remember that he kept the house quite dark. His stove sat on the dirt floor. His bunk consisted of a foot deep mat of horse hair with an old feather bed and canvas cover. A hollow cow horn stuck in a crack between two logs served as a very convenient urinal.

Neighbors remember him as being a frugal man. His lifestyle was rather primitive in this isolated location. He lived pretty much off of the land and river, his main staple being beans. A friend remembers him talking about the wild game he ate. "He said porcupine is "very" good. He said it tasted just like pork. He said he even tried beaver, which wasn't too good. He told of eating prairie dogs, which weren't too bad, and of "borrowing" a few chickens now and then. He ate a lot of fish which he caught from the river."

Another friend remembers having a meal of boiled venison with George one time, "George said he had taken the deer without using a cartridge. A coyote drove the deer out on river ice and killed it. George took the deer away from him."

The township was surveyed in 1916, and the plat map was approved in 1917. George filed a homestead entry in January of 1919. In 1919 he planted five acres of corn and potatoes, but, "harvested nothing." In 1920 he farmed ten acres of clover hay. In 1921 he added ten acres of rye to his crop land. He kept a few cows and quite a few horses.

From what people have said, George was very good with horses. Besides his own, he broke horses for other people. He told how he earned $50 once for riding an unbroken horse to Havre and back, about a 160 mile trip.

He was also very good with leather. He used to cure his own hides and tan them for leather. He then braided reins and bridles and such.

George filed final proof on the homestead in May of 1921. However, his final certificate was delayed until February of 1922 when the General Land Office discovered that his entry had been on 182 acres rather than the allowed 160 acres. A twenty-two acre lot on the eastern edge of his spread, the one containing his house, was eliminated from the entry. He received patent in March of 1925. Besides his house, he had a 14' x 16' log barn, a pole corral, and a "cave" (root cellar) at the time of proof.

George never married. He shared with a friend, "how he came pretty near to marrying once, but when he found out the "lady" already had twelve children he decided against it! He said he could hardly take care of himself let alone all those kids."

George is fondly remembered for passing out little gems of knowledge. "I quit taking baths years ago because water weakens you." "I quit eating lima beans because lime is bad for your system." When visiting a neighbor and someone started to sweep the floor, he'd hastily put on his cap, "because the dust will get in your hair." In about 1943 inflation had hit him, "No matter how I save, it costs me $10 a year to live." "War time cartridges are no good. It took three shots to get a deer."

George never learned to drive a motor vehicle. He rode horseback every where he went, although he's remembered pushing a two-wheel cart down a high ridge or "hogs back" to his place. When he could no longer get on a horse because of his arthritis, he sold the place to a rancher "up on top" and moved to a house in Winifred.

A stove accident in Winifred burned him badly, and he was forced to spend time in the Lewistown hospital. He liked it so well, they had a hard time getting rid of him. After that, he stayed in Lewistown.

He never really liked town life. He said he loved his old life and the river, and when asked if he was ever lonesome or bored down there, he answered, "No. There was always something new and different every day. The scenery was beautiful, a lot of wildlife passed by and the river was just a little different each day."

JOHN ERVIN

River Miles 121.2 to 123.0 Left

John Ervin was born in Texas, and as far as he knew, he was an orphan. He wasn't even sure if John Ervin was his real name or one that had just been given to him. Others had trouble with his name too, and it's recorded as Erwin, Irwin, and Irvine.

John's education is another mystery. Some say he claimed to have a second grade education. He confided to at least one friend that he'd lived with a sheep herder for awhile to get some education, but as soon as he learned his ABCs he left because he then knew as much as his teacher. During these early years, he had to wrangle horses to pay for his board. He was on his own and working as a cowboy when he was twelve, and he received $6 a month for his work on the range.

He spent most of his pay for ammunition so that he could learn how to shoot a revolver. The attitude in Texas at the time was that you shouldn't pack a gun unless you could shoot six bottles off of six continuous posts while riding a horse on a dead run.

He made two cattle drives from Texas to Montana. The notorious "Billy the Kid" worked on the same ranch, and made one of those drives with him. After the second drive, John stayed in Montana, and finally settled on the bottom land around the mouth of Bullwhacker Creek. He was well established in the area before the turn of the century.

Montana was spared much of the conflict that occurred between cattle men and sheep men in other parts of the country. Sheep were seen as a good way to get a start - they didn't require so much investment, and they yielded two crops a year, wool in the spring and lambs in the fall. John Ervin proved to be the exception to cow man, sheep man relations.

During the late 1890s he was running cattle along the southwest fork of Cow Creek. A sheep man by the name of Fred Garber herded his flock across John's range, and little or no grass remained after their passage. John warned him that it better not ever happen again. The next year, following an absence of some time, John returned to his place, and one of the first sounds he heard was the tinkle of a sheep bell. He went into his cabin, got his saddle gun, and that was the end of Fred Garber. The coroner found two bullet holes in the sheep man; one through the skull after entering at the center of his forehead, the other through the torso after entering at the back of the right hip and ricocheting up and out of his chest.

Ervin turned himself in for the killing at Chinook on December 27th of 1899, saying he had shot the man in self defense. A coroner's jury was impaneled, and the judge came through Chinook on January 2, 1900. John was charged with murder, and he pleaded not guilty. The charge was reduced to assault and battery with a deadly weapon with malice aforethought. Ervin again pleaded not guilty to the reduced charge. Bail was set at $2,000, and January 12th was set for a preliminary hearing. Four cattlemen signed the bonds and secured his release. Interest in the case was high, because the area around Chinook was primarily sheep country.

At the January 12th hearing, Ervin was bound over to appear in District Court in Fort Benton on the assault and battery with a deadly weapon charge. Bail was again set at $2,000, and bond was again secured.

In District Court on February 9th, Ervin was arraigned on the charges and trial date was set for February 20th. Names for jury service were also drawn, and in this case, forty-two names were drawn rather than thirty which was normal.

It took all afternoon and evening of the first day of the trial to secure a jury, and that was only accomplished after an additional six names were drawn. The first witness to testify was J. A. "Canada Jim" Potter. He said that he was at Ervin's cabin the day of the shooting and saw Garber, the herder, fire the first shot. He said there were other shots, but he could not say who fired them. He admitted that the shooting was done in plain view from where he stood and not far away. He saw Garber start toward his cabin (sheep herders wagon), which was but a few hundred feet away, and then he went home, returning later.

Garber's employer, Ed Bentel, testified regarding the "wereabouts" of the band of sheep Garber was herding. The Chinook coroner testified regarding facts bought out at the hearing. And, Dr. Hopkins was examined regarding Garber's wounds.

The case went to the jury on February 28th, and fourteen hours later they came back into court reporting that they were "unable to agree." Sixty-four days after he turned himself in, John Ervin was freed by the hung jury. At the outcome of the trial, the *Chinook Opinion* had some comment about the jury make up - only four of the jurors were from the area around Chinook, the rest were from Fort Benton, Highwood, Warrick and Havre.

It's not known when John settled here, but the *Chinook Opinion* identified the mouth of Bullwhacker as his home when reporting on the Garber shooting. A neighbor who arrived in the area in 1915 recalls that he was already well established. He raised good Percherons, and he had 150 of the large draft horses by this time. He also had about twenty-five head of cattle.

John built a two room log cabin on the west side of Bullwhacker Creek a short distance off the Missouri. He lived there by himself, and he preferred to be left strictly alone. He was never without a gun, and it's said that he kept it within reach even when he slept. He seemed to be always on guard, as if he was afraid of something.

He supposedly had two notches on his gun, both earned here in Montana. One was for the sheep herder, and the other was for a man he caught stealing his horses. One time when he was drinking, he boasted to a friend that he'd been involved in a bank robbery somewhere in northcentral Montana. John liked his whiskey, which he made himself. The "brew" also supplemented his income from time to time.

John has been described as a tall, lean man with a long mustache. It's said that his cowboy overalls were always clean. His day started at 2 a.m. Following a breakfast of sour dough hotcakes, he managed his livestock, including things like branding, alone. He was usually in bed by 7 p.m.

He received patent for his 320 acre river bottom homestead in May of 1929.

John couldn't swim. To cross the Missouri, he'd ride his horse out to where it was swimming, slide back over the saddle and grab the tail, and let the horse drag him across. One time his horse started floundering and he was almost drowned.

John Ervin sold out to John and George Sanford on November 15, 1930. John Sanford had homesteaded along the north side of the river some twenty-eight miles above here in 1926. Ervin moved to Hayes, a small community on the west side of the Little Rocky Mountains northeast of here. There he lived in a little cabin, alone, almost blind, and still afraid and on guard.

A new ranch headquarters was built east of Bullwhacker Creek, further back from the Missouri. Title eventually was transferred to the Gist family, and they farmed and ranched here until 1980. In 1980, the spread was purchased by the Bureau of Land Management as part of the management program for the Upper Missouri National Wild and Scenic River.

BULLWHACKER CREEK

RIVER MILE 123.5 RIGHT

Bullwhacker Creek is a major drainage that flows through an expansive area of wilderness badlands that provides extensive and interesting off-river hiking opportunities, as well as some old buildings and farming equipment. The area is interesting geologically, and provides opportunities to view spectacular folds and faults, to hunt for fossils, and to visit a diatreme, which is a rare type of igneous intrusion (diatremes are described in the geology chapter). From Bullwhacker Creek the site of Captain Clarks "first view of the Rocky Mountains" can be accessed (see accompanying map)

CAPTAIN CLARK VIEWS THE ROCKY MOUNTAINS

RIVER MILE 124.2 LEFT

It was common practice with the Lewis and Clark Expedition for one of the captains, and a couple of men, to walk ahead of the remainder of the expedition as it toiled with moving their boats upstream; the second captain remained on the river to manage affairs there. On a typical day the boats were able to travel about fifteen miles upriver, while the party on foot would easily log thirty miles. One of the

As the Lewis and Clark Expedition traveled up the Missouri in Montana, they were keenly interested in knowing what lay ahead. As the men struggled to paddle, pole, and pull the boats upriver, one of the captains usually hiked ahead, and frequently climbed to the bluffs above the river, to survey the land ahead, and hopefully to gain a view of the Rocky Mountains. On May 26th, 1805, Captain Clark hiked to a prominence above river mile 124.2 left, and had his first view of one of the ranges of the Montana Rockies - probably the Little Belt Mountains. Detail of Capt. Clark is from the Bob Scriver sculpture in Fort Benton.

objectives of the foot party was to gain a distant view up the Missouri and scout the route from high points above the river. On this particular day, Clark was on foot, traveling up today's Cow Creek to a high point on the Cow/Bullwhacker divide, where he first viewed the Rocky Mountains. His initial reaction is one of awe, followed by a realization of the challenge the mountains will pose in crossing them. Clark concluded his journal entry for the day with an admirable expression of optimism, a component of Clark's character which undoubtedly played a significant role in the success of the expedition.

[Clark - Sunday, May 26th, 1805]

I took one man and walked out this morning, and ascended the high countrey to view the mountains which I thought I saw yesterday, from the first sumit of the hill I could plainly see the Mountains on either side which I saw yesterday and at no great distance from me, those on the Stard Side is an errigular range, the two extremeties of which bore West and N. West from me (today's Bears Paw Mountains). those Mountains on the Lard Side appeared to be several detached Knobs or Mountains riseing from a level open countrey (today's Judith, North Moccasin and South Moccasin Mountains), at different distances from me, from South West to South East, on one the most S. Westerly (today's Big Snowy Mountains) of those Mountains there appeared to be snow. I crossed a Deep holler and assended a part of the plain elivated much higher than where I first viewed the above Mountains; from this point I beheld the Rocky Mountains for the first time with certainty

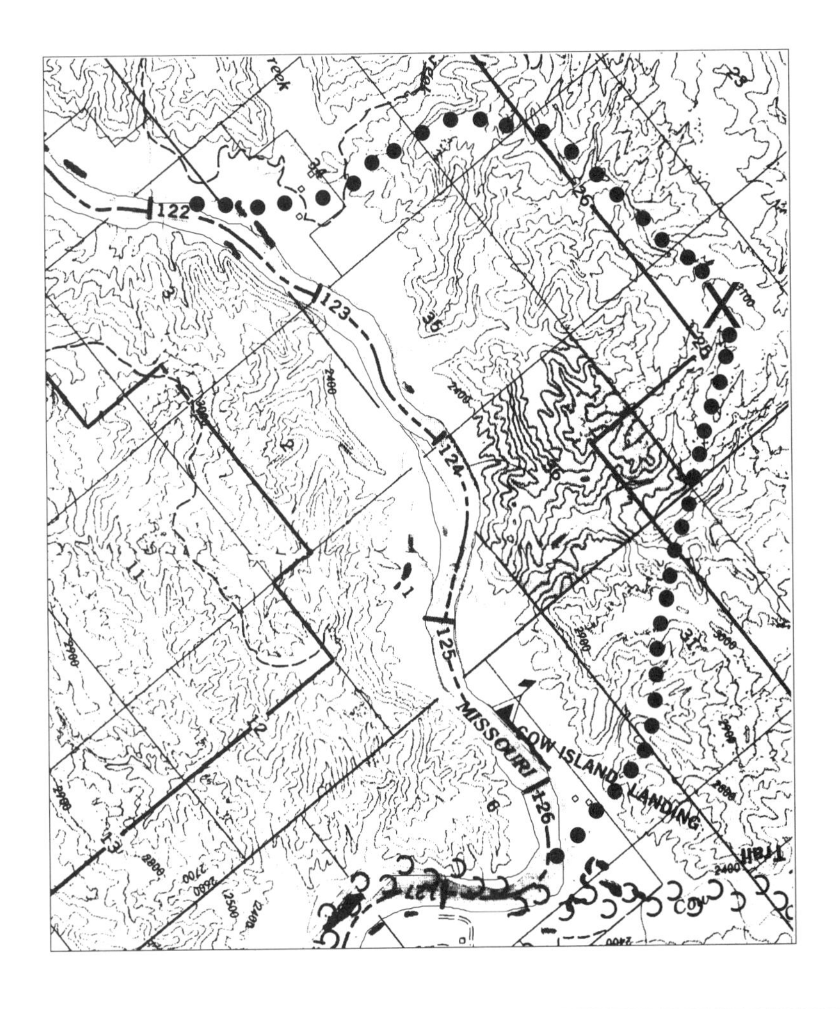

This detail from the BLM Floaters Guide map shows the route (dotted line) that Captain William Clark followed on the day he gained his first view of the Rocky Mountains. Clark hiked up Cow Creek (rm 126.5) to a high prominence (marked with an "X"), and then down Bullwhacker Creek (rm 122.3). The site is on public land and can be accessed by floaters. The terrain is rugged, but the views are rewarding.

(today's Little Belt Mountains, an outlier of the Rockies), I could only discover a fiew of the most elivated points above the horizon, the most remarkable of which by my pocket compas I found bore S. 60 W. those points of the rocky Mountain were covered with Snow and the Sun Shown on it in such a manner as to give me a most plain and satisfactory view. whilst I viewed those mountains I felt a secret pleasure in finding myself so near the head of the heretofore conceived boundless Missouri; but when I reflected on the difficulties which this snowey barrier would most probably throw in my way to the Pacific Ocean, and the sufferings and hardships of my self and party in them, it in some measure counter ballanced the joy I had felt in the first moments in which I gazed on them; but as I have always held it little Short of criminality to anticipate evils I will allow it to be a good comfortable road untill I am compelled to beleive otherwise.

MOUTH OF COW CREEK

River Mile 126.5 Left

The confluence area at the mouth of Cow Creek offers an excellent example of both prehistoric and historic use of the Missouri River Valley. Throughout time, people seem to have favored these parts of the valley that are broad and flat with good access to the prairie above. These factors combine beautifully at Cow Creek and are expressed in a rich and varied human record.

Archaeological investigations have just begun in the area, but important clues to understanding its prehistoric use are being found. Scattered remains of bones and stone tools are being found along the river banks and below the rim of the Missouri Valley. These remains indicate that as long as six thousand years ago, people here were making tools, camping, gathering vegetable and animal foods, and using the river corridor as a travel way.

For prehistoric people, the area around Cow Creek would have been a good place to make a living. The once extensive, woody bottoms and tributary coulees were rich in game and other wild foods. In the summer available water would have been of prime importance while shelter from cold winds and available fuel wood made the bottoms attractive in the winter.

The area had not changed much by May 26, 1805, when Lewis and Clark passed Cow Creek and recorded it as follows:

We came to the mouth of a creek on the north, 30 yeards wide, with some running water and a rocky bed, we called it Windsor's Creek, after one of the party.

After the "Corps of Discovery" passed Cow Creek it must have been passed by Maximilian, Bodmer and the parade of European and North American visitors who traveled up the Missouri River.

In 1863 there was an increase in historic activity at Cow Creek. Steamboats had been making their way upriver toward Cow Creek and what historian William E. Lass describes as "the short, 172-mile 'Rocky River' reaching from Cow Island to Benton." These boats had reached Fort Union at the confluence of the Missouri and Yellowstone in June of 1832, but it would be another thirty years before steamboats reached Cow Island.

In low water years like 1863, navigation often ended at Cow Island. This area wasn't necessarily as difficult an obstacle to navigation as was Dauphin Rapids or other problem areas further upriver, but Cow Creek provided a good off-loading area with excellent road access out of the Missouri Valley and across the prairie to Fort Benton. Freighting of the goods that were off-loaded from the steamboats was accomplished with wagons, usually drawn by teams of oxen. A typical freighter was composed of six oxen and three wagons, driven by two bullwhackers. Oxen were preferred over horses and mules because "they required less food and water, they didn't wander during storms, and the Indians didn't steal them because they couldn't ride them and they were too tough to eat". The road out of the breaks was steep in places, necessitating unhitching two of the three wagons, and then making two more trips for the remaining wagons.

The road from Cow Creek to Fort Benton had its actual beginning in 1864 and while the best available, was not an easy trek. As described by William Gladstone in 1864, it was "a very bad one and in ascending a very steep hill one of the wagons went over the precipice, draging four pairs of oxen with it. The tumble of 300 feet of course killed the oxen and I had hard work getting the wagon mended."

The exact amount of freight off-loaded at Cow Island varied from year to year depending on water levels in the Missouri. In 1866 most steamboats were able to navigate as far as Fort Benton into July, so little effort was needed to move goods from Cow Creek. But 1868 was a different story. Joel Overholser reports in the Fort Benton River Press, "At year end (1868) the Montana Post reported that 2,500 men, 3,000 teams and 20,000 oxen had been involved in freighting to Fort Benton."

Photograph of the Cow Island Landing in 1880, with a steamboat and an encampment in the background. Haynes Foundation Collection, Montana Historical Society.

While the amount of cargo off-loaded at Cow Creek varied, how it was treated once ashore was not. As soon as possible it was on the road to Fort Benton and the huge profits it would bring. Therefore, no warehouse or other storage facilities were constructed on the Cow Creek bottoms. The Army Corps of Engineers did attempt to improve the channel in the area in the 1870's, but virtually no remains of that effort can be seen today.

On September 23rd, 1877, a band of Nez Perce Indians, with Chief Joseph, crossed the Missouri River at Cow Island. General Sherman called the saga of the Nez Perce "the most extraordinary of Indian wars." Pressed into a fight by the rash actions of a few revengeful braves, some seven hundred-fifty "non-treaty" Nez Perces fought for their lives in two pitched battles in Idaho, then sought escape from the pursuing Army. Their circuitous route through four states, dictated by terrain and strategy, measured over 1,170 miles. From first to last, a warrior force never exceeding two hundred-fifty men fought twenty engagements with pursuing forces which totaled some two thousand soldiers plus uncounted civilian volunteer and support from Nez Perce enemies.

Joseph, chief of the Nez Perce Indians of Idaho. His tribe undoubtedly aided the Lewis and Clark Expedition more than any other, and in the years following the expedition, had a long history of good relations with whites. However, as the appetite for Indian land for white settlers increased, the pressure on the Nez Perce casued some of them to strike out against the flood of white settlers. This brought the wrath of the U.S. Army upon the entire tribe, and they chose to flee to Canada, a journey that took them across the Upper Missouri near Cow Island. Haynes Foundation Collection, Montana Historical Society.

The Nez Perce campaign, with its series of battles and skirmishes, yielded greater casualties than the Battle of Little Bighorn. About three hundred of the seven hundred-fifty fugitive Nez Perce men, women, and children died before reaching the Bears Paw Mountains, or shortly thereafter as prisoners.

The Nez Perce campaign was a "Freedom Flight," a life-or-death effort by peaceful people, demonstrably wronged, to escape from their violated homeland to seek distant lands in which they might again live their own lives. Their fighting was defensive, not aggressive. Their primary goal was to avoid conflict with the Army!

There is irony in the fate of the Nez Perce. In contrast to the behavior of some other tribes, their actions were exemplary. Their help to Lewis and Clark assured the success of the famed explorers. Fur traders admired the Nez Perce. They were superb warriors and horseman. They were the first Indians in the Pacific Northwest to request missionaries. When miners and ranchers invaded their homelands, they showed great patience despite growing abuses, while looking vainly to the Government for justice.

They left their Oregon and Idaho homeland in May, and with the U.S. Army in pursuit, made their way east to Yellowstone National Park and then north through their old hunting grounds in central Montana. The route was familiar to them. They followed traditional trails, which had long been a source of joy and sustenance. But the fond memories of hunting the buffalo, trading with old friends and visiting, were replaced by the reality of flight and conflict; their route now became a trail of sorrow.

The beleaguered Indians reached the Missouri River on Sunday, September 23, 1877. Some fity tons of steamboat freight at Cow Island Landing was being guarded by Sergeant William Moelchert, eleven soldiers and five civilians. The Nez Perce asked for supplies, and at first were refused. Eventually, Sergeant Moelchert and his troops gave them some of their own hardtack and bacon. It wasn't enough, and the Indians returned in force, this time taking what they wanted and burning the rest. They continued their flight up Cow Creek (rm 126.5 left), eventually camping six miles north of the Bears Paw Mountains where they were finally captured on October 5th. by Col. Miles, just forty-five miles short of their Canadian goal.

Chief Joseph's surrender speech is well know:

Tell General Howard I know his heart. What he told me before I have in my heart. I am tired of fighting. Our chiefs are killed. Looking Glass is dead. Toohoolhoolzote is dead. The old men are all dead. It is the young men who say yea or no. He who led the young men is dead. It is cold and we have no blankets. The little children are freezing to death. My people, some of them, have run away to the hills, and have no blankets, no food; no one knows where they are - perhaps freezing to death. I want to have time to look for my children and see how many I can find. Maybe I shall find them among the dead. Hear me my chiefs. I am tired; my heart is sick and sad. From where the sun now stands, I will fight no more forever.

As recounted by Joel Overholser, about twenty-nine volunteers rushed to Cow Island when it became obvious Joseph and his people were headed there. Overholser says:

They arrived at Cow Island the 24th (of September, 1877) to find that Sgt. Moelchert, eleven soldiers and five civilians had manned the rifel pits for two days ... The whites were unable to prevent burning of about fifty tons of freight.

James Kipp in his later years. Kipp was an important figure in the early days of the fur trade in Montana. He was sent by the American Fur Company to build the first fur trading post in Montana, Fort Piegan, at the mouth of the Marias River (river mile 22 left). His descendants settled in the Cow Creek area. Montana Historical Society photograph.

On the left is Joe Kipp, son of James Kipp who is pictured on the predeeding page. Joe was an Army scout at the Cow Island encounter with the Nez Perce, in 1877, and during the Baker Massacre against the Piegans on the Marias, in 1870. On the right is Joe Kipp's son, Jim, and grandson, Joe. Montana Historical Society photograph.

Sergeant William Moelchert left his own account of the fight with the fleeing Nez Perce; as he remembered the facts fifty years after they took place:

Things went along for a while quietly till we saw an indian coming between our breast-works and the foothills stripped naked when we know this means fight. Having previously destributed the ammunition and giving each man his place we were standing around and taking our supper as I jokingly remarked to the men that this might be their last sow belly and hard tack when without further warning they commenced to fire from the hills, the balls going in every direction between us.

Sgt. Moelchert goes on to describe a battle during which, "They charged us three times during the night through high willows, impossible to see anyone, and the burning of freight that included 500 sacks of bacon." The next day he and his men were relieved by Maj. Ilges and reinforcements from Fort Benton. Moelchert goes on to say:

Well, the Major looked over the whole thing and then sent for me and said to me, ''Sargeant, you have done very well to save yourself and men, it was impossible for you to save the freight."

Another perspective on the military activity with the Nez Perce is from Joseph Kipp, a long-time resident of the Cow Creek area and the great grandson and grandson of men who made names for themselves as pioneer traders and businessmen on the Upper Missouri River in Montana. Kipp relates the following story about his grandfather who was working as an army scout at Cow Creek:

He heard shooting and by the time he got to the river they were running around, so he jumped off and turned the mule loose. The only things he had of real value was a gun that he hid and a watch. He put the watch in his mouth and he went and laid in the driftwood where they couldn't see him. Then after the fighting was over he came out of the river and got his mule and then crossed.

Joseph Kipp lived on a farm homesteaded by his father, James Kipp just upstream from Cow Creek. The homestead immediately south of the mouth of Bull Creek and the Kipp place belonged to the Jones family, relations by marriage to the Kipps, so a large, extended family provided a backdrop for Joseph Kipp's childhood. Both families farmed the area and raised cattle. They depended on traveling salesmen on flat-bottomed boats for what they did not produce for themselves. According to Joe Kipp, life at Cow Creek was not dull, with amusements including cards, visits to and from other river valley dwellers and an occasional trip outside the valley to Zortman or Lewistown. Not everyone was suited to the isolated life along the river, as is illustrated by Kipp's Grandmother Jones, who only spent visits to the homestead, preferring instead the more gentile lifestyle in Lewistown.

IKE DeWEESE HOMESTEAD

River Miles 127.5 - 128.5 Right

Isaac "Ike" DeWeese was born in Kirkesville, Ohio, in February of 1889. His first try at homesteading was when he was eighteen years old. On December 17, 1907 he filed near Folsom, New Mexico. He relinquished that homestead on October 20, 1910.

The Jones homestead, at river mile 126.9 left, in the Missouri River badlands in the Cow Creek area. The Jones' were relatives of the Kipp family by marriage.

He settled on this 148 acre tract on August 1, 1915, prior to survey by the General Land Office. His name appears on the original township map, which was surveyed in 1916.

In 1916 he had eighteen acres in oats and alfalfa, and an additional five acres of sweet clover. He harvested fifteen tons of hay that year.

In 1917 he had eighteen acres in alfalfa, but before the crop was ready he was inducted into the Army. He reported to Fort George Wright, Washington, on June 22, 1917, and served in Battery A, 14th Field Artillery between July of 1917 and March of 1919.

Upon returning home, he finally filed his homestead entry papers on March 24, 1920. By 1921 he again had the land under cultivation, with fiteen acres in oats and a acres in sweet clover. The crop yielded five tons of hay.

In 1922 he had twenty acres in rye and five acres in sweet clover. The yield was again five tons of hay. In December of this year he finished proof and received his final certificate for patent.

Ike was a single man. In proving up his homestead he had constructed a 14' by 40' log house, an 18' by 20' log barn, a 16' by 16' store house, a 10' by 12' chicken house, a 16' by 20' shed, and a cave (root cellar).

On February 17, 1940, the entire homestead was returned to Federal ownership under the Bankhead-Jones Farm Tenant Act of 1937. Under terms of this Act, submarginal lands incapable of producing sufficient income for a family were purchased by the Government and the owners relocated. These actions were known as Land Utilization projects.

RUSSELL OPERATION and DRY ISLAND

River Miles 128.4 - 136.3 Left and River Miles 129.4 - 134.7 Right

Over a period of twenty-six years, Charles F. "Frank" and Estel Mary Russell homesteaded, bought, or inherited some 1,441 acres in nine separate tracts of land along the river. Uniquely, these lands lay along both sides of the river, and they also acquired an island. In the process of proving-up on the different tracts of land, they built three houses on the left side of the river, a cabin on the right side, purchased houses on each side of the river, and inherited a seventh place on the left side.

Charles was born in 1882 in Ellensburg, Washington. Estel was born in 1893 in Fourney, Texas. They met in 1910, probably near Zortman, Montana, where Charles was proving-upon a Desert Land Entry tract of land. Charles went by his middle name, Frank, possibly to avoid being confused with the cowboy artist Charlie Russell who was gaining so much fame about this time.

The river side story begins with Estel, who settled here on the left side of the river between miles 131.3 and 132.2 with her husband Bud Seacrist in September of 1914. Within a month they were building an 18' by 24' house, and the following summer she had a very good three acre garden under cultivation. The couple had a son, Clarence.

Bud Seacrist was shot and killed at a dance at the Kipp place above the mouth of Cow Creek. The murder was never investigated. The Blaine County sheriff insisted that the Kipps lived in Phillips County, which was out of his district and responsibility. The Phillips County sheriff refused to get involved, since he maintained that the incident occurred in Blaine County.

The year 1915 marked the beginning of a lot of activity on the north side of the river in this area. Just two miles down river from Estel's house, a coal fired electrical generating plant was under construction (see river mile 134.1 left). The following year it was completed, and Frank Russell was appointed superintendent of the operation.

Frank and Estel were married in 1917. By this time, Estel had thirty-five acres broken and in barley. Drought cost them the crop. The following year they planted the land with oats, and broke another twenty-five acres and seeded it to winter rye. Drought again took its toll.

In December of 1918, Estel filed a homestead entry on a total of 160 acres. Two months later she filed intention to make three year proof. Additional improvements at the time included a 12 foot by 14 foot bunkhouse and an 18' by 36' barn. Patent to the land was received in July of 1919.

The next land transaction was also Estel's. In November of 1920, she made an application to purchase a twenty-two acre isolated tract at the up river end of her property. She was successful, but it cost her $4.50 per acre.

The next move was Frank's. In March of 1921, he filed a homestead entry on 136 acres of river bottom land adjacent to Estel's tract. This extended their operation down river to mile 133.4. They had established residence there and built a 14' by 28' house the previous spring. By 1923 he had forty acres of the new place under cultivation, but drought took his crop that year and the next. In 1925, he harvested ten tons of rye hay. By the time he proved-up in 1926, he also had a 20' by 20' log barn, a 35' by 50' shed, a 16' by 16' hen house, two corrals and $2^{1}/_{2}$ miles of fence. Patent to the land was received in December of 1926.

During the years of construction and operation of the power plant, a ferry had been operated just down river from it. Frank continued to operate the ferry after the power plant shut down, but he moved it up river to the site of their new headquarters (river mile 132.5). He also continued to operate the mine, and he sold the coal at the mining towns of Landusky and Zortman in the Little Rocky Mountains.

In May of 1929, Frank purchased 142 acres south of the river at a sheriff's auction (see river miles 133.6 - 134.7 right).

In August of 1931, Estel submitted another application to the General Land Office to purchase an isolated tract. This time it was for the twenty-four acre island near the right side of the river just above the land that they'd purchased at the sheriff's auction. They wanted the island for its hay potential. "Dry Island" cost them $1.75 per acre.

The next two land transactions were also Estel's. In December of 1931, she filed for an Additional Stock Raising Homestead Entry on 113 acres along the left side between river miles 134.4 and 135.1. This was followed in February of 1932, by a like filing on 108 acres along the right side between river miles 132.5 and 133.4. The river was the dividing line between General Land Office areas of responsibility. Consequently, the first filing was in Great Falls, the second was in Billings. The applications were eventually consolidated into one file at Great Falls.

They were allowed five years to make the necessary improvements on the land, and to show proof that they had. This latest entry was jeopardized when the Russells failed to meet the deadline. The reason given was that those who could legitimately witness their proof left the country for the winter of 1936-37, and the winter itself was so severe that the Russells were snowed in for 10 weeks. The excuse was accepted, and they received patent to the land in November of 1939. In proving-up, they'd built a 12' by 14' house and a 30' by 30' shed on the north tract, and a 12' by 14' cabin on the south tract.

That same November of 1939, the Russells purchased Gus Nelson's 293 acre homestead. Gus had been their neighbor for twenty-three years. Gus lived across the river and just above Estel's original homestead (see river miles 129.4 - 131.1 right).

Neighbors along the river were few and far between. Frank and Estel's closest neighbor up river on the left side was George Shepherd. He'd settled there in 1925, and built a 14' by 28' log house along the bank three miles above the Russell's. A strong friendship formed. In May of 1933, George filed for a Stock Raising Homestead Entry on 276 acres along the river between miles 128.4 and 129.7 left.

In proving up, George also built a 12' by 14' stable and a 12' by 14' cellar. He annually cultivated a one acre garden.

In February of 1936, George Shepherd died. At the time he was about seventy-five years old. In 1931, he'd executed a will, and since he had no known relatives, he named Frank Russell as sole devisee. Frank was also named as executor. Frank made final proof on this tract in June of 1937, but in October of 1938 the General Land Office found that there had been insufficient improvements. Frank and Estel had just completed proving-up on her Stock Raising Homestead entry, so they now set out to correct the situation on Shepherd's place. They were successful, and in March of 1940, Frank received patent to this tract.

On January 19th, 1944, the Russells purchased 166 acres from Claude and Dorothy Loomis, their down river neighbors on the north side of the river (see river miles 135.1 to 136.3 left).

Frank and Estel stayed along the river for another five years. Then in May of 1945, they sold all of their holdings to Elwell "Frip" Ekegren of the Bar Diamond E Cattle Company of Harlem, Montana. Frank was sixty-three years old at the time. The Russells moved to Roundup, Montana, where they resided until their deaths. Frank's ferry continued to be the main north-south access across the river in this part of the country until the Fred Robinson Bridge, some sixteen miles down river, was dedicated in 1959.

GUS NELSON HOMESTEAD

River Miles 129.4 - 131.1 Right

On March 21,1951, residents of Central Montana were shocked and saddened to learn that an eighty-one year old pioneer of the area had gotten tired of living and put a bullet through his head at a cow camp sixteen miles east of Winifred. August "Gus" Nelson had been a hunter, trapper, stage driver, rancher, cook and an employee of the original James Fergus Ranch. He was a bachelor, and he presented a crusty exterior - friends said that was just to hide his kindliness. Gus was described as a "good-hearted, tough old bird." He had been ill and was dreading the possibility of hospital confinement when he ended it all.

August Nelson was born in Kristianstad, Sweden, on March 7, 1870. He immigrated to this country, and on October 22, 1902 he received his naturalization papers in Lewistown, Montana.

During his early years in this country, he drove the mail stage between Judith Landing and Big Sandy to the north. He was also hired by the P N Ranch, which was headquartered at Judith Landing, as a wolf hunter.

One time when Gus was driving his stage on the way to Big Sandy, he noticed his horses ears moving in a strange way. He looked up on the skyline of a ridge and counted thirty-two big grey wolves. He knew he didn't have much of a chance and there was only one thing he could do. Gus whipped his horses into a run, and soon the wolves were running along side. He said if one of his horses had stumbled or faltered in any way, it would have been the end. Luckily, they didn't, and eventually the wolves gave up the chase.

Another time when he was hunting wolves, he found a cave where there were some pups. Gus knew that the mother was in there also, so he crawled in prepared to shoot. To his surprise, there were two mother wolves present. He was a good shot and killed them both - but he couldn't hear for many a day.

Gus established residence along the river in this location in July of 1916, the same year the township was surveyed. The General Land Office plat map identifies a Watson as living here, so Gus probably bought out a previous settler. That same year he harvested oat hay from twelve acres that were under cultivation.

In 1917, Gus broke another three acres of land and planted everything to oats. Drought took his crop. The following year he broke another severn acres, and planted twelve acres in oats, five acres in rye, and five acres in alfalfa. Drought again took its toll, but he did get some hay. In December of this year he filed his homestead entry papers on the up river half of the place.

Improvements on the land that December of 1918, included a 16' by 22' log cabin, a 20' by 26' log barn, an 11' by 14' storehouse, a 10' by 12' hen house, a 30' by 40' cow shed and two miles of three-wire fence. The following summer Gus filed final proof on the homestead, and received patent to the 145 acres of land in February of 1920.

In September of 1920, Gus filed an application to purchase an isolated tract, the land that would make up the down river half of his place. The General Land Office valued the land at $3.625 per acre. In May of 1921, Gus was the successful bidder, and the $538.28 purchase brought the size of his place to 293 acres.

Gus would keep this ranch for more than twenty-three years. He told a story of one 4th of July during that period. He was getting ready to go to a celebration at a neighboring ranch, and was out by the barn saddling his horse when he saw two men in a boat coming down river. The previous year, over the July 4th holiday, someone had burglarized a number of the river side places, so Gus kept hidden to see what would happen. Sure enough, one man came up and checked the place out, and then he motioned to the other, a man named Shorty, that the way was clear. They soon had many of Gus' supplies and valuables down by the river. One man was bent over lifting a bag of dried fruit when Gus decided to shoot. Gus said, "I never wanted to kill a man, so I shot just below his nose! " The men left in a hurry! Sometime later, two bodies were found on an island down river, possibly the same two, and possibly the victims of thievery themselves.

Gus also ran cattle with a partner up on top on the south side some twenty miles from here. When he was working the river bottom place, he would ride out about once every two weeks to get his mail at a neighbors.

Among many of his friends, he was known as "White Gus," a tribute to his honesty. At age sixty-nine, Gus decided to stay up on top, and in November of 1939 he sold the river bottom place to Frank and Estel Russell (see previous write-up). He had a place in Winifred, but he preferred to stay at any of the surrounding cow camps. During these years, he often worked as a cook. If he liked you, the food was good - if he didn't, he'd serve you the "damnedest mess imaginable. " It was at one of these cow camps that he died, and he was buried near by beneath the pines in the Breaks he loved.

WOODHAWK CREEK

River Mile 131 Right

Woodhawk Creek is named for the men who set up shop on the banks of the Missouri to supply the steamboats with fuel-wood for their boilers, which consumed as many as twenty-five to thirty cords per day. The 'woodhawks' were an independent breed of men, and the work they performed was physically demanding. They led an isolated existence and were extremely vulnerable to attacks by hostile Indians. Their lives were dangerous, and often short.

Since the steamboats could only navigate the river during a short high-water period from April through June, the woodhawks spent the winter months cutting down trees, and bucking the logs to lengths that fit in the steamboat boilers. The cottonwood trees that grow only along the river were quickly depleted, so the woodhawks had to venture off-river into the breaks for the pine trees that grew there, which the steamboat captains preferred due to their greater heat value. Logs were skidded, either by hand or with horses, substantial distances to get them to the river banks; here the wood would be stacked for sale to the passing steamboats.

Although the woodhawks preferred cash for their wood, the steamboat captains much preferred bartering with supplies such as flour, tobacco, sugar, whiskey, and other necessities which the boats had bought cheaply in St. Louis.

A glimpse of a woodhawk's life can be had from reading the following journal excerpts. They were written in 1869-70 by Peter Koch, a young Danish immigrant who joined a woodhawking crew at the mouth of the Musselshell River, located just a few miles below James Kipp Recreation Area. They are printed with permission of the University of Montana.

Oct. 4. Commenced chopping. Blistered my hands and broke an ax handle.
Oct. 8. Twenty five years old and poor as a rat. Cut down a tree on the cabin.
Oct. 20. Cutting while Joe is on guard. Snow tonight.
Oct. 24. Killed my first buffalo. He took 7 Spencer and 6 pistol balls before he died. River full of ice.
Nov. 7. A Gale of wind. Those Arapahoes who camped abt.10 days at Jim Wells woodyard have moved down the river after shooting into his stockade.
Nov. 15. Chopped hard all day. B.M. says 3 cords. Fred came back all wet. He had started in a skiff with Dick Harris, both drunk, and upset at Squaw Creek.
Nov. 25. Fred and Olsen started out wolfing. We stopped chopping on account of shooting and shouting in the hills. Joe and I found 4 wolves at our baits.
Dec. 10. Sick. No meat.
Dec. 11. Sick yet. Bill, Joe and Mills went to Musselshell, said Indians had attacked and stolen 3 horses and mule but lost one man.

View looking up the Upper Missouri from above the mouth of Woodhawk Creek. This is in the heart of the badlands section of the river. This area is remote and wild and provides excellent cross-country hiking opportunities.

Dec. 24. Christmas eve. No wolves.
Jan. 16. Awful cold. Froze my ears.
Jan. 17. Too cold to work. Went up to Musselshell. Froze my nose.
Jan. 24. Thawing heavily. Mills drunk.
Jan. Mar. 22. Saw three geese. (Spring has come, gentle Annie.) Martin sick.
April 24. Sixty Crows went up the river after Sioux to avenge the killing of 29 Crows. They were all looking dreadful, had their hair cut off, their fingers and faces cut, with the blood left on their faces.
May 9. One hundred and seventy cords on the bank. We put fire to the brush piles. The fire spread and burnt up 50 cords. We were played out before we got it checked. Nothing to eat.
May 13. Wind turned and started the fire again. About 20 cords burned.
May 22. The 'Nick Wall' passed about two o'clock in the morning without stopping.
May 23. 40-50 Indians showed themselves at Musselshell the 20th. The crazy Frenchman started toward them and was badly beaten but when firing started they turned and ran.
May 24. Raining. The 'Ida Reese' passed about daybreak without our knowing it.
May 28. Sold 'Deerlodge about 10 cords of wood.
June 13. The 'Sallie' passed after midnight and took on 15 cords of wood.
May 16. The 'Ida Stockdale' passed without stopping. We threw 6 cords back from the bank to keep it from falling into the river.
July 4. Indians firing at us from nearest cottonwood trees and all through the sage brush. The balls whistled pretty lively but we returned the fire and drove them from their shelter. We went out and found one young warrior killed by a shot through the upper thigh. We got his gun, bow and arrows and two butcher knives and threw his body in the river. Waring scalped him.

After 1870, Peter Koch quit woodhawking, and worked for a time as an Indian trader and surveyor, eventually making good as a director of the First National Bank in Bozeman, Montana.

Woodhawks were frequently targets of Indian attacks. In some cases the woodhawks were simply a convenient target towards whom the Indians could vent their anger for the injustices that whites had heaped upon them. However the Indians frequently attacked the steamboats, and they knew that a steamboat without a wood supply was in trouble.

In the early years of the steamboats, they carried their own 'wooding' crews, but later began to purchase from woodhawks. One of the very first woodhawks, was a man named John Johnson, who later became known as 'Liver-Eating' Johnson. Johnson was known to have come up the Missouri in 1843 and to have set up shop on the Missouri, near the mouth of the Musselshell in 1846. His primary activities at first were trapping and hunting, but as the steamboats began to come into Montana, he diversified to woodhawking.

Johnson was described as being a 'mountain man' who was burly, red-headed, quick, strong, and wilderness savvy. He married a Flathead Indian woman, and while he was away on a trapping foray, his pregnant wife was murdered in their cabin by a Crow war party.

In revenge for this Johnson became a nightmare for the Crow tribe. He would hunt down Crow Indians and began killing and scalping them; it became known among the Crow that he was also eating his victim's livers - raw.

Crow chiefs then selected twenty braves to track down Liver-Eating Johnson and kill him. The braves were to act singly until one of them succeeded in tracking him down and killing him.

By 1855 it was rumored that eighteen of the hand picked assassins had failed in their attempts on Johnson's life, and in fact had lost their lives - along with their scalps and livers - in the process. Apparently the Crow decided upon a truce with Johnson, and the feud subsided.

Whether Johnson actually ate the livers is an open question. Some of his companions swore that he did, "only spitting out the gristle", while others said that he would cut out his victim's livers and simply rub them over his face and beard, which in itself would have impressed any of his victim's companions who may have been hiding while observing the attempted assassination.

By the time the Upper Missouri entered its heyday of steamboating in the 1860' s and 70's, Johnson was aging and had taken on some younger partners in his woodhawking business. It is said that even then he experienced little Indian trouble. A journal entry that was made by a passenger on a Missouri River steamboat that passed Johnson's woodyard recounts that, "Along the brink of the riverbank on both sides of the landing a row of stakes was planted and each stake carried a white, grinning, Indian skull. They were evidently the pride of the inhabitants and a little to one side, as if guarding them, stood a trapper well-known throughout eastern Montana by the sobriquet of Liver-Eating Johnson. He was leaning on a crutch with one leg bandaged, and the day being hot his entire dress consisted of a scant, much shrunken red undershirt reaching just below his hips. His matted hair and bushy beard fluttered in the breeze and his giant frame and limbs, so freely exposed to view, formed an exceedingly impressive picture."

LEWIS & CLARK CAMP OF MAY 25,1805

River Mile 132.9 Right

The Corps of Discovery made 13.3 miles during this day. The thoroughness with which Lewis described biological specimens is illustrated with this journal entry.

[Lewis - Saturday, May 25th]

as we ascended the river today I saw several gangs of the bighorned Anamals on the face of the steep bluffs and clifts on the Stard side and sent drewyer to kill one which he accomplished; Capt. Clark and Bratton who were on shore each killed one of these anamals this evening. The head and horns of the male which Drewyer killed weighed 21 lbs. it was somewhat larger than the male of the common deer, the boddy reather thicker deeper and not so long in proportion to it's hight as the common deer; the head and horns are rema[r]kably large compared with the other part of the anamal; the whole form is much more delicate than that of the common goat, and there is a greater disparity in the size of the male and female than between those of either the deer or goat. the eye is large and prominant, the purple of a deep sea green and small, the iris of a silvery colour much like the common sheep; the bone above the eye is remarkably promenant; the head nostrils and division of the upper lip are precisely in form like the sheep. there legs resemble the sheep more than any other animal with which I am acquainted tho' they are more delicately formed, like the sheep they stand forward in the knee and the lower joint of the foreleg is smallest where it joins the knee, the hoof is black & large in proportion, is divided, very open and roundly pointed at the toe, like the sheep, is much hollowed and sharp on the under edge like the Scotch goat, has two small hoofs behind each foot below the ankle as the goat sheep and deer have. the belley, inerside of the legs, and the extremity of the rump and butocks for about two inches arround the but of the tale, are white, as is also the tale exce[p]t just at it's extremety on the upper side which is of a dark brown. the tail is about three inches in length covered with short hair, or at least not longer than that of the boddy; the outher parts of the anamal are of a duskey brown or reather a leadcoloured light brown; the anamal is now sheding it 's winter coat which is thick not quite as long as that of the deer and appears to be intermixed with a considerable quantity of a fine fur which lyes next to the skin & conceald by the coarcer hear; the shape of the hair itself is celindric as that of the antelope is but is smaller, shorter, and not compressed or flattened as that of the deer's winter coat is, I believe this anamal only sheds it's hair once a year. it has eight fore teeth in the under jaw and no canine teeth. The horns are largest at their base, and occupy the crown of the head almost entirely. they are compressed, bent backwards and lunated; the surface swelling into wavy rings which incircleing the horn continue to succeed each other from the base to the extremity and becoming less elivated and more distant as they receed from the head. the horn for about two thirds of its length is filled with a porus bone which is united with the frontal bone. I obtained the bones of the upper part of the head of this animal at the big bone lick. the horns of the female are small, but are also compressed and bent backwards and incircled with a succession of wavy rings. the horn is of a light brown colour; when dressed it is almost white extreemly transparent and very elastic. this horn is used by the natives in constructing their bows; I have no double but it would [make] eligant and usefull hair combs, and might probably answer as many valuable purposes to civilized man, as it dose to the savages, who form their water-cups, spoons and platters of it. the females have already brought forth their young, indeed from the size of the young I suppose that they produce them early in March. they have from one to two at a birth. they feed on grass but principally on the arromatic herbs which grow on the clifts and inaccessable hights which they ususally frequent. the places they ge[ne]rally celect to lodg is the cranies or c[r]evices of the rocks in the faces of inacessable precepices, where the wolf nor bear can reach them and where indeed man himself would in many instancies find a similar deficiency; yet these anamals bound from rock to rock and stand apparently in the most careless manner on the sides of precipices of many hundred feet. they are very shye and are quick of both sent and sight.

LEWIS RETURN CAMP OF JULY 30,1806

NEAR RIVER MILE 133 LEFT

The return contingent under Captain Lewis was reunited on July 28,1806, near the mouth of the Marias River (river mile 22 left). Sergeants Gass and Ordway with fourteen of the men had made the portage around the Great Falls. Lewis, Drouillard and the Fields brothers had explored the Marias River and experienced the Two Medicine River fight and resulting run from the Blackfeet. They camped about ten miles below the Marias River confluence that night.

On July 29th they traveled some forty-five miles down river to their outbound campsite at Slaughter River. Then on July 30th they boated an additional fifty-seven miles to this location.

[Lewis - Wednesday, July 30th]

The rain still continued this morning it was therefore unnecessary to remain as we could not dry our baggage I consequently set out early as usual and pursued my rout downwards. the currant being strong and the men anxious to get on they plyed their oars faithfully and we went at the rate of about seven miles an hour. we halted several times in the course of the day to kill some bighorns being anxious to procure a few more skins and skeletons of this animal; I was fortunate enough to procure one other male and female for this purpose which I had prepared accordingly. seven others were killed by the party also 2 buffaloe cone Elk, 2 beaver with & a female brown bear with tallons 6-$^{1}/_{4}$ inches in length. I preserved the skin of this bear also with the tallons; it was not large and in but low order. we arrived this evening at an island about 2 m above Goodriches Island and encamped on it's N.E. side. the rain continued with but little intermission all day; the air is cold and extreemly disagreeable. nothing extraordinary happened today."

On July 31st the Corps of Discovery camped eight miles below North Mountain Creek (today's Rock Creek) in the C.M. Russell National Wildlife Refuge. The following day they passed the Musselshell River.

They reached the mouth of the Yellowstone River, where they were supposed to meet Captain Clark, on August 7th. However, Clark had arrived there on August 3rd, but finding the mosquitoes unbearable and the country lacking in buffalo, which he wanted for dried meat, he proceeded on the following day.

Finding the remnants of a note from Captain Clark at the Yellowstone, Captain Lewis continued down river. Upon passing the Yellowstone they departed present day Montana.

On August 11th, Lewis and Cruzatte were pursuing a herd of elk on a willow choked sandbar, when Cruzatte who had but poor vision in one eye mistook Lewis' buckskin clothing for an elk and shot the Captain. Lewis was hit in the buttocks, the bullet going through his left cheek an inch below the hip bone, and making a 3 inch, bullet deep crease across his right cheek.

The next day, August 12th, the Lewis contingent caught up with Captain Clark's group. They headed out down river, reaching St. Louis on September 23rd.

HILLIARD BELLAH HOMESTEAD

River Miles 133.6 - 134.7 Right

The Bellah brothers settled on adjacent tracts along the south bank of the Missouri. Hilliard established himself on this tract in April of 1918. Cyrus claimed the tract just down river in November the same year. They were born in Hood County, Texas, and the record indicates that they may have been twins. Cyrus was born on November 3, 1881. These homestead entries were both second attempts by the Bellahs.

Hilliard filed his first claim on 160 acres southwest of Havre, Montana, near the community of Box Elder in May of 1914. During May, the ground looked good between the patches of snow, and there was an abundance of water. Box Elder had a railroad siding, and it was only eight miles away. Hilliard was encouraged. As the summer progressed, however, the water turned very alkaline and unusable. The more he surveyed the land, the more convinced he became that less than half of it was tillable, and that was in small scattered plots surrounded by rough and rocky land. He abandoned the tract after less than six months.

This river side tract had been previously settled, and Hilliard purchased the improvements. When he filed his homestead entry the following November, the improvements listed included a 28' by 36' three-room house, a 12' by 14' lean-to on the side of the house which served as a kitchen, a 16' by 32' log barn, a 40' by 40 ' shed of sawed lumber with a "brush" roof, a 16' by 16' granary, and sixty-five acres of broken ground. The whole place was fenced.

Hilliard filed final proof on the place in May of 1925, almost two years over the five year time limit. He'd added a chicken house to the improvements, and he normally harvested thirty to forty tons of hay. The last couple of years had produced poor crops, however, and he was late filing because he was "physically and financially disabled." He received patent to the land in November of that year.

Hilliard's problems continued. Unable to meet his mortgage payments, he lost the place in a foreclosure in May of 1926. In May of 1929, it was sold at sheriffs auction. Frank Russell was the high bidder at $604.18.

CYRUS BELLAH HOMESTEAD

River Miles 134.7 - 136.1 Right

Cyrus Bellah waited until the next spring after his November 1918 filing to move to the river bottom. He started his house in May. He was thirty-seven years old at the time, and single.

His first homestead entry had been made in 1916, and like Hilliard's had been in northcentral Montana. He'd filed in December, and again like his brother, he found the following spring that it was not suitable for agriculture, the water was very strong alkaline, and there was scant growth of grass for stock grazing. He abandoned this entry.

In addition to building his house the first year here on the river bottom, he broke eleven acres and planted it to oats. The crop "dried out." The following year he rotated his crop to millet, and he developed another twenty-nine acres for hay. Both were cut for hay and yielded a fair crop. In 1921 he again tried eleven acres of oats, and the crop was again hayed. He cut hay for another couple of years, but the crops were poor and by 1924, he was convinced the land was more suitable for grazing.

During the years that he was proving-up, Cyrus married Mrs. Delta Hertel who was born in Morrisonville, Illinois. Delta brought two sons and a daughter to the homestead. During the years that followed, the couple would have another son, and in 1927, one child would be still born.

Cyrus filed his final proof in July of 1924. Improvements at the time included an 18' by 22' log house, a 16' by 24' log barn, a 40' by 60' board stock shed with a "hay" roof, a mile of three-wire fence and the forty acres under cultivation.

Patent to the land was received in February of 1925, and it stayed in the family until 1951. Cyrus died in 1945, Delta in 1950. The heirs sold the land to Juanita Heller of Winifred, and the Heller family still farms the bottom raising fine melons and other produce.

POWER PLANT

River Mile 134.1 Left

Depending upon the source consulted, gold was discovered in Montana in 1852, 1856, or 1858. Apparently, the first definitely recorded discovery was in 1858. By mid-1862, however, a major gold rush had developed.

Although there was a reasonable suspicion of gold in the Little Rocky Mountains by 1865, it would be nineteen years before a gold rush would materialize in this area. The initial rush was to the southwest, the Bannack and Virginia City areas, then to Last Chance Gulch and other areas around Helena.

In 1865 two Catholic fathers visiting the Gros Ventres were shown Little Rockies' gold, but cautioned the Indians not to reveal it to the white men. On Thanksgiving of 1868, two officers at Fort Browning dreamed up a scheme to get the secret from a Gros Ventre named Nepee. The officers got the Indian so drunk that he showed them a pouch containing gold dust and nuggets, but after three days of food and drink, Nepee still would not reveal where he'd found it. Later, a party of fur company men tried to dig on the eastern side of the range. They found color, but nothing in paying quantities and departed in fear of hostile Indians.

In 1865, Kris Kies sent a message to John Lepley at Fort Benton to join him down river where he'd struck it rich. Lepley, three men and three Indian women went, but were later attacked by a Sioux war party near Cow Island. All but one of the Gros Ventre women were killed. The Sioux slit open the gold sacks and dumped the dust into the Missouri and "(a)nother fortune had vanished into mystery."

The Little Rockies gold rush began in 1884. The story goes that "Dutch" Louis, a rustler hiding from vigilantes with his friends "Pike" Landusky and Frank Aldrich, made the discovery on June 15, 1884. Since the discovery was made on reservation lands, they managed to keep it a secret until the beginning of September. Miners swarmed into the area, almost two thousand of them. Troops were called out from Fort Assiniboine to maintain order in the area. The town of Landusky came into being, and "Pike" Landusky himself later discovered the gold quartz that would prolong the mining in the Little Rocky Mountains. Pete Zortman, for whom the town of Zortman was named, discovered the Alabama mine in Alder Gulch, and erected the first cyanide mill for processing the quartz ore.

Although the boom itself was short lived, the mines continued in operation for many years. Until the late 1970s when the price of gold went up so sharply, the period between 1903 and 1923 saw the most intensive development in the Little Rockies.

In 1903, Charles Whitcomb sold a ranch he owned and operated to B.D. Phillips, the leading sheepman of northern Montana. Whitcomb then moved to the mining country and obtained an option on the Independent claim. Together with Bob and Bill Coburn, he obtained a loan from Phillips in the amount of $7,000 to finance development. They organized as the Little Rockies Exploration Company, and carried out prospecting and development work over the next few years.

At this point the Alder Gulch cyanide mill was the only one in the mining district that worked. Whitcomb and his associates again approached Phillips for financing, this time for funds to build their own mill. Phillips put up $75,000 and received two-thirds of the stock of the newly organized Ruby Gulch Mining Company.

The new company developed the mill and bought up a number of adjacent claims. The mill eventually reached a capacity of three hundred tons. It had a No. 3 Gates crusher, a screening system that sent the fines from the crusher on to the leaching tanks, while the oversized rock was run through three sets of roll crushers. The plant had six three-hundred ton tanks and six one-hundred-ten ton tanks. Ore was usually leached for a week. The mill was powered by a steam engine, using wood for fuel. It consumed eight cords a day at a cost of $8.00 per cord.

The company continued to buy up mining claims until they owned most of the better claims in the district. The growing mining industry was one of the factors that led to a realignment of the governmental units in the area. Blaine County was first split from Chouteau County, and then was divided to yield Phillips County, which under B.D. Phillips' influence, was designed to include the gold districts. The gold production in the district amounted to $264,910 in 1908, rose to $700,000 in 1909, and remained at a high level until 1913. In that year, fire destroyed the Ruby Gulch Mill.

The Whitcomb and Phillips' interests had access, by this time, to considerable capital. In 1913-1914 they constructed a modern fine-grinding mill of six hundred ton capacity. Cordwood was by this time in short supply and too expensive for boiler fuel, so the developers cast about for another source of power. Unable to negotiate a successful agreement with the Montana Power Company, the company bought a ranch that contained a large warm water spring. They then built a dam and penstock to carry this water and then installed a two hundred horsepower Pelton wheel and generator set.

This coal-fired power plant (river mile 134.1 left), completed in 1916, provided power for the Little Rockies gold mines.

This supplemented the steam plant at the mills, but they needed still more power for full production. So they opened a lignite coal vein near the Missouri River. The coal was of poor quality, but it was the only answer to the problem. Consequently, a steam-driven electric power plant was immediately designed and construction started. The plant was completed in 1916 with the final installation of two water-tube boilers, weighing eighteen tons each. These were bought from the City of Lewistown where they had been used in the municipal power plant. The new plant had a capacity of 750 horsepower and burned seventy tons of coal per day. It was operated by Frank Russell.

Moving these huge boilers by pioneer freighter Joe Hartman is a story of great achievement in itself. The boilers were shipped to Winifred from Lewistown by railroad. It was still forty miles to the power plant over a wagon trail across the rolling prairie and then down through the rough badlands to the Missouri River and finally across the river by ferry to the power plant.

Because of the great weight of the boilers, they had to be moved in the winter when the ground was frozen hard. Hartman used heavy logging sleighs or very heavy trucks, depending on the condition of the trail, and sixteen horses to the team. The moving was done through the months of January, February, March and into April, 1916. This was, without doubt, one of the heaviest moving jobs, under the most difficult conditions, ever accomplished with horses.

With completion of the power plant and some twenty-three miles of electric transmission line, the mines ran at peak activity through 1917. Early in 1918 a number of problems arose. Average ore values dropped, the miners' union struck for higher wages, and this, in the midst of a general labor shortage, brought about by the demands of wartime industries, shut down mining operations after taking out only 219,350 tons of ore averaging $1.94 per ton.

During the years of the shutdown, Walter W. Phillips (son of B.D. Phillips) completed work on a degree in mining engineering. In the spring of 1920, he went to the Ruby mine and carried out an extensive prospecting and sampling program, while George Whitcomb (son of Charles) evaluated the repair work needed to get the mine back into operation. By November of that year, Phillips had assayed enough ore to be confident about the prospects for reopening the mine.

The Anaconda Copper Mining Company took an option on the property soon after that, but, on making their own examination, relinquished the option. So, with Walter W. Phillips as superintendent, the company set about reopening the mine. They rebuilt the power line, dehydrated the oil in all the transformers, overhauled the mill and power plant, developed a new water source in Alder Gulch and ran a mile of five-inch steel pipe to the mill.

Operations resumed in December of 1922, and with the discovery of additional promising ore bodies, prospects looked good.

Unfortunately, new problems developed. An eight-day rainstorm brought sixteen inches of rainfall and flooded the lower mine workings. In October of 1923, the mill burned down and operations at Ruby Gulch came to a halt. At this point the company decided not to rebuild, since rising costs could not be supported by the then current gold price, of $20.67 per ounce.

Through the rest of the 1920's, the mining district was in a slump, with only Whitcomb generating small scale activity. The 1930's saw renewed activity and a mining boom that lasted until the onset of World War II. During the 1930's, the mining interests took advantage of the changing technology of power production and turned to diesel engines at the mines.

LOOMIS HOMESTEAD

River Miles 135 to 136.3 Left

Only citizens of the United States could receive patent to lands under the homestead laws. On June 6, 1927, the clerk of the Seventeenth Judicial District in Malta wrote to Claude Loomis, "It is with the greatest chagrin and disappointment for me to be obliged to tell you that you are one of the most unfortunate persons I ever knew when it comes to naturalization." He concluded the letter with, "I am more sorry for this than I can tell; you have a splendid family, and I have been convinced that in your Deer Lodge (the Montana State Prison) trouble you were guilty of no wrong." The clerk's statement was profound, and only hints at some of the problems that plagued Claude Loomis during his attempts to acquire title to this 166 acres of river bottom land.

Claude John Loomis was born July 9, 1893, in Spirit Lake, Iowa. He was the second child born to Eugene Loomis, a twenty-five year old painter from Wisconsin, and Eva C. Wylder, a nineteen year old from Illinois. The family immigrated to Canada during the spring of 1910. In 1911, Claude filed on a homestead near Gull Lake, Saskatchewan. In Swift Current on August 11, 1913, he became a naturalized citizen of the Domain of Canada. He proved up on his homestead during 1914 or 1915.

Claude married Dorothy Lilian from North Dakota, and in 1915 their first child, a daughter, was born. They eventually moved to East End, Saskatchewan. In 1917, Claude sold his Canadian homestead, and the family "trailed cross country" (not going through a port of entry) to Montana, arriving in Harlem about July 2, 1917.

By August of 1917, the family had settled at this river side location. The tract had already been settled, and Loomis paid $1,000 for the improvements. The General Land Office plat maps identify the original settler as Shorty Croft, and he'd built a 16' by 24' log house here during the summer of 1915. Croft had forty acres in alfalfa, and Loomis harvested a few loads of hay.

On October 16, 1917, Loomis filed his declaration of intention "to become a citizen of the United States and to permanently reside therein."

In 1918, Claude replaced the original log cabin with a 32' by 46' frame house. The house had four rooms, a large fireplace and a stone walled basement. There was also a 16' by 32' frame barn, a 16' by 40' frame cow shed and a mile of fence. He had a mixture of alfalfa and oats planted on the forty acres under cultivation, and the crop yielded fifteen tons of hay.

To help support his family, Claude worked in Malta. In 1918, their second child was on the way, and Dorothy required hospitalization. When he went to collect his wages, he confided to his employer, J.A. Remple, that he lacked sufficient funds to cover the medical expenses. The paycheck was filled out with the amount left open to cover the situation. A son was born in Chinook, and the medical bill came to $179, the amount which Claude entered on his paycheck. Something went wrong, possibly the amount was for considerably more than Remple had anticipated, for Remple had Loomis arrested for forging the check.

On May 2nd, Claude's homestead entry for this tract was approved by the General Land Office.

In mid-August of 1919, Claude appeared before Judge Cosner in Malta Justice Court. He pleaded innocent to the charge, and was arraigned on a charge of grand larceny felony for writing the "bad" check and bound over to District Court. He subsequently plead guilty before Judge Hall in District Court in Malta, and on September 22nd was sentenced to not less than one nor more than two years in the Montana State Prison in Deer Lodge.

With good behavior, Claude was released from prison the following May. He then established a pattern that eventually almost cost him the homestead. He would visit the homestead for about a month in the spring, probably just long enough to get a crop in, and then go work at East End, Saskatchewan. He'd revisit the homestead in the fall, again probably just long enough to harvest the crop. Presumably he found the environment around his old homestead in Canada more comfortable for supplementing his income than that around northcentral Montana following his Malta experience.

In May of 1921, a second son was born.

In 1922, Claude was late in returning to the homestead. Enroute to the river, he stopped by his attorney's office in Havre, and learned that a hearing had been held on May 21st contesting his claim to the homestead. On November 29, 1921, Arthur Kendall (see river miles 142.5 to 146.0 left) had filed the contest against the entry charging that Loomis had not resided on the land for the last six months, and that he had "wholly" abandoned the land. Charles W. Duvall and Marcus Logan corroborated the statement. A letter sent to Claude on January 9, 1922, informing him of the hearing had failed to reach him in Canada.

At the hearing, Samuel H. Duvall testified that he'd leased the tract from Loomis between April and November of 1919, and that during that time period Loomis hadn't lived there at all. He also testified that Loomis hadn't lived there for six months prior to December 3, 1921 (the date the contest was recorded). John R. Smith testified that he'd leased the tract for a similar time period the following year, and that during the times he was there putting in the crop and then later putting up the hay, he'd not seen Loomis or any signs of his having been there. Arthur Kendall testified that he'd known the land for eleven years, that Loomis hadn't lived there since he filed the homestead entry, that he'd accompanied Loomis to Canada after his release from the pen, during which time Loomis said he would "never live down there any more." Kendall went on to say that what Loomis didn't take to Canada with him he sold.

Claude found the record of testimony to be "false to a very great extent" and claimed to have resided on the tract for more than thirty-two months. He said that the only reason he'd left the land was to seek employment and obtain means to support his three children and wife. An appeal was filed and a new hearing was granted.

July 10, 1923, was selected for reopening the contest for Loomis. Kendall objected to reopening the hearing because of the cost of getting his witnesses back, etc.. On the day of the hearing, Kendall filed motion to dismiss, and on August 10th the motion was sustained and the contest dismissed.

Whenever a homesteader was going to be gone from his entry for any length of time, he was supposed to file an "application for leave of absence" with the General Land Office. Claude and Dorothy had failed to do this. The day of the hearing, five such documents were filed to cover this oversight.

On August 30, 1923, Claude filed final proof on the homestead. By now he'd built corrals, a chicken coop, a 12' by 16' log store house, another one-half mile of fence, and a road that included three bridges. The General Land Office investigation approved on October 19, 1923, found that the "law as to residence, cultivation and improvements, have been well complied with, and issuance of patent in regular order of business is recommended, if *proper evidence* of citizenship is furnished." The issue of naturalization would plague Claude for another ten years, but on January 27, 1927, patent to the land was issued.

After his stay at Deer Lodge, Claude was required to "take out new first papers and start over again" to get his naturalization. He did in 1924. Then he was required to start all over again in 1927 because he had not entered the country through a port of entry in 1917. In both 1917 and 1924, a person could prove his date of entry into the country with an appropriate affidavit with two witnesses. Such was not the case in 1927. In 1926, a court ruling made it necessary, "In applying for second papers an alien must first secure from the immigration department, a certificate showing that he had been regularly admitted into the country and had paid a head tax of $8.00." It was no longer legal to issue a certificate and date it back to the time of arrival.

Loomis had to take his family to Havre and have the immigration inspectors there document their "arrival" into this country. In essence, he was starting all over again.

On March 26, 1934, citizenship was finally restored to Claude Loomis

In January of 1934, Claude had filed for an additional stock raising homestead entry on 244 acres of land adjoining his original homestead. The following May a special agent from the General Land Office was working in the Landusky area, when Charles Duvall and Benjamin Phillips alleged that Loomis' original homestead entry was secured by fraud. They charged that he had forfeited his citizenship and was a naturalized citizen of Canada. During the investigation that followed, it was discovered that indeed Claude had not been a citizen when patent was issued. In July, the special agent recommended that a suit be instituted to cancel Loomis' patent. He based his recommendation on allegations that: patent was secured through fraud, the entryman was not a citizen, and Loomis had not made a valid declaration of his intention to become a citizen.

In considering the case, the General Land Office recognized that they had erred, that Loomis had not tried to conceal the issue of his citizenship, and that after more than six years since patent was issued the government would be subject to the charge of negligence if they tried to cancel his patent. On August 31, 1934, the Commissioner of the General Land Office closed the case against Loomis, but on June 27, 1935, the additional stock raising homestead entry which had been allowed a year and a half earlier was canceled.

Claude had been severely injured in a horse related accident in Canada. As a result, he had a steel plate in his head. If he received a sudden jar, the plate would slip, causing a vibration on the brain. The condition would nearly drive him mad. By 1943, his condition had deteriorated to the point that he was declared incompetent. Dorothy was appointed his guardian, and on January 19, 1944, she sold the place to Frank and Estel Russell.

They'd maintained a place in Landusky since the late 1920's, and they established permanent residence there.

A couple of years later when visiting along the river, Claude confided to his old friend Charley Kendall that he had little left for which to live. A couple of days later in Landusky he shot himself.

After Claude's death, Dorothy spent some time in Idaho, and then spent the rest of her years in Malta.

HIDEAWAY COULEE

River Mile 138.9 Left

Because of the inaccessibility and remoteness of the Breaks, many settlers with questionable backgrounds or occupations were attracted to them. Blank chapters in many histories hint at situations where the search for solitude was the primary motivator for living here.

Among those with questionable motivation was Harvey Logan, alias Kid Curry. He had a place some five miles up Hideaway Coulee north of here. Kid Curry was Montana's contribution to the era of bank robberies and train holdups made famous by such characters as Butch Cassidy and the Sundance Kid, with whom he was allied.

While Wyoming and Colorado were the scenes of most of the big train robberies, the last and most dramatic was pulled off in Montana when Kid Curry and his gang held up Great Northern train No. 3 at Wagner, west of Malta, on July 3, 1901. This action spelled the doom of its perpetrators, and for all practical purposes, put an end to that wave of crime.

Kid Curry was one of a family of four brothers whose family name was Logan. They were natives of Virginia, and were probably orphaned at an early age. They were reared by an aunt, Mrs. Hiram Lee, on a ranch near Dodson, Missouri. Her contribution to the group was her son, Bob Lee, who joined the gang and participated in its activities.

In the 1880's the Logan brothers, Henry, Harvey (the Kid), Johnny and Loney, with their cousin, Bob Lee, left their aunt's home and rode northwest.

The general consensus is that on their way west, they stopped in Wyoming and became acquainted with the notorious Flat-Nose George Curry, a member of the Hole-in-the-Wall Gang led by Butch Cassidy. At any rate, when they arrived in Montana they were no longer Logans, but had assumed the name of Curry, presumably because of their admiration for Flat-Nose George.

Some authorities say that they drove a herd of stolen cattle into north central Montana and were being pursued by a posse. Others say that they brought no cattle into the state, hired out as cowboys on ranches, appeared to be law abiding young men, and at length bought a ranch of their own near Landusky in the Little Rocky Mountains.

In 1894, Henry, the eldest of the brothers, died from either pneumonia or tuberculosis. Henry is credited with having exercised a controlling influence over his three younger brothers - with his death they were set free to pursue the wilder careers for which they yearned.

In 1894, another event took place which is credited with driving the Currys into the ranks of the outlaws, if they had not been there before. That was the killing of Pike Landusky by Kid Curry.

The town of Landusky had been named for Pike, who had discovered gold in the area. Pike was as tough as they come. He hated Indians because a bullet from an Indian's gun had taken off half of his lower jaw. It was said that he had never killed a white man, but no one kept track of the number of Indians he had killed.

At first the Currys and Landusky apparently got along well together. The trouble started when Landusky borrowed a plow from the Currys, broke it, and returned it without repairs.

The trouble intensified when Loney Curry became overly friendly with Elfie, Pike's stepdaughter. Two years later she would bare Loney's child, a boy named Harvey in honor of Kid.

It became more intensified when another neighbor, Jim Winters, swore out a warrant against the Currys on charges of cattle stealing and brand changing. The charges were possibly trumped up because Johnny Curry and Winters were quarreling over water rights on the Winters ranch. The ranch had been previously owned by another man whose widow "took up" with Johnny.

The sheriff of Chouteau County took Kid and Loney into custody, and then he deputized Pike Landusky to take charge of the two prisoners while he went after Jim Thornhill. Thornhill had become a ranch partner with the Currys after Henry's death.

There wasn't any jail, so Pike hobbled the Kid's feet with leg irons and hog-tied Loney. While they lay helpless on the floor, Pike worked them over with his fists until their faces looked like chopped meat. Then he stomped on them and kicked them around until he got tired. Pike was working on a quart of whiskey and enjoying his job. He was chewing tobacco and kept spitting the juice on their faces and calling them all the filthy fighting names he could lay tongue to.

The Kid promised he would get even.

The sheriff returned, took his prisoners to Fort Benton, and the Circle C ranch posted bail to secure their release, taking Curry cattle as collateral.

The climax of the feud came on December 27th. Pike was in Jew Jake Harris's saloon in Landusky. Evidently Kid knew his whereabouts. Thornhill and Loney entered first, followed by the Kid. Landusky was at the bar wearing a heavy overcoat. He had a whiskey bottle in his hand, but as the Kid passed he hit Pike hard enough to loosen his grip on the bottle. Immediately Thornhill and Loney drew their guns and warned the onlookers to draw back.

The fight that followed was brutal and ruthless. Pike Landusky, at fifty, was still a powerful man and he fought with every ounce of his strength. If he had not been handicapped by the bulky fur-lined coat. the outcome might have been different. But Kid Curry was younger and more active, and although the older seasoned battler outweighed him by fifty pounds, the Kid was able to out maneuver him and give him a sound beating. Finally Pike pleaded, "Lemme up Kid, I got a-plenty."

Pike got to his feet and reached into his overcoat pocket. The Kid said he thought that he was pulling out a handkerchief to wipe the blood from his face. Instead, Pike drew a new automatic revolver. He pointed it at the Kid, fumbled with the unfamiliar mechanism and pulled the trigger. But the gun failed to go off. If it had fired, Kid Curry would have been killed.

Then the Kid pulled his own Colt .45, shot twice into Pike's body, then fired a third time but missed as Pike fell to the floor.

After the killing of Landusky, the Curry boys weren't seen in the Little Rockies for some 13 months. The evidence indicates that they went to Wyoming and became affiliated with the Hole-in-the-Wall Gang, which was led by their old friend, Flat-Nose George. Flat-Nose pretended to be a rancher, and the gang did whatever was opportune in order to make a living. The principal occupation was probably cattle rustling, but there was also an occasional train robbery or bank holdup.

The Currys returned to the Little Rockies area during the winter of 1896. One morning in February, Jim Winters and his partner, Abe Gill, heard a galloping horse approaching. Winters grabbed his loaded shotgun and opened the door. Johnny Curry was approaching. Johnny was at a disadvantage because he had lost one arm after being wounded in a gunfight in Wyoming. He saw Winters, dropped his reins and started to pull his gun. He was too late! Winters shot first and Johnny was killed. Winters was later acquitted by a jury which held he had shot in self defense.

After Johnny's death, the Kid and Loney rode back to Wyoming to rejoin the Hole-in-the-Wall Gang. In June of 1897, after an unprofitable bank holdup in Belle Fourche, South Dakota, the Kid, Loney and two other men spent a few days in the Deadwood jail, but they didn't linger - it was not a very strong jail.

Fearing that the Pinkerton detectives were getting close, Loney Curry fled to Missouri to hide with Mrs. Lee, the aunt who had raised him. One morning in February of 1900, the Lee home was surrounded by a posse who shouted for Loney to come out. He came out shooting, but the posse returned his fire and he died with a bullet in his head

Thus, by the time of the big train robbery at Wagner, Kid was the only one left of the four brothers. Most authorities agree that Butch Cassidy was the planner and the boss of the gang which held up the train on July 3, 1901. There is some discrepancy about who participated. The majority of writers say that Kid Curry got on the baggage car when the train stopped at Malta on its way west, and that the Sundance Kid bought a ticket and was in the passenger area. Apparently, Butch Cassidy waited at a bridge near Wagner where the train was to stop, and a Mexican named Camilla or Camillo Hanks guarded the horses to be used in the getaway.

The robbers were experienced and efficient and the holdup was accomplished quickly. Kid Curry crawled from his place on the baggage car over the tender to the engine, and with gun in hand gave the engineer specific instructions about where to stop the train. Cassidy and Hanks were waiting as planned with horses and dynamite and the safe was quickly blasted open, the currency and some gold taken. The four robbers mounted their horses and fled the scene. They eluded the posses which were sent in pursuit, and made their way to Kid Curry's Hideaway Coulee hideout.

The Kid apparently had one task to complete before leaving Montana - get even with Jim Winters. On the morning of July 25, 1901, Winters stepped outside his cabin door and was shot to death. No one knows that it was Curry who did it, but no one doubts it either. Tracks and empty cartridges behind the corral fence showed where the riflemen were hidden.

There are various stories as to how much the robbery amounted to, some saying $80,000, others note $61,000, but most agree that it was $41,000 in unsigned notes consigned to the National Bank of Montana in Helena. The currency was valueless without the signatures of the president and cashier of the bank. Several attempts were made to forge the signatures and to pass the notes, but it was risky and almost proved to be the outlaws undoing. The notes were recognized in Great Falls and reported to authorities as far away as Nashville, Tennessee and St. Louis, Missouri.

Kid Curry turned up in Knoxville, Tennessee. He was playing pool in a saloon, quarreled with his opponent and hit him over the head with his pistol. The police were called. The Kid wounded two of them, escaped from town and walked all night, but he was overtaken and arrested the next day and returned to jail in Knoxville.

He had to wait months for his trial in Federal court on train robbery charges, but at length he was tried, convicted and sentenced to 130 years in the Federal penitentiary in Columbus, Ohio. His old partner, Jim Thornhill, is reported to have visited him in Knoxville and provided him with a supply of money. Police had found the Kid's suitcase in a checkroom, empty, indicating that all the Montana bank notes had been disposed of.

Still in jail two years later in Knoxville, the Kid was waiting for the outcome of an appeal. The officials were fearful that he would escape, and so a guard was stationed outside his cell at all times.

On June 27, 1903, he had apparently made all necessary preparations. He asked for a broom to sweep his cell, and while the guard was not looking, took it apart and made a loop of the wire that bound it. Then, in casual conversation with his guard, he in some way lured the man close to the bars, got him to look in the other direction, and looped the wire around his neck.

One story says that he forced the guard to unlock the cell. Another is that he used the broom handle to reach between the bars and retrieve a box in the corridor which he knew contained guns. Then he called the jailer and threatened to kill the guard unless the cell was unlocked and he allowed to flee. No matter what the sequence of events, the Kid was free. He found the sheriff's horse in the jail yard and calmly rode out of town, never to be certainly identified again.

Following his jail escape, the record gets pretty confused about what happened to Kid Curry, with claims and counter claims about him continuing his career both in this country and South America or being caught or killed or going straight. It's fairly certain that Butch Cassidy and the Sundance Kid made their trip to South America following the hold up of Great Northern train No. 3, but from that point on their story also gets pretty confused.

GRAND ISLAND

River Mile 139

From *Floating on the Missouri,* Schultz; refer to narrative at river mile 1.2 left for background.

Leaving our lunching place, we pushed off, and a stretch of swift water took us quickly down around a bend and in sight of Crescent and Grand Islands. We arrived at the head of the latter about one o'clock, and having made twenty-five miles since daylight, decided to camp. This is one of the largest islands on the river, a mile and a half long and half a mile wide. At its upper end there is a magnificent grove of tall old cottonwoods, and a growth of smaller timber completely belts it. The rest of the island is a level plain, covered with buck brush and tall grasses. We soon had the tent up under a large cottonwood, and then proposed a hunt up in the breaks of the south side of the valley, for mule deer. There were numerous tracks and trails of whitetail where we were, also more wolf signs than in any place we had yet seen, but after finding the dead deer on Dry Island, we did not care especially for that kind of meat.

Directly opposite the island a long high-cut bank shuts off sight of anything beyond it. After crossing the river we were obliged to walk up the shore some distance to find a place where we could climb it, but when we did finally arrive on the summit, a typical view of the badlands country was spread out before us; long ridges and deep coulees sloping up for miles; hills of blue clay absolutely devoid of vegetation; here and there patches of juniper brush and groves of pine, especially in the heads of the coulees, and back of them cut walls of sandstone. We started up the nearest ridge, following a well-beaten game trail. After traveling a mile or more we stopped to rest a bit, and I caught sight of a deer as it was entering a pine grove at the head of a short lateral coulee not far away. We were not long in getting to the lower edge of it, but there was so much underbrush that I did not like to go in, fearing that I would scare the animal out without getting sight of it; so I decided to circle around to the upper edge of the timber and have Sah-ne-to try to drive it to me. Another climb of half a mile and I stood on top of a high cliff; at its foot there was a boulder-strewn slope of some fifty yards, and then the pines. I waved my hat to Sah-ne-to, saw her start into the timber, and then sat down to await the result of my plan.

In order to have this story read right, I suppose I ought to make my pencil say that the deer suddenly bounded out of the timber several hundred yards away and ran as fast as it could, and that at the crack of my trusty rifle it gave a convulsive spring and fell dead. What really did happen was this: I had been looking over the ridges and groves to my left, trying to spot some game, and again turning my attention to the business in hand, was surprised to see five deer, one of them a good-sized buck, standing on the slope right under me and looking curiously into the timber from which they had likely just emerged. Back and forth they swung their great ears, and occasionally stamped the ground with their forefeet. I allow that it was unfair, but we needed meat, and I took a careful sight on the buck's back just back of its withers and dropped him. The others made a few jumps, but did not know which way to run, until I threw a rock at them and shouted, when they hurried away along the edge of the timber and turned up the nearest coulee.

I was obliged to go back several hundred yards to get around the end of the cliff, and by the time I got to the fallen deer Sah-ne-to appeared a little further on. She said she had heard the deer run when she scared them up, and remarked that she had found an old "war house".

The buck was larger than I thought when I saw him from the cliff, and still very fat, for the rutting season had barely commenced. He was too heavy to be packed whole, so I skinned out the forequarters and hung them on the nearest tree. But before starting back the "war house" had to be inspected. It stood in the thickest part of the timber, and was a large one, some sixteen feet in diameter inside. Like all others of its kind, 'twas built of a number of long poles set up cone shape. The many layers of pine and balsam boughs which had covered it had long since slipped down and decayed, and the flooring of brush was in a like condition. We poked around inside where the warriors had sat and slept, hoping to find some little trinket they had lost or forgotten, but all we found were mice-gnawed ribs of deer or mountain sheep. There are hundreds of these "war houses" hidden in the breaks of the Missouri, or rather, there were. Most of them have fallen down and rotted away. They were built by parties of Indians on the warpath in order to screen the flame of their fire from observant eyes, and also as a protection from the cold and storms. We wondered what tribe had built this one, where they were bound, and what had been their success. More than likely they had their eyes on some woodhawk's little band of horses, and perchance secured them and his scalp also.

KENDALL BOTTOMS

RIVER MILES 142.5 - 146.0 LEFT

Charles E. Kendall was born in Stetsonville, Wisconsin, on October 16, 1891, the son of Charles H. Kendall and Margaret Knoblock. C.H. worked for the Milwaukee Railroad, and his job as a station agent took him west, leaving Margaret to raise Charley and his brothers and sisters. By 1906, C.H. had found his way to the Missouri River where he filed a Desert Land Entry claim in this vicinity.

The first settler of record here was named Fisk. His name appears on the General Land Office Plat map, which was surveyed in 1906. At the time of survey, Fisk had a number of roads, ditches, and fences built, and had a gasoline irrigation pump installed at river mile 142 left.

Charley was large for his age, and at fourteen was able to get a job as a carpenter's helper for the Milwaukee Railroad. He made his way west working on depots. When he found himself in the vicinity of Butte in 1907, he decided to join his father. He bought a bald-faced horse in Butte and headed for his father's claim, passing through Pipestone, Helena and Utica along the way.

This photograph, taken in Fort Benton, shows three of Charley Kendall's 'store barges'. Charley loaded these barges with provisions for homesteaders living along the Upper Missouri and delivered them as he traveled downriver. The barges were made of building materials that were sold to homesteaders, so the barges were being dismantled and sold as they progressed downriver.

C.H. had filed (prior to approval of the GLO survey) in the vicinity of river miles 145.3 to 146.0 left. Charley got a job breaking horses for a neighboring homesteader soon after he arrived at his dad's claim, then he filed on 165 acres immediately up river from his dad's place in March of 1910. He later thought better of it, and in May of 1911 he relinquished his first claim. He then filed on the next tract up river from his dad's, and then turned around and filed for a supplemental homestead entry on the original tract in between.

In the mean time, C.H.'s desert land entry had been canceled (1915 or 1916), and he refiled on the tract for a regular homestead entry. Patents for this and both of Charley's entries were received in 1919.

Charley undertook many ventures during his years along the river, but the most unique was between 1911 and 1918 when he operated a floating grocery and hardware store on the Missouri River. His territory extended from Fort Benton down river to Fraser (just below today's Fort Peck Dam).

Charley would inform homesteaders along the river of his plan, and then take orders. With enough orders to make a profit he went to Fort Benton, purchased timbers and lumber and proceeded to make a large raft. He then purchased the supplies from a local wholesale dealer and loaded them on the barge. At times his cargo made it necessary for the construction of two or more barges. Homesteaders would order flour, sugar, tea, coffee, canned vegetables, canned milk, repair items for farm and ranch machinery, muslin and yard goods for the women to make into clothing. In fact, almost anything needed by a household and ranch to help see them through the winter was loaded aboard.

The news that Kendall's barge or barges were coming down the river preceded him, and families eagerly awaited the arrival of their supplies. If someone had overlooked an item or had unexpectedly run out of something, all they had to do was send one of the kids to the river bank to hail the barge. Charley would pull over and ask what they needed. He usually had a few extras on board and would deliver what they needed. Another service was relaying news of neighbors and friends up river.

The barge or barges would be dismantled at the end of the trip, sometimes partially during the trip. and Charley would sell the lumber to those in need of building materials.

Charley married Ruby Henry of Missouri in 1914. They floated down the river on their wedding trip. In 1915, he worked at the August Mine near Landusky in the Little Rocky Mountains north of here. He and Ruby also operated a boarding house for the miners in Landusky. The marriage lasted only two years - it ended when he got so angry with her that he stuck her head first into a rain barrel. As soon as someone pulled her out, she departed for Chicago.

Hard times were brought on by the spring break-up in 1916, and this possibly contributed to the failing marriage. Because of ice jams and flooding, everyone in the vicinity lost all of the livestock that was wintering along the bottom lands.

The barge mercantile business came to an end after the fall trip in 1917. The trip was made in October, but an early freeze caught them in the ice just above the Hagadone place (see river mile 95.3 to 99.3 right). A valiant effort was made to save the barges and their cargo, but Charley still lost $3,000 worth of supplies. He must have had the supplies on consignment, for it's said he repaid Brown's of Great Falls at the rate of $40 a month.

A brother, Art, is also mentioned in conjunction with the place, and apparently he was a character. Charley broke his land with a bull team, and Art decided to liven them up. He hooked up some batteries to the chains of the singletree. Parts of the plow were still being found in 1938. In 1920, Art wanted to take their dad on a motorcycle ride. C.H. said okay, but first he went in and strapped on his gun. "Son, you buck me off and I will shoot you!" he said. Away they went. Art took off across a plowed field and bucked C.H. off. When C.H. collected himself, Art was long gone. When they heard from him again, he was in Deadwood, South Dakota.

Alfalfa was raised on Kendall Bottoms. In 1924, Charley bought his first threshing machine. It was an all wood International. They separated the alfalfa seed and hauled it to Landusky where it was shipped to various places by parcel post.

Charley supplemented his income by trapping beaver along the river bottoms. He sold hundred of hides since beaver coats were very popular at the time.

In 1928, Charley bought the old Fisk place.

In 1929, Charley married Mrs. Ruby Noordam Shellito. This Ruby was born on August 27, 1905. She was the first white girl born in Ruby Gulch, a mining district in the Little Rocky Mountains north of here. When they married, she had a daughter, Emma. The new Mrs. Kendall worked side by side with Charley as ranch hand, ranch cook, cook at Ruby Gulch Mine, riding for cattle, operating farm and ranch machinery and stacking hay. She assisted with the difficult job of herding cattle across the river for shipment to market from Roy (the closest community to the south). She even made two trips to Sioux City with shipments of cattle. A son, Charles Elvin, was born in 1933.

The marriage did not last however. In 1935, the U.S. Army Corps of Engineers condemned the property at Kendall Bottoms for the new Fort Peck Reservoir. The family was allowed to continue occupying the land under a lease arrangement. In 1936, the Kendalls divorced. Ruby remarried, but was widowed in 1943. In 1945, she and Charley remarried. In 1948 at the age of fifty-eight, Charley died of a heart attack while roping a horse.

The Kendall family continued to use the Bottoms until 1952 when they could no longer afford the lease.

ARMELLS CREEK

RIVER MILE 149.5 RIGHT

From *Floating on the Missouri;* Schultz; refer to narrative at river mile 1.2 left for background.

The breeze freshened and we ran the six miles from this point to the mouth of Armell's Creek in an hour. This is a fair-sized stream, heading near the Black Butte, thirty miles south. The latter part of its course is between high, rough, pine-clad hills. It was named after Charles Armell, a trader for the American Fur Company, who once managed a branch post here for some time. Sah-ne-to said that her people called this creek It-tsis-ki-ot-sop-Crushed, or, more liberally, Trapped. Somewhere along its course, in the long ago, she said, the Piegans were camping and hunting, and some one discovered a seam of soft, red ochre, or burnt clay, in a high cut bank. The news quickly spread through camp and cre-

ated great excitement, for the substance was not common, and in great demand for making a sacred paint for the face. In other words, 'twas great medicine. Early the next morning more women flocked to the place than could work at it at one time, for the seam was not long. They dug and gouged and scraped with such implements as they had, sharp-pointed sticks and shoulder blades of buffalo, and had mined in for a considerable distance when a large portion of the high bank fell, completely burying twenty-seven of them and seriously injuring several more. All of the twenty-seven were dead when the people finally uncovered them.

ROBINSON BRIDGE

RIVER MILE 148.8

Fred L. Robinson came to the Malta Montana area in 1911, and settled on a 320 acre homestead north of Wagner. He was twenty-two years old at the time. Born in Tennessee, he'd spent his early life on the family farm there.

In the years that followed, Fred farmed, rode irrigation ditch for the Bureau of Reclamation, served twenty months in the Army during World War I, operated a general store, and helped organize the Malta Auto Company. He married a local school teacher in 1923, and the couple had two children.

Fred Robinson had a record of serving in an elective office of some kind or another, including the State Senate, for a period of forty years. He said that he always had two main objectives for which he resolved to work. One was the construction of a north and south road through Phillips County, and the second was the building of a hospital. Both of these objectives were accomplished, and the bridge across the Missouri River on Highway 191 was dedicated to Fred Robinson in 1959.

The adjacent park was dedicated the same year to preserve the memory of James Kipp. It was Kipp who opened the upper river to the fur trade in 1831 with the establishment of Fort Piegan at the mouth of the Marias River (see river mile 22 left)

An outcrop of the Virgelle Member of the Eagle Formation; this white to cream-colored sandstone is commonly referred to along the Upper Missouri as the Eagle Sandstone. This photograph, taken in the vicinity of Eagle Creek, shows an intact arch on the right, and a collapsed arch on the left. Arches are formed as a small hole forms in a wall of sandstone, permitting wind to accelerate through the hole. The wind carries away loosened sand grains, and over time the hole continues to enlarge. As the hole becomes increasingly larger, it eventually loses the ability to support its roof, resulting in collapse.

Chapter 5

Geology

Introduction

The Upper Missouri flows in a general east to northeasterly direction across the Northern Great Plains of Central Montana, where it occupies an impressive canyon of up to a thousand feet deep. Downcutting by the river has exposed rocks of both sedimentary and igneous origin, which range in age from approximately 90 to 55 million years old.

The most abundant rocks along the Upper Missouri are sedimentary rocks, derived from marine muds and sands which were deposited during a period of time when central Montana was covered by seawater of the Western Interior Seaway. The marine conditions occurred during the Cretaceous Period, beginning about 90 million years ago and persisting until about 70 million years ago. Significantly, the Western Interior Seaway was characterized by cyclical oscillations which caused the seaway to alternately shrink or expand, which in turn resulted in both fluctuating depths, and migration of coastlines. This oscillating seaway provided a basin for the deposition of the shale, sandstone, and siltstone that form the valley walls and cliffs along the Upper Missouri.

Igneous rocks of the Upper Missouri were emplaced approximately 55 million years ago as areas of central Montana were influenced by massive quantities of molten rock, or magma, that rose from great depths along faults and invaded the upper crustal rocks, where it solidified. In some areas adjacent to the Upper Missouri River the magma forced its way to the surface where it produced volcanic eruptions, whose solidified lava today forms many of the beautiful mountain ranges that spread across central Montana. Geologists call this region the Central Montana Alkalic Province, in reference to the chemical composition of the rocks; the province contains a number of rare types of igneous rocks, as well as some unusual structures in which the rocks occur.

Between about 2 million and 10 thousand years ago, during the “Ice Age”, central Montana was influenced by several pulses of advancing glacial ice which moved south from Canada. These glaciers caused severe disruptions to central Montana’s surface geology, including the rerouting of river drainages. Prior to glaciation, the Missouri River flowed northeasterly through central Canada, and into the Arctic Ocean via Hudson’s Bay. As a result of disruption by glaciers, the present day Missouri flows into the Atlantic, via the Mississippi River and the Gulf of Mexico.

The river today continues to actively erode its channel, where the combination of relatively soft sedimentary rocks, erosion resistant igneous rocks, and a semi-arid climate produce a spectacularly varied landscape that is known locally as the “Missouri Breaks”.

Overview of the Crustal Rocks of Central Montana

In the surrounding plains that border the river, there is little opportunity to view central Montana crustal rocks; all that is visible is vegetation and soil. However as the Upper Missouri follows its path to the Gulf of Mexico, it erodes, or downcuts, through the crust of central Montana, thereby exposing crustal rocks in the walls of its valley, in effect providing a cross section of the region's geology.

Sedimentary Rocks

The dominant class of rock that is exposed along the river corridor is sedimentary rock. These rocks, listed in order of decreasing grain size, are composed of hardened layers of sand, called sandstone, hardened layers of silt, called siltstone, and hardened layers of clay, called shale; occasionally, layers of mud containing lime, or calcium carbonate were deposited, resulting in the formation of limestone. All of these rocks formed during a period when central Montana was covered by a large body of water that geologists today call the Western Interior Seaway. The sands, silts, and clays were muds that formed on the bottom and shores of this sea.

Geologists who study sedimentary rocks group similar layers of sandstone, siltsone, shale, and limestone into identifiable packages, which are called formations; an example of a formation in the Upper Missouri area is the Eagle Formation, also called the Eagle Sandstone. Typically a formation will consist of many layers of rock, ranging from between tens to thousands of feet in thickness, all of which were deposited under similar geologic conditions. As conditions change, the type of sedimentation changes, and a different formation will be deposited. In the Upper Missouri area different sets of geologic conditions were caused by episodes of growth or shrinkage of the Western Interior Seaway across central Montana.

Igneous Rocks

A second class of rock found along the course of the Upper Missouri is igneous rock, which is formed from liquid, molten rock, called magma. About 55 million years ago, Central Montana experienced episodes where magma from deep within Earth was pushed upward, along existing or newly created faults. Although magma is well known for its role in producing volcanoes, great quantities of this material in fact wind up cooling underground. Central Montana is riddled with outcrops of igneous rock which originally cooled underground, and have since been exposed by erosion; this is the case along the Upper Missouri. In other places the magma did rupture the crust at the surface, resulting in volcanic eruptions that produced lava flows and ash deposits. Many of central Montana's mountain ranges such as the Highwoods, Judiths, Little Rockies, and Bear's Paw are piles of igneous material that formed where great masses of magma were focused, frequently resulting in volcanic eruptions.

Along the Upper Missouri, all of the igneous rocks were formed by underground cooling of magma, which resulted in the formation of features such as dikes, plugs, and sills; there is no evidence of volcanic eruptions. The specific type of rock that is found in most of these igneous features is an unusual and rare rock named shonkinite.

Another type of igneous rock landform that occurs in a localized area along the Upper Missouri are called diatremes. They are small features, and none are visible from the river. They are interesting in that they show evidence of having been forced explosively into the surrounding rock, and in some areas of the world are associated with diamond deposits.

Sedimentary Rocks of the Upper Missouri

How Sedimentary Rocks Form

Sedimentary rocks typically form in large bodies of water, as rivers ceaselessly deliver massive amounts of sand, silt, and clay into them, over vast amounts of time. These particles, in turn, are distributed by bottom currents, tides, and waves until they eventually settle out as layers of sediment. As new layers accumulate, they compress the earlier layers with their weight, and cause them to lithify, or turn to stone. Lithified sand particles become sandstone, silt particles become siltstone, and clay particles (the finest in size) become shale. Since the sedimentary rocks are composed of materials that were laid down in horizontal layers, this layering is an important visual identifying characteristic of sedimentary rocks.

The Cretaceous Period of Geologic Time

From Fort Benton to James Kipp Recreation Area, the Missouri flows past, and has cut down through, sedimentary rocks that were deposited during the Cretaceous period of geologic time. The Cretaceous began about 135 million years ago and ended about 65 million years ago; it was the last geologic time period during which the dinosaurs flourished. During much of the Cretaceous period, much of west-central North America, including the part of Montana through which the Upper Missouri flows, was covered by the waters of an inland sea, called the Western Interior Seaway; the sand, silt, and clay which were washed into the sea became the sedimentary rocks of today. These rocks range in age from 70 to 90 million years old. Fossils of marine organisms such as clams, snails, and ammonites are preserved in the rocks, as well as the remains of dinosaurs. Most of the sedimentary rocks contain quantities of volcanic ash, which was produced by numerous volcanic fields that were active in the western U.S. during the late Cretaceous; this airborne ash either fell into the seaway, or was washed in by rivers.

The Western Interior Seaway

The Western Interior Seaway was long and narrow, and it formed as all of west-central North America, including the land which is now central Montana, was subsiding, or sinking, to an elevation which was below sea level. As this occurred, ocean waters from both the Gulf of Mexico, to the south, and from the Arctic Ocean, to the north, began filling in the resulting depression, and the waters eventually joined, forming a long, narrow sea which extended from north to south across the entire North American continent. During the late Cretaceous period, tectonic forces were just beginning to uplift the Rocky Mountains in western Montana and Idaho, and rivers flowing eastward from the newly uplifted Rockies delivered massive amounts of sediment to the Cretaceous sea, which was deposited as layers of sand, silt, clay, and lime. As the sedimentary layers became deeply buried they were compressed and turned into sandstone, siltstone, shale, and limestone.

Much evidence exists that the coastline of the Western Interior Seaway was a favorite habitat for dinosaurs, and some of their remains have been found in the Judith River Formation, within the the monument boundaries. In the Fort Peck Reservoir area, located downstream from James Kipp State Park, outcrops of the Hell Creek Formation are world famous for their rich deposits of dinosaur remains. The Hell Creek rocks were deposited above the Bearpaw Shale by rivers which flowed over the area formerly occupied by the seaway.

Low grade coal is fairly common in many of the sedimentary rocks of the Upper Missouri, lying between the layers of sandstone, siltstone, and shale. These coals are easily recognized by their black color, and they represent the remains of plant material which accumulated in coastal swamps and estuaries of the Cretaceous sea, and which were later buried by younger sediments as the sea level rose. It takes about thirty inches of vegetation to make a one inch layer of coal, and the warmer climate which prevailed in Montana during the Cretaceous provided conditions favorable to lush vegetation and the resulting coal deposits.

Sea Level Fluctuations

The Western Interior Seaway grew and shrank many times during the Cretaceous, as forces within the earth caused the land to oscillate between periods of uplifting and subsidence. During periods of uplift, the connection between the Gulf of Mexico and the Arctic Ocean was broken, and parts of central Montana temporarily rose above sea level; in places that were still covered by water, the depth decreased. It was during these times - when the sea was shrinking - that deposition of sand, in the

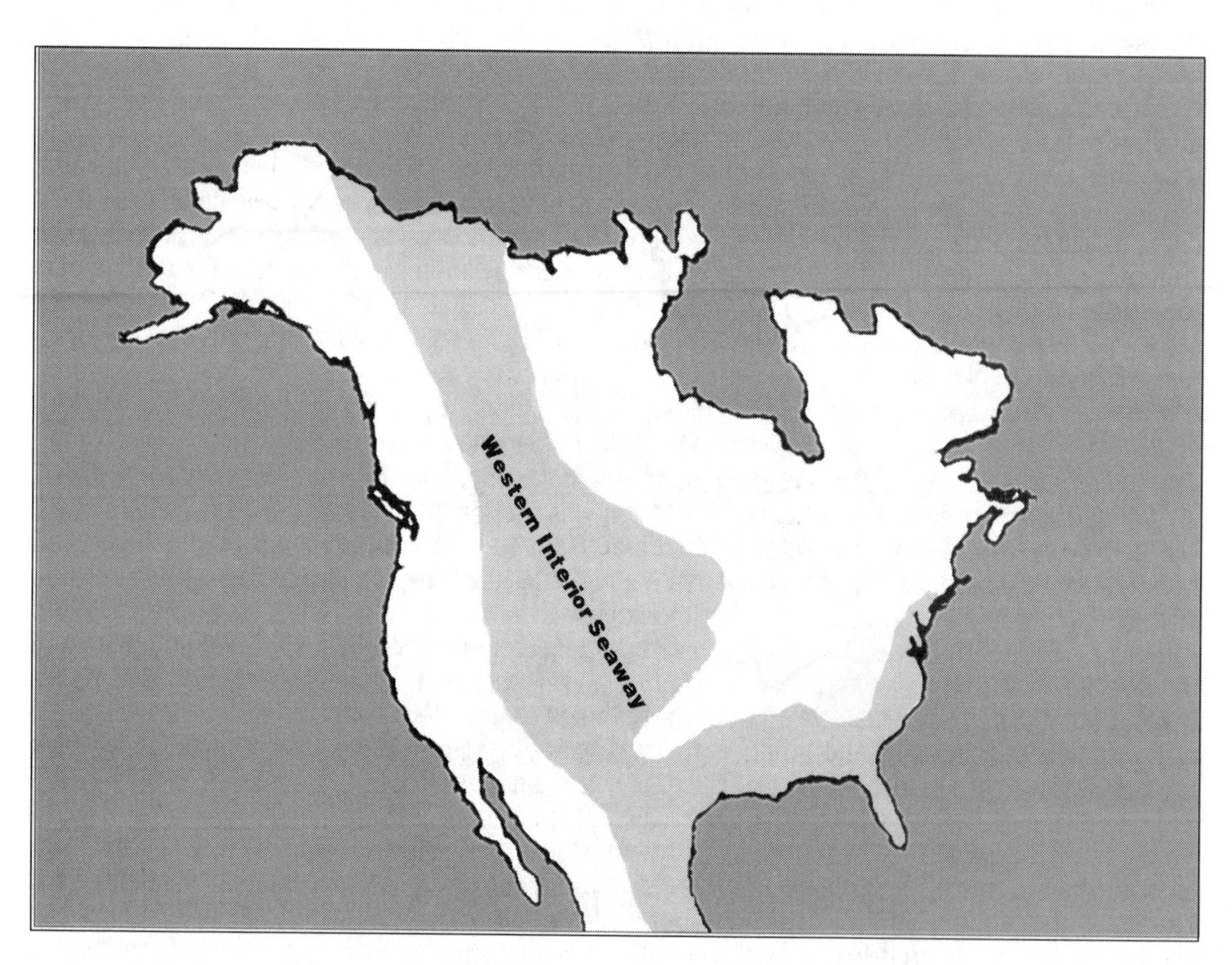

Map of present-day North America, showing the location of the Western Interior Seaway, extending from the Gulf of Mexico to the Arctic Ocean and covering eastern and central Montana. The seaway existed from 70-90 million years ago during the Cretaceous Period. Rivers draining into the seaway deposited thousands of feet of sediments which today make up the rocks of the Upper Missouri area. In Montana, as the land cycled between periods of uplift and subsidence, the seaway expanded or shrank, resulting in dramatic east-west shifts in the position of the coastline.

form of beach deposits and offshore sand bar deposits was dominant. The receding, migrating coastline left behind a blanket of coastal sand in its wake, and this sand later became the sandstone layers through which the Upper Missouri is presently flowing. Examples of these sandstones are the Telegraph Creek Formation, the Eagle Sandstone, and the Judith River Formation.

Correspondingly, during times when the land was subsiding to below sea-level depths, the sea was expanding - in both depth and area, and the connection between the Gulf of Mexico and the Arctic Ocean was reestablished. Rivers flowing into the seaway deposited thick layers of fine-grained silt and clay into the deepening water, and predominately shale-rich rocks resulted, such as the Marias River Shale, the Claggett Shale, and the Bearpaw Shale.

Final Retreat of the Western Interior Seaway

About 70 million years ago, central Montana experienced a final period of uplift which was sufficient to cause a permanent retreat of the sea from Montana. The Bearpaw Shale, which is the youngest of all of the sedimentary rock layers that occur withinin the momument, represents the last accumulation of sediments to be deposited in the Western Interior Seaway in Montana. By the end of Bearpaw time sedimentary rocks totaling several thousand feet in thickness had accumulated in central Montana.

Names, Descriptions, and Features of the Sedimentary Rocks of the Upper Missouri

Geologists have given the sedimentary rock formations names which are related to the locales where the individual formations had been first identified and studied. Thus the six formations through which a floater passes are called: Marias River Shale, Telegraph Creek Formation, Eagle Sandstone, Claggett Shale, Judith River Formation, and the Bearpaw Shale. Each of these formations is described below.

Due to the "layer cake" arrangement of the sedimentary rocks along the Upper Missouri, identifying the different formations is relatively easy, and can add to the enjoyment of a float trip. Following are descriptions of the formations, and the locations along the river where they can be found in outcrop.

Marias River Formation

The Marias River Formation (Marias River Shale) is the oldest of the sedimentary rocks seen along the Upper Missouri. It dominates the banks at river level along most of the upper reaches of the river, between Fort Benton and Coal Banks Landing, and is common as well through the White Cliffs, between Coal Banks Landing and Judith Landing. The Marias River Formation can be easily identified as a black (when moist) to dark grayish-blue (when dry) outcrop of shale, composed predominately of fine clay particles, with some silt mixed in, and some thin layers of sand.

As with most shales, it tends to form slopes rather than cliffs, which can help in identifying this formation. However at Black Bluff Rapids (rm 19), aggressive undercutting by the river has produced a striking black shale cliff of the Marias River Formation, perhaps the best outcrop of this formation on the river.

The fine-grained sediments of the Marias River Formation were deposited in quiet waters, distant from the shoreline. Such conditions would have predominated during a period when subsidence of central Montana was causing the inland sea to deepen and expand. Its thickness is about 500 feet. It contains occasional spherical masses of limestone, called concretions, which weather out of cliffs and can be found on the banks of the river.

Telegraph Creek Formation

The Telegraph Creek Formation is younger than the Marias River Shale, and therefore lies above it. Its thickness is about 100 feet. It can be identified as the band of yellowish rock which form the tops of the breaks in the Fort Benton area, and downriver for about forty miles. In some places the Telegraph Creek dips down to river level.

An excellent place to examine the Telegraph Creek Formation is at the highway rest area immediately above and to the east of Fort Benton, in the old railroad cut.

The Telegraph Creek Formation is composed of alternating beds of yellowish, fine-grained sandstone and gray shale, and was deposited at a time when the inland sea had stabilized after its previous advance during Marias River time; this stable environment allowed the deposition of these intermediate sized sedimentary particles in near shore locations.

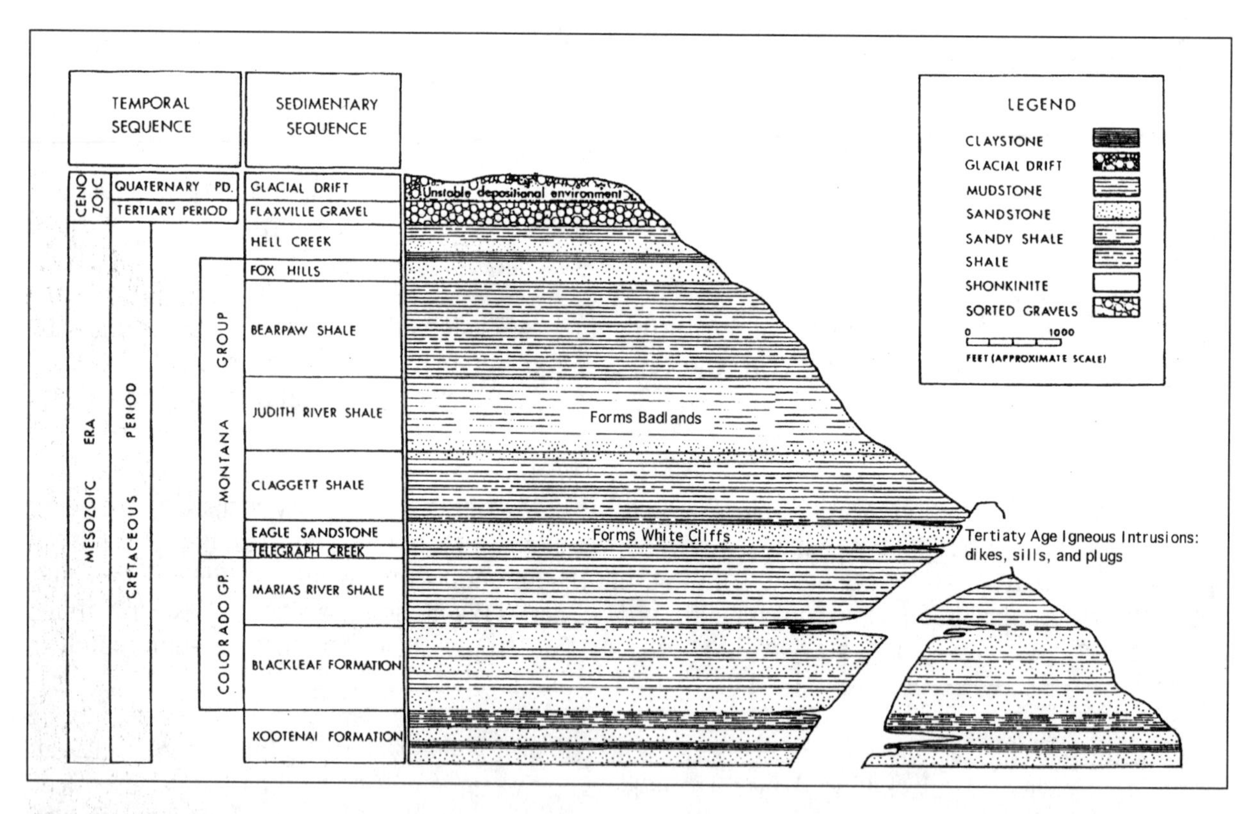

A stratigraph chart that shows the "layer cake" geology of the Upper Missouri area. The oldest sedimentary rock exposed along the river is the Marias River Shale (about 90 million years old), and the youngest is the Bearrpaw Shale (about 70 million years old). The igneous rocks intruded into these rocks about 55 million years ago, after the Western Interior Seaway had disappeared. Through the entire length of the monument, the rocks are slightly tilted towards the east - downriver. Therefore as floaters travel downriver the rocks get older. At Fort Benton the river banks are composed of Marias River Formation, while at James Kipp Recreation Area the rocks are Bearpaw Shale.

Eagle Formation

The Eagle Formation (Eagle Sandstone) begins to make its appearance in the vicinity of Coal Banks Landing (rm 41), located near the town of Virgelle, where the spectacular White Cliffs of the Missouri begin. Although it lies above the Telegraph Creek Formation, it can be difficult to actually identify the boundary between the two formations, because the Telegraph Creek becomes thinner and finer to the east.

The Eagle has a prominent member, called the Virgelle Sandstone Member, which forms the srtiking White Cliffs of the Missouri; it is composed primarily of sand particles with subsidiary pure white clay. Above this white sandstone is a layer of low grade coal and black shale.

The Eagle Formation can be easily identified by its characteristic creamy-white color, and its tendency to form striking cliffs, up to a couple of hundred feet high, in many places capped by the black coal/ shale layer. Traveling downriver from Coal Banks Landing, the Eagle soon becomes the dominant formation, culminating in the White Cliffs region, (rm 53 to 77), perhaps the most impressively beautiful stretch of the Upper Missouri.

Since the Eagle figures so prominently in the scenery of the White Cliffs, and because it displays so many interesting features that can be easily observed, it is discussed below in greater detail than the other formations. The information that follows will help individuals understand the geologic story behind many of the landforms that appear in the White Cliffs.

A typical view on the upper third of the river, a few miles below Fort Benton. The rock outcropping at river level is the Marias River Shale, which tends to form slopes; it ranges in color from black when moist, to medium-gray when dry. Above it is the Telegraph Creek Sandstone which tends to form cliffs; its color is a light yellowish-brown.

Eagle Formation: Location of Outcrops

The first place that the Eagle begins to outcop is in the Virgelle area (rm 39.5 right). At White Rocks (rm 53 left), and at Eagle Creek (rm 56 left), the Eagle Sandstone occurs near river level, but below Eagle Creek faulting has uplifted the rocks along the river corridor, resulting in the Eagle outcropping higher up in the breaks, and allowing the Marias River Shale to again make an appearance at river level. Finally, at Slaughter River (rm 77 right), the Eagle returns to river level, and soon dips below the water line; downriver from Slaughter River the Eagle makes occasional appearances at or above river level, where it has been lifted by faults, for example in the vicinity of The Wall (rm 81 left), and again at Sugarloaf Rock (rm 101.5 right)

Eagle Formation: Environment of Deposition

The Eagle Formation was formed during a retreat of the coastline of the Western Interior Seaway, and was probably accompanied by uplifting of central Montana, and a shallowing of the sea. Along the coastline of the retreating sea would have been a beach of white sand that was being worked by wave action. Some of the sand would have been deposited as off-shore sand bars. As the coastline retreated to the east, a continuous layer of white sand was left behind; later, these sand grains became cemented together to form sandstone.

Several spherical concretions are visible in this photograph of the Eagle Sandstone in the White Cliffs, near Dark Butte (rm 69). Since the surrounding sandstone erodes more easily than the concretions they are often seen protruding from the sandstone, as well as littering the ground near outcrops.

Eagle Formation: Cementing Material

The cementing substance which holds the individual sand grains together in the Eagle Formation is called calcite, and is the same material that sea shells are made of. Calcite is not a particularly strong cement, and the Eagle Formation actually erodes quite easily. However, other components within the Eagle, such as concretions, different cementing materials, and igneous intrusions, combine to help it resist erosion, and are responsible for the array of unusual features which contribute to the beauty of the White Cliffs.

Eagle Formation: Concretions

The white colored Eagle Formation is comprised of sand and clay particles that are cemented together with a mineral called calcite; this is a fairly weak cement, that is easily attacked by rain water, resulting in disintegration of the sandstone. In places however, structures called concretions protect the Eagle from rapid erosion. Concretions are the result of concentrations of an iron-rich cement, called hematite, which replaces - and is much more erosion resistant - than the calcite cement. Typically, this red-brown colored cement aggregates in spherical pods within the sandstone, some as large as eight feet in diameter. The hematite cement is more erosion resistant compared to the bulk of the white,

Castle Rock, located at river mile 56.5 Right. The bottom vegetated part of this butte is Marias River Shale, here displaying its characteristic slope forming quality. The prominent white cliff is Eagle Sandstone, in which the sand grains are cemented with light colored calcium carbonate. The dark band visible at the very top of the cliff is composed of a thin layer of Eagle sandstone that is cemented with hematite, which can be identified in the field by its rusty-brown color; this layer is quite resistant to erosion by falling rain, and although it is only a few inches thick, it is responsible for protecting the soft white sandstone beneath it from eroding away.

A large pedestal rock, resembling a toadstool, off the river in the White Cliffs region. The light-colored stem is composed of easily weathered Eagle sandstone, and the individual sand grains are cemented with weak calcium carbonate. The darker capping segment is also Eagle sandstone, but it is cemented with rusty-colored hematite, a much stronger cement that withstands dissolving by rainwater.

calcite-cemented sandstone, and in places where a concretion lies on the surface, it forms a protective cap above the more easily eroded white sandstone. This cap protects the sandstone from the erosive effects of rain, allowing it to remain standing while all of the other white sandstone around it erodes away. The result is the formation of exquisite pedestal rocks, columns, towers, and other unique features of the White Cliffs. The capping concretions, being iron-rich, can be identified by their rusty, red-brown color, which contrast sharply with the underlying white sandstone. Concretions are also responsible for the hole-studded, pock-marked appearance of some of the cliffs of Eagle Sandstone. This results from concretions which have loosened and fallen out of the cliff faces, leaving holes in the sandstone; these are frequently inhabited by rock pigeons, swallows, and other birds. While hiking in the White Cliffs keep an eye open for concretions lying on the ground; they often resemble cannon-balls.

Geologists believe that the concretions formed after the sandstone was originally laid down. There is evidence that a minute concentration of iron, possibly associated with a dead organism trapped within the sand, acts as a nucleus to which ions of iron, traveling in migrating ground water, are attracted. As more iron continues to accumulate around the nucleus, it grows in a spherical shape, forming a concretion.

Eagle Formation: Iron-Cemented Layers

At some locations, particularly at the top the white Eagle Sandstone, entire layers of sand particles are cemented together with hematite rather than with the easily dissolved calcite cement. Since the hematite is much more difficult for rain water to dissolve, this layer is instrumental in protecting many of the cliffs, spires, towers, walls, and pedestal rocks. Hematite is the same iron-rich mineral that is responsible for the concretions, mentioned above. As with concretions, the hematite cement layers in the Eagle can be identified by their rusty-brown color, which contrasts sharply with the characteristic white sandstone; they occur as layers, typically a few to several inches thick.

An excellent location to observe the protective effect of this layer of hematite cemented sandstone is Castle Rock (rm 56.5 Right). This massive landform owes a great part of its existence to the protective capping of hematite cement, just a few inches in thickness, that covers its top.

Eagle Formation: Arches and Holes

If a vertical slab of Eagle sandstone wears in such a way as to form a small hole, wind becomes able to blow through the hole, which greatly accelerates the removal of additional sand particles, resulting in the formation of an arch or a hole, such as Hole-In-the-Wall (rm 64)

Eagle Formation: Igneous Intrusions

Other erosion-resistant materials were introduced into the Eagle Sandstone during the period of intrusive igneous activity, described below in the section on igneous rocks. Like the concretions, the igneous rock is more resistant to erosion than the Eagle Sandstone, and it too, acts to protect the sandstone from erosion. Many cliffs and buttresses of Eagle sandstone are supported by igneous rocks which have been injected into fractures in the Eagle, a dramatic example of which is Hole-in-the-Wall (rm 64). The wall in which this feature occurs is a thin, erosion-resistant intrusion of igneous rock that is sandwiched between two sheets of sandstone, which the tougher igneous rock is supporting. This interaction between the igneous and sedimentary rock can be easily observed by climbing to the top of this ridge, via the trail on its upriver side.

Claggett Shale

The Claggett Shale, about 500 feet thick, is composed of a thick brownish-gray shale, with a prominent yellowish-gray sandy layer near the top. The Claggett was deposited on top of the Eagle Sandstone, in deep offshore waters as the Cretaceous inland sea was expanding in size and depth, likely caused by subsidence of the land in central Montana.

The shale erodes easily, forming slopes, while the sandy layer tends to form cliffs, resulting in 'badlands' topography. The thick, sticky mud found along the banks of the river, which proved so troublesome for the men of the Lewis and Clark Expedition as they pulled their boats upriver, is composed of clay that has weathered out of the Claggett Shale. The Claggett appears at river level beginning below Arrow Creek (rm 78), and continuing to Stafford Ferry (rm 102), and beyond to the old power plant site (rm 134). In places the contact between the top of the Claggett and the bottom of the overlying Judith River Formation can be identified by a conspicuous band of pine trees, whose roots are exploiting groundwater that is pooling in the Claggett's porous, sandy upper layer.

A typical scene in the 'Badlands' of the Upper Missouri. Badlands topography occurs along the river beginning at Judith Landing, where the Claggett Shale and the Judith River Formation start to outcrop along the banks of the river. The Judith River Formation contains alternating layers of sandstone and shale. The sandstone layers are more resistant to erosion than the shale layers, form small bands of cliffs, and help protect the shale from rapid erosion.

Judith River Formation

The Judith River Formation was deposited on top of the Claggett shale. This formation consists of layers of sand, silt, shale, limestone, and coal; it is about 600 feet thick. Because this formation is composed of alternating beds of erosion-resistant sandstone, and erosion-prone shale, it (along with the underlying Claggett) forms a striking topography known as 'badlands', characterized by slopes comprised of steep sandstone cliffs interspersed with gentler slopes of shale.

The Judith River Formation, as evidenced by its predominance of sand, represents another episode of retreat of the inland sea, when the land in central Montana was again experiencing uplift. The Judith River outcrops along the Missouri at the top of the breaks below the mouth of the Judith River, but does not appear at river level until the area around the Power Plant (rm 134).

Some of the beds in the Judith River show evidence of having been laid down in fresh water environments, probably in large, flat flood plains that bordered the retreating coastline.

Large iron concretions are found in the Judith River formation. Some thin limestone beds contain abundant fossil shells; dinosaur remains have been discovered in the Judith River, and petrified wood occurs in some locations.

An eye-catching feature that's scattered throughout the Judith River Formation is the presence of orange-red colored *scoria* beds. Scoria is formed when coal seams become ignited, perhaps by lightning, and as they slowly burn they bake the overlying rock, causing the color change. Some are visible below Dauphin Rapids (rm 103).

The Bearpaw Formation

The Bearpaw Formation (Bearpaw Shale), about 900 feet thick, is a dark gray to black shale with some intermittent silt and sand. The Bearpaw does not appear at river level until just a few miles above James Kipp Recreation Area, but further upstream it can be seen at the tops of the breaks, overlying the Judith River Formation, where it tends to erode into relatively gentle, dark-colored slopes. A good place to examine the Bearpaw is in the vicinity of Lower Woodhawk Bottom camping area. By hiking up the access road about a mile or so, one passes through the Judith River Formation and, where the road levels off, into the Bearpaw Shale. At this location the shale supports very little vegetation and the Bearpaw is nicely exposed as a dark grey to black-colored mound of several acres in area. At this location the Bearpaw also contains abundant crystals of the mineral selenite, which is described below.

When the Bearpaw was being deposited, central Montana was likely subsiding, causing the Western Interior Seaway to make its final advance across central Montana. Conditions were characterized by increasing water depths, and an advancing coastline. The fine grained clays and silts were deposited in quiet water distant from the shore. Following the deposition of the Bearpaw, the land was uplifted and the sea permanently retreated from Montana.

The Bearpaw contains layers of the mineral gypsum, in a form called selenite, and some large, handsome crystals may be found. The presence of the gypsum, which is geologically classified as an evaporite type of mineral deposit, indicates that the Bearpaw Shale was deposited in a marine environment where salts - in this case calcium sulfate - were being concentrated in the waters; this process would be expected to occur where a hot, evaporating climate existed. As massive quantities of seawater evaporated, the salts became so concentrated that they precipitated out of solution, and settled to the bottom to form layers of selenite gypsum.

Igneous Rocks of the Upper Missouri

A small, but important part of the rocks that outcrop along the Upper Missouri are igneous rocks, which have their origin as magma, or molten rock. Not all magma reaches the surface to erupt as volcanoes; in this case it cooled underground as the magma was injected into the pre-existing Cretaceous sedimentary rocks. Geologists refer to these rocks as intrusive, or plutonic, igneous rocks, in reference to their forming underground. Most of the intrusive igneous rocks are classified as shonkinites, which help to form some of the most spectacular scenery within the Upper Missouri National Wild and Scenic River corridor. A far less common type of igneous intrusion that occurs in a few locations off the river are diatremes.

All of the igneous rocks of the Upper Missouri area originated about 55 million years ago, during the Tertiary Period of geologic time, as large volumes of hot magma were injected into several locations in central Montana. Collectively, geologists call the part of central Montana where the igneous activity occurred the Central Montana Alkalic Province. Alkalic refers to the unique chemical composition of these rocks - they are enriched in potassium and sodium.

Near the Missouri River, the shonkinitic igneous activity was centered in the Highwood Mountains to the south, and in the Bearpaw Mountains to the north. A line on a map connecting these two centers of intense volcanic activity passes right through the White Cliffs, suggesting that all of these rocks have related origins. However in the White Cliffs the magma never reached the surface but instead cooled within the exsting rocks, most notably the Eagle Formation.

Along the Upper Missouri corridor these shonkinitic igneous rocks are easily identified. From a distance they display a distinctive rusty-brown color, and they do not exhibit any bedding, as in the sedimentary rocks. Freshly broken pieces display a medium to dark gray color, and when viewed up close can be seen to contain crystals of black minerals, biotite and augite. In some locations the shonkinite dikes develop a series of intersecting fractures which give it the appearance of a wall of hand-laid rectangular stones.

The effects of this intruding magma are especially visible today in the stretch of the river between Pilot Rock (rm 51) and Dark Butte (rm 69), where the magma was injected into joints and fractures in the Eagle Sandstone. Upon cooling it formed a maze of dark-colored dikes, sills, and plugs that permeate the white sandstone.

Dikes are masses of solidified magma oriented in a generally vertical position which crosscut the bedding in the sandstone, while *sills* are horizontally oriented, resulting from the magma flowing and hardening between layers of sandstone. Along the Upper Missouri dikes are by far more common than sills. Erosion by the river has today exposed these dikes and sills, which have spent most of their existence underground. The area above and around Eagle Creek (rm 51 - 57) contains numerous dikes, the most impressive of which is Grand Natural Wall (rm 57 right). Sills can be seen on the opposite side of the river from Hole-in-the Wall (rm 64 left).

Plugs are irregularly-shaped masses of igneous rock which vary in size from tens to hundreds of feet across. LaBarge Rock (rm 56), named for the steamboat captain Joseph LaBarge, is a plug that is visible across from the Eagle Creek camping area. Plugs represent major conduits that were feeding molten magma from depth into a locale. An especially large, impressive plug, called the Eagle Buttes, is located across the river from Citadel Rock (rm 62). One can easily trace this plug as the source of the numerous radiating dikes, sills, and associated masses of hardened magma that permeate the surrounding sedimentary rocks, mostly Eagle Sandstone. Another large plug is Dark Butte (rm 69)

'The Grand Natural Wall', river mile 56.9, is a dike - a vertically oriented mass of igneous rock that was intruded into a fracture in the white-colored Eagle Sandstone about 55 million years ago, when the Eagle was buried deep beneath the surface. Dikes are common in the White Cliffs area, and are all composed of a type of rock called shonkinite. This photograph also displays the geologic phenomenon of "differential erosion". The dikes are more resistant to erosion than the sandstone, so as the sandstone is stripped away by erosion the dike, which is a much tougher rock, is left standing.

The type of rock which forms the intrusives is rare; it is named *shonkinite* after Shonkin Sag in the Highwood Mountains. The rock is similar to basalt, but is unusual in that it contains high levels of potassium. Large black crystals of the minerals augite and biotite are common in shonkinite, and aid in its identification.

A second, distinct type of igneous intrusion found in the Missouri Breaks is the *diatreme*. Diatremes occur in the vicinity of Bullwhacker Creek, as part of the Missouri Breaks Diatreme Field, but are nowhere visible from the river. They are an unusual and uncommon type of igneous intrusion, but are important because in some places in the world they are associated with diamond deposits. They are quite small, typically covering no more than a couple of acres where they have intruded into the sedimentary rocks. They consist of a matrix of hardened magma, with included fragments of deeper rocks through which the magma passed as it rose from unusually great depths. This texture indicates that they were emplaced with great explosive force, perhaps due to the presence in the magma of highly pressurized carbon dioxide gas that helped the magma to blast its way upward, fracturing the rock that was in its path, and then transporting these broken fragments upward to be incorporated within the solidifying magma. Bullwhacker Creek, just a couple of miles back from the river, contains a spectacular diatreme along its west side.

LaBarge Rock, river mile 56 right, is a classified as a plug; it is seen here in the middle of the photograph, surrounded on both sides by the lighter-colored Eagle Sandstone. It is the result of a relatively large mass of magma that pushed its way upward from great depths into the layer of Eagle Sandstone, at a time when the Eagle was deep underground. Uplift and erosion has now exposed these rocks at the surface. The plug is made of shonkinite, which is more resistant to erosion than the sandstone, causing it stand higher than the sandstone cliffs.

Structural Disturbances of the Sedimentary Rocks

The sedimentary formations which have been exposed by the Missouri River have not been severely disturbed by tectonic forces since their deposition, as evidenced by the fact that they are generally oriented close to their original horizontal positions. Continued uplift of the Rocky Mountains to the west has, however, uplifted them more in the west, causing them to be very gently inclined downward towards the east. As a result, by floating down the Upper Missouri - to the east - one passes through a cross section of sedimentary rock layers which progress from older to younger.

There are a number of places along the Upper Missouri where faults can be seen to disrupt the predictable near-horizontal layering that is so common along the Upper Missouri. These can be identified by watching for abrupt changes in the layered rocks along the canyon walls. For example, if a prominent cliff of white Eagle Sandstone that lines the river bank suddenly terminates, the likely cause is a fault; the same rock may possibly be visible at a level above or below its original level, depending upon which direction the fault moved.

Spectacular zones of folding and faulting, where the layered sedimentary rocks have been tilted ninety degrees and more, occur along the lower stretch of the Upper Missouri beginning in the vicinity above Dauphin Rapids (rm 101) and continuing past the power plant ruins (rm 136).

Many of the faults seen along the Upper Missouri are classified as thrust faults. Thrust faults occur when layers of rock are compressed laterally and break; the layers on one side of the fault are pushed (or thrust) upward and over the same rock layers on the other side of the fault. When an area that has been affected by thrust faulting is viewed from the river, the same layers can often be seen at two different levels above the river. Perhaps the easiest formation in which to identify the presence of thrust faults on the Upper Missouri is the white Eagle Sandstone. In unfaulted sections of the river, only one layer of the Eagle is present. However in areas that have been affected by thrust faulting, two layers of Eagle can be seen, one above the other, separated by a layer of dark shale. An excellent place to observe the phenomenon of two repeating layers of Eagle Sandstone, caused by thrust faulting, is in the vicinity of Steamboat Rock and Dark Butte (rm 69 left), on the left side of the river. The first layer of Eagle sandstone is about a hundred feet above the river, and the second layer is a few hundred feet higher, forming the rampart of Steamboat Rock; the two sandstone layers are separated by dark shale, probably Marias River Formation.

The cause of the thrust faulting along the Upper Missouri has been identified by geologists as having its origin to the north in the Bear's Paw Mountains. These mountains were being uplifted by igneous activity approximately 55 million years ago, and the layers of sedimentary rock which covered them began sliding southward, off of the top of the uplift and towards the Missouri River, as the uplifting progressed. At some distance from the uplift, the sliding layers buckled and broke - forming a thrust fault, resulting in individual layers sliding over themselves. The soft shales in the area, such as the Marias River Formation, provided an excellent glide plane for the thrust faults to move on.

Glaciation and its Effects on the Upper Missouri

The Pleistocene Epoch of geologic time, which began about two million years and ended about ten thousand years ago, was a time of cold climates and ice ages, leading to the formation of glaciers. Mountain glaciers formed in the Rockies, while massive continental glaciers formed in the northerly latitudes and flowed south from Canada into northern Montana, where ice thicknesses of fifteen-hundred to two-thousand feet occurred.

A spectacular example of both folding and faulting in the Judith River Formation. The location of the photo is the Bullwhacker - Cow Creek area, river mile 122-127 left. In most places along the river the parallel beds of the Judith River Formation are in a near horizontal position, however in this vicinity they have been subjected to intense forces exerted over a long period of time. At first the rocks responded to the stress by bending, or folding; as the stress continued the rock experienced brittle failure and the fault developed. The fault is highlighted with a superimposed dashed line; the rocks on either side of the fault are intensly folded.

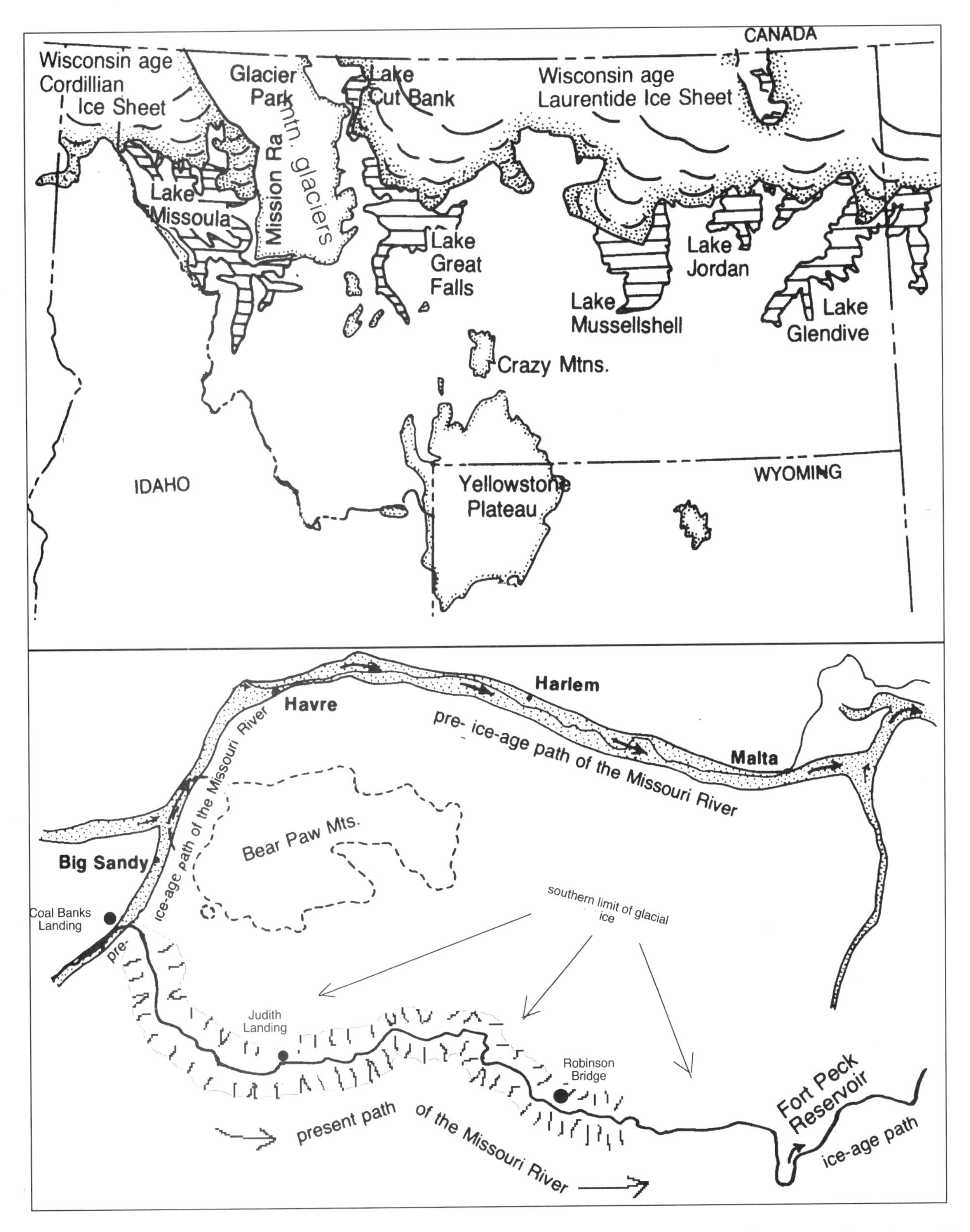

Top. During the Ice Age, central Montana was strongly affected by glaciers which were flowing southward out of Canada. The northward-flowing Missouri was dammed by the ice, forming 'Glacial Lake Great Falls'. Bottom. The Upper Missouri with Coal Banks Landing on the left showing changes in the river's course caused by glaciers. Before the Ice Age, the Missouri flowed northeast past Big Sandy, and on to Havre. As the glacier advanced, the river was diverted to the east, around the southern edge of the ice, where it cut a deep channel for itself in which it remained after the ice retreated. (From Alt and Hyndmnan, Roadside Geology of Montana; courtesy Mountain Press, Missoula)

In the vicinity of Great Falls, where the Missouri is flowing generally northward, the edge of the glacier at times formed a dam across the river's channel, resulting in the formation of a huge lake called "Glacial Lake Great Falls".

At other times, the ice simply changed the course of the Missouri. Where the northward flowing river met the southward moving ice, the river was diverted to the east and flowed around the edge of the glacier. In this new position, running around the toe of the glacier, the river began to actively cut its way down through the soft Cretaceous sedimentary rocks, quickly establishing a well-entrenched channel for itself.

The ice persisted for tens of thousands of years, but when a warming climate finally heralded the end of the Ice Age, and the glacier retreated towards Canada, the Missouri remained in its newly formed channel. The retreat of the ice also exposed the Missouri's old, more northerly channel, which today is occupied in places by the Milk River.

Evidence of the effect of the glacier on the Missouri is easily observed. As one travels down the Missouri from Fort Benton, the first several miles of the river's channel are wide, with a well developed flood plain, and a lack of steep-walled banks. These features are characteristic of a mature river valley, and geologists believe that this part of the river's course is part of its original channel, which the Missouri occupied both before and after the Ice Age.

At Virgelle (rm 41), the river enters a long, sweeping curve which results in a radical, ninety-degree change in its direction of flow - from northeast to southeast. Beyond this curve (rm 46), the river's channel undergoes a dramatic and visible change. The previously wide valley gives way to a narrow, steep-walled gorge in which the river is entrenched. There are fewer islands, and the map shows that the river is straighter, with fewer meanders. These are features indicative of a young channel, where downcutting by the river is very active, and geologists believe that downriver from Virgelle, the Missouri is flowing through the new channel that it had cut for itself as it was diverted around the edge of the glacier. By the time the glacier began retreating, the new channel was so well established that the Missouri could not return to its old channel.

Geologists have identified a portion of the Missouri's old, pre-Ice Age channel just northeast of Virgelle. Big Sandy Creek, which presently flows to the northeast, around the west flank of the Bearpaw Mountains, and into the Milk River, occupies an exceedingly wide channel for such a small stream. Big Sandy Creek lines up nicely with the present channel of the Missouri from Ft. Benton to Virgelle. This oversized valley appears to be the part of the Missouri's channel which connected the present channel (from Fort Benton) with the Missouri's pre-Ice Age channel that is today occupied by Milk River, further to the north.

Weathering, Erosion, Downcutting, and Mass Wasting

The rugged nature of the Upper Missouri corridor is due primarily to the geologic processes of weathering and erosion, and to another process called mass wasting.

Weathering is the chemical and mechanical breakdown of rock caused by exposure to conditions at earth's surface; ultimately weathering produces soil from rock. There are a number of different processes that contribute to rock weathering, the most important of which are exposure to moisture, oxygen, carbon dioxide, and solar radiation. An example of weathering along the Upper Missouri is the breakdown of the Eagle Sandstone, which is composed of grains of sand that are held together by a cement called calcium carbonate. As rainwater passes through the atmosphere it absorbs carbon dioxide and as a result forms a weak acid called carbonic acid. This acid dissolves the calcium carbonate cement and liberates individual sand grains, thus disintegrating the sandstone.

Erosion is the process whereby loose, weathered materials become transported by earth processes such as running water and wind. Along the Upper Missouri running water is dominant among these processes. Rain and melting snow that runs across the sedimentary and igneous rocks that line the river's banks pick up small rock fragments, such as sand grains, that have been loosened by weathering processes and transport them downhill where they eventually wind up in the river. Ultimately this material will be transported by the Missouri's current into the Mississippi River and the Gulf of Mexico. Wind is responsible for features such as sandstone arches that occur in the White Cliffs, as it removes loosened sand grains from what began as a small hole in a wall of sandstone.

Although the above processes of weathering and erosion occur at slow rates, at least in human perspective, the key to understanding their dominant role in forming today's landscape is the concept of geologic time. Grain by grain, the removal of material from the river corridor over vast amounts of geologic time has resulted in the creation of the canyon through which the Upper Missouri today flows.

A steep shale slope along the Upper Missouri that is experiencing undercutting by the river. As the river's current attacks the bottom of the slope it removes material, undercutting the entire slope. Eventually the overhanging material can no longer support itself and a landslide occurs. This entire slope displays signs of ongoing landsliding, as evidenced by a lack of vegetation, general steepness, and the presence of a very recent small slope failure near river level.

In addition to the main canyon of the Upper Missouri, an intricate system of side canyons, called coulees or ravines, border the river. These are formed by smaller rivers and streams that drain into the Missouri, and they are responsible for the rugged topography that is locally known as the Missouri Breaks. The formation of the breaks is a function of the fact that the Upper Missouri is carrying far more water that these smaller tributary streams, and is therefore downcutting into the rocks and deepening its canyon at a much faster rate than are the tributaries. As the Missouri's canyon continually deepens the tributaries must respond by increasing their gradient, or steepness, particularly at the upper ends of the ravines, where they border the surrounding plains. This steepening of their gradient causes these tributary streams to have a more vigorous, turbulent rate of flow which is capable of eroding material at a more aggressive rate, and leads to a process called *headward erosion*, whereby the tributaries continue to cut further and further into the flat land along the uppermost rim of the canyon, the result being that the canyon is continually widening and deepening over time.

Mass wasting is the downslope movement of loosened rock material by gravity, without the aid of a transporting medium, such as water. Along the Upper Missouri the most common type of mass wasting is *landslides*, taking the form of both *rockfalls* and *slumps*. The overwhelming cause of landslides on the Upper Missouri is undercutting by running water. Undercutting typically takes place along the outside curve of bends in the river, where the current is directed against the river's banks. At such locations the removal of bank material by the river is accelerated and the slopes and cliffs above these locations become undercut. As undercutting progresses, support for the overlying material weakens until the slope or cliff fails and collapses. A *rockfall* is a rapid failure of an undercut slope, the results of which can be seen in the White Cliffs where vertical cliffs of Eagle Sandstone have been undercut, resulting in large boulders having fallen and collected along the river's banks. A *slump* is a type of landslide that typically moves slowly, perhaps over the course of days to weeks. On the Upper Missouri slumps typically occur where the river has undercut a relatively gently sloping shale outcropping. As these slopes fail they typically give the appearance of a mass of gooey mud that has slid downhill into the river and they leave behind concave shaped scars that appear as if they were produced by a giant ice-cream scoop.

Additional Information

The Montana Bureau of Mines and Geology, located in Butte, Montana is a good source for additional information about the geology of Montana. They have produced geologic maps of the Upper Missouri area which can be purchased by the public.

In 1833 Karl Bodmer sketched a large herd of buffalo crossing the Missouri River. This was a common scene on the river, and steamboats were often held up for hours as these magnificent animals forded the river. Courtesy Joslyn Art Museum, Omaha, Nebraska; gift of the Enron Foundation

Chapter 6

Wildlife

Introduction

The abundance and diversity of wildlife along the Missouri River breaks area has been noted since the days of the Lewis and Clark Expedition. At the present time, sixty species of mammals, two hunderd thirty-three species of birds, twenty species of amphibians and reptiles, and forty-nine species of fish have been reported to inhabit the wild and scenic corridor. This chapter provides a survey of some of the more common and interesting inhabitants of the Upper Missouri River Breaks.

The climate of the central Montana region is semi-arid, and water is a limiting resource for wildlife. The river area provides several special and unique habitats which provide for the abundance and diversity of wildlife found near the river. Unique habitats consist of cliffs, talus slopes, and caves. Cliffs and talus habitats are located primarily between Coal Banks Landing and the mouth of the Judith River - locally known as the "White Rocks" area. Several species of animals are more abundant along this section of the river because they require these habitats in their life cycle.

An important habitat type is the riparian area associated with surface water. The riparian habitat exists as scattered narrow bands of mixed vegetative types on the river banks, supplying diverse foliage and a greater number of habitat types for wildlife. The majority of the riparian habitat is confined to one-half of the total river: Fort Benton to Little Sandy Creek - forty-seven miles; mouth of Arrow Creek and Judith River - three miles; Cow Island to Robinson bridge - twenty-two miles. Most wildlife species in the river area require riparian habitat in their life cycle.

Snags are important raptor perches and nest sites for tree cavity nesters.

River islands are in a near primitive state and provide major deer fawning, elk calving, and goose nesting sites by providing an area free of livestock disturbance. Increased recreational use of islands could adversely affect wildlife use, and the Bureau of Land Management discourages recreational use of islands until after July 31st to reduce stress on young animals.

Cliffs, talus slopes, caves, riparian zones, and islands are special and unique wildlife habitat areas, since they occupy a small percentage of the total area, are restricted in locations, and dependent wildlife are concentrated into small areas.

The expansion of small grain farms on the flat lands above the river has reduced wildlife habitat such that wildlife species are more dependent upon the river area to meet their key habitat requirements.

Large mammals that live within the Upper Missouri River Breaks National Monument are shown here. Clockwise, beginning at top left, they are Elk, Bighorn Sheep, Mule Deer, and White Tail Deer. All images are courtesy of Montana artist Robert Neaves of Hamilton.

Mammals

Members of the Lewis and Clark Expedition observed bison, bighorn sheep, mule deer, white-tailed deer, elk, antelope, beaver, black bear, grizzly bear, wolves, swift fox, and mountain lion along the wild and scenic segment of the Missouri River. The coming of fur traders and the establishment of trading posts marked the permanent presence of white men in the area. Later, cattlemen settled the area followed by dryland farmers. All these demands on the land greatly reduced the native prairies and marked the decline of wildlife. The bison, black bear, grizzly, wolves, and swift fox are no longer found in the river area.

The major emphasis of most wildlife studies by state and federal agencies and universities has been on game species. Detailed studies of many non-game species have not been extensive for the Missouri Breaks, and much undoubtedly remains to be learned about the region's animal life. Likewise the effects of recreational use in the river area on these species is unknown.

Large Mammals

Mule deer are common along the river. They are closely associated with the breaks and adjacent agricultural lands. Low mule deer populations in the lower half of the river are due to poor productivity and/or survival. Populations in the upper half of the river are in somewhat better condition. Seasonal distribution of this species shows a preference for grassland-sagebrush and riparian type vegetation in the spring and summer, moving to the heads of the breaks and benches in winter. River islands are an important area for fawning, free from livestock disturbance.

White-tailed deer are restricted to the narrow riparian habitat and agricultural lands along the river bottoms. During periods of heavy snow, these animals will move to the sagebrush-grasslands of the breaks. The river islands provide a major fawning area as well as supplying food and cover.

Where the terrain is open, with easy access to the river, small bands of antelope will utilize the sagebrush-grasslands on the river bottom in summer. During the spring and fall, antelope utilize adjacent small grain fields. During severe winters, antelope will migrate into the breaks for shelter and food.

The last native elk was believed to have vanished from the breaks during the 1860's. This species was reintroduced in 1951 and they continue to increase in numbers as well as to expand their range. Recent reports show a westward expansion of their range along the river, as far west as Stafford Ferry. River islands and riparian zones are major calving areas for elk in the management area.

Lewis and Clark reported seeing bighorn sheep along the river bluffs. This species, the Audubon Bighorn Sheep, became extinct by 1916. In 1958 and 1961 the Montana Department of Fish, Wildlie, and Parks reintroduced forty-three Rocky Mountain Bighorn Sheep, a close relative of the extinct Audubon Bighorn, on the river within the C.M. Russell National Wildlife Range. The herd grew to at least ninety animals, but then a series of die-offs reduced the herd to nine animals. In 1980, another twenty-seven sheep were planted in the Chimney Bend area (river mile 108). These animals have done exceedingly well and at the present time their progeny appear to have repopulated all of the areas once inhabited by the Audubon sheep. Floaters frequently observe bighorns on both sides of the river from Judith Landing to Robinson Bridge.

Small Mammals

Coyotes are numerous in some locations along the river, and are frequently heard at night, adding immeasurably to the wilderness experience. The Red Fox's range includes the Upper Missouri River.

The black-footed ferret is an endangered species with historical presence in the river area. Presumptive evidence of ferret activity has been found in the area, although no ferrets have been observed. Blacktailed prairie dog towns provide the necessary habitat requirements for the ferret. A number of prairie dog towns near the river might support a population of this species. Eleven prairie dog towns have been identified on the river flood plains.

Beaver, the largest rodent in North America, are common on the Upper Missouri. Its value as a fur animal was the singular most important reason for the arrival of the fur trade in Montana in the late1820's. Beaver lodges, constructed of sticks and mud, are a common sight on the river, as is the sight of a beaver swimming in the river and slapping its large paddle-shaped tail as it dives to avoid an approaching canoe. Beaver are plant eaters, who will consume leafy vegetation in summer and woody vegetation year-round. In length they range from thirty-four to forty inches, and they weigh from thirty to sixty pounds.

Muskrat are another aquatic rodent which habitate the Upper Missouri; they resemble beaver, but are smaller, and lack the flat tail of the beaver.

Among other mammals that occur within the Upper Missouri River Breaks National Monument are bobcat, skunk, raccoon, mink, badger, and weasel.

The beaver is common along the Upper Missouri. They are often seen swimming in the river, and their lodges, composed of piles of sticks and mud can be seen lining the banks of the river. Image courtesy of Montana artist Robert Neaves, of Hamilton.

Birds

A complete list of all bird species that have been observed on the Upper Missouri National Wild and Scenic River is included at the end of this chapter.

The great diversity and number of birds found along the river can be attributed to a diversity of special habitats. The scattered narrow bands of riparian habitat contains the greatest diversity of bird species by providing more diverse foliage and a greater number of niches for food, cover, and nest sites.

Canada geese and mallards are the primary waterfowl species nesting on the river. Early spring is marked by the arrival of thousands of Canada Geese, many of whom remain to nest. Canada geese almost exclusively nest on river islands. The largest number and variety of waterfowl occur during the fall migration when the birds utilize standing grain crops and marshes long distances from the river and return to the river for resting, cover, and some feeding.

The white pelican, a large, magnificent bird is common on the river, especially in spring and early summer.

A variety of shorebirds are found on the river throughout the spring and summer.

Cottonwood groves provide nesting sites for great blue herons, cormorants, ospreys, and raptors. To date, four great blue heron rookeries have been identified within the wild and scenic corridor.

Further back from the river where vegetation is available to provide nesting habitat and protection, several upland game birds occur. These include sharp-tailed grouse, sage grouse, gray partridge, pheasants and Merriam's turkey. Sharp-tailed grouse are common and widely distributed on the benches.

The most common birds of prey include the buteo hawks, such as the redtail hawk and Swainson's hawk. Golden eagles are common and nest along the river. Bald eagles over-winter along the river, with some nesting pairs being reported.

Burrowing owls are commonly associated with prairie dog towns. The endangered peregrine falcon and prairie falcon have a history of nesting along the river. The Montana Department of Fish, Wildlie, and Parks has reported that peregrine falcons are presently nesting on the river.

Eighty percent of the passerine birds (these include perching birds and songbirds) found within the river area are year-around residents. The range of eastern and western species overlap where suitable riparian habitat exists. Late summer concentration of nearly one-half million doves have been reported by Montana Department of Fish, Wildlie, and Parks observers.

Amphibians

Amphibians are primarily concentrated along side drainages and stream channels where there is riparian vegetation and surface water. The Upper Missouri is within the known range of the Western Toad, Woodhouse's Toad, the Western Chorus Frog, and the Northern Leopard Frog.

Reptiles

Numerous reptiles inhabit the river corridor, including turtles in the river environment, and snakes and lizards occupying the river banks and the dry lands adjacent to the river.

Perhaps the reptile which commands the greatest attention of river recreationists is the Western Rattlesnake. They range in length from fifteen to sixty inches, and the most obvious identifying characteristic is the rattle at the end of the snake's tail, which emits a high-pitched 'rattle' when the snake is threatened. Rattlesnakes have two venom sacks in their heads, from which venom is injected through two hollow fangs as a means of disabling small prey.

Other snakes which occur along the Upper Missouri are the Racer, the Gopher (or Bull) Snake - which bears a resemblance to the Rattlesnake, the Common Garter Snake, Western Terrestrial Garter Snake, and the Plains Garter Snake.

Two species of turtles inhabit the Upper Missouri, the first being the Snapping Turtle, which ranges from thirteen to thirty pounds, and the second being the Spiny Softshell, which range up to eighteen inches in length.

A single species of lizard that is found along the Upper Missouri is the Short-Horned Lizard, sometimes erroneously refered to as the Horned Toad. They are from about two six inches in length, with small horns on their head, and a distinctive row of pointed scales on either side of the body. They can be seen scurrying suprisingly fast across the surface, and are very active during the day, feeding largely on ants. They do not seem to require a proximity to water and can be found far up into the breaks.

Fish

The Missouri River supports a significant fishery, with greater use being placed on this resource annually. The river has a greater diversity of aquatic habitats with a larger variety of fish species than many river drainages in Montana. Forty-nine species representing fourteen families are known to occur in the river and its tributaries. Thirty-five species are found in the Missouri River proper, primarily warm water fisheries, with the remaining fourteen species in tributaries, primarily cold water fisheries.

A unique species of fish that occurs in the Upper Missouri River is the Paddlefish. Only seven known spawning populations of Paddlefish exist today. The population that inhabits the Upper Missouri spends much of its time in Fort Peck Reservoir, and spawning runs come up the river in the spring. This is one of the last known "stable" populations of paddlefish. The State of Montana allows a short fishing season for Paddlefish, during which time fishermen gather near Fred Robinson Bridge.

Two other unique fish in the Upper Missouri are the Pallid Sturgeon and the Shovelnose Sturgeon. Of the two, the Pallid Sturgeon is an endangered species, while the Shovelnose Sturgeon populations appear to be stable.

Pallid Sturgeon are large fish, as much as five feet in length, whose numbers in the Upper Missouri above Fort Peck Dam are estimated at less than one hundred. It is likely that damming of the Missouri has altered the natural environment of the river bottom - where these fish live, to such an extent as to make their survival questionable. A captive breeding program has been successful and is providing new stock to bolster natural populations; efforts are also underway to restore habitat.

The Shovelnose Sturgeon population in the Upper Missouri seems to be healthy. They are somewhat smaller than the Pallid Sturgeon. The State of Montana allows a short fishing season for Shovelnose Sturgeon.

Among other species of fish that inhabit the Upper Missouri are the Goldeneye, Northern Pike, Channel Catfish, Black Bullhead Catfish, Burbot, White Crappie, Yellow Perch, Walleye, and Sauger.

Threatened and Endangered Species

The black-footed ferret, and peregrine falcon have been sighted in the Missouri Wild and Scenic River area in the past century. The present status of these species is uncertain, but evidence indicates that the peregrine falcon is probably occupying nesting sites along the river today, indicating they are making a comeback.

Extinct and Displaced Species

As white civilization began encroaching on the Upper Missouri, the pressures that were exerted on wildlife populations caused the extinction or displacement of some of the species that had roamed these lands for thousands of years. In the case of the buffalo, wolf, Audubon bighorn sheep, and the plains grizzly the eradication was intentional and surprisingly swift. Fortunately, some of these species are now being reintroduced into parts of their former ranges.

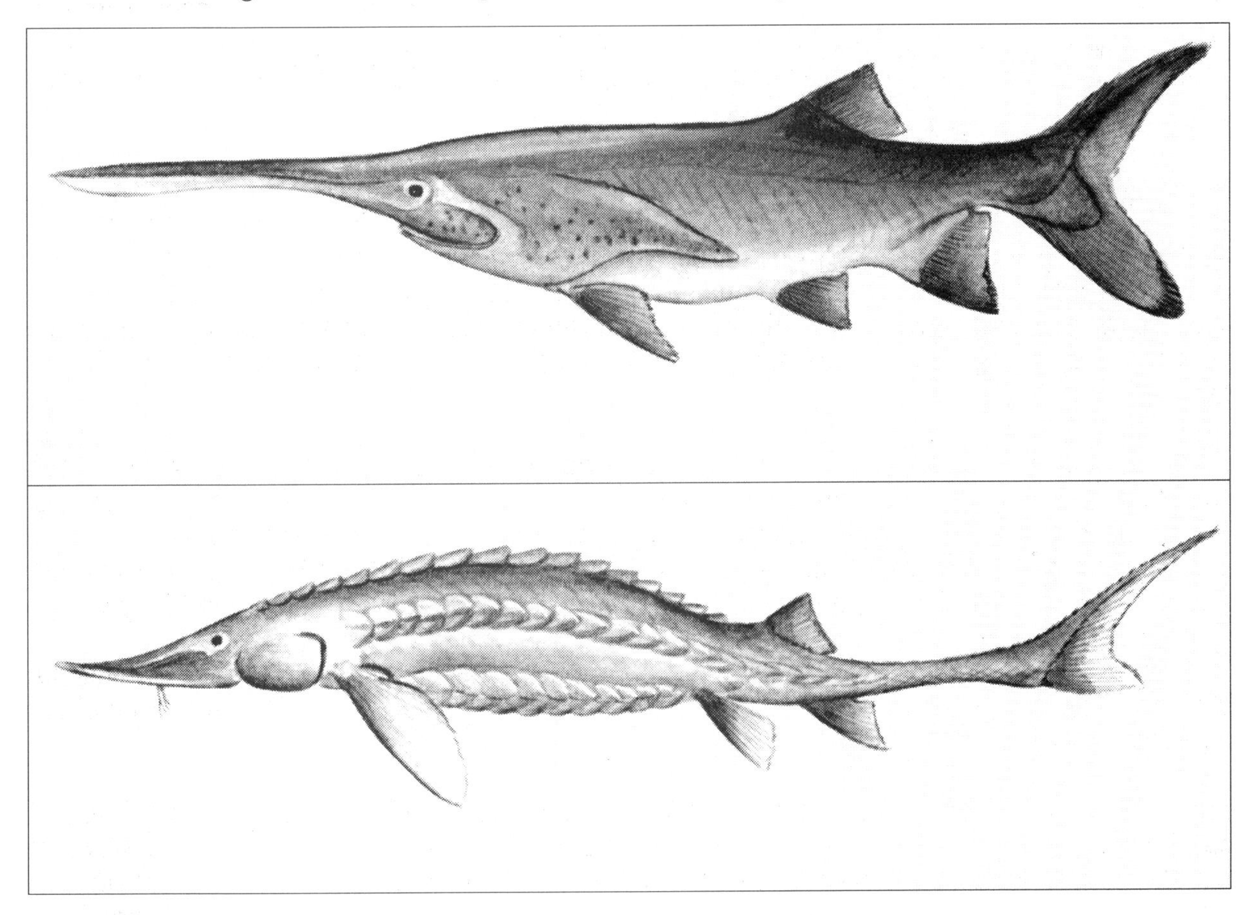

Two unusual fish that inhabit the Upper Missouri River are the Paddlefish, top, and the Shovelnose Sturgeon, bottom. Images courtesy Montana artist Glenn West of Billings.

Buffalo

The sight of a herd of buffalo crossing the Missouri, or blanketing the plains above the river, must have been a truly impressive sight - sadly, one that today's visitors to the Upper Missouri National Wild and Scenic River can only imagine. Lewis and Clark's journals are filled with entries that reflect the captains awe at the size of the herds. Steamboats were sometimes held up for hours, or even days, as buffalo herds crossed the river. Today there are small remnant herds in places such as Yellowstone National Park, and the Moeise National Bison Range. Perhaps it will be possible some day to reintroduce buffalo in the Missouri Breaks.

Wolves

Another animal that Lewis and Clark frequently commented on was the wolf. Lewis and Clark recorded in their journals that the herds of buffalo were always accompanied by "their constant shepherds, the wolves". James Willard Schultz in his book, "Many Strange Characters" (1982, Univ. of Oklahoma Press), devoted a chapter to the 'Eagle Creek Wolfers', where the method of the day for killing wolves for their hides was described. It involved killing a buffalo and lacing the carcass with strychnine. As an example of the brutal effectiveness of this method, Schultz recounts that four such baited carcasses drew in a total of sixty-seven wolves in a two-day period, along with foxes, coyotes, and other unfortunate souls. Hopefully the wolf introduction program will result in the return of the wolf to the Missouri Breaks.

Audubon's Bighorn Sheep

As Lewis and Clark traveled through the Upper Missouri National Wild and Scenic River corridor, they made many journal entries about the "bighorned animal", and marvelled at the sure-footedness of these animals, as they bounded across the near-vertical breaks above the river. These animals, Audubon's bighorn sheep, were hunted to extinction in the early twentieth century. Attempts at replacing them with transplanted Rocky Mountain Bighorn Sheep appear to be successful.

Grizzly Bear

Today, the Grizzly Bear is well known as an inhabitant of the mountains and high plateaus in Montana's two national parks, Yellowstone and Glacier. But in the days of the Indians, Lewis and Clark, and the fur traders, the grizzly was common along the Upper Missouri. The Indians had great respect for the grizzly, and the members of the Lewis and Clark Expedition quickly learned that their single shot rifles were inadequate for dispatching a grizzly. As people and stock began to populate the Upper Missouri, there was no place for the great bear, and they were eliminated from the plains.

Bird Species of the Upper Missouri National Wild and Scenic River

LOONS & GREBES
Common Loon
Pied-billed Grebe
Horned Grebe
Eared Grebe
Western Grebe

PELICANS & CORMORANTS
American White Pelican
Double-crested Cormorant

BITTERNS & HERONS
Great Egret
Snowy Egret
American Bittern
Great Blue Heron
Black-crowned Night Heron

SWANS & GEESE
Tundra Swan
Trumpeter Swan
Snow Goose
Ross' Goose
Brant
Canada Goose

DUCKS
Wood Duck
Green-winged Teal
American Black Duck
Mallard
Northern Pintail
Blue-winged Tea
Cinnamon Teal
Gadwall
Eurasian Wigeon
Northern Shoveler
American Wigeon
Canvasback
Redhead
Ring-Necked Duck
Lesser Scaup
Oldsquaw
White-Winged Scoter
Common Goldeneye
Barrow's Goldeneye
Bufflehead
Hooded Merganser
Common Merganser
Red-breasted Merganser
Ruddy Duck

HAWKS, FALCONS, & VULTURES
Turkey Vulture
Osprey
Bald Eagle
Northern Harrier
Northern Goshawk
Sharp-shinned Hawk
Cooper's Hawk
Broad-winged Hawk
Northern Goshawk
Swainson's Hawk
Red-tailed Hawk
Ferruginous Hawk
Rough-legged Hawk
Golden Eagle
American Kestrel
Merlin
Peregrine Falcon
Gyrfalcon
Prairie Falcon

GROUSE, PHEASANTS, & TURKEYS
Gray Partridge
Ring-necked Pheasant
Blue Grouse
Ruffed Grouse
Sage Grouse
Sharp-tailed Grouse
Wild Turkey

CRANES & RAILS
Virginia Rail
Sora Rail
American Coot
Sandhill Crane
Whooping Crane

PLOVERS & SANDPIPERS
Black-bellied Plover
Lesser Golden-Plover
Semipalmated Plover
Killdeer
Mountain Plover
Black-necked Stilt
American Avocet
Greater Yellowlegs
Lesser Yellowlegs
Solitary Sandpiper
Willet
Spotted Sandpiper
Upland Sandpiper
Long-billed Curlew
Marbled Godwit
Hudsonian Godwit
Sanderling
Semipalmated Sandpiper
Least Sandpiper
Baird's Sandpiper
Pectoral Sandpiper
Long-billed Dowitcher
Common Snipe
Wilson's Phalarope
Red-necked Phalarope

GULLS & TERNS
Franklin's Gull
Ring-billed Gull
California Gull
Herring Gull
Caspian Tern
Common Tern
Forester's Tern
Black Tern

DOVES
Rock Dove
Mourning Dove

CUCKOOS
Black-billed Cuckoo

OWLS
Great Horned Owl
Snowy Owl
Northern Pygmy Owl
Burrowing Owl
Long-eared Owl
Short-eared Owl
Northern Saw-whet Owl

GOATSUCKERS
Common Nighthawk
Common Poorwill

SWIFTS
White-throated Swift

HUMMINGBIRDS
Calliope Hummingbird

KINGFISHERS
Belted Kingfisher

WOODPECKERS
Lewis' Woodpecker
Red-headed Woodpecker
Red-naped Sapsucker
Downy Woodpecker
Hairy Woodpecker
Northern Flicker

Both Bald Eagles, left, and Golden Eagles, right are frequently seen on the Upper Missouri. Images courtesy Montana artist Joe Thornbrugh, of Victor

Bird Species (continued)

FLYCATCHERS
Olive-sided Flycatcher
Western Wood-Pewee
Willow Flycatcher
Least Flycatcher
Dusky Flycatcher
Cordilleran Flycatcher
Say's Phoebe
Western Kingbird
Eastern Kingbird

LARKS
Horned Lark

SWALLOWS
Purple Martin
Tree Swallow
Violet-green Swallow
Northern Rough-winged Swallow
Bank Swallow
Cliff Swallow
Barn Swallow

JAYS & CROWS
Gray Jay
Blue Jay
Pinyon Jay
Clark's Nutcracker
Black-billed Magpie
American Crow
Common Raven

CHICKADEES
Black-capped Chickadee
Mountain Chickadee

NUTHATCHES & CREEPERS
Red-breasted Nuthatch
White-breasted Nuthatch
Brown Creeper

WRENS
Rock Wren
House Wren
Winter Wren
Marsh Wren

DIPPERS
American Dipper

KINGLETS
Golden-crowned Kinglet
Ruby-crowned Kinglet

THRUSHES
Western Bluebird
Mountain Bluebird
Townsend's Solitaire
Veery
Swainson's Thrush
Hermit Thrush
American Robin

THRASHERS
Gray Catbird
Northern Mockingbird
Sage Thrasher
Brown Thrasher

PIPITS
American Pipit
Sprague's Pipit

WAXWINGS
Bohemian Waxwing
Cedar Waxwing

SHRIKES
Northern Shrike
Loggerhead Shrike

STARLINGS
European Starling

VIREOS
Solitary Vireo
Warbling Vireo
Red-eyed Vireo

WARBLERS
Orange-crowned Warbler
Yellow Warbler
Yellow-rumped Warbler (audubon's?)
Blackpoll Warbler
American Redstart
Ovenbird
Northern Waterthrush
MacGillivray's Warbler
Common Yellowthroat
Wilson's Warbler
Yellow-breasted Chat

TANANGERS
Western Tanager

GROSBEAKS & SPARROWS
Rose-breasted Grosbeak
Black-headed Grosbeak
Lazuli Bunting
Indigo Bunting
Spotted Towhee
Green-tailed Towhee
American Tree Sparrow
Chipping Sparrow
Clay-colored Sparrow
Brewer's Sparrow
Harris Sparrow
Vesper Sparrow
Savannah Sparrow
Baird's Sparrow
Lark Bunting
Grasshopper Sparrow
Song Sparrow
Lincoln's Sparrow
White-throated Sparrow
White-crowned Sparrow
Dark-eyed Junco

LONGSPURS
McCown's Longspur
Lapland Longspur
Chestnut-collared Longspur
Snow Bunting
Bobolink

BLACKBIRDS & ORIOLES
Red-winged Blackbird
Yellow-headed Blackbird
Western Meadowlark
Brewer's Blackbird
Common Grackle
Brown-headed Cowbird
Northern Oriole (Bullock's and Baltimore)

FINCHES
Pine Grosbeak
Cassin's Finch
Purple Finch
Grey-crowned Rosy Finch
Red Crossbill
White-winged Crossbill
Common Redpoll
Hoary Redpoll
Pine Siskin
American Goldfinch
Evening Grosbeak

WEAVER FINCHES
House Sparrow

Chapter 7

Floating the Upper Missouri

Introduction

Although there are a few places where the Upper Missouri is accessible by roads, most of the river and its adjacent wilderness must be accessed by boats. For thousands of people every year, the river offers a welcome dose of natural beauty and serenity; it is largely unchanged since Lewis and Clark Expedition traveled through in 1805 and 1806. Floating the Upper Missouri offers individuals opportunities to view and visit numerous historic sites from several periods of our country's history, to enjoy the varied plants and animals which inhabit the river corridor, to gaze upon a striking geologic landscape, and to experience the rejuvenating effects of a trip through a wilderness.

The Fort Benton Visitor Center, operated by the U.S. Bureau of Land Management, is open during the main floating season, typically from Memorial Day to Labor Day. Before taking off on a canoe trip on the Upper Missouri, floaters should check with the BLM for updates on river conditions and regulations.

Management and History

The Upper Missouri is managed by the Bureau of Land Management (BLM), a division of the United States Department of the Interior. Originally, in 1976, the Upper Missouri was designated as a National Wild and Scenic River, largely due to the efforts of Montana Senator Lee Metcalf. In 2001, President Clinton, acting upon the recommendation of Interior Secretary Bruce Babbitt, signed an executive order creating the Upper Missouri River Breaks National Monument, which includes lands bordering the river corridor.

As of this writing there are no permits required to float the Upper Missouri, and there are no restrictions on the number of parties that can launch on a given day. Its possible that this may change, and its always worth checking with the BLM, should a permit system be instituted.

There are two locations from which the BLM manages the river, each of which can provide extensive and current information for individuals seeking information about the river. During the floating season, from Memorial Day to Labor Day, the BLM has a visitor center located in Fort Benton, where the monument begins, which is staffed with highly knowledgeable personnel. The visitor center also has some fine displays of the natural and human history of the river. The Fort Benton visitor center can be contacted at (406) 622-5185. During the remainder of the year the BLM can be contacted at its Lewistown office: Bureau of Land Management, River Manager, PO Box 1160, Lewistown, MT, 59457; (406) 538-7461.

There are also seasonal ranger stations (Memorial Day to Labor Day) at the other major launch and take-out points located at Coal Banks Landing, Judith Landing, and James Kipp Recreation Area.

Paddling in the White Cliffs; view upriver near Eagle Creek.

Maps and Printed Information

The BLM offers an excellent set of maps for the Upper Missouri, which are indispensable for those planning a float trip. The maps can be purchased at the Fort Benton visitor center, or they can be ordered by mail or phone from the Lewistown office. The BLM also provides additional information about camping, safety, drinking water, outfitters, etc., which can be requested or picked up in person. It is always a good idea to stop at a visitor center just prior to embarking on a trip to get the most recent updates about river conditions.

Planning and Preparation

Outfitters

There are a number of professional outfitters that operate on the Upper Missouri who offer a variety of services ranging from fully guided trips to equipment rental, and vehicle shuttling services. In general outfitters are well-versed on the river's history, geology, and the location of many of the river corridor's unique places. These individuals are licensed by the BLM, and the BLM maintains a list of these individuals, with information on how to contact them. This list also contains contact information for canoe and equipment rentals, and shuttle services.

View upriver in the Badlands section of the river, between Judith Landing and James Kipp Recreation Area.

Going on Your Own

The Upper Missouri is considered an easy river to float, but anyone who is considering a trip down the river must consider the fact that it a wilderness excursion. Once on the river, there is no access to telephones (including cellular), towns, and emergency services. Paddling parties must have everything in their boats that they'll need until arriving at their take-out point. Should an emergency occur, it is likely that it will take at least 24 hours to get help. Preparedness is therefore essential.

The primary prerequisites for anyone embarking on an Upper Missouri paddling trip are basic wilderness travel and camping skills, a fair to good level of physical conditioning, and quality equipment, as well as a basic familiarity with handling and packing a canoe.

Launch and Take-Out Points

Following is a list of the launch and take-out points, and their position on the river, that are easily accessed by automobile:

Fort Benton, river mile 1; accessible by paved road from within the town of Fort Benton. Rest rooms, camping, drinking water available.

Loma Bridge, river mile 18; accessible by gravel road one mile from town of Loma; from the bridge follow the BLM signs to launch area. Vault toilets, camping, no water.

Coal Banks Landing, river mile 41, accessible by gravel road, eight miles from Highway 87 at milepost #66. Vault toilets, camping, water source not always dependable, seasonal BLM Ranger Station.

Judith Landing, river mile 88; accessible by paved/gravel road forty-four miles from the town of Big Sandy. Vault toilets, camping, no water, seasonal BLM Ranger Station, and a seasonal store (ice, film, beverages, etc.).

James Kipp Recreation Area/Fred Robinson Bridge, river mile 149; accessible directly from Highway 191 on the south side of the river; boat launch is located about one-half mile from entrance; rest rooms, drinking water, and camping available.

Tripping Options

There are three contiguous segments which make up the 149-mile Upper Missouri National Wild and Scenic River. Each segment possesses different scenic and geologic characteristics, different types of wildlife viewing possibilities, and access to different historical sites. The major access sites for starting or ending a trip are located at Fort Benton (rm 0), Wood Bottom (rm 20) Coal Banks Landing (rm 42), Judith Landing (rm 88), and James Kipp Recreation Area (rm 149)

Trips of varying distances are possible and include: 46 miles, 61 miles, 88 miles, 103 miles, and 149 miles. The shortest trip takes 3-4 days, and the longest takes a minimum of 6-7 days. Trip duration depends on the rate the river is flowing, and your group's desired pace of travel. The most popular trips are described below.

Fort Benton to Coal Banks Landing (42 miles) This segment of the river is entrenched in a mile-wide, steep-walled valley composed of black-colored Marias River Shale, capped by the yellow Telegraph Creek Sandstone. The Missouri River here has a meandering habit, with bottomlands and islands, many covered with lush groves of cottonwoods. This is rich habitat for deer, pelicans, geese, ducks, eagles, and many other birds. There are four Lewis and Clark campsites, including their camp at the mouth of the Marias River, the site of an extremely important decision point for the captains. Several important fur trading posts, most notably the American Fur Company's Fort McKenzie, were located on this stretch of the river. A high percentage of the land bordering this segment is private; nevertheless, this is a beautiful stretch of river that is enjoyable to float. Small BLM holdings provide a number of camping sites, almost all of which are in the "undeveloped recreation area" category (described below in the section on camping).

Coal Banks Landing to Judith Landing (46 miles) Considered by many to be the most spectacular stretch of the Upper Missouri River, this is also the most popular. The percentage of public land begins to increase, as compared with the upper segment of the river. Along this stretch of the Upper Missouri floaters pass three Lewis and Clark campsites, Indian habitation sites, petroglyphs, and several still-standing homestead buildings. Adventurous floaters can take a vigorous climb up to the "Hole-In-The-Wall". No longer meandering in nature, the river follows a relatively straight course, and has cut a spectacular 800 foot-deep canyon through the white-colored Eagle Sandstone, which forms breath-taking 300 foot high cliffs. Weird and unusual formations, called "pedestal rocks", resembling large toadstools, are common, and in many places are so numerous as to form "gardens". The sandstone cliffs contain an intricate labyrinth of dark brown-colored veins, called dikes and sills, some over 20 feet thick, that were formed by the injection of hot magma. These dikes and sills are highly resistant to erosion, and frequently form spectacular vertical walls. Geologists who visit this area consider it to contain textbook examples of landforms produced by intruding magma. Captain Meriwether Lewis was awe-struck by this area, and in a lengthy journal entry described "scenes of visionary enchantment". Most of the campsites in the White Cliffs are classified as "minimally developed recreation area" (see camping section, below).

Judith Landing to Kipp Recreation Area (61 miles) This stretch of the river is probably the least traveled. Combined with the White Cliffs section it makes an excellent 5 to 6 day trip. The amount of public land increases dramatically, providing countless hiking opportunities. Many old homestead buildings are found here, as well as some important sites in the Upper Missouri's steamboat history, and five Lewis and Clark campsites. The Nez Perce National Historic Trail crosses this stretch of the Upper Missouri. Excellent opportunities to view herds of Rocky Mountain Bighorn Sheep exist in some locations. The dominant rocks are those of the Judith River Formations (70 million years old), which is made up of strong, thin layers of sandstone, and alternating thick layers of weak siltstone and shale. This combination produces the landform known as badlands, where erosion has run rampant and produced hauntingly beautiful scenery. The Upper Missouri here has cut a one-thousand foot deep canyon that is bounded by steep, mud-like walls. There are spectacular examples of geologic faults and folds. Lucky explorers may view a few fossils. The banks of the river do not support many groves of trees, and shady campsites are more scarce; most campsites here are classed as "undeveloped recreation areas", and there are numerous "dispersed recreation area" camping opportunities (both described below in the camping section).

Trip Duration

According to the BLM the average floater travels about 20 river miles per day and the average current in the river is 3.5 miles per hour. Paddling, rather that simply drifting in the current, can obviously increase the rate of travel. Using these numbers, along with an evaluation of one's fitness level, individuals can determine the amount of time that they choose to allocate for a trip, and how much of the river they wish to paddle.

Some may wish to build in an extra day, or more, for exploring old homesteads, or for hiking in the hundreds of thousands of acres of public lands that border parts of the river. It is also a good idea to build an extra day into the schedule in the event that inclement weather, such as a storm or high winds, interfere with travel plans.

Water Craft and Accessories

A number of different water craft are used to float the Upper Missouri, including canoes, touring kayaks, rafts, and rowboats. Larger craft can sometimes be taken down the river during high water. Before using any motorized craft individuals should first check with the BLM to determine its most current regulations regarding motors; such regulations vary at differnet times of the year.

The Upper Missouri River is the premier segment of the Lewis and Clark Trail, having changed little since the expedition came up the river in 1805 on its way to the Pacific, and passed downriver in 1806 on its return trip to St. Louis. The expedition spent more time, and traveled more miles in Montana than in any other state.

Canoes are by far the most popular craft, due to their combination of shallow draft, stability, gear carrying capacity, maneuverability, and user friendliness. Rafts tend to be much slower than canoes, and are probably a poor choice; they don't handle well in the upriver winds that sometimes occur on the Upper Missouri. Sea, or touring kayaks perform well, provided they have sufficient storage capacity for gear.

Since the Upper Missouri is a large and normally calm river, which does not require a lot of maneuvering, canoes with little or no rocker, which track well, are a good choice. Since paddling the Upper Missouri is a multi-day venture, short canoes may not have sufficient capacity to safely hold people and gear; the most popular canoes in use on the river are seventeen feet in length.

Montana state law requires that every adult individual be in possession of a lifejacket, and that children be wearing their lifejacket at all times while on the water.

Floating Season

The main floating season on the Upper Missouri is from Memorial Day to Labor Day. This is the time of year when the weather is probably the most predictable, and is the time of year when the BLM will have rangers patrolling the river, which is comforting in the event of an emergency. Obviously, it is also the time of year when the river experiences the greatest number of travelers. Weekends tend to be a little busier, since local Montanans often float short sections on their days off. The Upper Missouri, as of this writing, has no permit system in place, nor are there any restrictions on numbers of boats that can launch on a given day.

The river is never closed to floating, and can be floated any month of the year. Obviously, each month brings with it different weather conditions, which in turn necessitates different levels of preparedness.

Weather and Climate

The Upper Missouri flows through a portion of central Montana that is classified as semi-arid, with a total yearly precipitation of approximately 13 inches, 7 inches of which falls between May and July. The climate is of a continental type, characterized by rather large differences between daily high and low temperatures. The greatest amount of precipitation falls in June, and the least in the winter months. The number of frost-free days numbers about 120.

During the main floating season, June through August, the weather is characterized by warm to very hot days, and cool nights. Relative humidity is usually very low. Particularly in July and August daytime high temperatures typically range from the low 80's to the high 90's, with a number of days hovering around 100. Summer night time temperatures typically cool to the 50's.

Extended rainy periods are not typical in the area. Summer precipitation is usually in the form of thunderstorms, which can produce large amounts of rain, but are short lived. Thunderstorms can be quite intense, and are typically accompanied by strong winds, lightning, and sometimes hail.

The following weather data is for the city of Great Falls, Montana, located near the Upper Missouri. Note that the temperatures in this table are average highs and lows; extremes will occur.

	APRIL	MAY	JUNE	JULY	AUG	SEPT	OCT
MAX T°	57.8	66.8	74.4	84.4	82.4	70.8	66.3
MIN T°	33.2	41.4	48.8	54.5	52.2	43.4	36.1
RAIN	1.07 in	2.31	3.10	1.47	1.15	1.36	.81
SNOW	3.4 in	0.8	0	0	0	0.9	2.0

Winds on the Upper Missouri are fairly common and sometimes blow strongly enough to be a problem for floaters. They can make the water choppy, and unsafe, and can make steering a canoe challenging. When winds are directed upriver, which is not an uncommon occurrence, they significantly increase the effort required to paddle downriver, sometimes totally negating the effect of the river's 3.5 mph current; when these occur its a good idea to take frequent rests, and to consider waiting out the winds on shore.

Drinking Water

The water in the Upper Missouri can not, unfortunately, be used for drinking or cooking; it contains agricultural chemicals, as well as micro-organisms that are harmful if ingested. The BLM does not recommend the use of river water that has been treated with commercial backpacking water filters. The BLM recommends that all individuals carry drinking water in containers that has been taken from reliable sources, such as municipal systems, or from wells at BLM facilities where testing has proven the water to be safe.

The BLM recommends that all parties carry one gallon of water per person, per day. During a hot, mid-summer trip this should be considered a safe minimum, and it would be prudent to bring along a little extra. The containers that are used should be strong, with well-fitting lids, puncture resistant, and should not leak if they are accidentally tipped on their side.

The most consistently reliable source of drinking water is that available from municipal systems, such as in Fort Benton. The BLM has wells at a number of it launch sites and at a few locations on the river, but these are frequently not reliable sources of safe water. The BLM tests these wells regularly and often must shut them down due to poor test results.

A mandatory contact that should be made immediately before embarking on a float trip is with the BLM, for example at the Fort Benton Visitor Center, for the purpose of getting up-to-the-minute information about the current status of all of its wells. If downriver wells are out of service, floaters will have to pack additional water in their canoes. Remember - one gallon per person per day.

Camping

Paddling parties have basically two choices when selecting campsites along the Upper Missouri, first are "developed" campsites, of which there are three varieties, and second are "dispersed" sites.

Developed sites have varying amounts of improvements. The accompanying table lists all of the developed sites with the improvements that are available at each. The three classes of developed recreation areas are described below.

Upper Missouri National Wild and Scenic River Camping and Recreation Sites

Recreation Area	River Mile	GPS Coordinates	Boat Ramp	Road Access	Shelter	Telephone	Toilet	Water
Fort Benton Launch	1.5 Left	N 47° 49' 14" W 110° 39' 46"	Yes	Yes	Yes	Yes	Yes	Yes
Evans Bend Recreation Area	5.7 Right	N 47° 50' 45" W 110° 34' 52"	No	No	No	No	No	No
Senieurs Reach Recreation Area	16.2 Right	N 47° 52' 49" W 110° 28' 23"	No	No	No	No	No	No
Black Bluff Rapids Recreation Area	19.2 Left	N 47° 54' 39" W 110° 28' 27"	No	No	No	No	No	No
Wood Bottom Recreation Area	20.3 Left	N 47° 54' 42" W 110° 29' 31"	Yes	Yes	No	No	Yes	No
Coal Banks Landing Recreation Area	41.5 Left	N 48° 1' 56" W 110° 14' 4"	Yes	Yes	No	No	Yes	Yes
Little Sandy Recreation Area	46.7 Left	N 48° 1' 44" W 110° 8' 5"	No	No	No	No	Yes	No
Eagle Creek Recreation Area	55.7 Left	N 47° 54' 46" W 110° 3' 27"	No	No	No	No	Yes	No
Hole-in-the-Wall Recreation Area	62.9 Right	N 47° 49' 13" W 110° 3' 50"	No	No	Yes	No	Yes	Yes
Dark Butte Recreation Area	68.8 Left	N 47° 65' 58" W 109° 57' 7"	No	No	No	No	Yes	No
Pablo Rapids Recreation Area	72.8 Left	N 47° 45' 39" W 109° 53' 15"	No	No	No	No	No	No
Slaughter River Recreation Area	76.8 Left	N 47° 43' 2" W 109° 50' 57"	No	No	Yes	No	Yes	No
The Wall Recreation Area	81.2 Left	N 47° 42' 14" W 109° 45' 12"	No	No	No	No	No	No
Judith Landing Recreation Area	88.5 Left	N 47° 44' 20" W 109° 37' 21"	Yes	Yes	No	Yes	Yes	Yes
Stafford Ferry Recreation Area	101.8 Left	N 47° 44' 15" W 109° 23' 27"	No	Yes	No	No	No	No
McGarry Bar Recreation Area	103.1 Right	N 47° 44' 48" W 109° 21' 34"	No	No	No	No	No	No
Cow Island Recreation Area	125.5 Left	N 47° 47' 35" W 108° 57' 16"	No	No	No	No	No	No
Upper Woodhawk Recreation Area	129.5 Right	N 47° 44' 57" W 108° 55' 58"	No	No	No	No	No	No
Lower Woodhawk Recreation Area	131 Right	N 47° 44' 31" W 108° 56' 50"	No	Yes	No	No	Yes	No
Hideway Recreation Area	136.2 Left	N 47° 43' 21" W 108° 51' 1"	No	No	No	No	No	No
Kipp Recreation Area	149 Right	N 47° 37' 26" W 108° 40' 36"	Yes	Yes	No	Yes	Yes	Yes

This table is reproduced from a BLM brochure and shows the location of all of the designated campsites and launch points on the Upper Missouri. In addition to these sites there are thousands of acres of public land that are available for wilderness camping. This table should be used in conjunction with BLM maps. ALWAYS check with the BLM regarding the status of the drinking water supplies before starting on a trip.

Developed Recreation Areas have drive-in access and boat launches. They also have fire rings and toilets, and most have picnic tables. Users at these sites include those preparing to begin a float trip, or those just getting off the river, as well as non-floaters who are fishing and car camping on the river.

Minimally Developed Recreation Areas are generally accessible only from the river, and not by road. They are designed to accommodate three to five parties and have toilet facilities and fire rings. Some of these areas are enclosed with fences to keep cattle away from the camping areas, and to protect riparian vegetation from damage by cattle.

Undeveloped Recreation Areas are accessible only from the river, and are generally intended for use by one party. Fire rings are present, but there are no picnic tables. There are no toilets and campers must be knowledgeable about proper waste disposal techniques whenever using these sites.

Dispersed Recreation Areas are simply river bank locations that are located on the thousands of acres of public land within the monument, and they offer the opportunity for primitive camping. Expect no improvements of any kind, and accept the responsibility of proper human waste disposal.

Low-impact camping techniques can go a long way in preserving the quality of an Upper Missouri float trip for future floaters. Use of stoves for cooking, keeping campfires small, and not putting soap or food wastes in the river are common wilderness courtesies.

Keep in mind that most parties who are floating the river are seeking solitude. If a campsite is occupied, respect that parties privacy and locate your camp a healthy distance away.

Islands

Because islands offer some protection from predators they are used by deer as fawning sites, and by geese as nesting sites. The BLM requests that floaters not camp on islands until after July 31st, to give these animals the solitude they need

Human Waste

The BLM has installed outhouses at a number of the most heavily used camp areas, almost all of which are located in the White Cliffs; the locations of these can be gotten from BLM brochures. However most of the camping areas along the river provide no outhouses, and proper disposal of human waste is a critical health and aesthetic issue for users of the river.

As of this writing, the Upper Missouri is one of the last rivers in the western U.S. that does not require overnight floaters to pack out all human waste; however, the BLM has announced its intention to implement such a requirement in the near future. Floaters should check with the BLM for its most current regulations.

If a portable toilet is not used, it is imperative that every party on the river know how to properly dispose of human waste, and insure that all of its members comply. Unfortunately, improper and grossly inconsiderate disposal of human waste is rapidly becoming a major problem on the Upper Missouri that is of great concern to BLM officials involved in managing the river.

Upon arrival at an evening camp location, the group should designate a latrine area, located at least 200 feet straight back from the river, and at least 300 feet from camp areas. Areas along streams that drain into the main river are not acceptable.

Every party must pack at least one trenching tool or sturdy shovel for the purpose of digging a hole for the burial of solid human waste; small garden trowels are unacceptable, because of the hardness of the soils in some areas. The trenching tool should be used to dig a hole, at least eight inches deep in which the solid waste is deposited, along with all toilet paper, and then buried using the dirt which was dug from the hole.

Hiking

Hiking possibilities abound within the monument. However, there is no trail system, so hiking is typically done on old roads and jeep trails, on game trails, and cross-country.

Some of the lands within the national monument are private property; some landowners don't mind people hiking on their property, while others do. If land is posted with 'no trespassing' signs, or with fluorescent orange paint, the landowners' wishes should be respected. The BLM maps of the river use color codes to show the locations of private versus public land.

Particularly in the stretch of the river between Judith Landing and Kipp Recreation Area, there are vast expanses of public land that offer unlimited hiking opportunities; six of these areas are wilderness study areas, and offer spectacular scenery in an unspoiled setting. The names of these wilderness study areas are Dog Creek South and Stafford, located on opposite sides of the river near Stafford Ferry (river mile 102), Ervin Ridge, located above Sturgeon Island (river mile 119), and finally Cow Creek, Antelope Creek, and Woodhawk, located on both sides of the river in the Cow Creek vicinity (river mile 127).

Safety and Hazards

The primary consideration for floaters on the Upper Missouri National Wild and Scenic River is the river's remoteness. For this reason floaters must realize that if a problem is encountered, that help from the river rangers will not likely be close at hand, and therefore all parties on the river should be aware of hazards, and prepared to deal with problems.

Following is a list of some of the hazards that exist on the Upper Missouri:

Shallow water and the presence of unanticipated large boulders in some parts of the channel make the river unsuitable for boats with a deep draft, and present capsizing potential for all boats.

In some locations, electric lines cross over the river, and sadly, boats with projecting masts have had deadly encounters with them.

There are two locations where ferry boats transport automobiles across the river: the Virgelle ferry (rm 39), and the Stafford ferry (rm 101.8). These ferries cross the river by means of a set of steel cables which are anchored on each bank. Depending upon the amount of water flowing in the Missouri's channel, these cables can be very close to the water's surface, sometimes making it necessary for canoeists to duck as they pass under them. Watch for these cables and plan your approach; to avoid capsizing, don't both duck to the same side of the canoe!

The ferry boats themselves should always be given a wide berth, whether they are docked on the bank, or crossing the river. Approaching them from upstream is especially dangerous because a boat can collide with the ferry, and be sucked beneath it.

Sun in mid-summer can be intense. Quality sunglasses, including a spare pair, are a necessity, as is a wide brimmed hat. Floaters should carry a generous supply of high protection sun screen or sun block (SPF 30-45) for exposed skin. A long-sleeved cotton shirt and full-length cotton pants can offer welcome protection from the sun. Use your maps, which show the locations of groves of trees, to plan breaks and camps in areas that have trees for shade.

Dehydration is a continuous threat. During hot weather floaters should make a conscious effort to drink plenty of water. Remember that water is superior to soft drinks and juices. Children especially should be encouraged to drink adequate water. The BLM recommends that each person carry at least one gallon per day; the river water is not drinkable, so carry a little extra.

Rattlesnakes are present throughout the area, and floaters must keep an eye out for them when hiking or exploring homesteads; boots and long pants offer some degree of protection since most bites occur on the lower leg. Rattlesnakes are not aggressive, and will flee if given adequate warning of your approach. Walk single file to avoid crossing the path of a snake that is avoiding another of your party. Keep your tent door zippered to discourage unwanted sleeping partners.

When exploring homesteads, the BLM is now cautioning floaters of the presence of deer mice, which are implicated in a sometimes fatal disease called hantavirus. The disease is carried in the mice's feces, and exposure can be minimized by avoiding contact by touch and by not stirring up dust where the mice have been.

Poison ivy grows in some locations along the river and floaters should know how to identify it. Several plants that grow along the Upper Missouri have sharp spines and leaves, and good footwear should be included for off-river hiking.

Mosquitoes and fly populations vary greatly from site to site and from year to year, so carry insect repellent, and a mosquito headnet.

Undercut river banks can collapse and should be approached with caution.

Old homesteads are neat places to explore, but hazards like nails, collapsing structures, and old barbed wire should be watched for. Rattlesnakes like to dwell in some of the old structures.

The rock along the river corridor are soft and crumbly, and any type of scrambling is fraught with danger; scrambling techniques that work well on good rock can not be relied upon - use caution and common sense.

Respecting the River

Congress had the foresight to set aside the Upper Missouri for the enjoyment and enrichment of all Americans. The BLM, as the agency responsible for managing the river, is doing its job to make the river a quality experience for floaters. The Upper Missouri is unique in many ways, and the cooperation of all users is essential to maintain the resources that make the river so special.

Old Homestead Buildings

Thanks to the Upper Missouri's dry climate and remoteness, many of the old homestead buildings along the river are still standing, and some are in relatively good shape. Regardless of their state of preservation, they are all priceless glimpses into a chapter of our nations short history, and all of them should be treated with respect. Do not remove anything from these buildings or from the grounds surrounding them. They are, in fact protected by Federal law. Tread lightly, and take only pictures.

Artifacts

Arrowheads, tipi rings, and other remnants of the habitation of the Upper Missouri area by Native Americans should not be removed from the area or disturbed from their original resting places. Detailed archaeological studies have not been undertaken in many area within the wild and scenic corridor, and these items are of great potential value to scientists. Pictographs, or rock paintings do occur along the river, and should be treated respectfully.

Geologic Features

Almost all of the rocks along the Upper Missouri are soft and fragile. This means that it is easy for hikers to cause significant damage to geologic features. In the White Cliffs, care should be taken to not disturb or loosen anything, and routes should be chosen that will avoid fragile ridges, as well as delicate arches, pedestal rocks, and spires. In other areas, a good rule to follow is to avoid walking anyplace where the material underfoot is breaking loose and sliding downhill.

Dinosaur fossils have been found along the Upper Missouri, and are especially numerous in the Fort Peck area, just a few miles below the wild and scenic corridor. Collecting them or disturbing them is not permitted, and finds should be reported to the BLM.

Invertebrate fossils, such as clams, snails, and ammonites are very abundant in some areas, particularly within the Judith River Formation, and collecting them is permitted, however it is a good idea to check with the BLM for current regulations regarding fossil collecting.

In Closing

Both the Upper Missouri National Wild and Scenic River and the Upper Missouri River Breaks National Monument are national treasures, and they belong to all Americans. In today's world there are continuous pressures on this area, including potential for natural gas and mineral development, cattle grazing, and overuse by recreationists. Places like the Upper Missouri have been protected because people have fought for their protection, and the challenge to keep such places wild will be ongoing. Please become involved in protecting the Upper Missouri and other wild places that are special to you.

BIBLIOGRAPHY

Abel, Anne Heloise, ed.; 1932; *Chardon's Journal at Fort Clark, 1834-1839.* Iowa City, Iowa.

Aldrich, Bess S.; 1942; *The Lieutenant's Lady.* Appleton, New York.

Allen, Irah I.; 1862; From St. Louis to Fort Benton in 1862. Microfilm 63. Montana Historical Society, Helena.

Allen, John Logan; 1941; *Passage Through the Garden: Lewis and Clark and the Image of the American Northwest.* University of Illinois Press, Chicago.

Alt, David and Hyndman, Donald; 1986, *Roadside Geology of Montana,* Mountain Press, Missoula

Anonymous n.d. *Progressive Men of the State Of Montana.* A.W. Bower & Co., Chicago.
1869a; Untitled. Helena *Weekly Herald,* April 1, 1869. Montana Historical Society.
1869b; Untitled. Helena *Daily Herald,* September 2, 1869. Montana Historical Society.
1875; Untitled. *Benton Record.* Fort Benton.
1880; Untitled. *River Press,* Fort Benton. forward
1899; *Society of Montana Pioneers.* 10 vol. Werner Co., Akron.
1975; *Hoofprints of the Yellowstone Corral of Westerners,* 5(1):6, Billings.

Atkins, C.J.;1908; Logs of Missouri River Steamboats. *Collections of the State Historical Society of North Dakota, vol.* II. Bismarck.

Audubon, Maria R., ed.; 1898; *Audubon and His Journals.* 2 vol.

Barrows, T. Eugene;1981; *Homestead Days.* Browstone Books, Chicago.

Beal, Merrill; 1963; *I Will Fight No More Forever.* University of Washington, Seattle.

Bradley, Lieutenant James H.; 1900; Affairs at Fort Benton From 1831 to 1869. *Contributions to the Historical Society of Montana, vol.* III. Helena.
1917; "Establishment of Fort Piegan as Told Me by James Kipp." *Contributions to the Historical Society of Montana, vol.* 8. Helena.

Brower, J.V.; 1896; *The Missouri River and Its Utmost Source.* Pioneer Press, St. Paul, Minnesota.

Brown, Mark H.; 1967; *Flight of the Nez Perce.* Putnam, New York.

Burlingame, M.G. and K.R. Toole; 1957; A *History of Montana, 3 vol.* Lewis, New York.

Canfield, A.N. and Sarah E. Canfield; 1868; Papers, 1866-1868. Microfilm 73. Montana Historical Society, Helena.

Chittenden, Hiram M.; 1903; *History of Steamboat Navigation of the Missouri River, 2 vol.* Francis P. Harper, New York.

Chittenden, H.M. and A.T. Richardson; 1905 *Life, Letters and Travels of Father Pierre Jean DeSmet,* 1801-1873, 4 vol. Harper's, New York.

Chittenden, H.M. and P.C. Phillips; 1902; *The American Fur Trade of the Far West,* 3 vol. Harper's, New York.

Cobban, Roy M.; 1880; Diary of a Trip to Montana. Small Collections 348. Montana Historical Society, Helena.

Coues, Elliot; 1893; *History of the Expedition Under the Command of Lewis and Clark,* 4 vol. Francis P. Harper, New York.

Curtis, Susan W. and David Conklin; 1975; Judith Landing National Historic District. State Historic Preservation Office, Montana Historical Society, Helena.

Cushman, Dan; 1962; Monsters of the Judith. *Montana, the Magazine of Western History,* 12(4):18-36.

Cutright, Paul Russell; 1976; A *History of the Lewis and Clark Journals.* University of Oklahoma Press, Norman.

Davis, Leslie B.; 1976; *Missouri River Breaks Area Archaeological and Historical Values - Montana.* Bureau of Land Management, Billings, Montana.

Davis, Leslie B. and Stephen A. Aaberg; 1978; *Upper Missouri Wild and Scenic River Followup Cultural Resources Investigation.* Montana State University, Bozeman.

Dawson, Andrew; 1855; Letter to Pierre Chouteau, October 10,1855, Judith River. Pierre Chouteau Collection, Missouri Historical Society, St. Louis.

Denig, Edwin Thompson (John C. Ewers, ed.); 1961; *Five Indian Tribes of the Upper Missouri.* University of Oklahoma Press, Norman.

DeSmet, P.J.; 1847; *Oregon Mission and Travels Over the Rocky Mountains in 1845-46.* Edw. Dunigan, New York.

DeVoto, Bernard; 1947; *Across the Wide Missouri.* Bonanza Books, New York.

1953; *The Journals of Lewis and Clark.* Houghton Mifflin Company, Boston.

Donnelly, Joseph P. Translator; 1967; *Wilderness Kingdom: Indian Life in the Rocky Mountains, 1840-1847. The Journals & Paintings of Nicholas Point, S.J.* New York.

Dusenberry, V.; 1957; Development of Montana's Indians. In *History of Montana, 3 vol .* by M. Burlingame and K.R. Toole, Lewis, New York.

Eide, Ingvard Henrey; 1969; *American Odyssey. The Journey of Lewis and Clark.* Rand McNally.

Ewers, John C.; 1958;*The Blackfeet: Raiders on the Northwestern Plains.* University of Oklahoma Press, Norman.

Ewers, John C., ed.; 1961; *Edwin Thompson Denig: Five Indian Tribes of the Upper Missouri.* University of Oklahoma Press, Norman.

Fahey, John; 1974; *The Flathead Indians.* University of Oklahoma, Norman.

Fine, Harry L.; n.d.; *Montana Territorial Post Offices, 1864-1889.* Montana Historical Society, Helena.

Flandrau, Grace; 1974; *Frontier Days Along the Upper Missouri.* (reprint of Great Northern Railway publication) Shorey Book Store, Seattle.

Fletcher, Robert S.; 1929; The End of the Open Range in Eastern Montana. *Mississippi Valley Historical Review* 16:188-211.

Frazer, R.M.; 1865; Diary. Steamboat papers, Missouri Historical Society, St. Louis.

Garraghan, Gilbert J., ed.; 1931; A Journey in a Barge on the Missouri From the Fort of the Blackfeet (Lewis) to That of the Assiniboines (Union). *Mid-America* 13(3). Chicago.

Geraldine History Committee; 1976; *Spokes, Spurs and Cockleburs.* The River Press Publishing Company, Fort Benton, Montana.

Goetzmann, William H.; 1979; *Army Exploration in the American West, 1803-1863.* University of Nebraska Press, Lincoln.

Hafen, LeRoy R., ed.; 1965; *The Mountain Men and the Fur Trade of the Far West,* 10 vol. Glendale, California.

Halsey, Jacob; 1837; Letter to Pierre Chouteau, St. Louis From Fort Pierre, Nov. 2 Pierre Chouteau Collection, Missouri Historical Society, St. Louis.

Hanson, Joseph M.; 1946; *The Conquest of the Missouri.* Murray Hill, New York.

Harkness, James; 1861; Diary, St. Louis to Fort Benton. *Contributions to the Montana Historical Society,* vol. II. J.S. Canner, Boston.

Hart, Herbert M.; 1963; *Old Forts of the Northwest.* Superior Publishing Co., Seattle.

Hatch, Edwin A.C.; 1857; Annual Report of the Blackfeet Agency, 1856. *Report of the Commissioner of Indian* affairs, for the Year 1856. Washington.

Hazard, J.T.; 1952; *Companion of Adventure.* Binfords, Portland.

Hewitt, J.N.B., ed.; 1930; Indian Tribes of the Upper Missouri, by Edwin Thompson Denig. *Forty-sixth Annual Report of the Bureau of American Ethnology.* Washington.

Hilger, David; n.d.; Early History of Fergus County. Montana Historical Society, Helena.

1928 Early History of Northern Montana and Chouteau County. Montana Historical Society, Helena.

Hogan, Martin E.; 1874; Letters Written to Andrew O'Connell of Helena From Camp Cooke, 1866-1874. Montana Historical Society, Helena.

Holabird, Samuel B.; 1869; Report. Executive Document 8, Senate Report Serial 1440, 41st U.S. Congress, 3rd Session. Montana Historical Society, Helena.

Hosmer, James Kendall, ed.; 1904; *Gass's Journal of the Lewis and Clark Expedition.* A.C. McClurge & Co., Chicago.

Kane, Paul; 1968; *Wanderings of an Artist Among the Indians of North America.* Rutland, Vermont.

Koury, Michael J.; 1970; *Military Posts of Montana.* Old Army Press, Bellevue, NB.

LaBarge, A.G. n.d. Untitled manuscript. Missouri Historical Society, St. Louis.

Larpenteur, Charles; 1898; *Forty Years a Fur Trader on the Upper Missouri.* 2 vol. Edited by E. Coues. Francis P. Harper, New York.

Lass, William E.; 1962; *History of Steamboating on the Upper Missouri.* University of Nebraska, Lincoln.

Leeson, M.A., ed.; 1886; *History of Montana,* 1739-1885. Warner, Beers & Co., Chicago.

Lepley, John G.; 1981; *Luxury Living Along the Levee: Frontier Homes in Fort Benton.* River Press Publishing Company, Fort Benton.

Lutz, Dennis and Meryl Lutz;1975; *Montana Postal Cache: Montana Post Offices, 1864-1974.* Montana Historical Society, Helena.

Mallory, Oscar L.; 1963; An Archaeological Appraisal of the Missouri Breaks Region in Montana; A Project of the Inter-Agency Archaeological and Paleontological Salvage Program. Midwest Archeological Center, Lincoln, NB.

Malone, Michael P. and Richard B. Roeder; 1976; *Montana: A History of Two Centuries.* University of Washington Press, Seattle.

Mattison, Ray H.; 1953; An Army Wife on the Upper Missouri: The Diary of Sarah Canfield, 1866-1868. North Dakota History 20(4):191-220.
1954; "The Army Post on the Northern Plains, 1865-1885." *Nebraska History* 35(1). (March 1954).
1956 "The military frontier on the upper Missouri." *Nebraska History* 37(3). (Sept. 1956).

McDonnell, Anne; 1940; "Notes and References, on Fort Benton, Alexander Culbertson, Fort McKenzie, and F.A. Chardon." *Contributions to the Historical Society of Montana,* vol. 10. Helena.

McWhorter, L.V.; 1952; *Hear Me, My Chiefs!* The Caxton Printers, Caldwell, Idaho.

Missouri Historical Society; 1866; Log of the *Lillie Marlin,* 1865-1866. Roper Collection, Missouri Historical Society, St. Louis.

Missouri River Commission; 1892-1895; Map sheet no. LXXIII. *Map of the Missouri River From its Mouth to Three Forks, Montana.* Washington.

Mitchell, David; 1837; Letter to P.D. Papin, from Fort Union, December 1, 1837. Pierre Chouteau Collection, Missouri Historical Society, St. Louis.

Montana Historical Society; n.d.; T.C. Power Collection. Montana Historical Society, Helena.

1862; List of Arrivals, Steamboats in Fort Benton. *Contributions to the Montana Historical Society, vol. I.* J.S. Canner, Boston.

Mueller, George D.; 1973; Historic Spots at the Mouth of the Judith. *Lewistown News-Argus,* Christmas edition.

Mueller, 0.0.; 1964; Ridding the Range of Renegades. In *Cowboys and Cattlemen,* edited by M.S. Kennedy. Hastings House, New York.

Mulloy, William; 1958; A preliminary Historical Outline for the Northwestern Plains. *University of Wyoming Publications* 22 (1):1-235. Laramie.

Murray, Robert A.; 1968; *Montana Historical Sites Inventory.* Montana Fish and Game.

1973 Inventory and Evaluation of Historic Sites. MS for Montana Department of Fish and Game.

National Archives: Record Group 92. List of Civilians, Citizens, Attaches, Camp Followers, Traders and Others, Camp Cooke, March 31, 1868. Washington D.C.
Record Group 98. Records of the United States Army Commands (Army Posts), Camp Cooke, Montana, 1866-69. Washington D.C.
Record Group 393. List of Interments, National Cemetery, Camp Cooke. Washington D.C.
Microfilm Group 94. Records of the Adjutant General's Office, Medical Histories of the Posts, Camp Cooke, vol. 15. Washington D.C.
Microfilm 617. Returns from U.S. Military Posts, Role 252, Camp Cooke 1866-1870. Washington D.C.

National Park Service; 1975; Lewis and Clark. U.S. Government Printing Office, Washington, D.C.

Neihardt, John G.;1910 ; *The River and I.* G.P. Putnam's Sons, New York.

Oglesby, R.E.; 1963; *Manuel Lisa and the Opening of the Missouri Fur Trade.* University of Oklahoma, Norman.

Osborn, Henry F.; 1931; *Cope: Master Naturalist.* Princeton University Press, Princeton.

Osborn, N.W.; 1870; Letter to commanding officer from the Lt. N.W. Osborn, Ft. Benton, February 10, 1870 on moving of troops and equipment from Camp Cooke and the abandonment of the latter post. In *Official letters and reports of army officials and Indian agents relating to affairs in Montana, 1867-1875,* by J.H. Bradley. Montana Historical Society, Helena.

Partoll, A.J., ed.; 1937; Blackfoot Indian Peace Council. *Frontier and Midland* 17:199-207. Missoula.

Phillips, Paul C.; 1962; *Medicine in the Making of Montana. MSU* Press, Bozeman.

Phillips, Paul Chrisler; 1961; *The Fur Trade,* 2 vol. University of Oklahoma Press, Norman.

Point, Nicolas; 1967; *Wilderness Kingdom.* Holt, Rinehart and Winston, New York.

Porter, Mary W.; 1949; *The Surgeon in Charge.* Rumford Press, Concord, NH.

Quaife, M.M., ed.; 1916; *The Journals of Captain Meriwether Lewis and Sgt. John Ordway Kept on the Expedition of Western Exploration, 1803-1805.* State Historical Society of Wisconsin, Madison.

Quaife, Milo M., ed.; 1933; *Forty Years a Fur Trader on the Upper Missouri.* Lakeside Classics Series. Chicago.

Russell, Osborne; 1921; *Journal of a Trapper or Nine Years in the Rocky Mountains, 1834-1843.* Boise.

Schmitt, Martin, ed.; 1946; "From Missouri to Oregon in 1860; the Diary of August V. Kautz." *Pacific Northwest Quarterly* 27(3). (July 1946).

Schultz, James Willard; 1979; *Floating on the Missouri.* University of Oklahoma Press, Norman (Forest and Stream, 1902).

Sharp, Paul F.; 1973; *Whoop-Up Country.* University of Oklahoma Press, Norman.

Sharrock, Susan R. and James D. Keyser; 1974; Cultural History of the Missouri River From Fort Benton, Montana to Garrison Reservoir, North Dakota: An Inventory of Prehistoric and Early Historic Sites. Unpublished special report of the University of Montana Statewide Archaeological Survey. Corps of Engineers, Omaha, NB.

Shumate, Maynard; 1973; Fort McKenzie (1832-1843): Historic Site Salvage Archaeology. *Archaeology in Montana* 14(2). Bozeman.

1974; Camp Cooke (1866-1870): Historic Site Salvage Archaeology. *Archaeology in Montana* 15(3):41-46.

Spence, Clark G.; 1975; *Territorial Politics and Government in Montana 1864-89.* University of Illinois Press, Urbana.

Stanton, T.W. and J.B. Hatcher; 1905; Geology and Paleontology of the Judith River Beds. *United States Geological Survey, Bulletin* 257. Government Printing Office, Washington D.C.

Stearn, Ester A. and A.E. Stern; 1945; *The Effect of Small Pox on the Destiny of the Amerindian.* Humphries, Boston.

Stevens, Hazard;1901; *Life of Isaac Ingalls Stevens,* 2 vol. Houghton Mifflin & Co., New York.

Stevens, Isaac; 1855; Narrative of 1855. In *Reports of Explorations and Surveys for a Railroad From the Mississippi River to the Pacific Ocean, 1853-1855. U.S.* House Executive Document 56, 36th Congress, 1st session, vol. 12, books 1 and 2.

Stocking, Lucy; 1882; Diary, 1871-1881. Small collections 142. Montana Historical Society, Helena.

Stout, Tom, ed.; 1921; *Montana, Its Story and Biography.* The American Historical Society, Chicago.

Stuart, Granville; 1925; *Forty Years on the Frontier,* edited by P.C. Phillips. Arthur H. Clark Co., Cleveland.

Sunder, John E.; 1965; *The Fur Trade on the Upper Missouri, 1840-1865.* University of Oklahoma Press, Norman.

Thwaites, Reuben Gold, ed.; 1906; *Early Western Travels: 1748-1846.* The Arthur H. Clark Company, Cleveland, Ohio. Vol. XXIII.

Thwaites, Reuben Gold; 1904; *Original Journals of the Lewis and Clark Expedition, 1804-1806,* 8 vol. Dodd, Mead, and Co., New York. Vol. 2.

Time-Life Books (text by Paul O'Neil); 1975; *The Rivermen.* Time-Life Books, New York.

Upper Missouri Outfit; 1844; Property of the Upper Missouri Outfit, American Fur Company, Fort McKenzie, March 19, 1844. Manuscripts Department, Missouri Historical Society, St. Louis, Missouri. Copy held by Historical Research Associates, Missoula, Montana.

1845; Inventory of Goods on Hand at Fort F.A.C., April 5,1845. Manuscripts Department, Missouri Historical Society, St. Louis, Missouri. Copy held by Historical Research Associates, Missoula, Montana.

Utley, Robert M.; 1973; *Frontier Regulars: The United States Army and the Indian, 1866-1890.* Macmillan, New York.

Wheeler, Colonel W.F.; 1940; Personal History of Mr. George Weippert, Chouteau County, Montana," and "Charles Mercier (Rondin), 1803-1891." *Contributions to the Historical Society of Montana,* vol. 10. Helena.

Woolworth, Alan R.; 1975; Fur Trade Posts of the Trans Mississippi West: An Examination of Their Design and Construction. Paper Read at the Society for Historical Archeology Meeting in Ottawa, Canada. In author's possession.

About the Author

Glenn Monahan lives in Anaconda, located in southwest Montana, about five miles from the Continental Divide. During the summer floating season he lives in Fort Benton, Montana, where he operates an outfitting and guide service on the Upper Missouri River.

Glenn holds degrees from Montana State University in Geology and Secondary Education. He has worked as a geologist, junior high science teacher, park ranger (in Yellowstone and Mt. Rainier), and cross-country ski instructor. He has also been a volunteer member of the National Ski Patrol, and of the Flathead County Search and Rescue Association.

Glenn is a member of the Montana Wilderness Association, Alliance for the Wild Rockies, Friends of the Missouri Breaks Monument, Geological Society of America, and the Montana Historical Society.

The history and geology of the Upper Missouri, and of Montana in general, are two areas in which Glenn has a particular interest, and he has taught college classes on various aspects of these two subjects.

Glenn enjoys many outdoor pursuits, which in addition to canoeing, include camping, hiking, cross-country skiing, bicycling, and ice sailing.

Northern Rocky Mountains Books is a Montana-owned and based company which publishes books about Montana, and books that are written by Montana authors. We welcome inquiries from Montana authors.